Designing Your Own Dress Patterns

Designing

Your Own

Dress Patterns

By Helen Nicol Tanous

Chas. A. Bennett Co., Inc.

PUBLISHERS • Peoria, Illinois

25P53

SET, PLATED, AND LITHOGRAPHED IN THE UNITED STATES

Contents

Letter to the Reader

Dear Reader:

I take this opportunity to explain to you who are the most concerned that this book was written for the express purpose of making it possible for interested parties to learn pattern making without having to go to school to do so.

Naturally, for anyone who is sufficiently interested in dress designing, it is highly desirable to go to a good costume-designing school. But, if it is not convenient or possible to go to school and you still wish to learn this fascinating and useful skill, then you can do so merely by a diligent perusal of this book.

It took several years to clarify and simplify this subject, which is usually clothed in mystery and buried under a mountain of words. In my opinion, the fewer words used to explain the diagrams the easier it is for the reader to understand.

When you take up a new subject you are naturally eager to progress and loathe to be hindered by pages of text from which you must extract the meaning like the kernel from a nutshell. This is time consuming and exasperating to most of us. Or perhaps it is just that people who love to work with their hands are impatient with words, which serve only to hold them back.

You will not be bothered by any such hindrance here, as the only words which are used are those few which are vital to the understanding of the diagrams. The nutshells have been thrown away. The kernels remain.

Sincerely yours,

Helen Nicol Tanous

Introduction

Most of us are well acquainted with the fact that making one's own clothes is a highly economical thing to do. There are, however, other factors which are equally important.

First, and perhaps the most important, is the glow of pure satisfaction which we all feel upon accomplishing a piece of creative work. This satisfaction has been increasingly denied to most of us who live in an age when machines have assumed the burden of work which used to fall to the homemaker.

Today, no mass-produced clothes can ever give the wearer the same sense of pride and accomplishment which she gets from having actually created the garment herself.

It is true that you can buy ready-made patterns with which to sew. But to have original clothes which are truly expressive of your own feelings and taste, you have to go a step further and *design* your own clothes.

If you are going to design them, then you must also make patterns for them.

Only by designing and making your own patterns can you achieve a perfect fit. Once you have adjusted a set of basic blocks to your own measurements, you will seldom have to have "fittings." Most clothes are completely thrown out of alignment by being altered. Unless you know how to make patterns, it is difficult even to alter a pattern successfully, and even harder to alter a finished garment. Then, too, you can make up your mind to just what you want, but even with the most diligent searching are unable to find a pattern that approximates the garment which already has taken shape in your head. You may say, "Yes, all that is true, but I am not artistic. I could never design a dress." Stop and think for a minute. Have you really never wished to yourself, "If only I had a dress in this luscious color, with a skirt like that one, and a bodice like this, and the marvelous new sleeves I saw in a magazine"? Of course you have. Everyone has. Well, as soon as you learn how to make patterns you can make that very dress. Or a suit incorporating ideas you saw that cost so much. And the very best part of it is that you will have fun doing it and experience that wonderful glow of satisfaction.

Last, but certainly not least, there is the possibility of making a career of dress designing. It is probably the best field there is for a woman. The work is pleasant, pays well, and the designer commands a certain respect which is not always forthcoming elsewhere as one of the rewards of earning a living. Again the excitement and satisfaction of doing creative work applies. To be a successful designer, it is essential to be a perfect pattern maker. As an artist is unable to paint a picture until he can control his paints, so a designer cannot present a dress unless she knows how to cut up a flat piece of cloth so that it comes out with the necessary contours.

Pattern making is a very interesting skill to learn. But it is a very particular skill and you must apply yourself with diligence. You must be precise. So, in working out the lessons is this book, bear in mind that this is not a reading book. It is a *working book*. Go slowly. Work out each diagram exactly as shown. When further work is recommended, be sure that you do that, too. Nothing has been included that is not absolutely essential, so don't skip a single lesson.

Materials and Tools Required for Pattern Drafting

1. A 6 or 8 inch ruler.
2. A 45-degree angle, small size.
3. Thick stack of paper. Typing paper, 8½ x 11 inches, is fine for quarter-size work.
4. A pair of sharp scissors for cutting paper.
5. A big table or desk with good light.
6. A large wastebasket.
7. Plenty of medium-soft pencils and a good pencil sharpener.

The above list provides for the things which you need for working out the quarter-size diagrams. Below you will find another list of the things which are needed for drafting full-size patterns.

1. A good pair of dressmaker shears. Blades should be at least 6 inches long. To be used for patterns and cloth.
2. A tracing wheel.
3. A notcher. (This is the one thing on the list which you can do without, but it is a very handy tool and can be bought at a reasonable price.)
4. A punch. (You can use an icepick cut off short and resharpened.)
5. Standard dress form closest to your own size. For anyone who intends to become a professional I recommend a size 14 as it is the accepted sample size.
6. Heavy paperweights. At least two.
7. A roll of heavy "kraft" wrapping paper for permanent patterns.
8. A ream or more of packing tissue, or any other tissue paper. Packing tissue is inexpensive.

Guide to the Symbols

C.F.	Center front.
C.B.	Center back.
R.S.	Right side.
	Right angle.
14/①	Size fourteen: cut one piece.
14/②	Size fourteen: cut two pieces.
4/④	Size four: cut four pieces.
⊙	Inside end of notch: or pocket or pleat guide.
	Clip pattern in, one-half inch.
gather ←→	Gather between notches.
↕	Cut on the vertical grain of the goods.
NOTCH	An indentation in the pattern paper used as a guide for matching two pattern pieces, or as a guide for folding, gathering, pleating, etc.

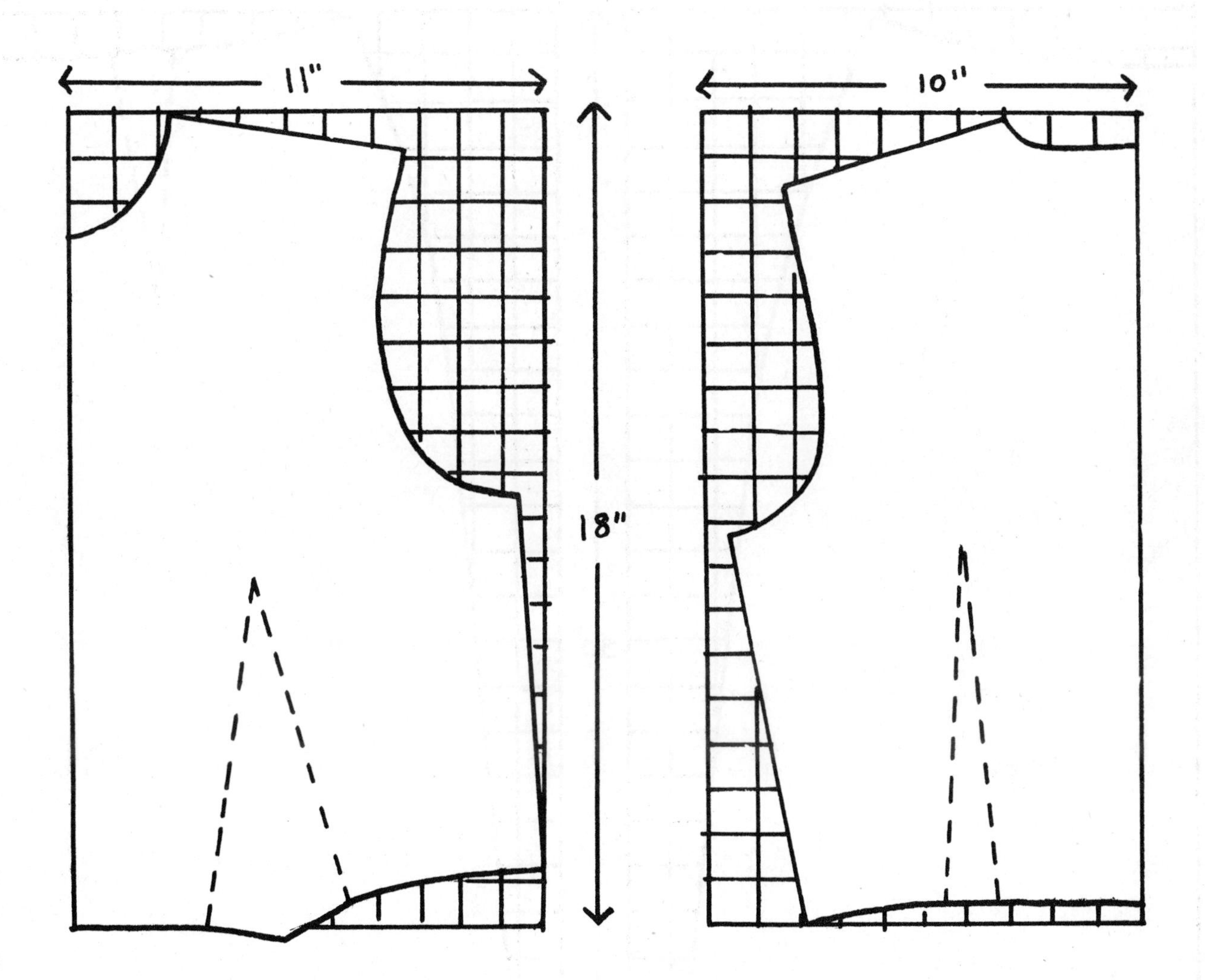

These are the blocks with which you will work out the diagrams. Trace them and cut out your copies. Use fairly stiff "kraft" wrapping paper so that they will not wear out with repeated tracing. If the blocks do become too worn around the edges, be sure that you take time to make fresh copies.

Seams have been allowed for on the blocks — ½ inch at waist, shoulder, side, and armscye; ¼ inch at the neckline.

To enlarge these patterns to full size, block off your paper in 1 inch squares and draw the blocks exactly as they show up on the ¼ inch squares in this diagram. *The basic blocks are all a size 14. Directions for changing the size 14 to any size required will be given later.*

Center front and center back have no seams.

Adjust the length of skirt blocks to conform to the current style.

Be careful in copying the back skirt; the dart must be placed exactly where it is on the diagram, 2¾ inches from the Center Back fold. The paper is not actually cut on the fold, but in cutting a garment, the C.B. has no seam and is meant to be placed on a fold.

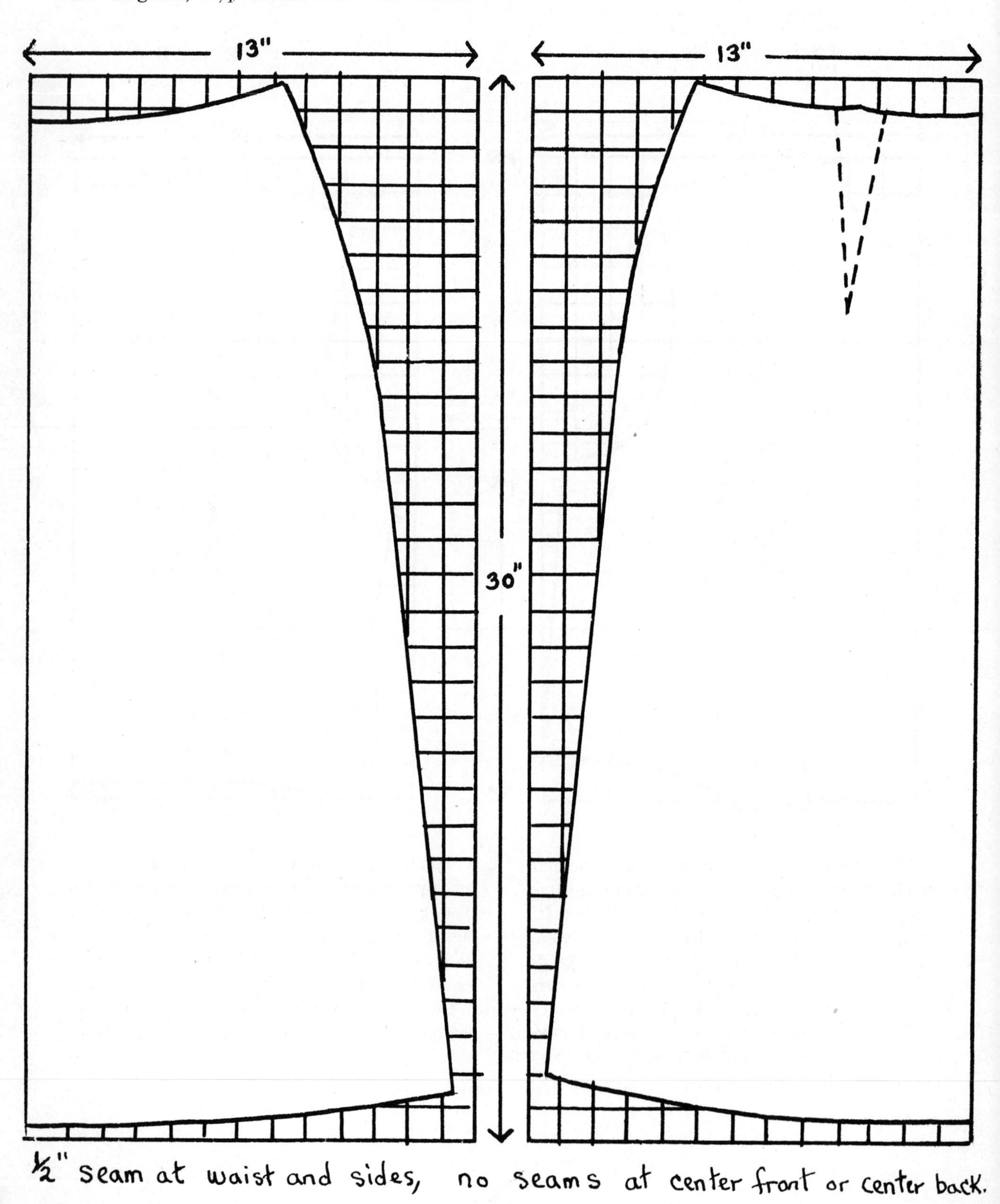

BASIC SLEEVE BLOCK

When you have all your copies of the basic blocks cut out, place them in a business-size, "kraft" envelope.

They are small enough to be easily lost if not kept in a special place.

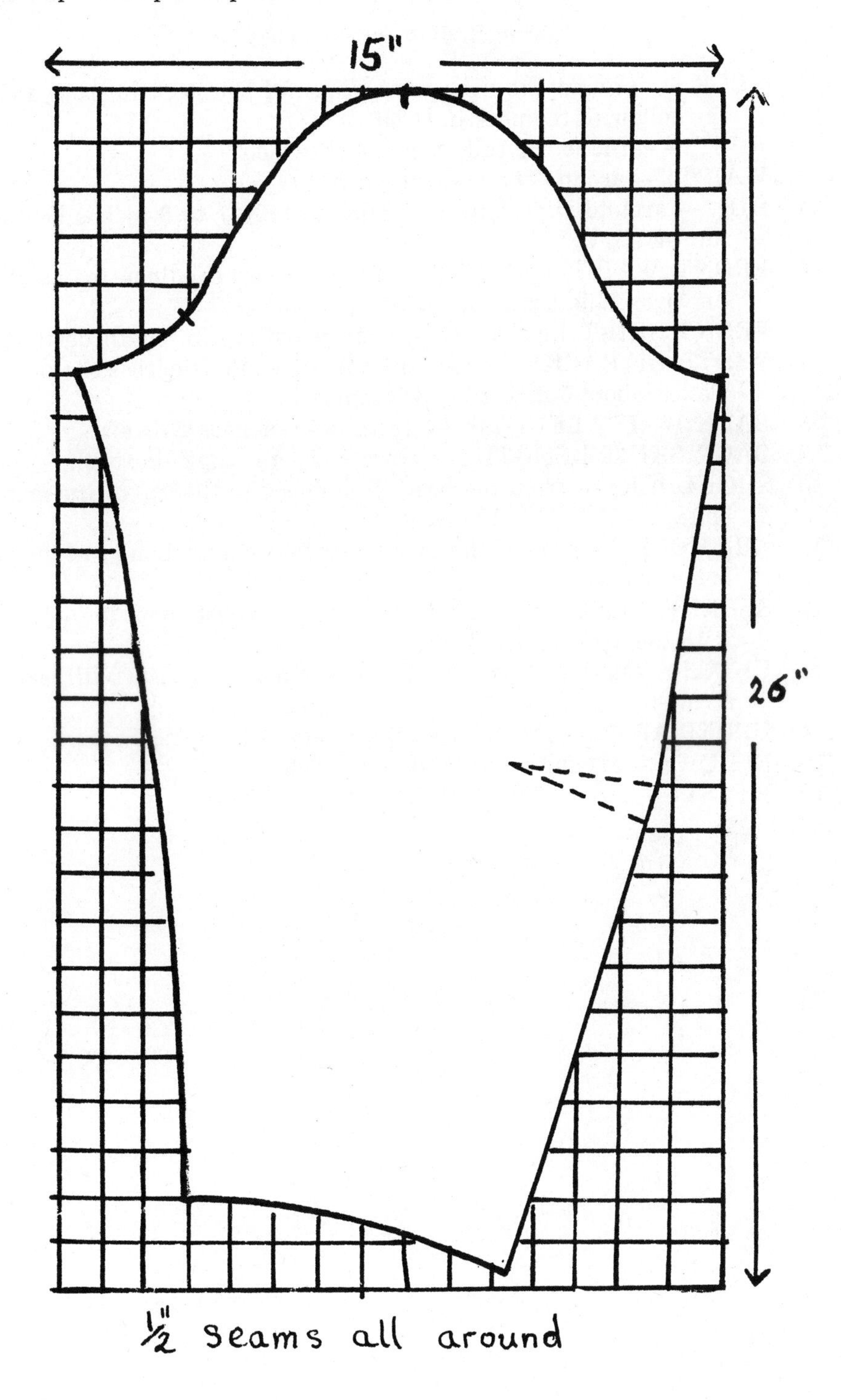

Taking Body Measurements

1. NECK: — around the neck at the base of the neck in back and the hollow of the neck in front.
2. BUST: — around the fullest part of the bust.
3. WAIST: — around the natural waistline.
4. HIP: — around widest part of hips, usually 7 to 9 inches below the waist.
5. FRONT WAIST LENGTH: — from center shoulder to waistline over fullest part of the bust.
6. FRONT SKIRT LENGTH: — from waistline to length desired.
7. WIDTH OF BACK: — from armhole to armhole across shoulder blades, about 5 inches below the neck.
8. BACK WAIST LENGTH: — from base of neck to waist.
9. BACK SKIRT LENGTH: — from waist to length desired.
10. SHOULDER: — from the base of the neck to the top of the arm bone.
11. ARMHOLE: — around the arm from top of arm bone to 1 inch below the armpit.
12. SLEEVE LENGTH: — from shoulder to wrist over the elbow with the arm slightly bent.
13. UNDERARM LENGTH: — from armpit to wrist with arm straight.
14. UPPER ARM: — around the fullest part of the arm.
15. ELBOW: — around elbow with arm bent.
16. WRIST: — around the wrist just above the hand.

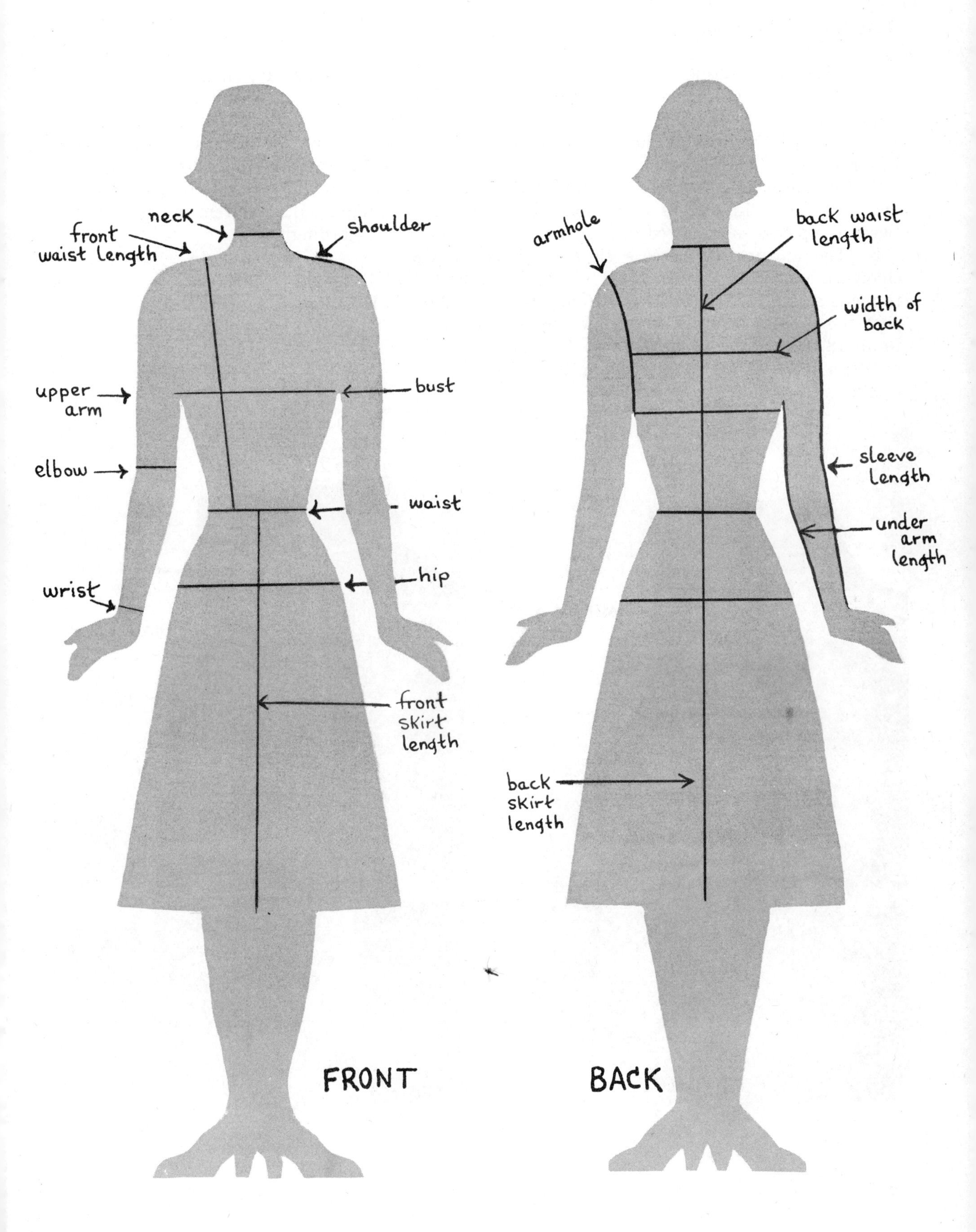
neck
front waist length
shoulder
upper arm
bust
elbow
waist
hip
wrist
front skirt length
FRONT
armhole
back waist length
width of back
sleeve length
under arm length
back skirt length
BACK

Grading to Other Sizes

The blocks used in this book are a standard size 14. In order to change to a smaller or larger size, proceed as follows:

1. Mark off the lines on the front bodice. Diagram A.

2. Cut the block apart on all of the lines and reassemble, leaving as much space between the pieces as indicated in Diagram B.

3. The amount of increase shown will change the size 14 to a size 16. If you wish to make a size 18, first make the 16 and repeat the process in order to change the 16 to an 18. Do not try to make a size 14 into an 18 in one step by merely doubling the increase.

4. To make a size 12, simply reverse the process — instead of spreading out the cut pieces, overlap them the specified amount.

The total amount of increase or decrease per size will be given here. However, in making a pattern to fit yourself, be guided by your own individual measurements and alter the blocks accordingly.

NECK	$\frac{1}{16}$	*Length*	
SHOULDER	$\frac{1}{8}$	*Bodice*	
ARMHOLE	$\frac{3}{4}$	FRONT	$\frac{3}{8}$
WAIST	$1\frac{1}{2}$	BACK	$\frac{1}{4}$

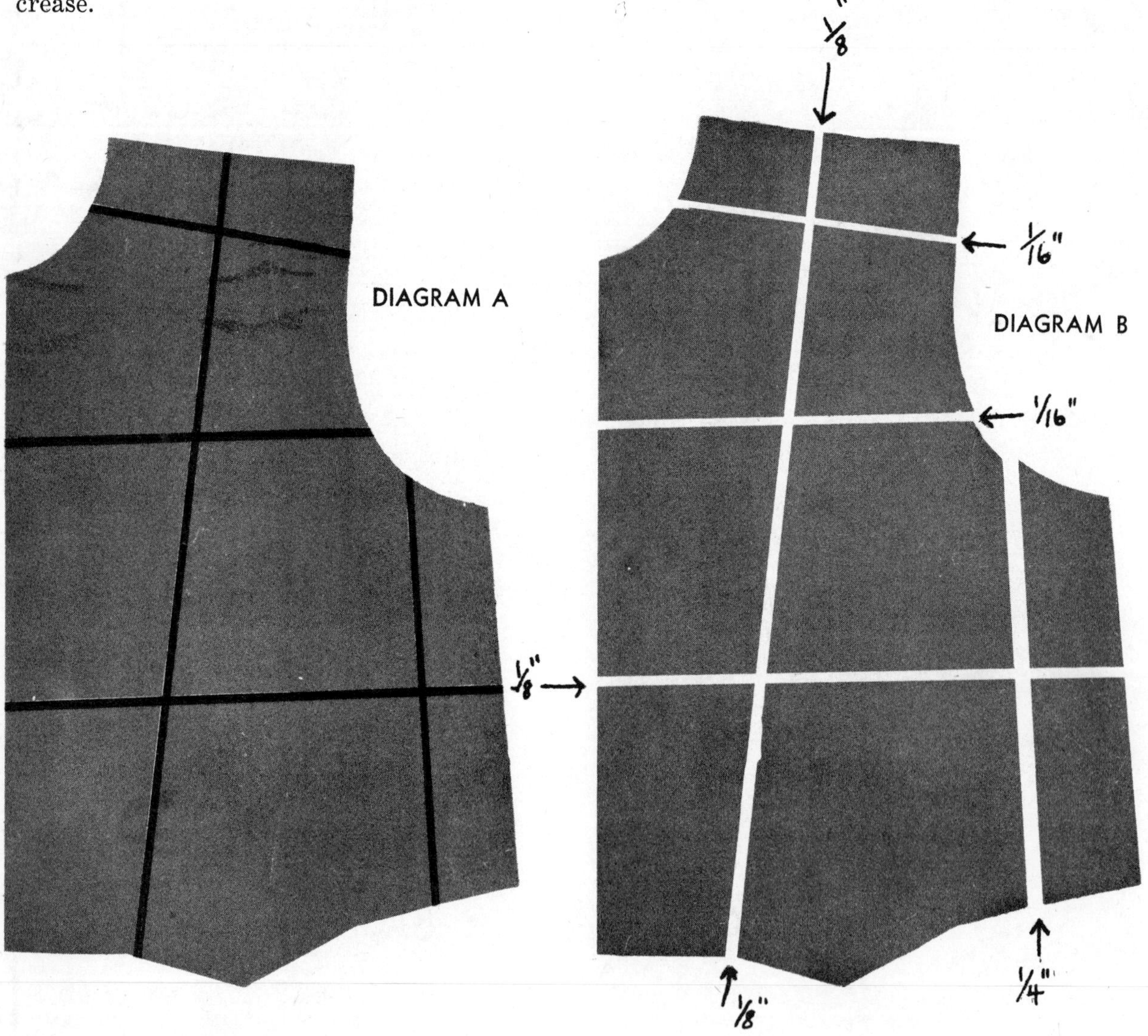

Grading to Other Sizes *(cont.)*

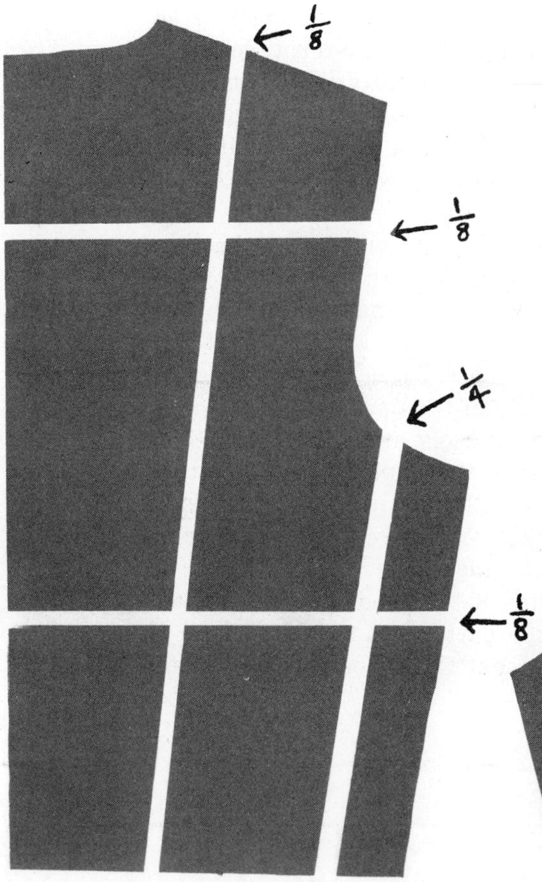

BACK BODICE

Proceed the same with the back bodice as with the front. Notice that there is no increase in the back neck measure. The neck increase is taken care of entirely in the front.

Do the same with the sleeve. Diagram B. The sleeve must increase *exactly* the same amount as the armhole of the bodice, which is $\frac{3}{4}$ inch to a size.

Skirts and Shorts or Slacks

Increase or decrease the waist and hip measurement $1\frac{1}{2}$ inches for every size.

Crotch measure increases or decreases $\frac{1}{4}$ inch every other size. Thus, a size 12 and a size 14 will have the same crotch length, and a size 16 and 18 will be $\frac{1}{4}$ inch longer in the crotch.

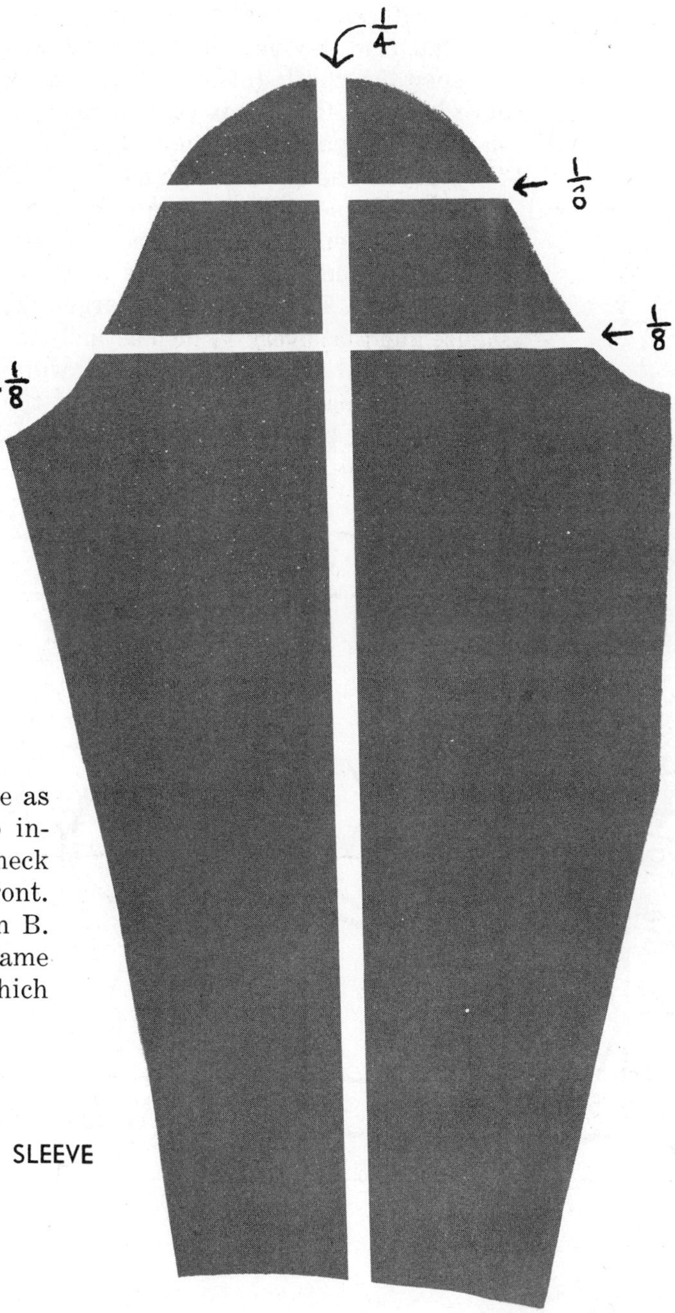

SLEEVE

Estimating Yardage

In order to estimate the yardage required for a pattern, it is necessary to lay out all of the pattern pieces, fitted together as closely as possible on a piece of paper the same width as the material selected.

Since it would be awkward to use a full-size pattern without professional facilities, it saves time to copy your pattern in quarter size for the purpose of estimating yardage. All pattern pieces should have a directional arrow marked on them to show in which direction the piece should be cut.

To determine exactly how much yardage you will need in cutting your garment, lay out all of the quarter-size pattern pieces on a piece of paper the width (also in ¼ inch scale) of the material which you have in mind. Or, to cut your garment on the fold, lay the pieces out on a piece of paper half the width of the material, being sure to mark "FOLD" on one side, and "SELVEDGE" on the opposite side.

When all pieces have been fitted in as closely as possible, with due regard for their proper direction, measure the paper that it required for laying them together. This amount will constitute your yardage requirements. However, don't forget that you have been working in ¼ size and that every ¼ inch actually is 1 inch.

Laying out a pattern on the full width of the goods generally takes a little less material than laying out the pattern on a folded piece of goods, but in cutting an individual garment the amount sayed is seldom worth the extra time and trouble.

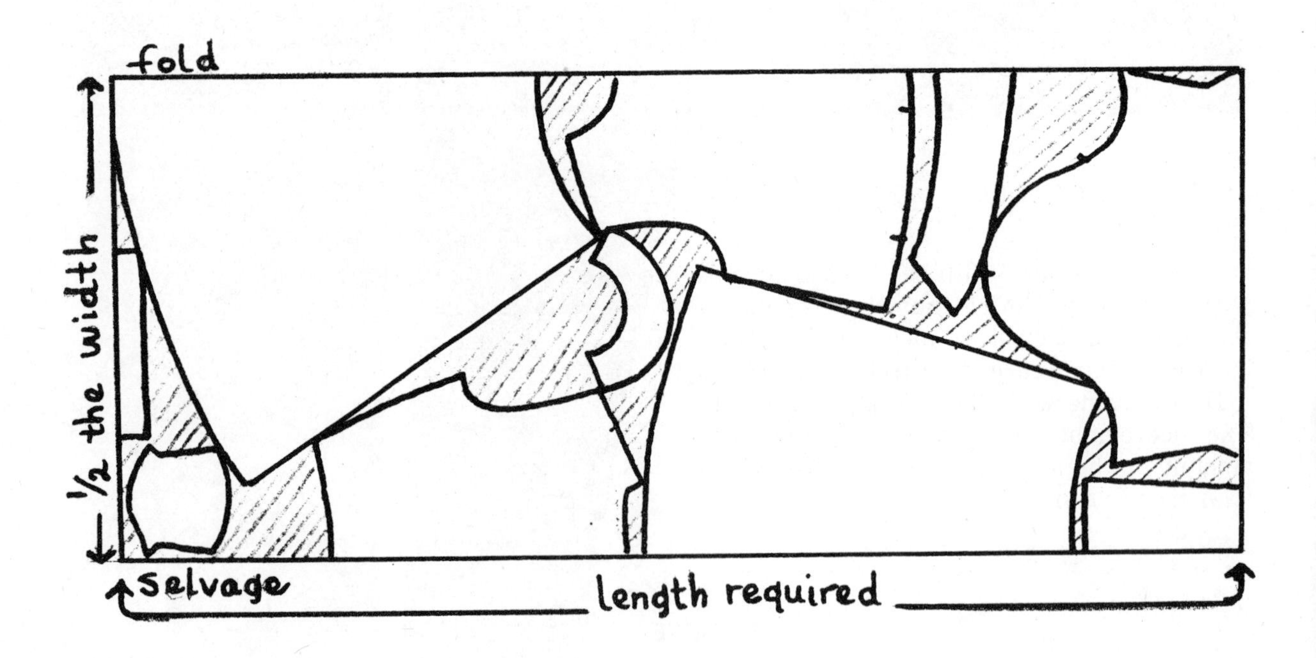

Special Considerations in Cutting a Garment

Prints, stripes, plaids, checks, and pile fabrics all require special consideration in cutting, and almost always take more material for a garment than a plain fabric.

Stripes, plaids, and checks must always match with absolute accuracy at openings and seams, and sleeves must match the bodice except where the design is being used specifically in opposing directions. If there are two or more pockets they, too, must be perfectly matched. It is a good idea to rule in the stripes, plaid, or checks on your full-size pattern so that there will be no danger of making a mistake in the cutting of the actual garment.

Some fabrics — such as corduroy, velvet, velveteen, velour and teddy bear cloth — have a pile surface and have to be cut in one direction. Run your hand over the cloth to determine in which direction the pile goes, and then lay all the pattern pieces on the cloth with the pile going *down* the garment. If you do make an error and have some of the pieces with the pile going *up*, you will find that there is a vast difference in the color, as light is reflected in a different manner with the pile going up from the effect of pile going down.

Prints, too, offer problems which must be borne in mind when cutting the garment. Some prints are one directional and, like pile fabrics, must be cut all one way. Be sure to cut the pieces the right way, and don't have the print upside down. With large prints, care must be used in placing the motif in strategic spots. Sleeves should match unless you are deliberately placing a motif on one sleeve and leaving the other plain. Care should also be used so as not to bisect a large design right at the waist. Better to have one complete motif appear on the bodice and another on the skirt.

Chapter One

Dart control in the bodice

The bodice block is a foundation garment cut to conform to the rounded shape of the upper torso. In order to have the block fit the form, it must have either a dart or some other control, to allow for the fullness of the bust and the proportionately smaller size of the waist.

A DART is a short seam bringing together the edges of a fabric where a V-shaped piece has been cut out of the goods. The dart is *usually* used as a method of controlling fullness. It can also be used for purely decorative purposes.

The dart is only one of the possible methods of controlling the excess material that is required to fit a garment over the contour of the bust. However, in this first chapter, only the dart will be discussed; the other methods of control will be taken up later.

It is sometimes necessary to move the dart from one position to another in order to change the style of a garment. For instance, in a basic block the dart goes from the waistline directly to the center of the bust. If your bodice design is such that the dart would not look good there, you will have to move the dart to another position — to the shoulder perhaps, or under the arm at the side seam. The first problem, then, is to learn to move the dart. This is called "swinging the dart." It is of great importance to learn this procedure, and for that reason, the subject will be discussed with thoroughness. Do not attempt to solve the more complex problems until you have completely absorbed all the information on "swinging the dart."

Swinging the Dart from Waist to Shoulder

This first lesson is concerned with "swinging" or moving the dart from its basic waist position to the shoulder position. Diagram A shows the basic bodice block with the waist dart. Diagram B shows the first step in moving this dart to another position. Follow the diagrams exactly, as this first step is the most important thing there is to learn about pattern drafting.

BASIC BODICE BLOCK: FRONT

DIAGRAM A

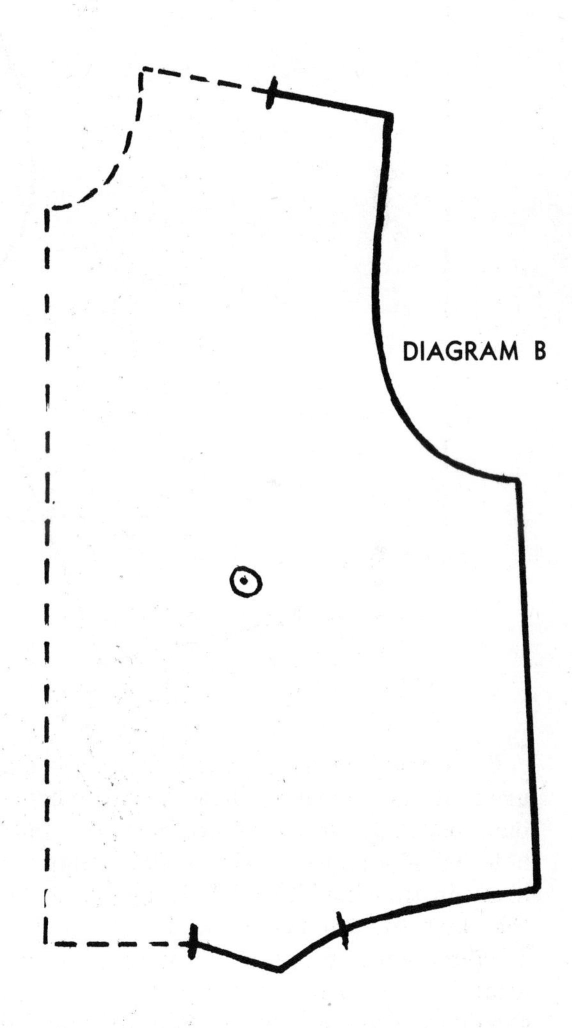

Directions

1. Make a mark at the approximate center of the shoulder.
2. Trace the block from the *front* waist notch around the center front *up to* the mark which you made at the center of the shoulder.
3. Put your pencil through the punch hole at the end of the dart and hold the block tightly to the paper.

4. While holding the block as described in step 3, swing it around so that the second waist notch overlaps the *front* waist notch, which was the starting point for your tracing.

5. Now trace the rest of the block, *from* the overlapped notches around the side *up to* the mark which you made at the center of the shoulder.

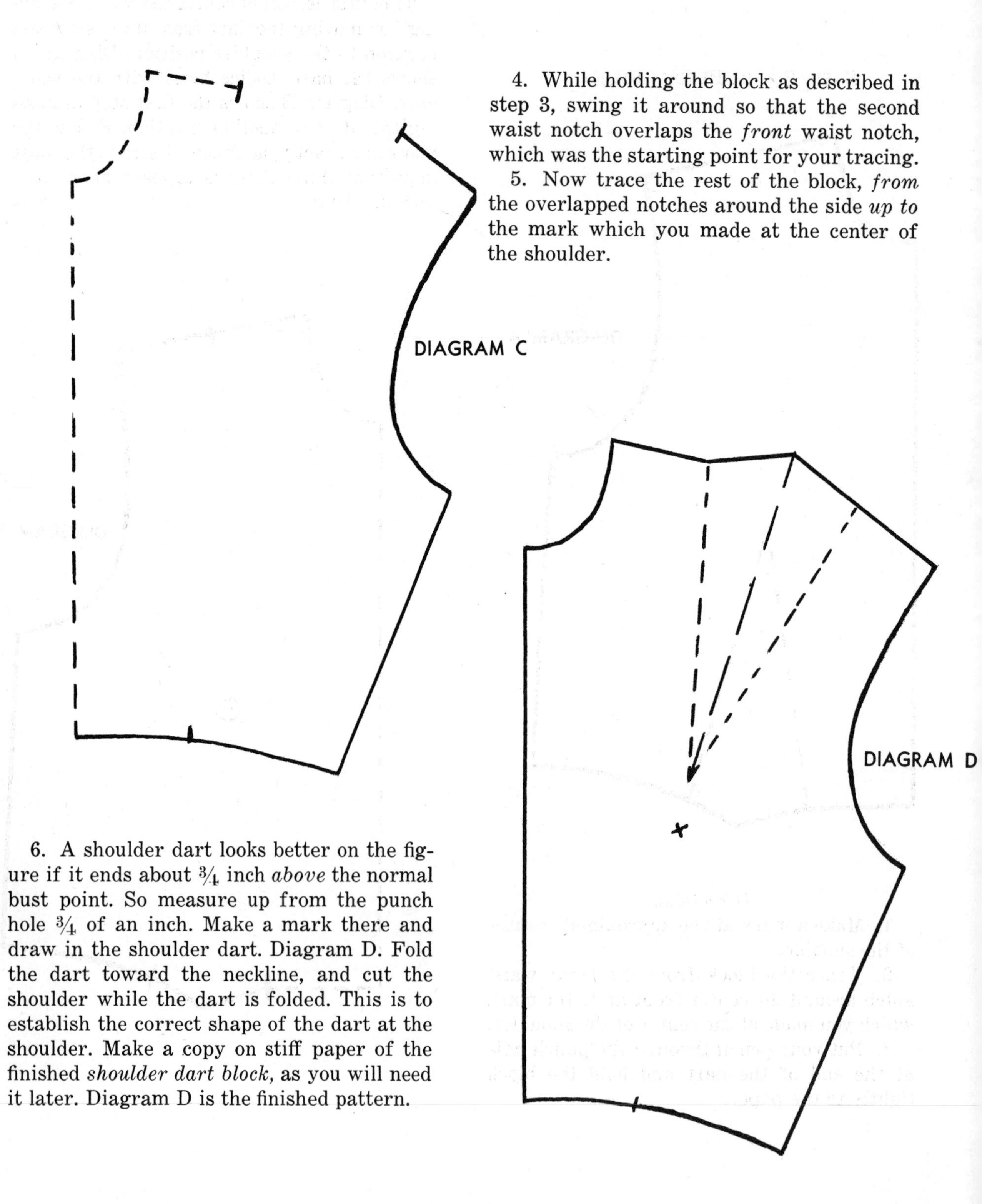

6. A shoulder dart looks better on the figure if it ends about 3/4 inch *above* the normal bust point. So measure up from the punch hole 3/4 of an inch. Make a mark there and draw in the shoulder dart. Diagram D. Fold the dart toward the neckline, and cut the shoulder while the dart is folded. This is to establish the correct shape of the dart at the shoulder. Make a copy on stiff paper of the finished *shoulder dart block*, as you will need it later. Diagram D is the finished pattern.

Swinging the Waist Dart to the Underarm Position

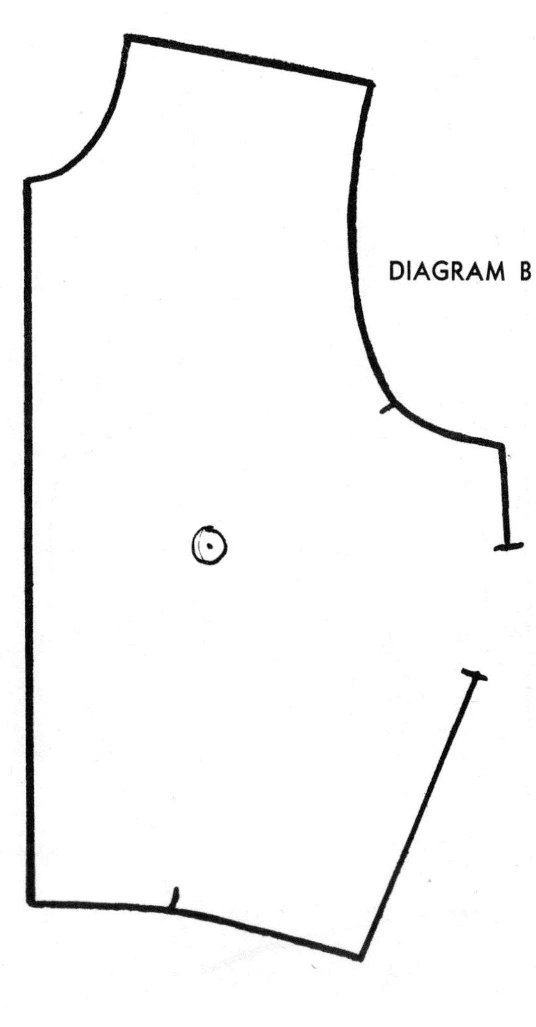

DIAGRAM A

Next, learn to swing the waist dart to the underarm position. To do this, proceed just as you did in Lesson One, except that here you must trace a little more of the block in your first step.

Directions

1. Trace as much of the block as is drawn with a broken line in Diagram A. Make a mark on your block at the side seam, at the point where you finished your tracing.
2. Next, holding the block firmly in place with your pencil point, swing the block until the two waist notches overlap. Then complete your tracing of the block. Should match Diagram B.

SWINGING THE WAIST DART TO THE UNDERARM *(cont.)*

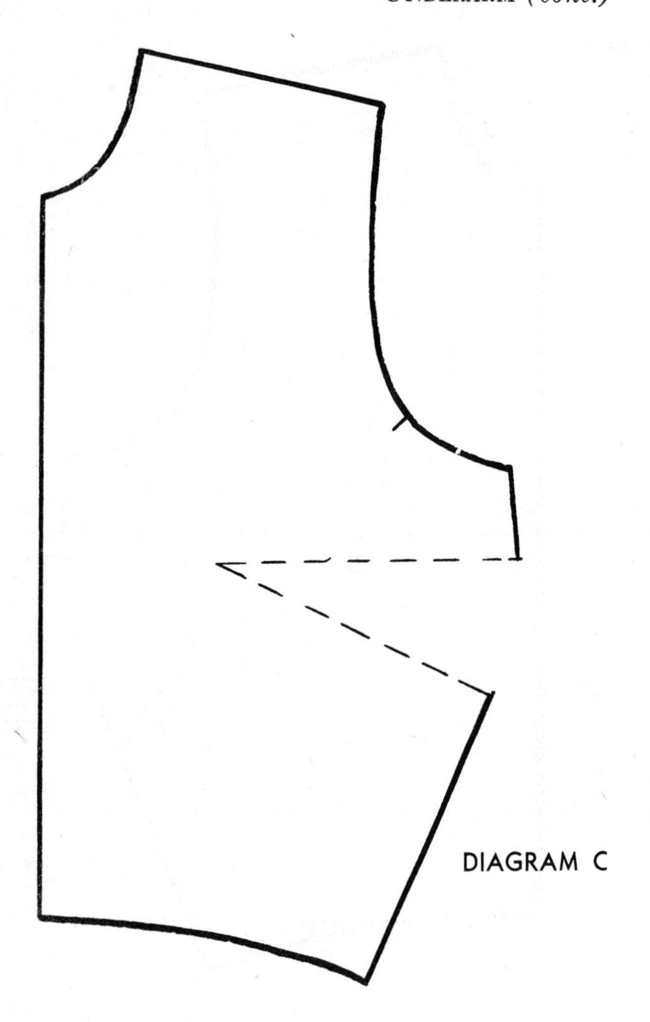

Fold in the new dart and cut the side seam with the dart folded. Diagram C shows the completed pattern. Check your results with this diagram.

DIVIDING THE DART IN TWO

Next, divide the dart in two, leaving half of the original width as a waist dart, and swinging the other half of the width to the underarm position.

DIVIDING THE DART IN TWO

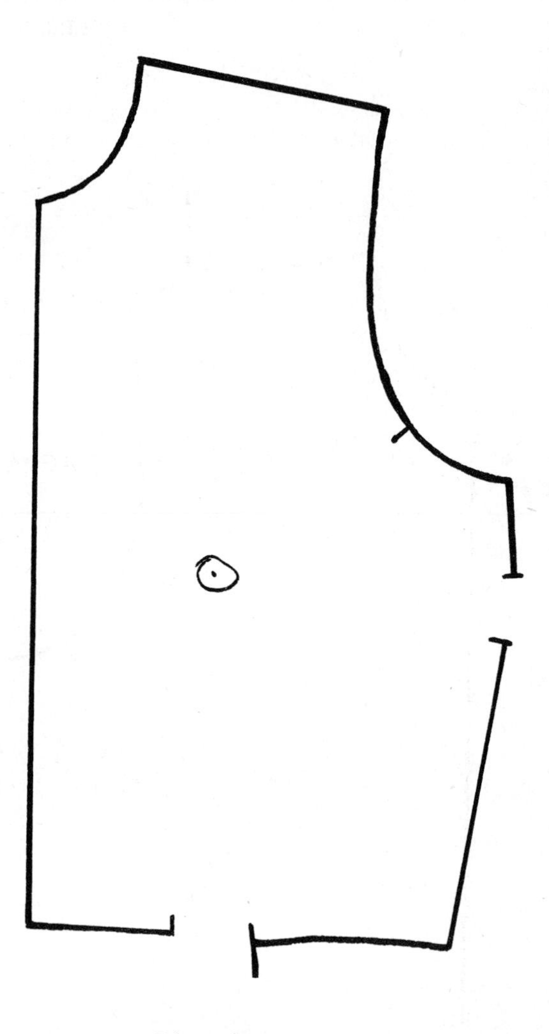

Directions

1. Start at the front notch of the waist dart and trace around the front of the block to the side seam, 2 inches below the armscye.
2. Mark off the center of the waist dart on the paper on which you are working; swing the block so that the *second* waist notch overlaps the mark which you made at the center of the dart. Your waist dart is now only half as wide as it was originally, and the other half of the width is used as an underarm dart.
3. Trace the block from the center-dart mark around the side to the underarm mark. Your result should be exactly the same as shown in the diagram.

Dividing the Dart in Two *(cont.)*

In general, a bodice which uses side darts for control will be more smoothly fitted if the side dart (or underarm dart) is only about 2½ inches in length. The fit will be still better if the width of the dart is divided into two or three shallow darts. It is possible to obtain a perfect fit with a single dart which is full length, but to do so you need to place the dart lower on the side seam. This will be discussed more thoroughly later. This lesson continues with dividing the underarm dart.

Using the block which you made in the last lesson, proceed as follows:

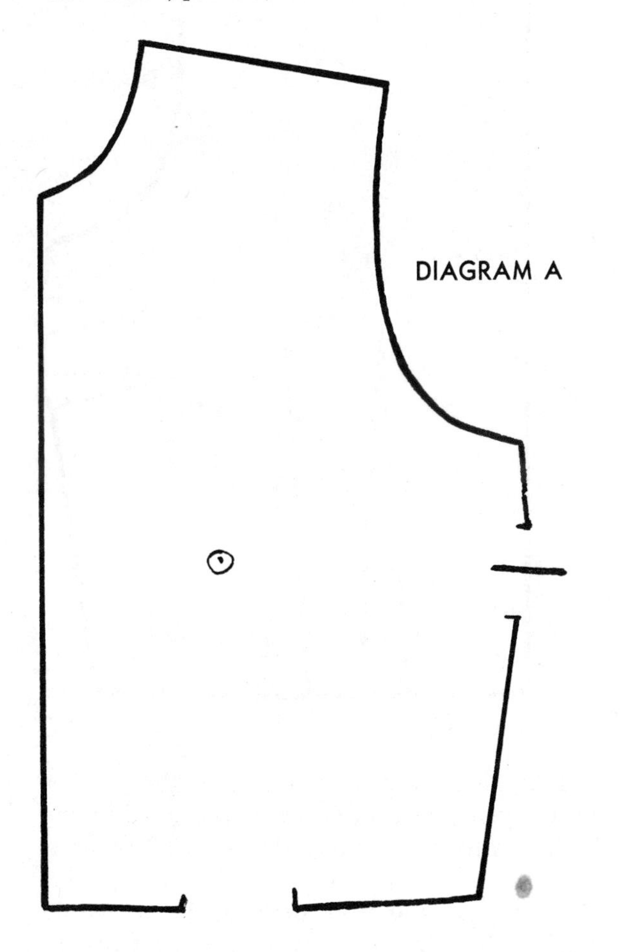

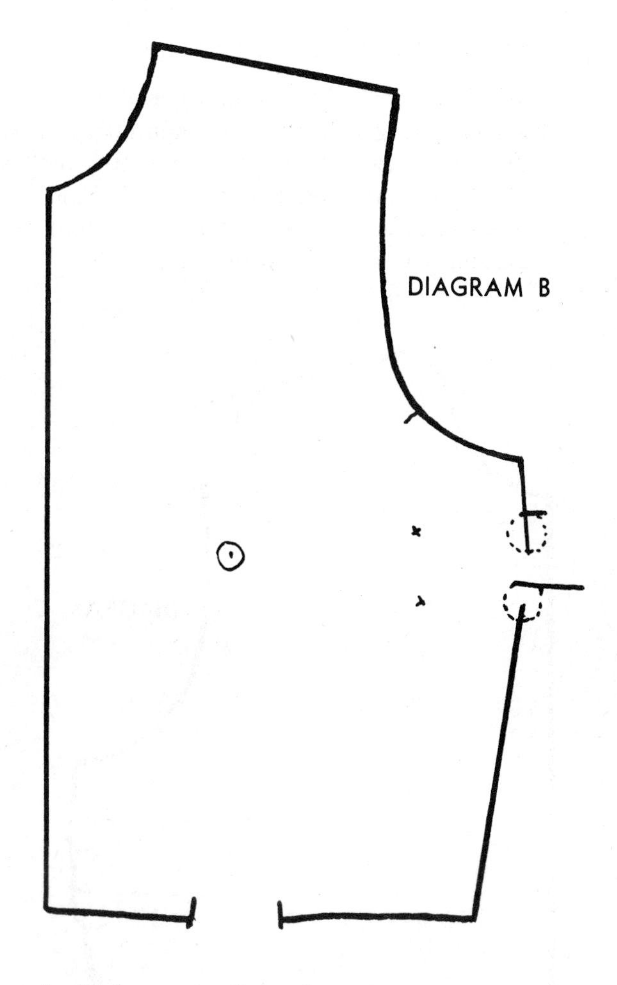

1. Make a pencil mark at the center of the underarm dart. Diagram A.
2. Make another mark on the side seam above the top notch of the original dart. Diagram B. The distance should be the same as half the width of the original dart.
3. The areas circled with dotted lines in Diagram B are the new darts.
4. Measure in 2½ inches from the exact center of each dart. Mark as in Diagram B.

Dividing the Dart in Two *(cont.)*

Dividing the Dart in Two *(cont.)*

5. Draw in the two underarm darts from the four marks which you made on the side seam to the two marks you made 2½ inches in from the side seam. Diagram C. Fold the darts closed and cut the side seam. Fold the waist dart and cut the waistline.

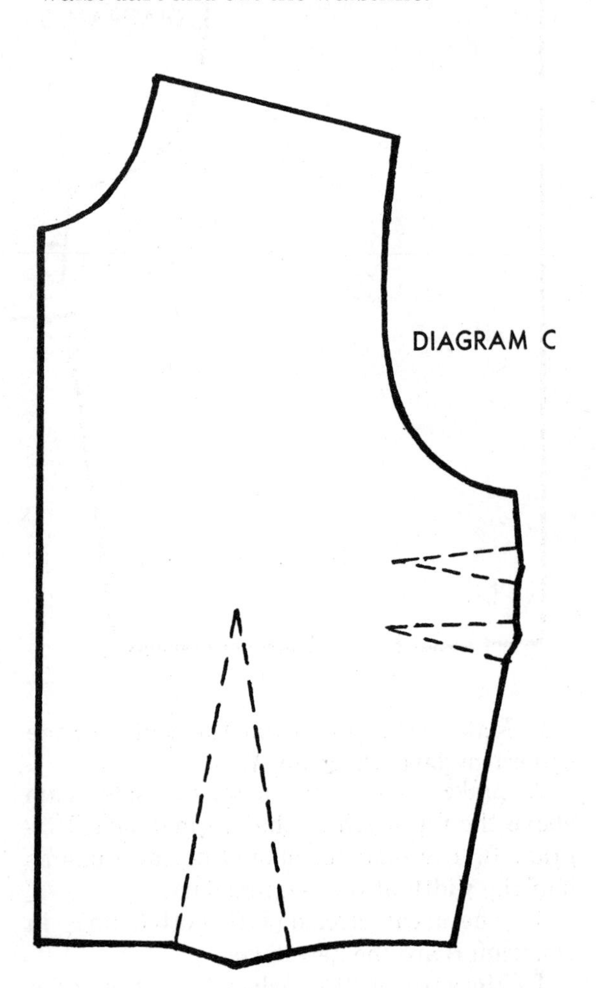

More Dart Divisions

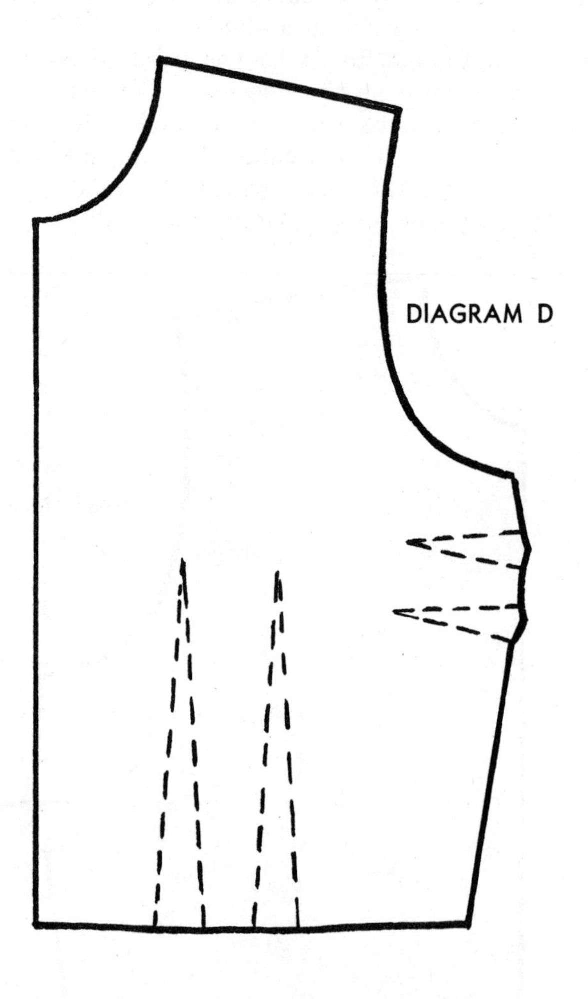

Make a copy in stiff paper of the pattern which you just completed. It is a good fitting basic pattern for many dresses and blouses.

To be sure that you can accurately divide the dart, make another draft of the preceding lesson, this time making two waist darts as well as two underarm darts.

SWINGING AND DIVIDING THE DART

This next step is a little more complicated — learning to divide and move the dart at the same time. Starting with the waist dart block, proceed as follows:

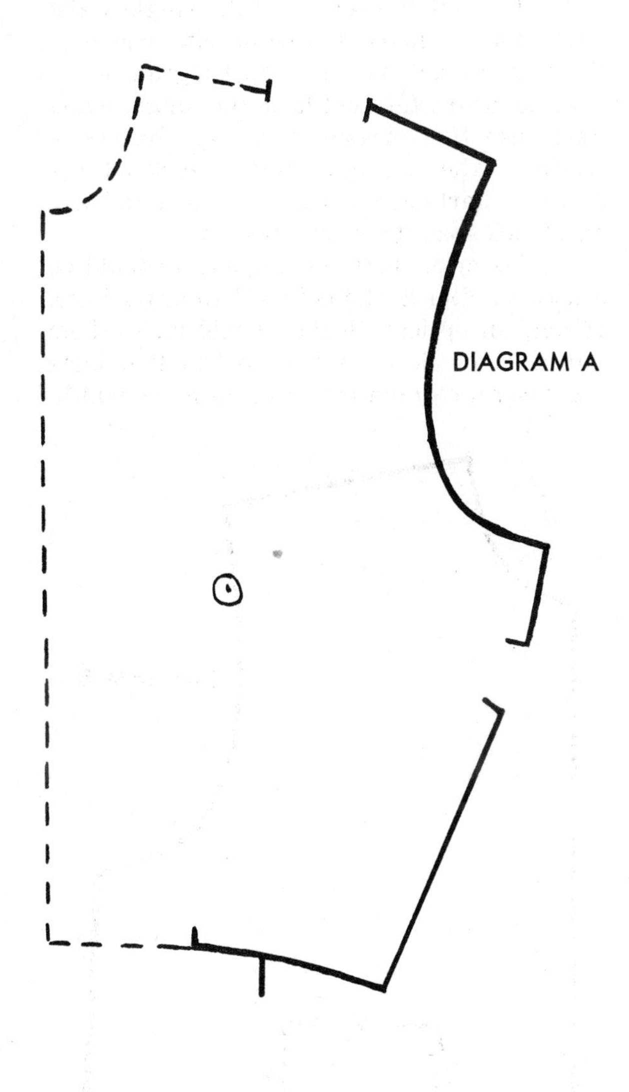

Directions

1. Starting at the front notch of the waist dart, trace around the front of the block to the center of the shoulder seam. Mark this place on both the paper on which you are working, and on the block which you are tracing. See dotted line, Diagram A.
2. Mark off the center of the waist dart and swing the block to that point. Trace the block from the center of the shoulder to the side seam 2 inches below the armscye.
3. Still holding the block in place with your pencil through the dart point, swing the block until the waist dart is completely closed. Continue tracing the balance of the block. Diagram B.
4. Draw in the darts, fold, and cut. Be sure to raise the bust point ¾ inch for the shoulder dart. The underarm dart is only 2½ inches in length.

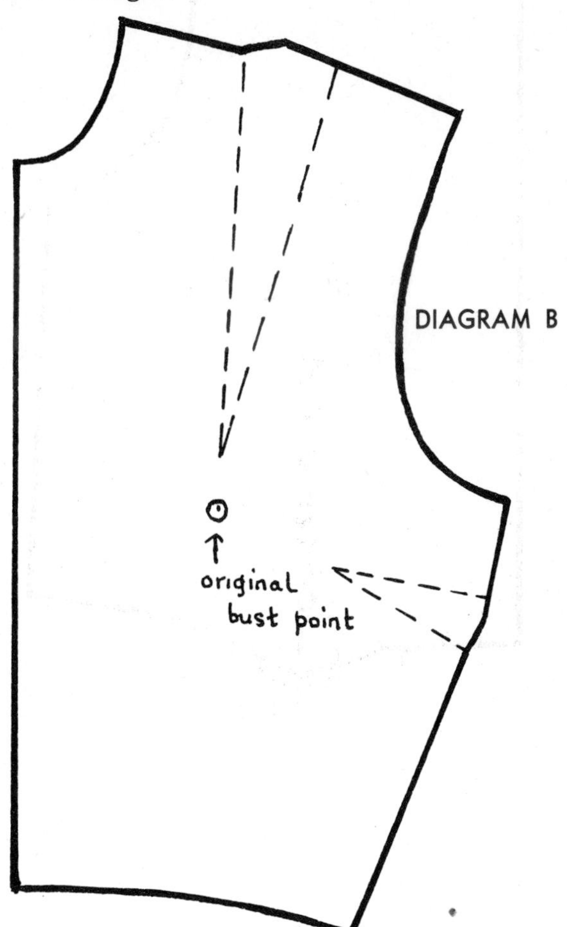

Dividing the Waist Dart Into Two Darts

The next few lessons are going to be more or less a review. It is so important to understand the process known as "swinging the dart" that you must repeat each step until you are able to do it with no conscious thought at all. This first review lesson is on dividing the waist dart.

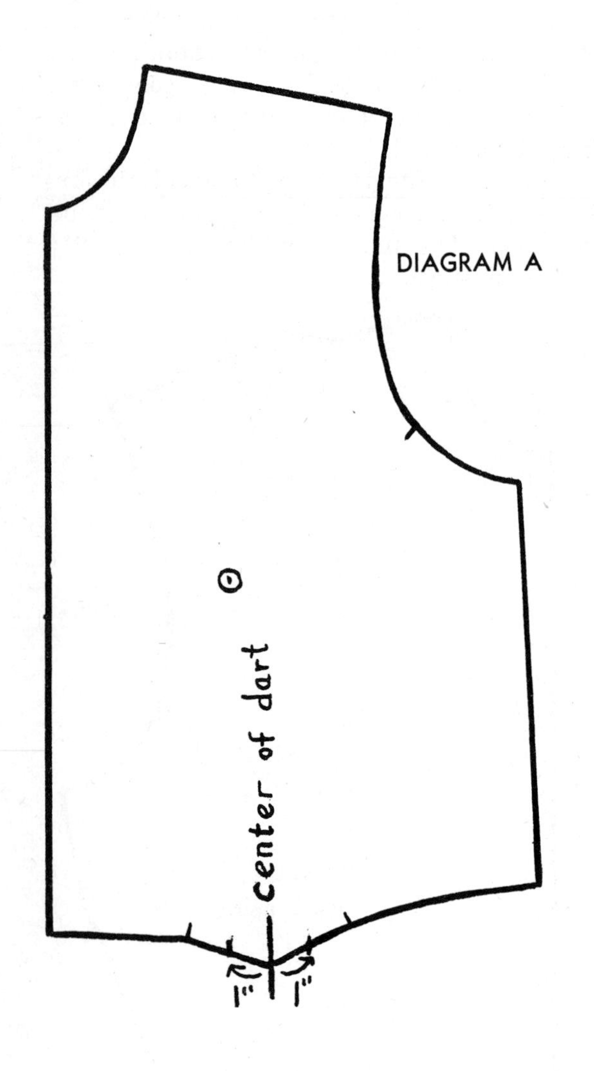

Directions

1. The first step is to determine how far apart you want the two darts to be. In this instance they will be 2 inches apart at the base.
2. Mark off the center of the single waist dart; make a mark 1 inch on either side of the center mark as shown in Diagram A.
3. Measure the width of the single waist dart; use this measurement for the entire width of the *two* new darts. Mark off the two new darts at the waist. Be sure to leave the 2 inch space between the darts.
4. The space between the darts should be a little greater at the points than at the base. If not, an optical illusion would make them appear to be closer at the top. The two darts *must be exactly* the same in length and width.

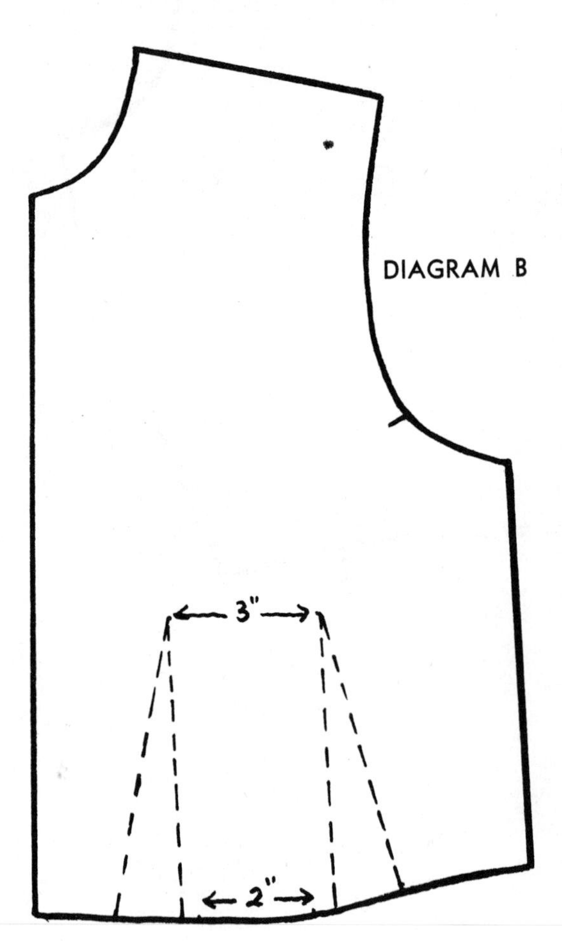

Darts With Released Fullness

A dart does not necessarily have to be sewn together its entire length. You may wish to release the fullness of the dart in order to achieve a soft bloused effect. The pattern will have to indicate this, so that the person who cuts and sews the garment will be able to put in the dart correctly.

Directions

Using the pattern which you made in the preceding lesson, first eliminate the punch holes. A simple way to do this is to paste little squares of gummed tape over the holes. Then make new punch holes lower down on the pattern. In the diagram, the punch holes are 2½ inches up from the waist.

Since the darts are sewed up such a short distance, it will not be necessary for them to be farther apart at the top than they are at the waist. Make your measurements carefully, being sure that each dart is the same length and width. Since there is a ½-inch seam at the waist the *finished* length of these darts will be 2 inches. As this is a matter of style, you may make your darts longer or shorter.

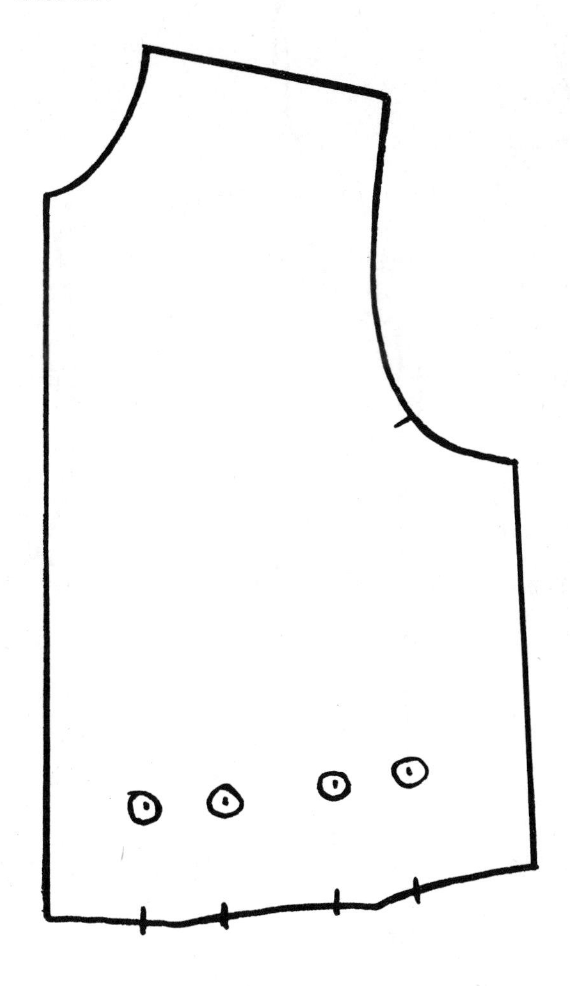

Dividing the Waist Dart Into Three Darts

Now, working exactly as you did in the preceding lesson, divide the waist dart into three shallow darts, as shown in the sketch.

To begin, measure the dart and divide that measurement into three to get the width of each of the new darts. Since the total width of the original dart is 3 inches, each of the new darts will be only 1 inch in width.

Directions

1. Make a mark at the center of the original dart. Use this mark for the center of the middle dart; measure ½ inch on each side of the mark you just made and draw in the center dart from those marks to the original bust point. This completes the center dart.

2. Make two marks; one 2 inches to the left of the center dart, the other 2 inches to the right of the center dart.

3. Make two more marks; this time 1 inch to the left of the center dart and 1 inch to the right of the center dart. These marks indicate the base of each of the remaining two darts.

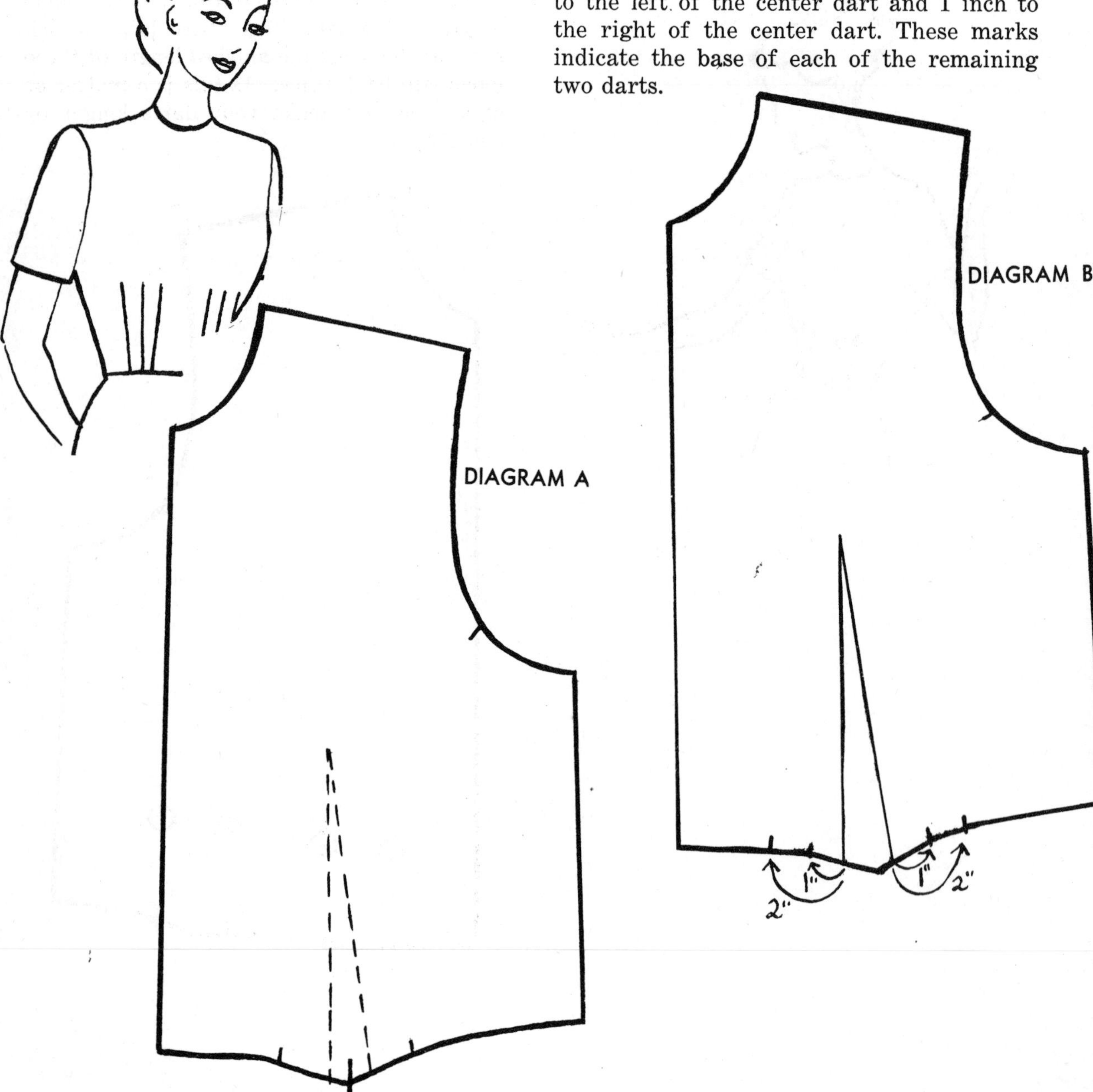

Dividing the Waist Dart Into Three Darts *(cont.)*

Next, establish the points of these two new darts; to do this, proceed as follows:

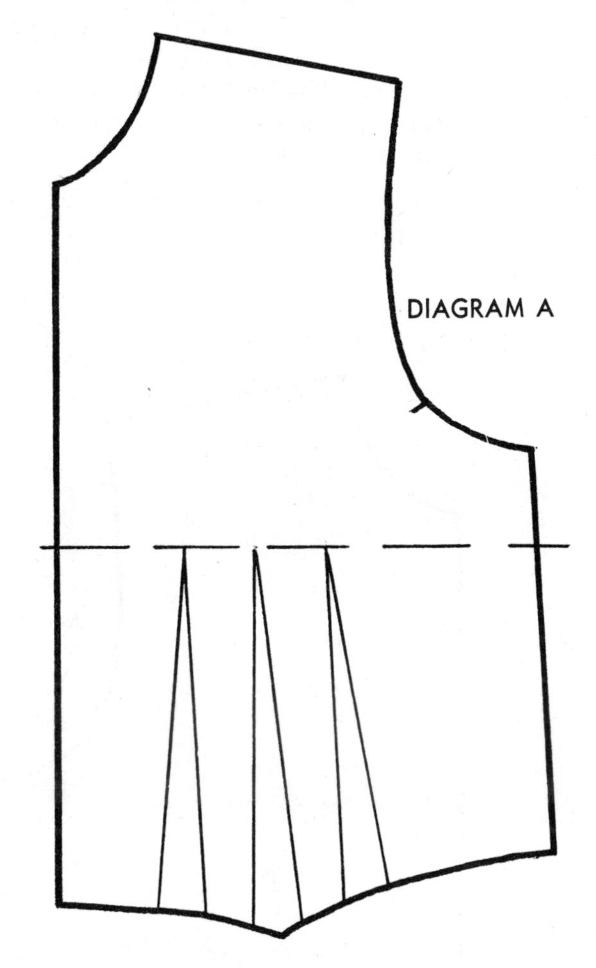

Directions

1. Using the right angle, draw a line across the block at the level of the center dart point. This is indicated with a broken line on Diagram A.
2. Make two marks on this line. One mark is 1½ inches to the left of the center dart point; the other is 1½ inches to the right of the center dart point.
3. Now draw in the two darts, connecting the base marks to the dart points just made.
4. To complete this pattern, fold in the three darts and, with them folded, cut the waistline. The reason for cutting with the darts folded, in case you have forgotten, is to establish the correct shape of the dart extensions at the waist.

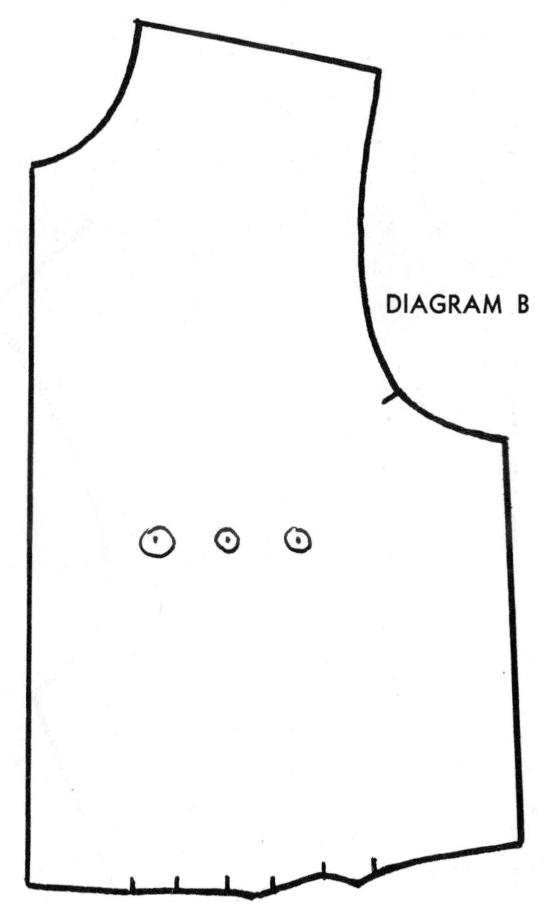

Diagram B shows the completed pattern notched and punched for three waist darts.

Swinging the Shoulder Dart to the Waist

The importance of learning how to swing darts cannot be overstressed. Before taking up other steps, it is essential that this basic step be not only mastered but completely "absorbed." This time, using the *shoulder dart block,* which you made by swinging the waist dart to the shoulder, reverse the process and swing the shoulder dart back to the waist.

Directions

1. Trace as much of the shoulder dart block as is shown with a dotted line in Diagram A.

2. Holding your pencil firmly in the punch hole, swing the block until the shoulder dart is completely closed. Then trace the balance of the block. The bust point will have to be lowered 3/4 inch, since you raised it that amount when you made the *shoulder dart block.*

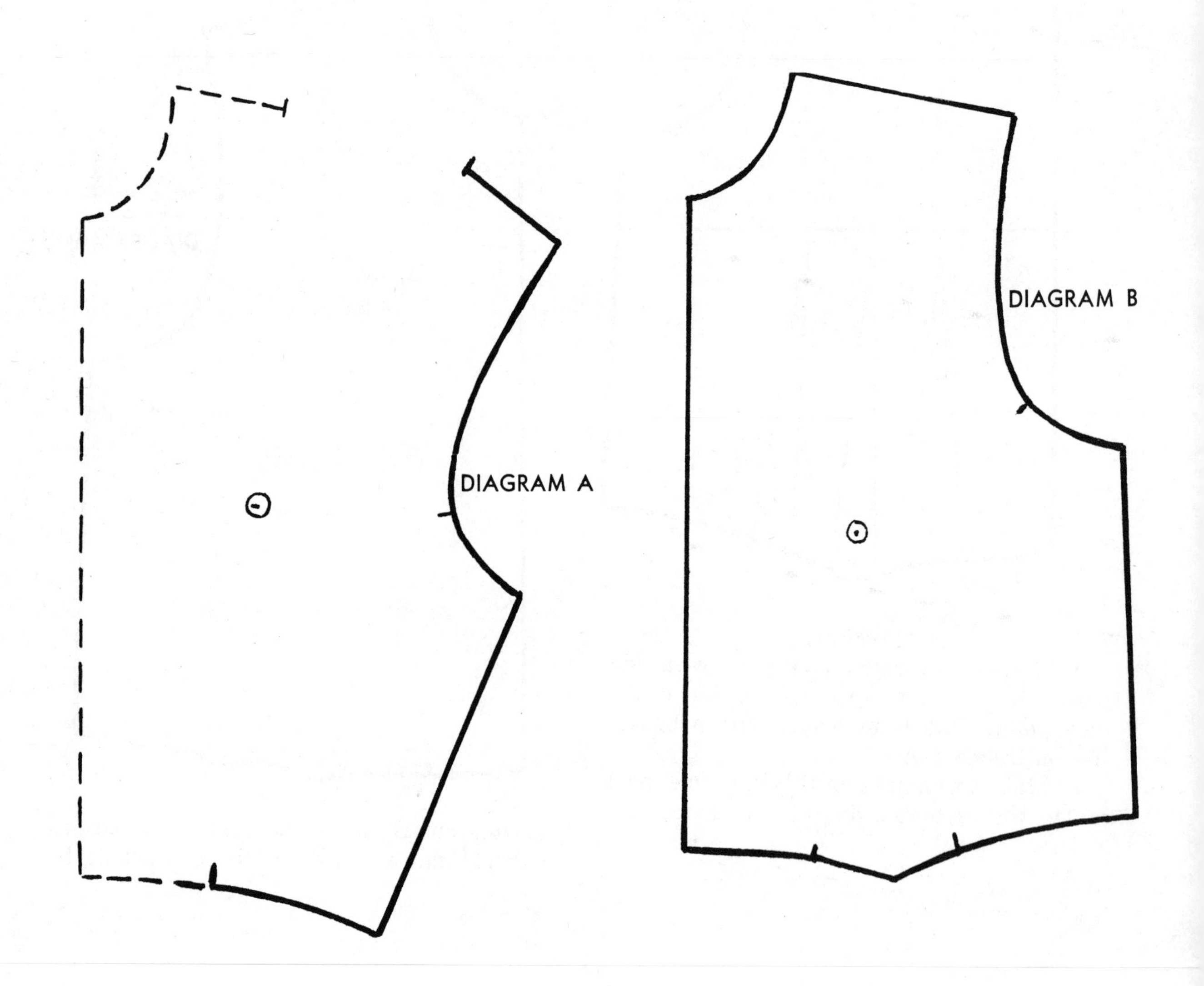

Dividing the Shoulder Dart Into Two Darts

To continue the review, divide the shoulder dart into two shallower shoulder darts. This is primarily a matter of careful measuring. A space of 2½ inches between the two darts will result in a well proportioned style.

First you will have to mark off the center of the shoulder dart. Measure 1¼ inches on each side of the center mark. Mark these two points. Next, measure 1¼ inches on each side of the dart point. Draw in the new darts, making the base, which is at the shoulder seam, 2 inches in width. Fold the darts closed and cut the shoulder seam.

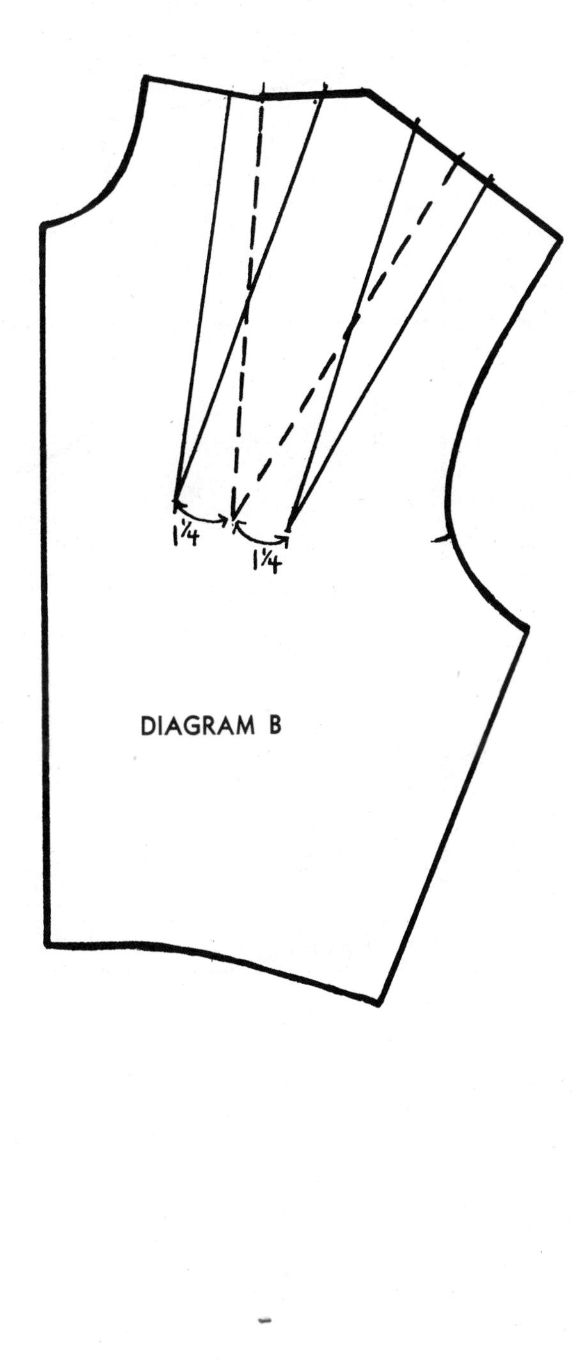

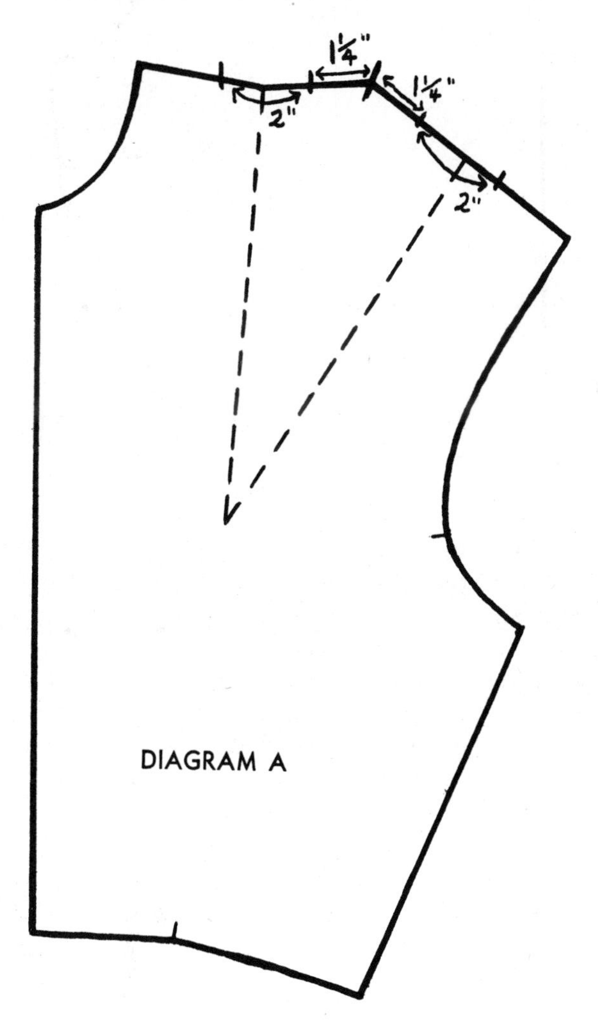

More Shifting of the Shoulder Dart

Next step in this review is to swing the shoulder dart to the underarm position. No detailed instructions are given here, as you should be able to accomplish this step with ease. Diagram A shows the completed pattern.

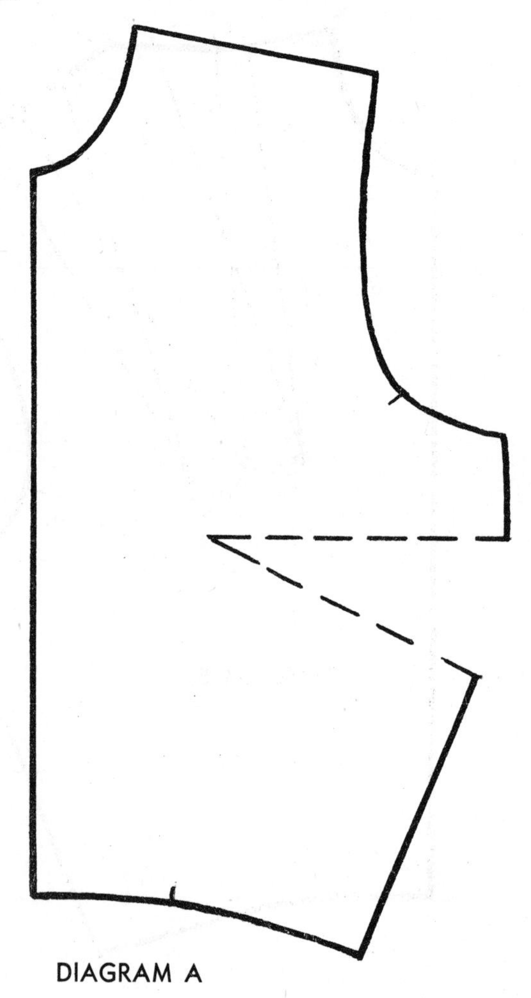

DIAGRAM A

DIAGRAM B

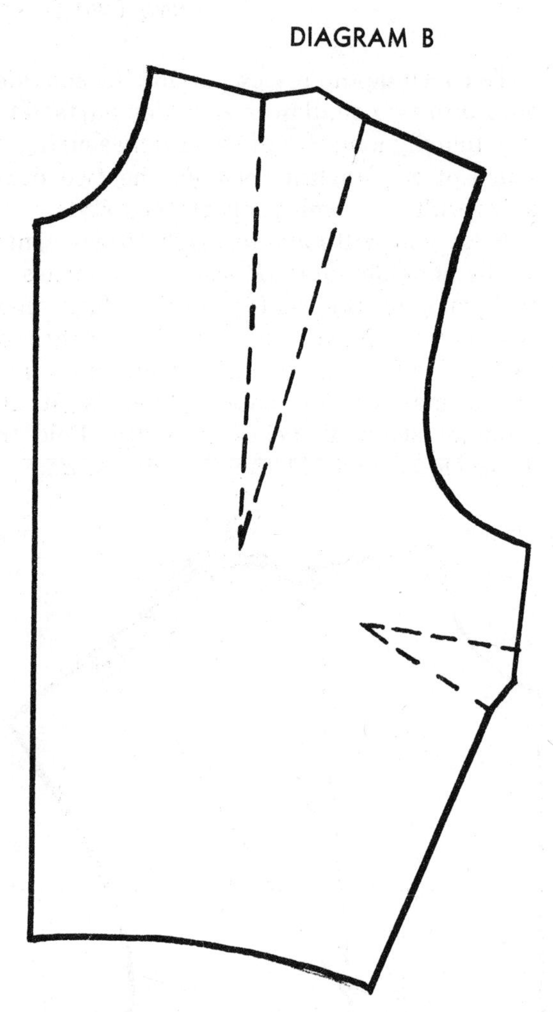

Diagram B shows the completed pattern for a bodice which has both a shoulder dart and an underarm dart. Using the *shoulder dart block* again, divide the dart and swing half the width to the underarm position. This time make the underarm dart 2½ inches long. Remember to complete your patterns by folding in the darts before cutting any seam line which has a dart extension.

Swinging Half the Shoulder Dart to the Waist

The next problem is to swing half the shoulder dart to the waist while retaining the other half as a shoulder dart. A few directions are given, although by now you should be able to shift the dart without advice.

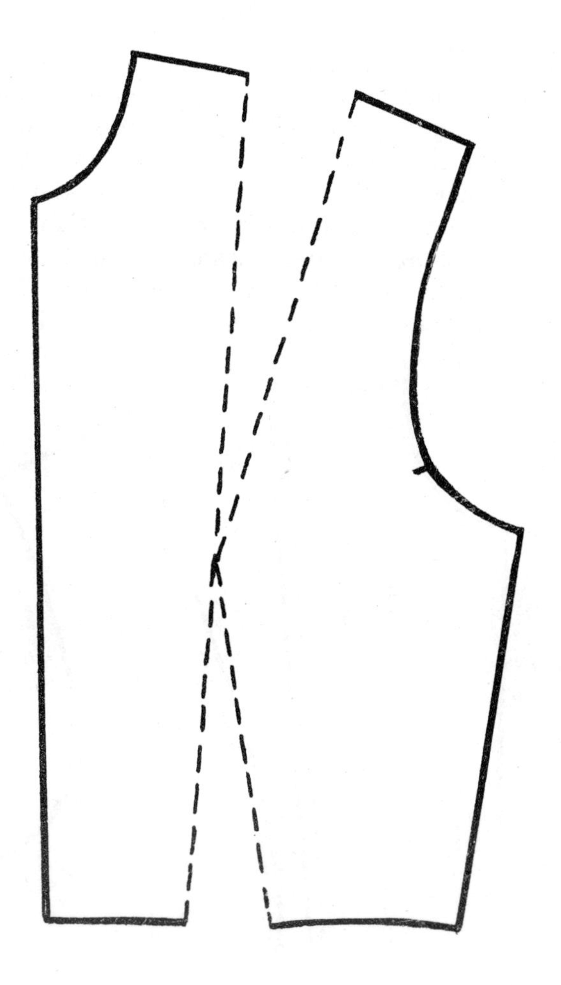

Directions

1. Starting at the waist notch (the one closest to the center front), trace the block around the front to the center of the shoulder seam. Make a mark at the center of the shoulder dart on the paper on which you are working.
2. Swing the block so that the shoulder dart is half closed; then continue tracing the block.
3. Be sure that you lower the bust point ¾ inch for the waist dart.

Two darts that almost but not quite meet at the bust point would give the garment a very poor fit. For that reason, cut this pattern into two pieces, which will give what is known as a "princess" bodice. Cut as indicated by the dotted lines in the diagram. The excess material which is in the darts will be cut away completely and the two pieces will be seamed back together.

FRONT "PRINCESS" BODICE

The preceding lesson is continued by adding seam allowance to the two pattern pieces which you made for the "princess" bodice. If the two pieces were to be sewed up as they are now, with no seam allowance, the finished garment would be much too tight. To avoid this, a ½-inch seam will have to be added to each of the two pattern pieces. This is indicated on the diagram by the dotted lines.

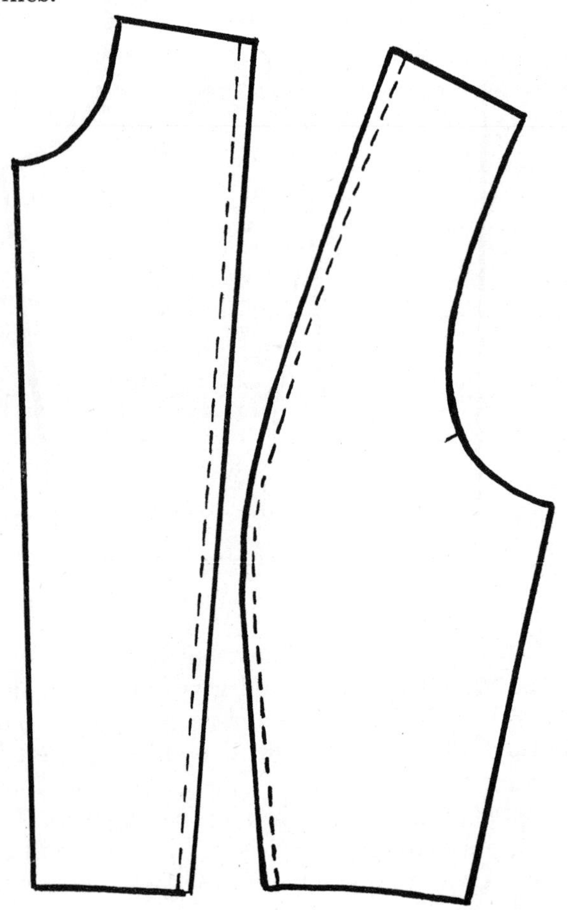

Before adding the seam allowance, round the bust contour slightly. The original pattern is rather sharply angled at the widest part of the bust. A smoother fit will be obtained by making the curve a little more gentle. The next step is to notch the two pieces so that they may be easily fitted together when sewed. In a style of this type, it is necessary to notch the pieces twice, once fairly near the shoulder, and again about 4 inches up from the waist. If the person who sews the garment is careful to match the notches, there will be little danger of its being pulled out of shape by handling.

Seam Allowance

Before going on to the back bodice, you should study seam allowance in general. You cannot make patterns unless you know how, when, and where to add seam allowance. To begin with, the seam allowance on the *basic block* will be explained.

Seam Allowance on the Basic Block

Neckline . . . ¼ inch	Waist . . . . ½ inch	Center Front . no seam
Armscye . . . ½ inch	Side Seam . . . . ½ inch	Center Back . . no seam
Shoulder . . . ½ inch		

Commercial patterns usually have ⅝-inch seams all over; this probably avoids a great deal of confusion, but in personal dressmaking it is better to know all the various reasons for different width seams. In inexpensive clothing, ½-inch seams are the rule. This means all over the garment. In more expensive clothing, which of course gets more careful handling, seam width varies considerably. Necklines, collars, and facings usually have ¼-inch seam. A ½-inch seam can be used on necklines and collars, but, in general, it is easier to turn a collar with a narrower seam, and for this reason the seam allowance is ¼ inch for both collar and neckline. Obviously two pieces which are going to be sewed up together must have the same seam width. Yokes usually have a ½-inch seam if they are faced rather than double. Double yokes usually have ¼-inch seams. But it is impossible to make a definite statement about seam allowance. Side seams in expensive clothing *usually* have 1-inch seams. However, sometimes the seams may be 1¼ inch, or again they may be only ¾ inch.

Shoulders and sleeves nearly always have the same amount of seam that the side seam has in any given garment. The idea behind these wide seams is to provide enough material for clean seaming — that is, to turn under ¼ inch of the material and top stitch to prevent the cut goods from fraying. If the seam allowance is 1 inch, you will still have ¾ inch to press open after clean seaming. This gives the inside of the garment a neat, tailored appearance. In the case of ¾-inch seam allowance, the finish will probably be either pinking or binding. The armscye in this so-called "better" garment which is under discussion will have a ½-inch seam. Since the sleeve cap is sewed into the armscye, it, too, will have a ½-inch seam. On the less expensive, factory-made garment, most of the seams will be overlocked, which is a rather loose buttonhole stitch applied by an overlock machine. This neither adds nor takes away material from the seam; hence the ½-inch seam allowance. Pockets, style lines, cuffs, belts, and waistbands almost always have ½-inch seams.

Chapter Two
Dart control in the back bodice

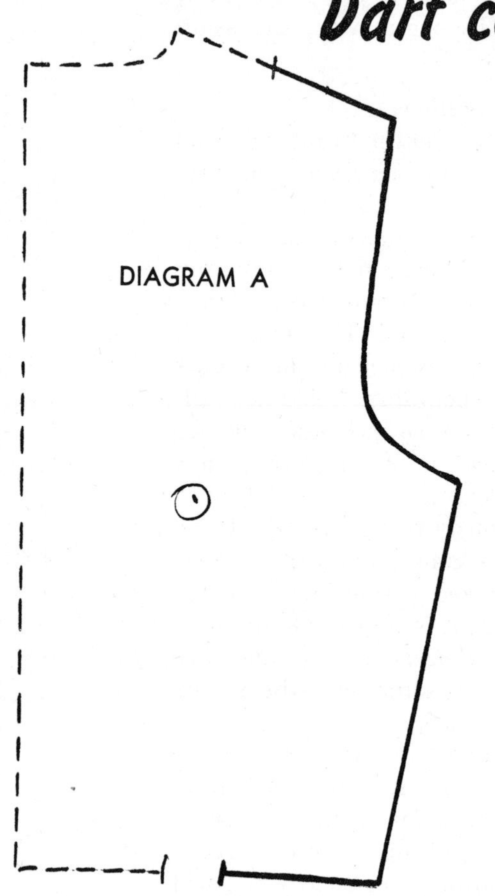

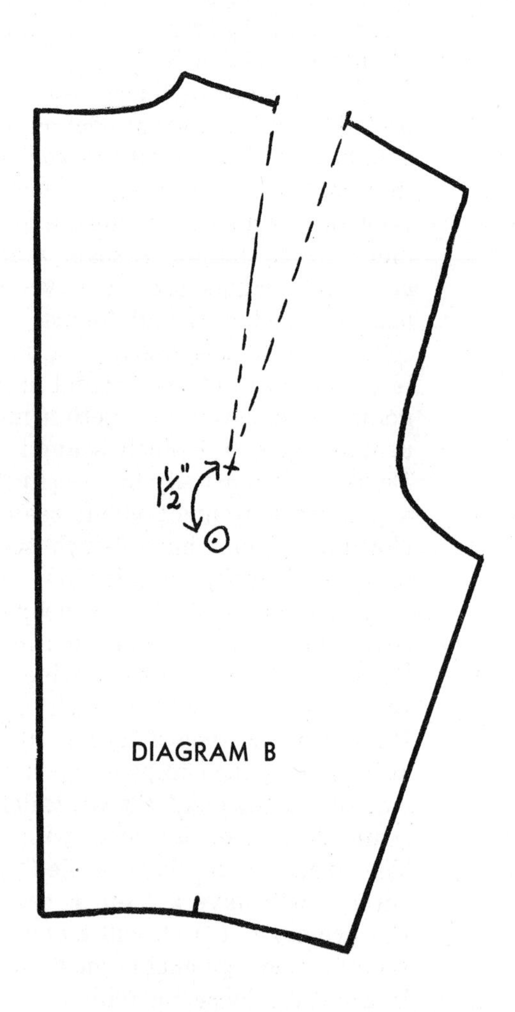

The first problem is to swing the waist dart to the shoulder position, but this will probably be no problem at all, for moving the dart in the back bodice is no different from in the front.

Directions

1. Trace as much of the block as is drawn with a dotted line in Diagram A.
2. Holding your pencil in the dart point, swing the block until the waist dart is completely closed. Then continue tracing the block. The result should be the same as shown in Diagram B.

A shoulder dart as long as the waist dart would give the garment a poor fit, because of the protrusion of the shoulder blade. So take away some of the length of the dart before completing this pattern. Raise the dart point about 1½ inches. Draw in the dart, fold the dart closed, and cut the shoulder seam.

Dividing the Back Waist Dart

The next step is to divide the back waist dart into two darts. Usually, two shallow darts in the back give a better fit than one deep dart. This is because of the gentle slope of the back in contrast to the more or less abrupt protrusion of the bust in the front bodice pattern.

Directions

1. Using the right angle, draw a line across the block at the dart point.
2. Now mark a point 1½ inches on each side of the dart point. Diagram A.
3. Again using the right angle, draw two parallel lines, from the new dart points down to the waistline.

The original dart is indicated by a dotted line.

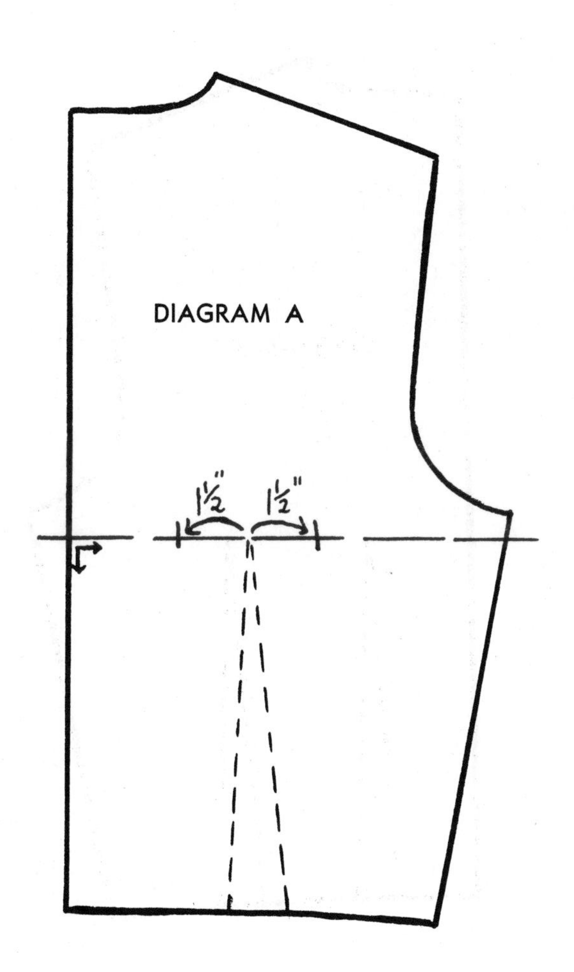

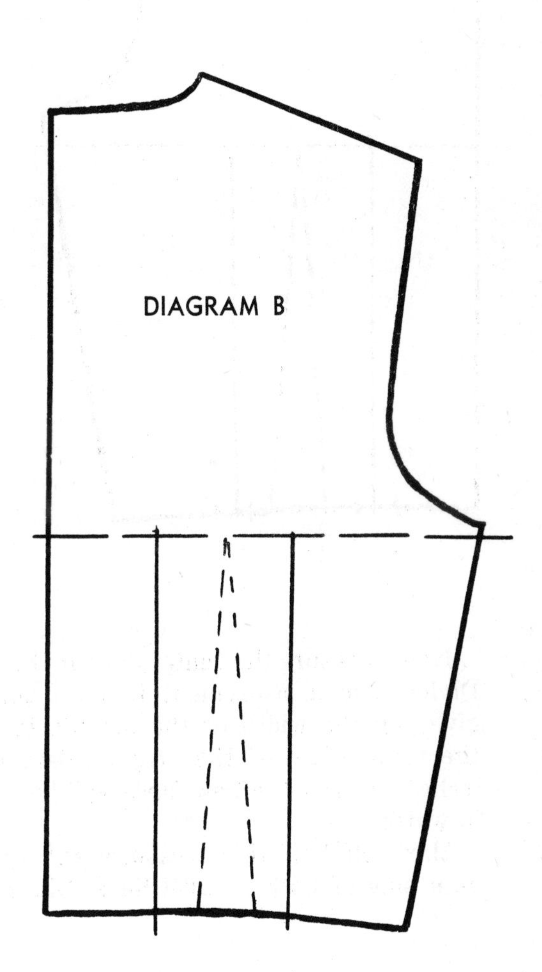

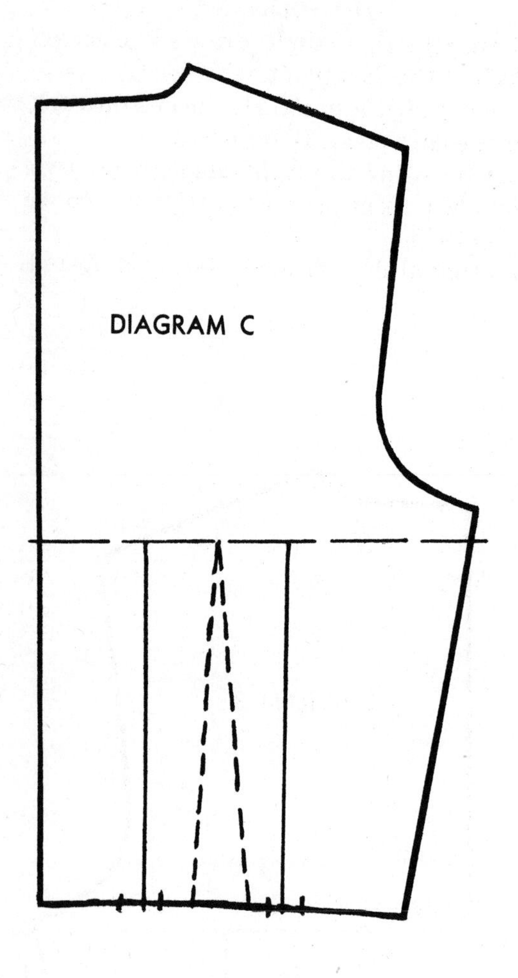

Now, measure the center dart at the waist. Divide this measurement in two; this will give you the width of the new darts. Since the total width of the original dart is 1½ inches, each of the new darts will be ¾ inch in width.

Mark off half this measurement (⅜) on each side of both parallel lines. Diagram C.

Draw in the new darts and the pattern will be complete. You may prefer to leave these darts open part way, and in that case, indicate this by making the punch holes as far up on the dart lines as you want the darts to be sewed. It is especially becoming to have the darts released in this manner on the back bodice. It gives a slightly bloused effect which is flattering to most figures.

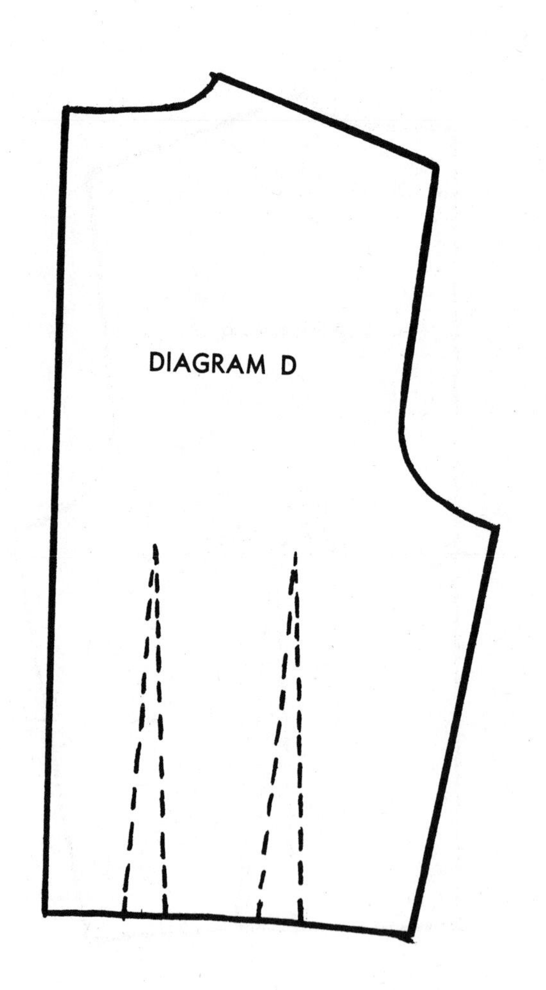

Adding a Back Neck Dart to the Block

A dart at the back of the neck will improve the fit of almost any garment. The reason for this is that the body rounds out from the neck over the shoulder blades. In order to get a dart into the back neck position, proceed exactly the same as you would to swing the dart to any other position.

1. Starting at the waist dart notch which is closest to the center back, trace around the back of the block to a point $1\frac{1}{2}$ inches into the neckline. Shown in Diagram A with a dotted line.

2. Holding your pencil in the dart point, swing the block $\frac{1}{2}$ inch away from the mark which you made at the neckline. Finish tracing the block. Make a mark on the C.B. 3 inches below the neck. Using the right angle, draw a line across the block at that point. Measure in 2 inches on the line. Make a mark. That mark will be the dart point.

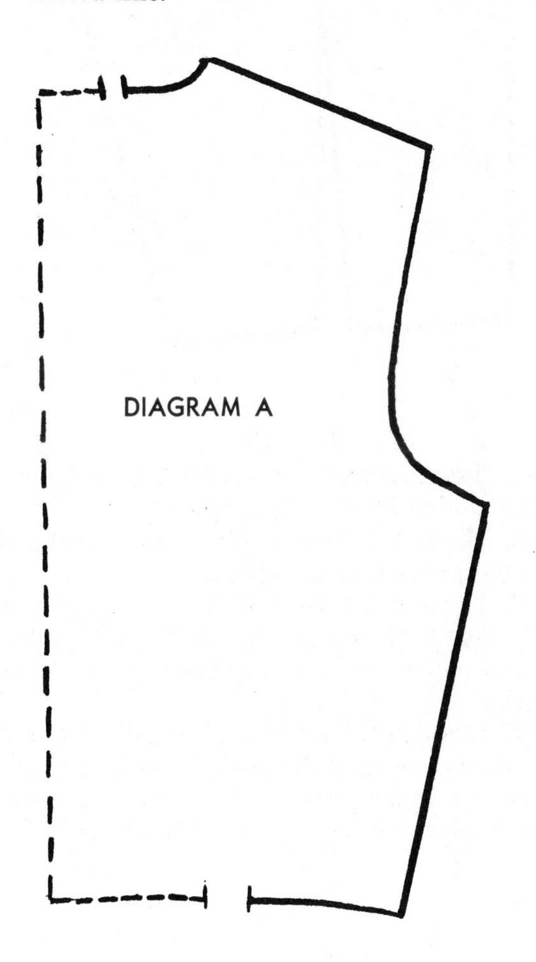

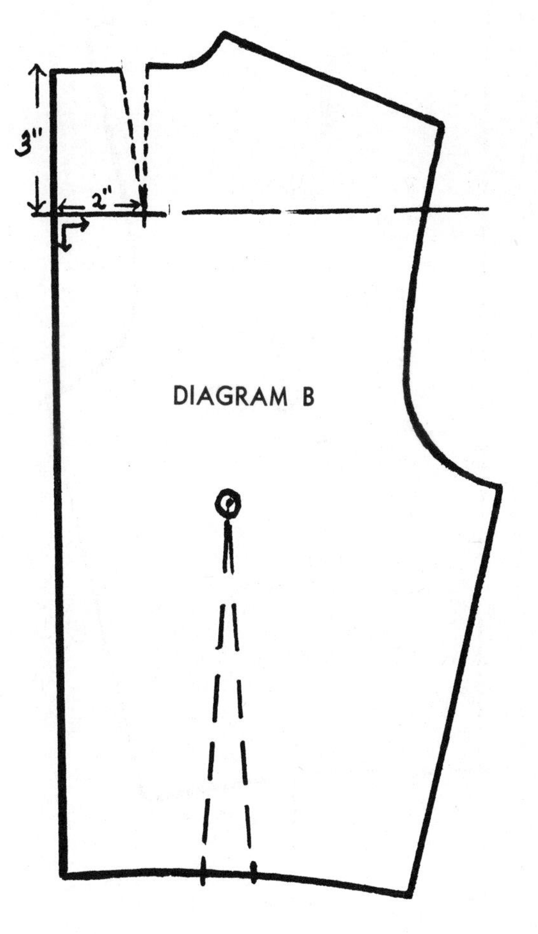

Back "Princess" Bodice

This lesson covers the fitted, two-piece back bodice, which is generally referred to as a "princess" silhouette. Proceed with the pattern exactly as for the front "princess" bodice — that is, by swinging half the waist dart to the shoulder position.

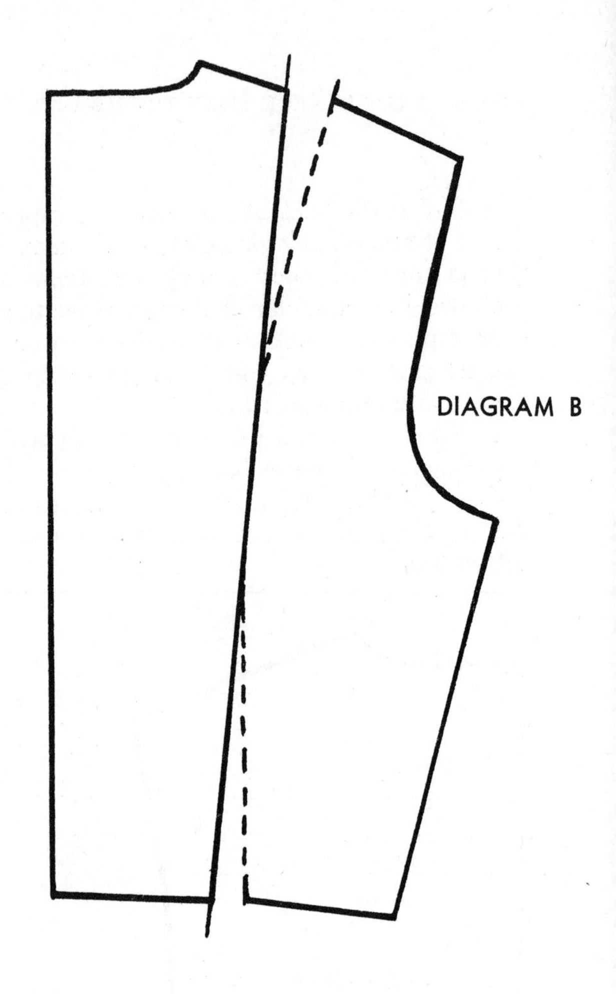

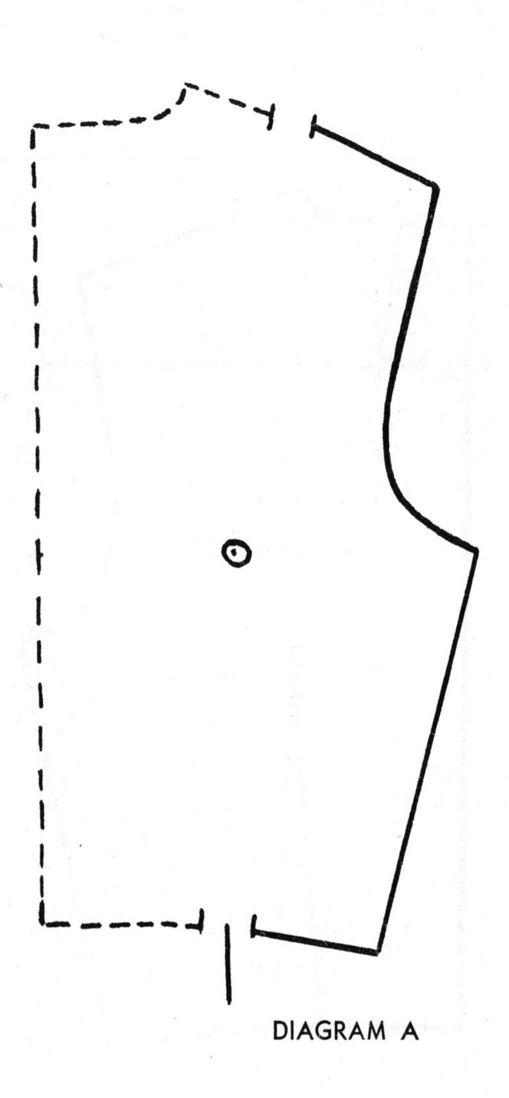

Directions

1. Trace as much of the block as is shown with a dotted line in Diagram A.
2. Mark off the center of the waist dart and swing the block to that point.
3. Draw a straight line from the center of the shoulder, through the dart point, to the waist notch which is closest to the center back.
4. Draw in the other pattern piece by connecting the center shoulder to the dart point, and then to the waist notch closest to the side seam. Make this last line gently curved.

5. Cut the pattern apart. Now you have the back "princess" bodice pattern. But there is still no seam allowance on either of the pattern pieces. So, as a final step, copy both pattern pieces and add a ½-inch seam allowance at the style line of each piece. It is a good plan to make a set of "princess" blocks for both back and front. Make them full size, in stiff paper. Keep these and use them when you need a fitted bodice. It saves time to keep your most-used patterns at hand so that you do not have to draft them each time they are needed.

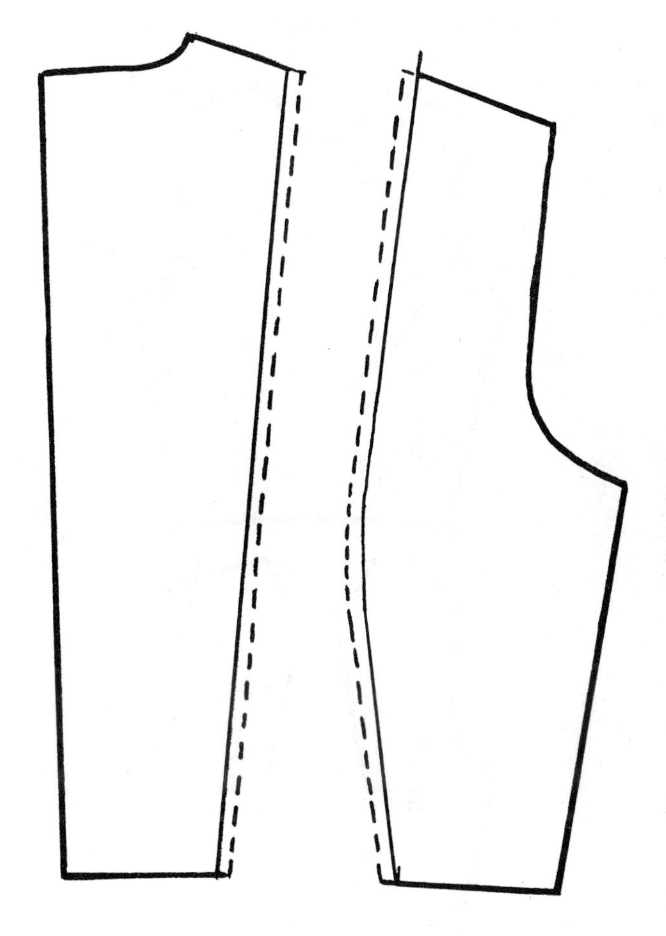

By this time you should have a clear understanding of the dart and how to move it from one position to another. To prove to yourself that you do thoroughly understand these basic problems, work out each of the bodice designs which are included in the test which completes this chapter. First work the patterns with the quarter-size blocks. When you are sure that they are correct, then work them out in full size on tissue paper. Pin and fit them on the dress form. Be sure that the darts always end at the natural bust point, or reasonably close to it.

Test

These bodice styles have been designed to test your knowledge of the dart swinging procedure. If you have carefully followed and worked out each lesson, you should be able to work out each of these styles.

Draft them first in quarter-size, then again in full-size patterns on tissue paper. Pin them on the dress form to be sure that they fit. The first six styles are for the front bodice, the last three for the back. Check your results with those which are included here. Then sketch six styles of your own design and draft each pattern.

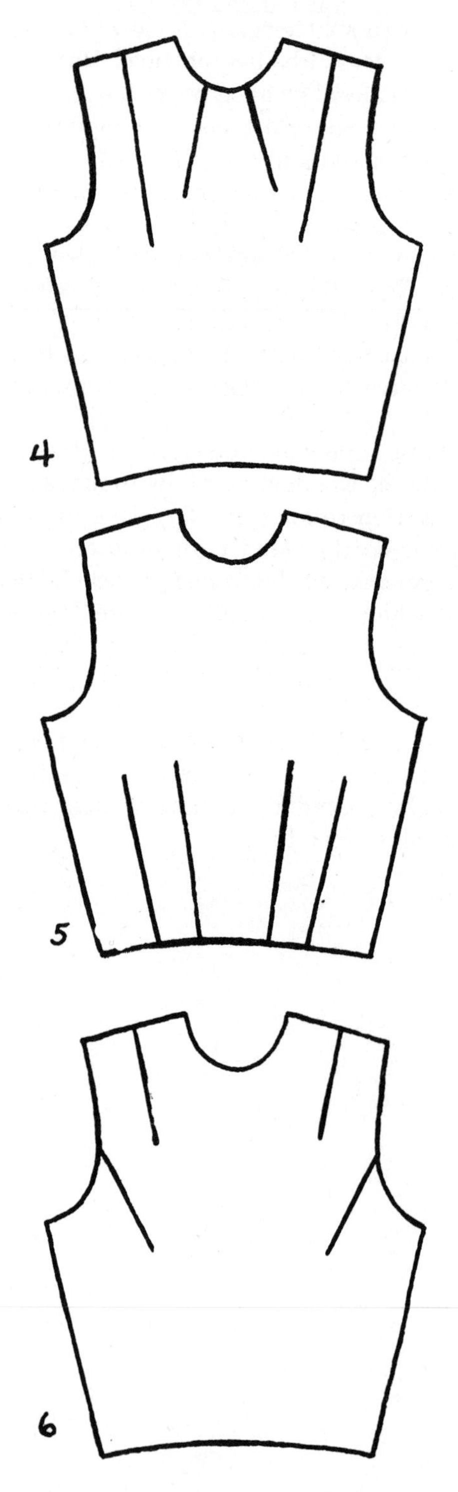

In some of the patterns shown on the next three pages, the excess dart material has not always been left to be folded into the seam. When the dart is especially wide, as in some of these patterns, it looks better on the finished garment if the dart material is cut away and the raw edges simply seamed together. Also, when the dart is placed so that it is nearly all cut on the bias, there is less danger of its being pulled out of shape than if it were folded. There is no rule to follow except to do what is best calculated to give the finished garment a neat appearance both inside and out. In folding the darts closed for sewing into the seam remember the following rule:

Darts at the shoulder, the back neck, the sleeve cap, and the waistline are folded toward the center. Darts in the elbow and the underarm are folded up.

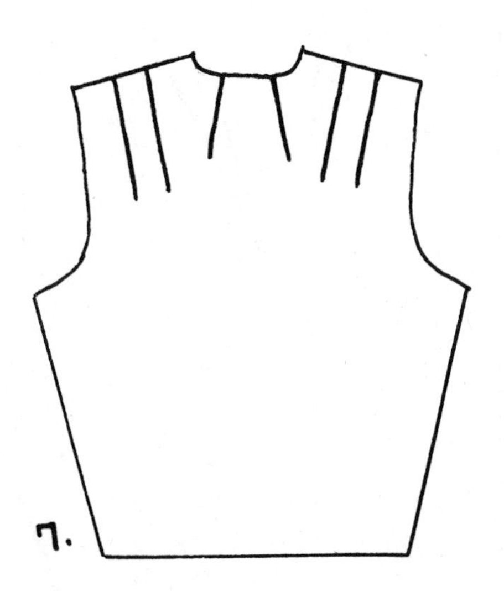

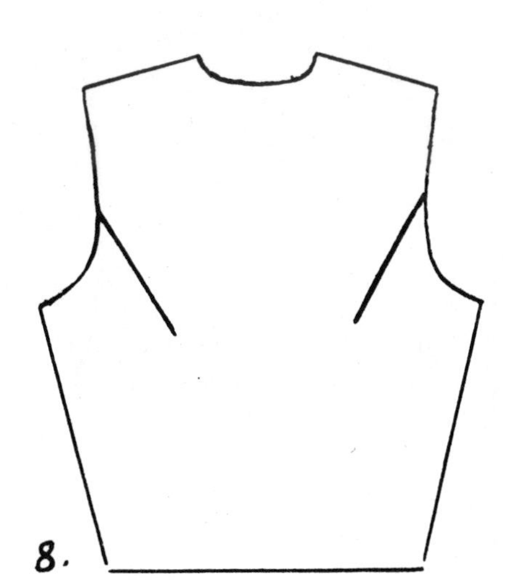

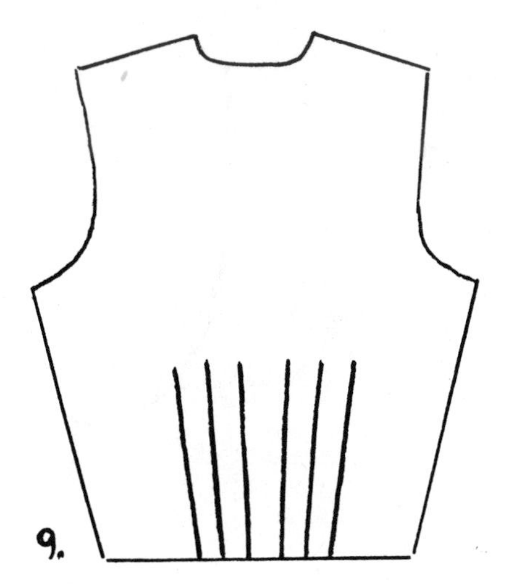

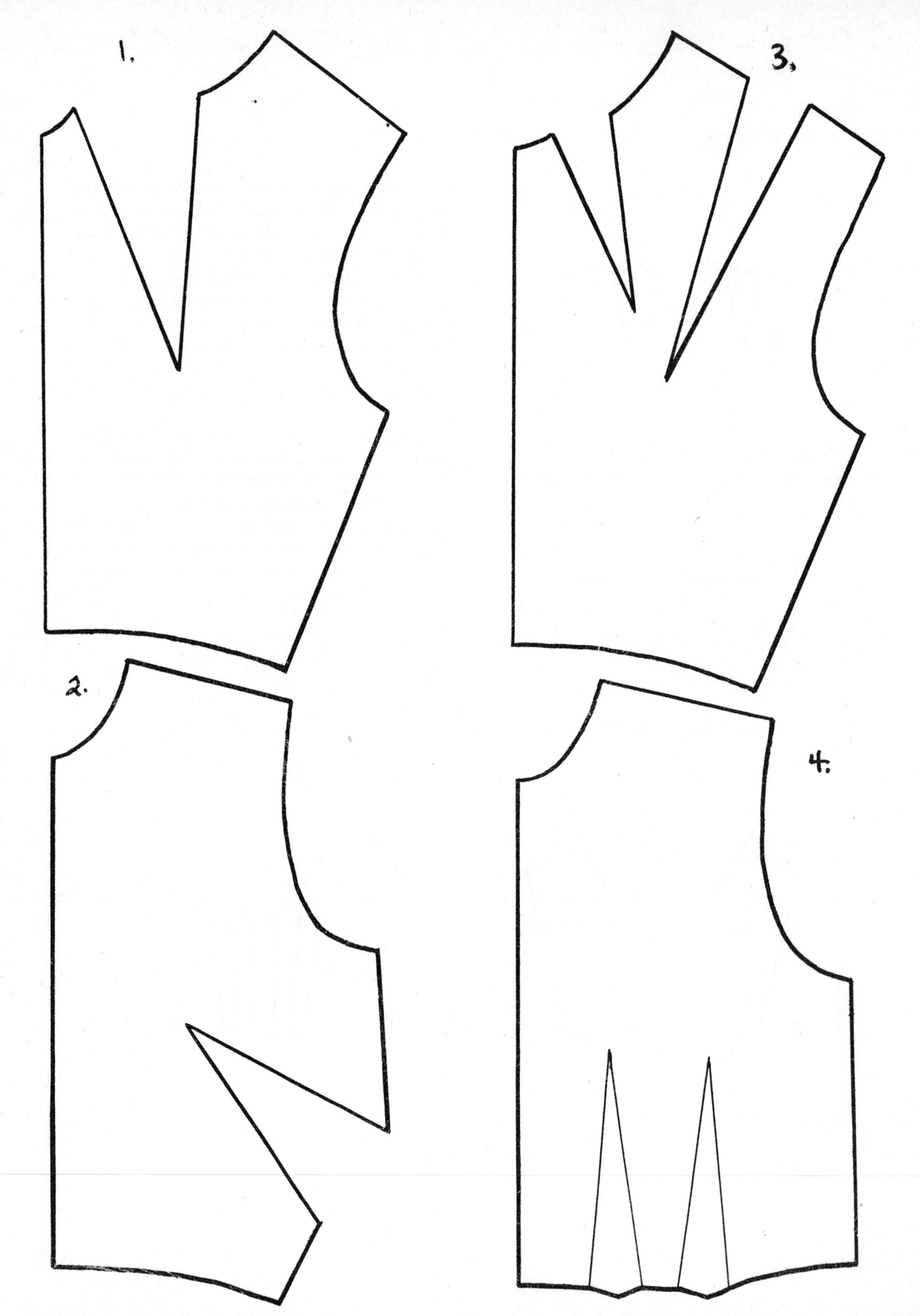
1.
2.
3.
4.

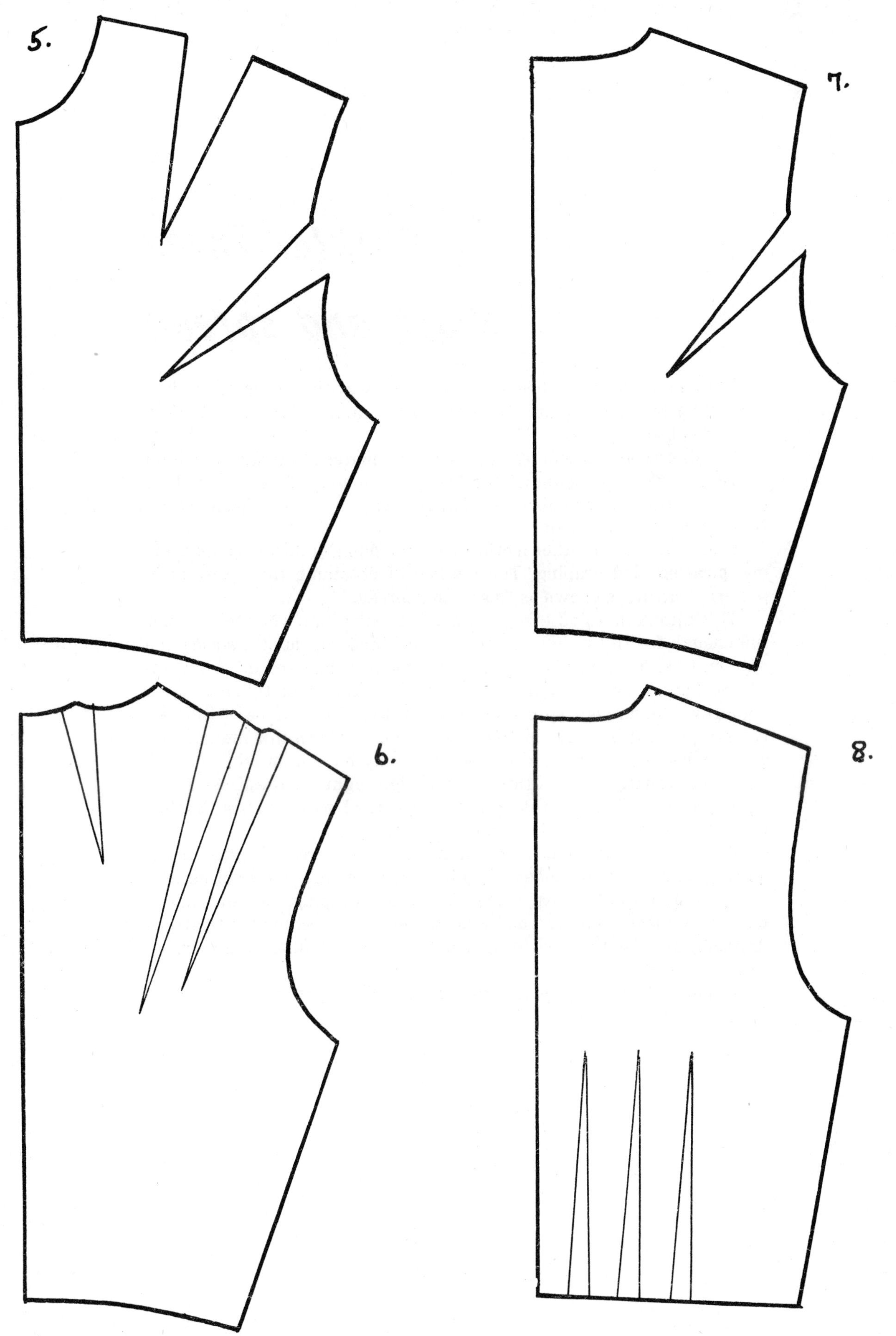
5.
7.
6.
8.

Chapter Three

Slash and spread

Until now you have been concerned only with the dart, used in controlling the excess material in fitting a straight piece of cloth over a rounded body contour.

In this lesson you will learn how to add material at various points in order to vary the shape of the bodice or to add softness or bulk to the silhouette. You will also find that there are methods of controlling fullness other than the dart.

Specifically, these other methods of controlling fullness are: gathering, pleating, and draping. The method of obtaining these results in pattern drafting is known as "slash and spread."

This means that you take your original pattern, if you feel it is not full enough for the style you have in mind, and you cut (or *slash*) the pattern in several parallel divisions; these are then *spread* apart until you have what you think is the correct amount of fullness. Then you draw around your spread-out pattern to get the shape of the new pattern piece. It is a very simple thing to do, yet with this method you can achieve almost any effect which you may have in mind.

The alternative is to drape your design right on the dress form, with muslin. But, since this book is concerned with *drafting* rather than draping, this method will not be treated.

Draping is a skill that is very important for a dress designer to acquire, and the serious student who intends to make a career of designing should certainly learn something about draping, but draping is more easily learned after you have mastered the technique of pattern drafting, and for this reason is usually the last course taught in designing schools.

In general, it is easier and quicker to draft a pattern than it is to drape it.

Slash and Spread

For the first problem in slash and spread, start, as always, with the basic front bodice. The design is extremely simple — a perfectly plain bodice that is softly gathered at the waistline. There are no darts.

Since the amount of material that is allowed for contour rounding in the basic block is not sufficient to give a soft, bloused effect, add a few more inches of material to the bodice. You cannot add the extra fullness to the center front or to the side seam without materially altering the fit of the garment. If you were to add the extra fullness to the center front, the bodice would pull diagonally from the center of the neckline to the side seam. If you added the additional material to the side seam, the position of the armscye would hold all the fullness right under the arm.

DIAGRAM A

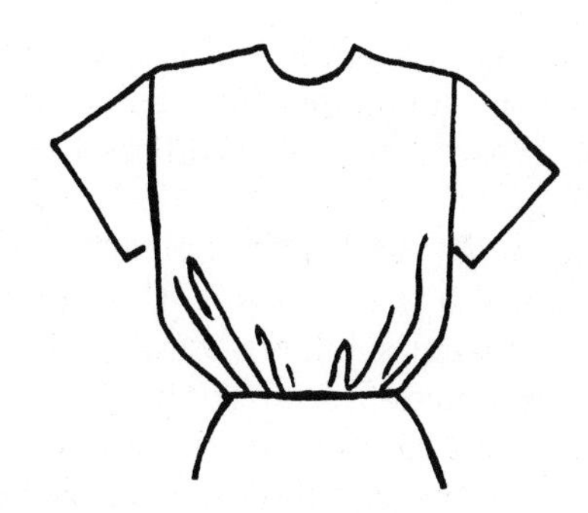

DIAGRAM B

Neither of these results would be what you had in mind. Diagram A shows a bodice in which the fullness is equally distributed in soft gathers all the way across the front waistline. In order to achieve this effect, the additional material will have to be incorporated right into the middle of the pattern.

To do this, slash the basic block (or rather a traced copy of the block) from waist to shoulder and spread the pieces at the waist to allow as much fullness as you think you need. See previous explanations.

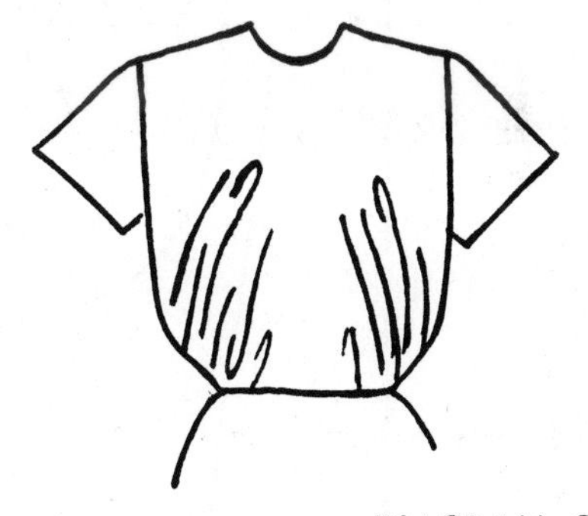

DIAGRAM C

Front Bodice With Waist Gathers

This bodice has added fullness at the waistline while the shoulder is still smoothly fitted. For this reason, you add fullness *only* at the waistline.

To do this, *slash* the pattern *from the waistline up to the shoulder.* Cut the pattern in three parallel slashes almost to the shoulder — close enough so that the pieces do not fall apart, but so you can spread them apart right up to the shoulder seam. Follow the diagrams carefully.

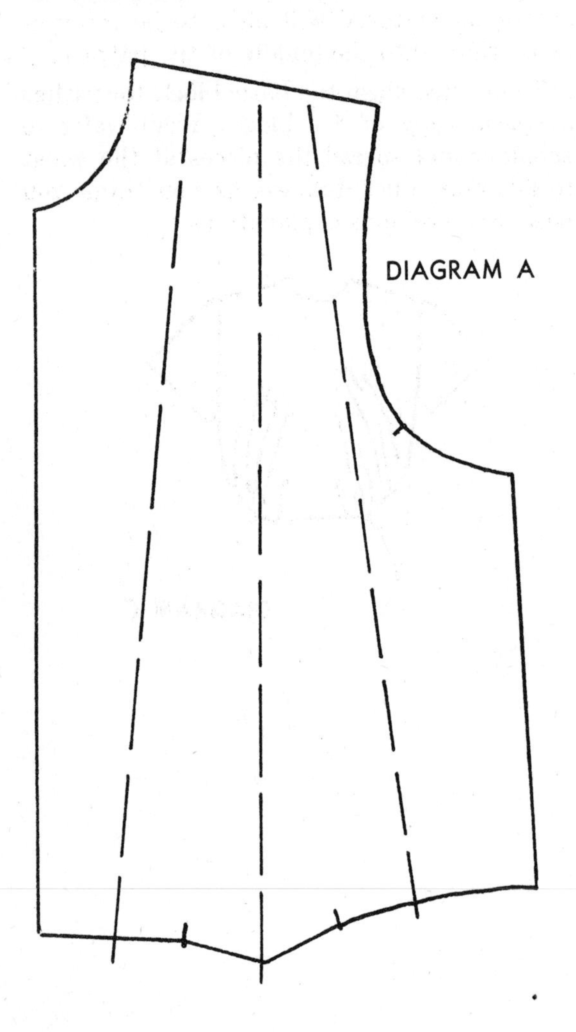

The next step is to *spread* the slashed pieces out far enough so that the bodice appears to have the amount of fullness which you had in mind. This is a matter with which you will have to experiment. In time you will be able to judge at a glance just how much fullness is needed. For the present, follow the diagrams for exact measurements. The slashed pieces are spread out 2 inches apart, which will give you a total of 6 inches of additional fullness for your gathers.

The *spread-out* pattern is shown in Diagram B.

FRONT BODICE WITH WAIST GATHERS *(cont.)*

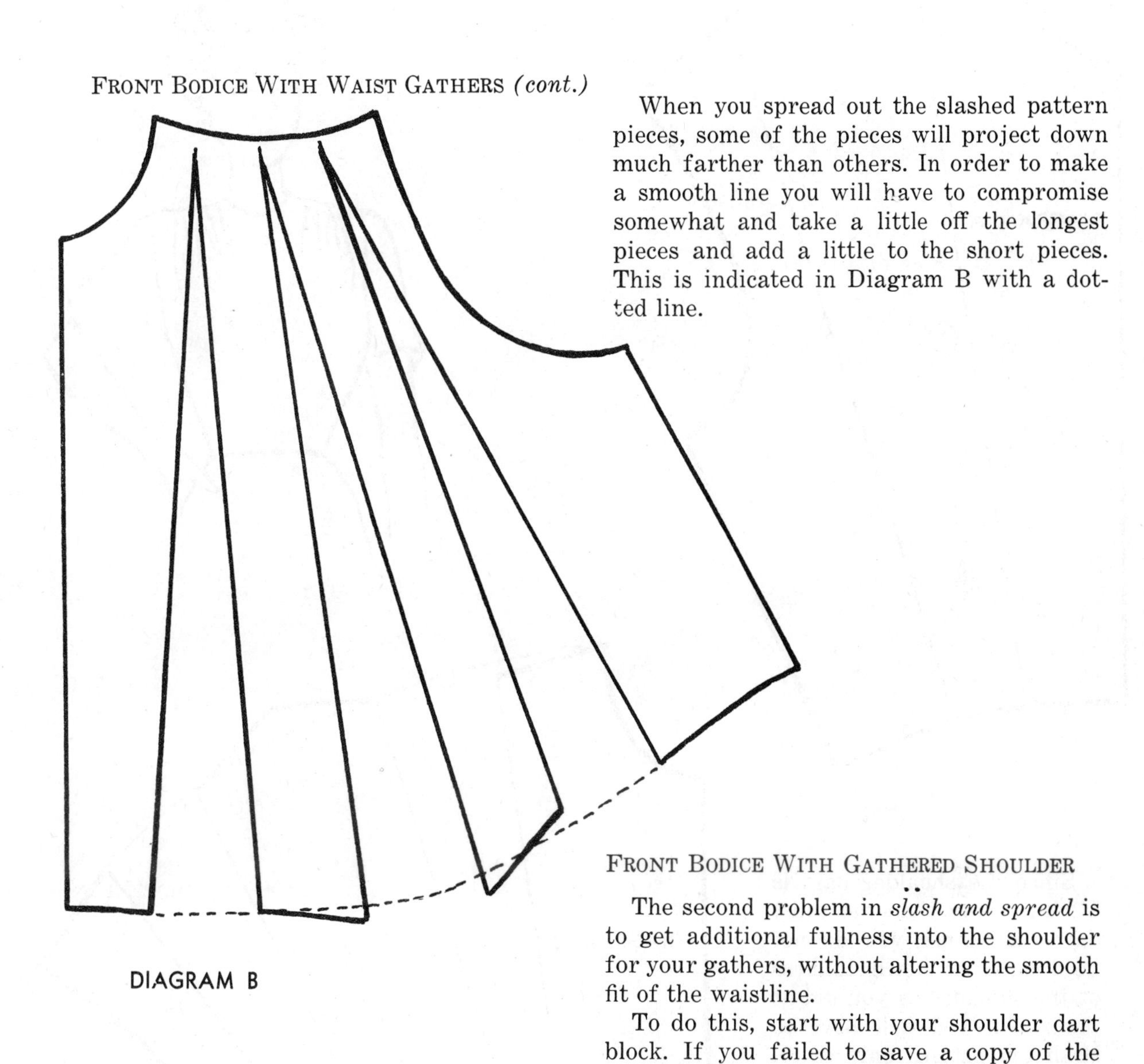

DIAGRAM B

When you spread out the slashed pattern pieces, some of the pieces will project down much farther than others. In order to make a smooth line you will have to compromise somewhat and take a little off the longest pieces and add a little to the short pieces. This is indicated in Diagram B with a dotted line.

FRONT BODICE WITH GATHERED SHOULDER

The second problem in *slash and spread* is to get additional fullness into the shoulder for your gathers, without altering the smooth fit of the waistline.

To do this, start with your shoulder dart block. If you failed to save a copy of the shoulder dart block, you will have to make one now, by swinging the waist dart to the shoulder.

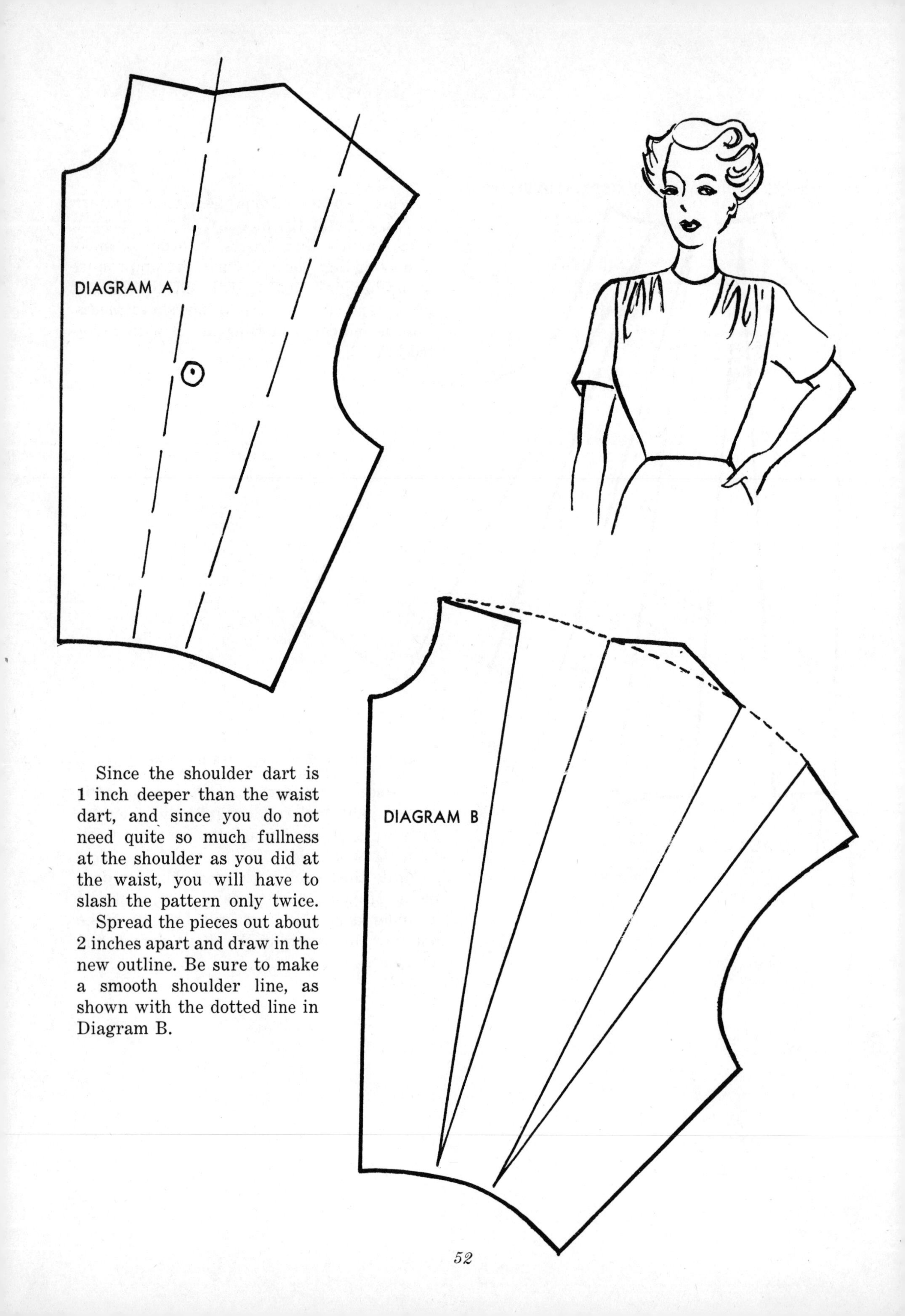

Since the shoulder dart is 1 inch deeper than the waist dart, and since you do not need quite so much fullness at the shoulder as you did at the waist, you will have to slash the pattern only twice.

Spread the pieces out about 2 inches apart and draw in the new outline. Be sure to make a smooth shoulder line, as shown with the dotted line in Diagram B.

Front Bodice With Neckline Gathers

The third problem in slash and spread is to get additional material into the neckline, and to control that extra fullness with gathers.

When you make the two slashes as indicated in Diagram A, cut the inner slash all the way through the pattern. In spreading the pieces out, overlap the two separate pieces so that the dart is no longer in evidence.

When overlapping the two pieces, be sure to be guided by the original dart notches and the punch mark. Remove *only* the dart, being careful not to overlap so far that the waistline is no longer the correct size. Draw in your new neckline with care, being sure to get a smooth line.

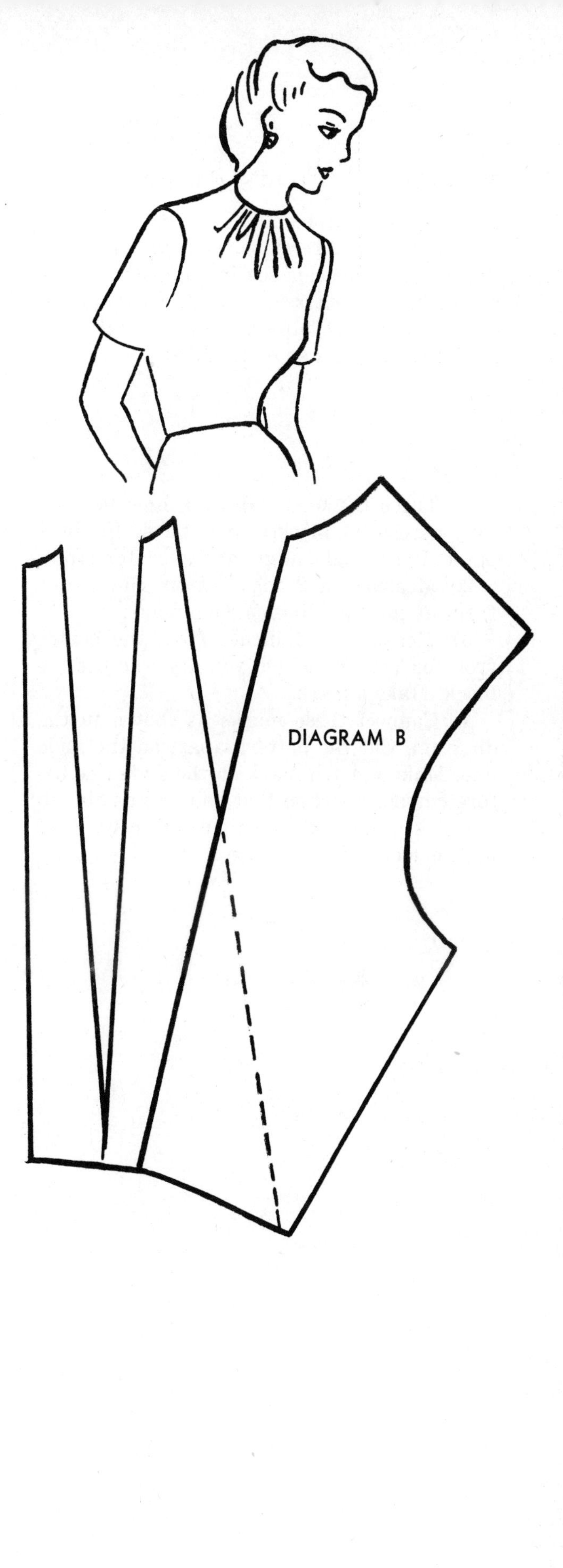

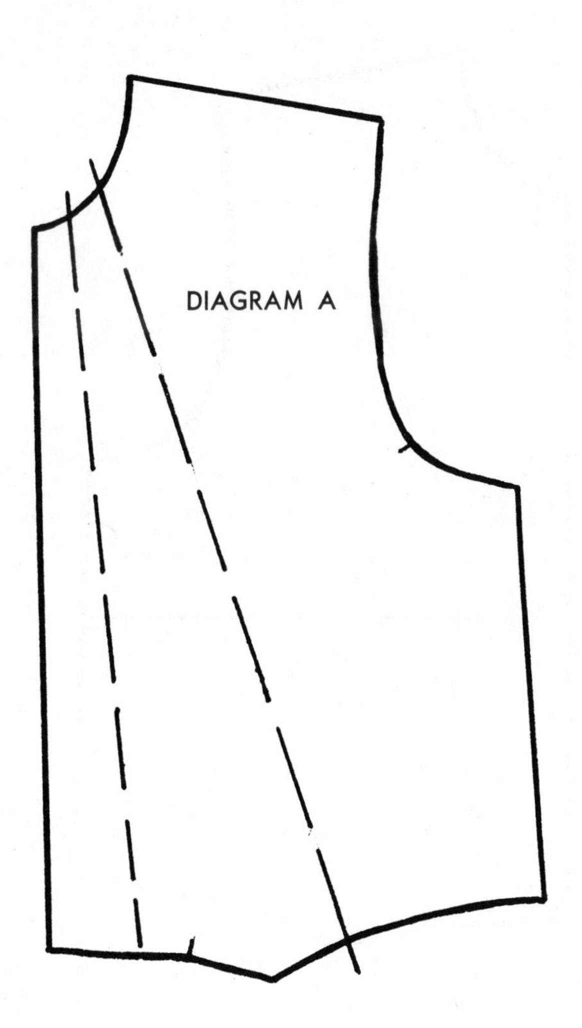

FRONT BODICE WITH BUST GATHERS

In the next problem, if you pay close attention to the directions, you will have no trouble. As you can see in the sketch, this bodice has the extra fullness underneath the bustline, and the fullness is divided into two sections, leaving a smooth midriff.

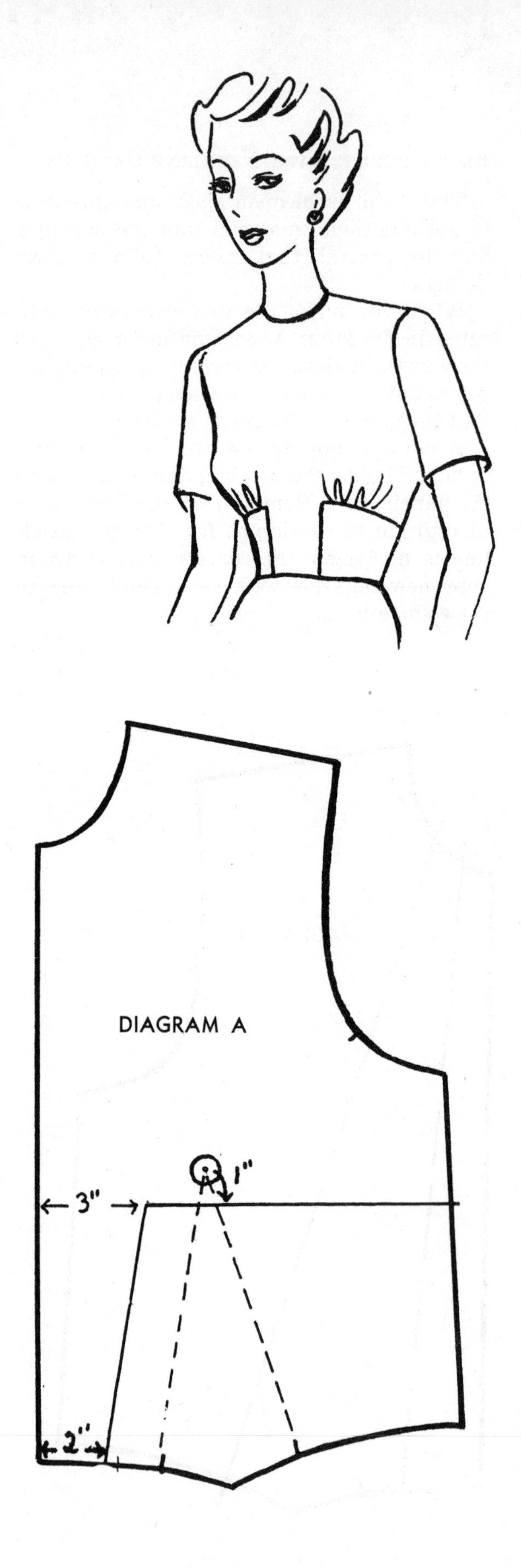

Directions

1. Trace the block. Draw a line horizontally across the block, 1 inch below the bust point. Use a right angle at the center front.
2. Measure in 2 inches from the center front at the waistline. Make a mark.
3. Measure in 3 inches from the center front on the line which you drew across the block. Make a mark.
4. Connect these marks as shown in the diagram. Cut the pattern apart on the style line. Make a notch mark on the style line before cutting apart so that you will be able to put the pieces back together correctly. Save both pattern pieces.

FRONT BODICE WITH BUST GATHERING *(cont.)*

5. Slash your upper pattern piece almost to the shoulder. Remember not to cut clear through the shoulder line. Make three slashes.

6. Next, spread out the slashed pattern, allowing plenty of fullness. In the diagram, about 6 inches of additional material has been allowed for the gathers.

Your pattern now has extra material for gathering, but as yet there has been no allowance made for the contour of the bust. For this purpose, additional length must be added from shoulder to bustline. An increase in length of 1½ inches is necessary for the garment to fit over the bust contour without pulling. This addition is made at the center of the horizontal style line, and is tapered to nothing at both the side seam and the center style line. This is shown with a dotted line on Diagram C. When this addition has been made to the pattern, you will then have to add seam allowance to the style line.

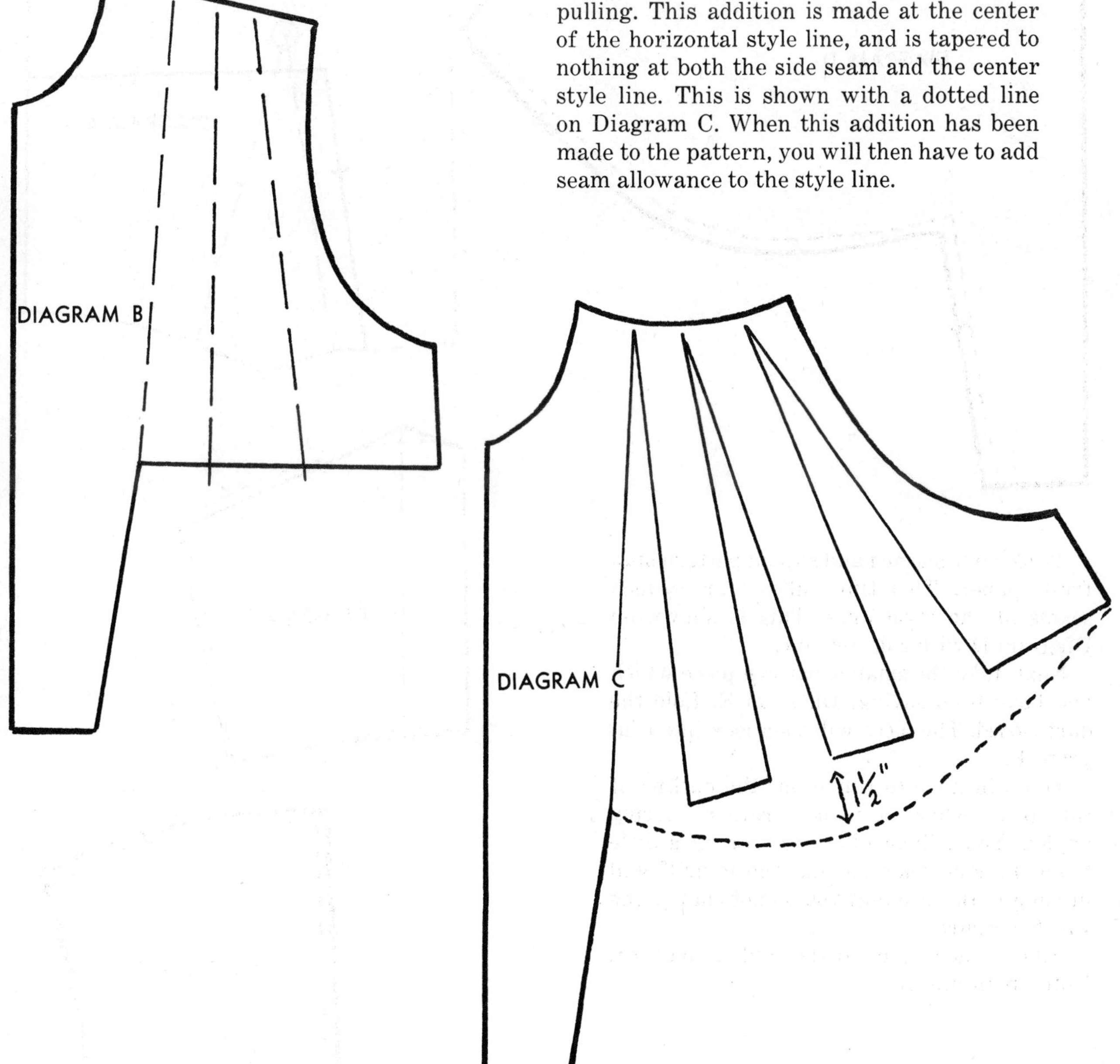

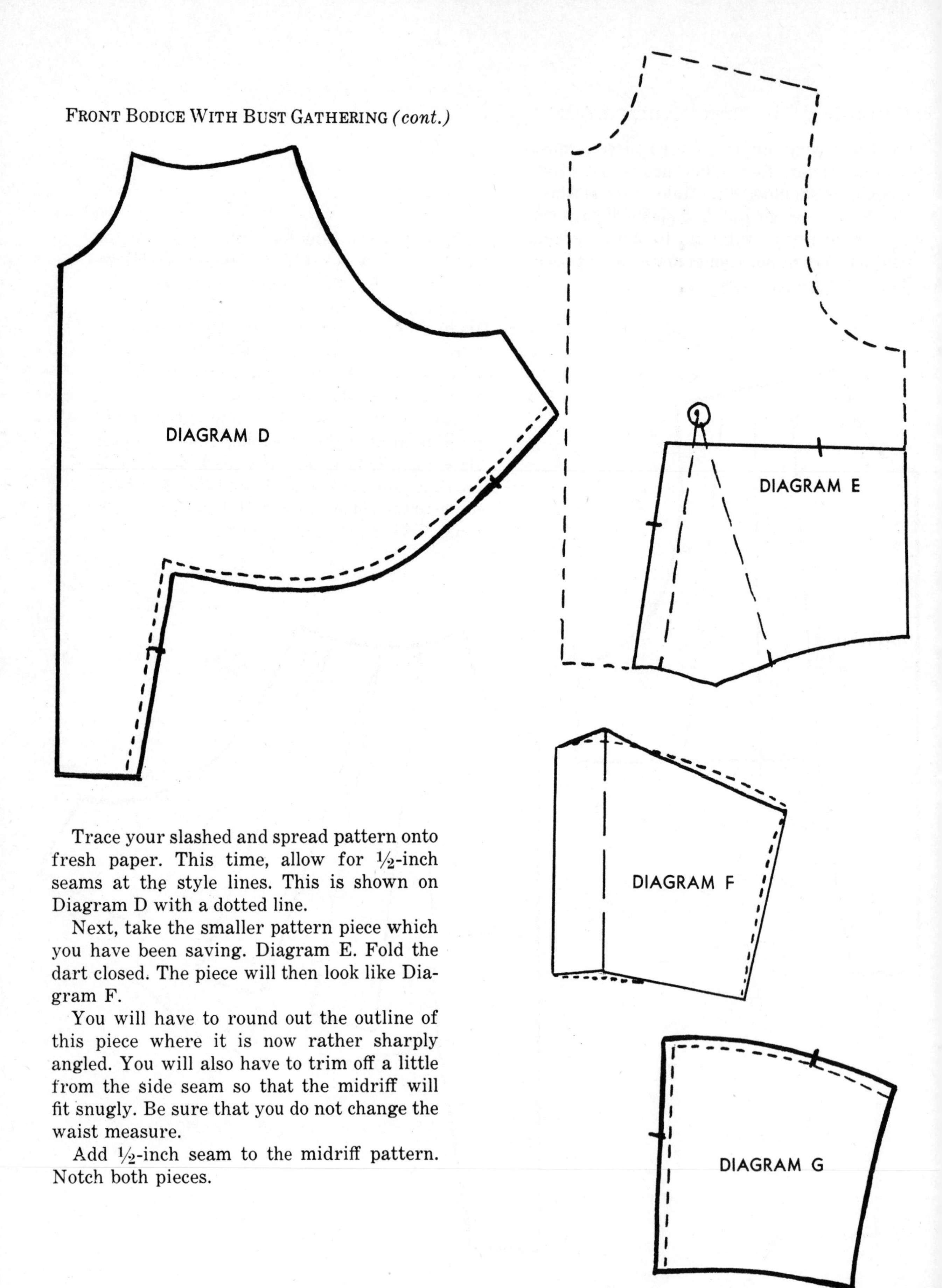

Trace your slashed and spread pattern onto fresh paper. This time, allow for ½-inch seams at the style lines. This is shown on Diagram D with a dotted line.

Next, take the smaller pattern piece which you have been saving. Diagram E. Fold the dart closed. The piece will then look like Diagram F.

You will have to round out the outline of this piece where it is now rather sharply angled. You will also have to trim off a little from the side seam so that the midriff will fit snugly. Be sure that you do not change the waist measure.

Add ½-inch seam to the midriff pattern. Notch both pieces.

SET-IN COLLAR WITH FRONT GATHERS

Next, combine slash and spread with *yokes*. The set-in collar shown in the sketch technically may not be a yoke, but it does present the same problems.

To begin with, decide how wide you want the collar to be. You may use either your own proportions or follow the measurements in the diagrams.

This collar is 2 inches wide. This means that the finished collar will be 1¾ inches wide, for ¼ inch of the width will have to be used as the seam at the neckline. The outside edge of the collar has, as yet, no seam allowance.

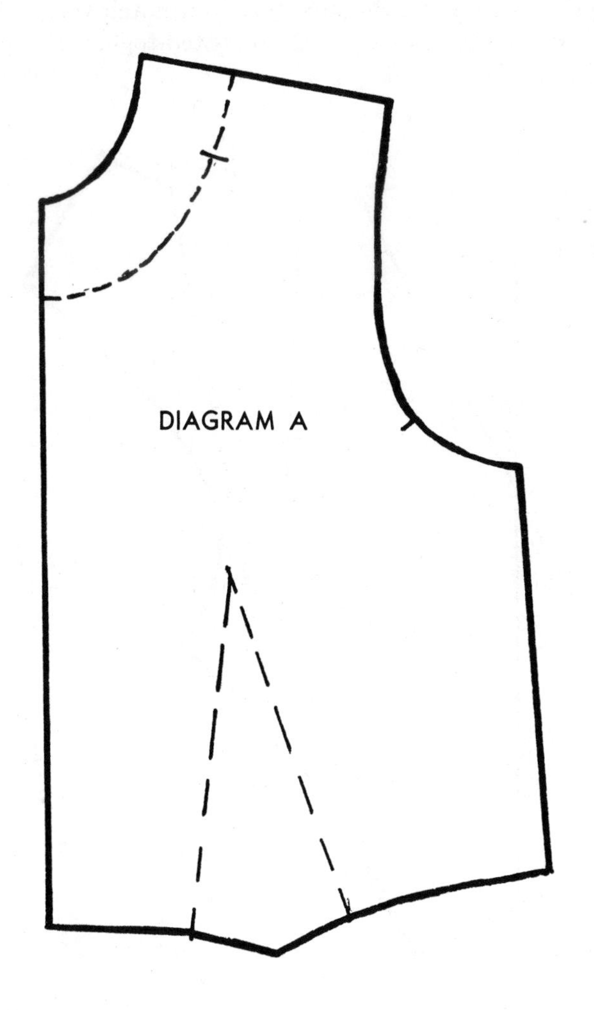

Cut the pattern apart on the style line. Be sure that you have first measured the collar carefully so that it will be the same width all over. Add ½-inch seam to the outside edge of the collar. The collar pattern will then be complete.

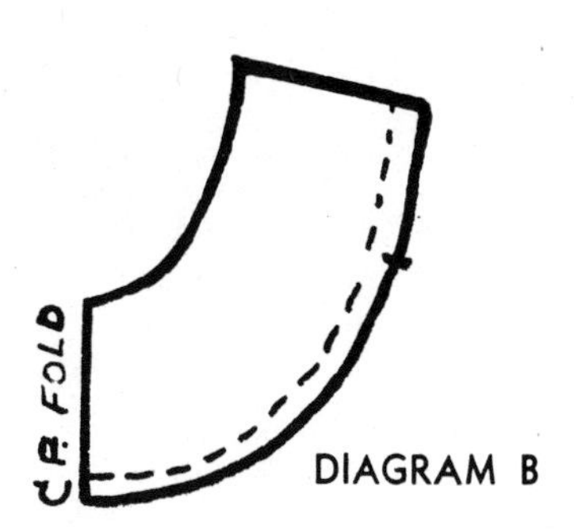

Next, slash your other pattern piece as shown in Diagram C. Cut from the neckline to the waist, being careful not to cut clear through the pattern. Since you have to eliminate the dart, you do have to cut clear through the center slash so that you have two separate pattern pieces.

In spreading out the slashed pattern, overlap the two pieces so as to close the waist dart completely. The center slash cuts right through the center of the dart. Diagram C.

Diagram D shows the slashed pattern spread out to allow the required fullness at the neckline. Check your pattern to be sure that you overlapped the entire dart.

Draw in a smooth line at the neck, trimming off the long projecting points. Add ½-inch seams to the style line and your pattern will be complete. Be sure that you notch the two pieces so that they can be fitted together again.

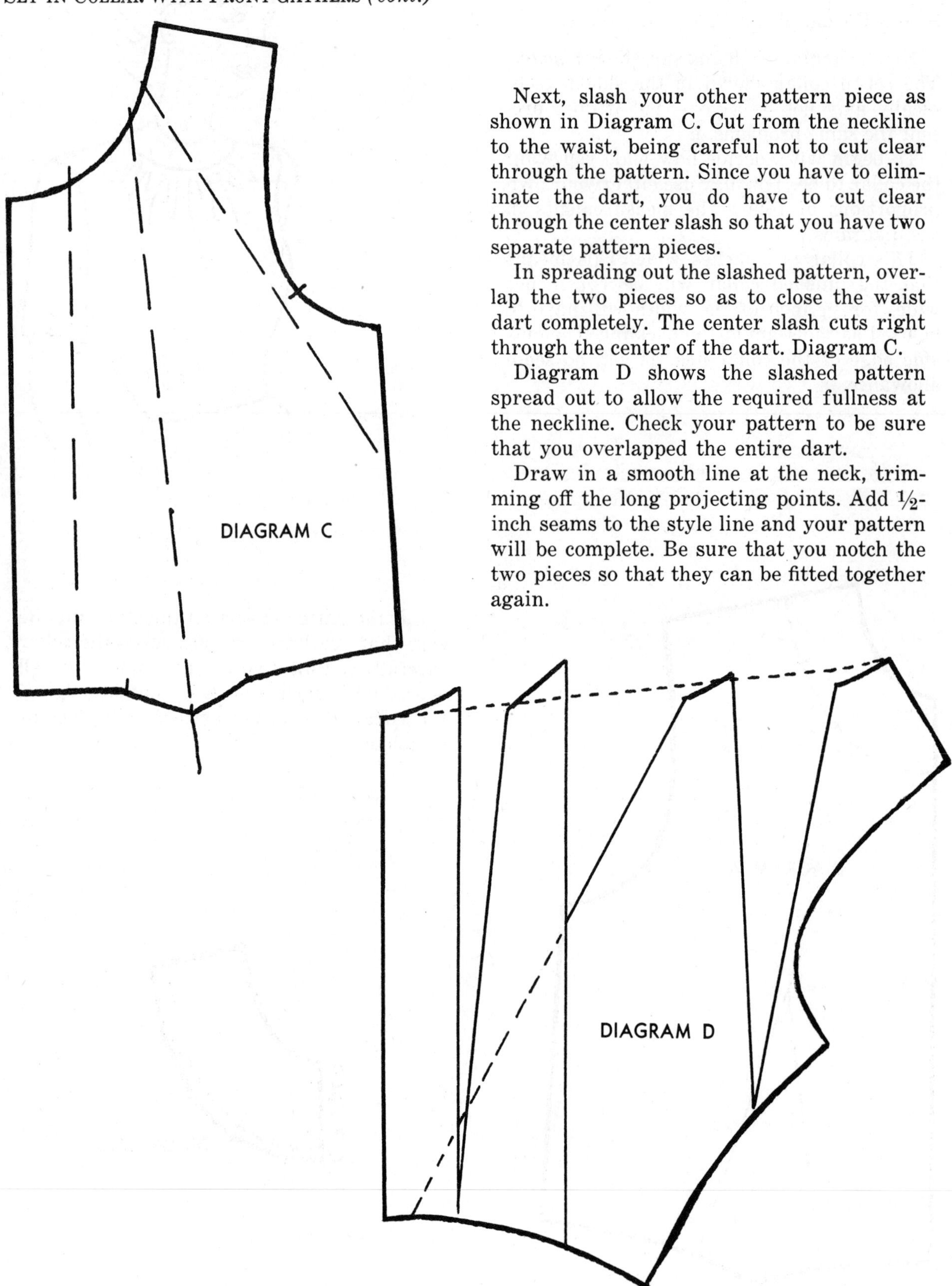

SPREADING THE DART

In this bodice, with soft gathers at the high waist and at the shoulder, it will be sufficient to slash only the shoulder dart and spread it out about 1 inch at the bust point.

In copying your midriff pattern remember to add a ½-inch seam at the style line.

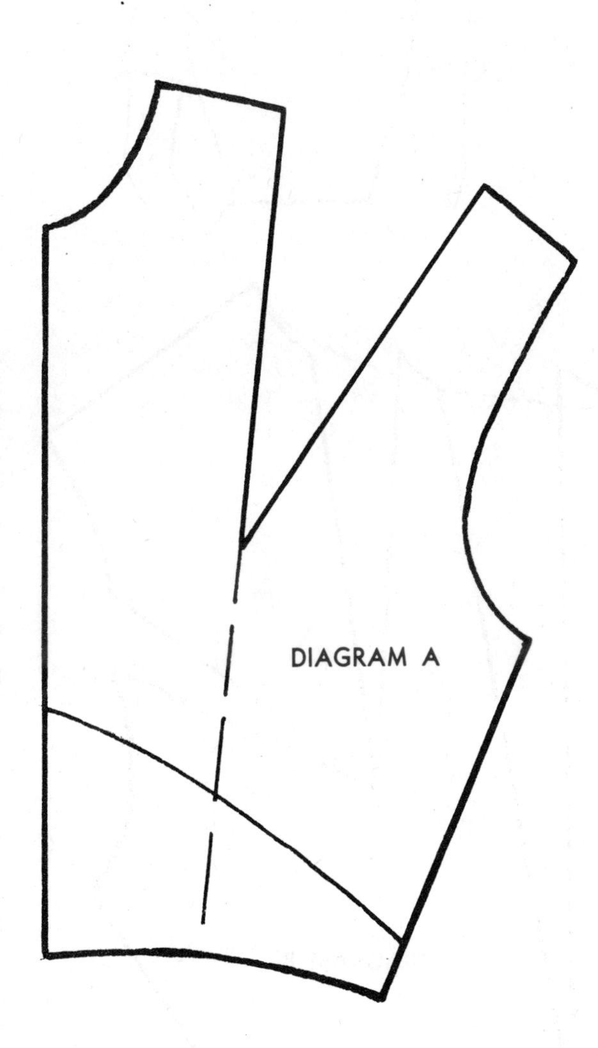

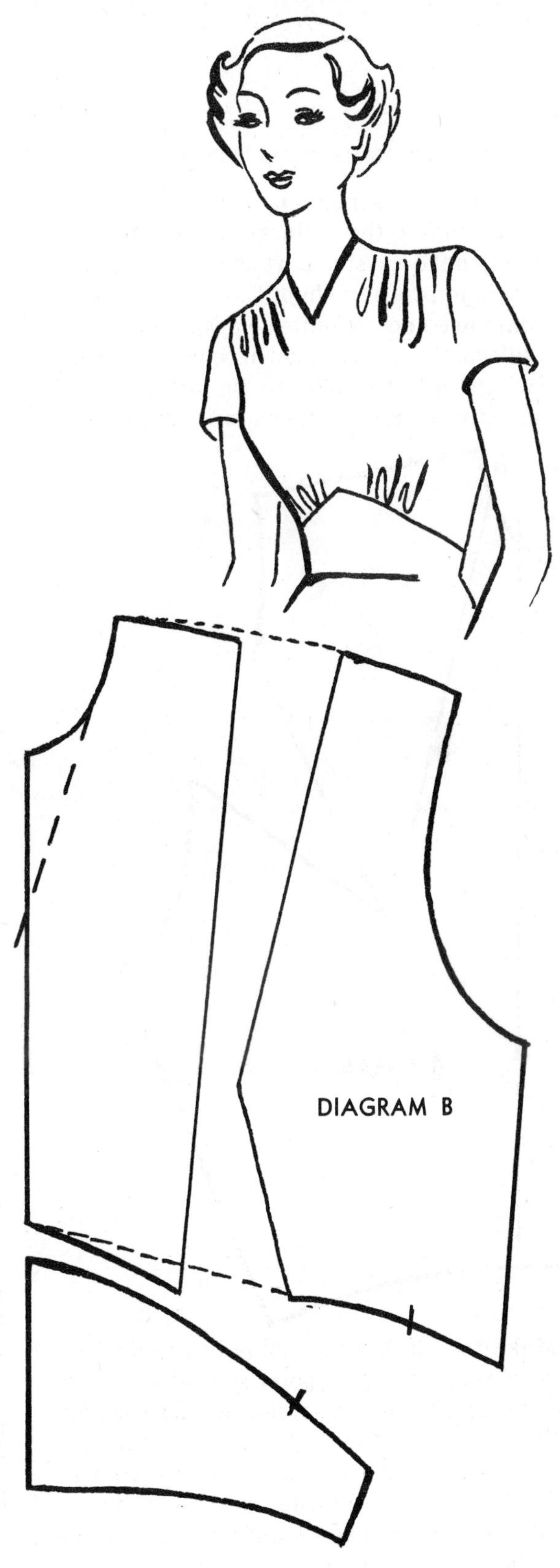

The amount of fullness added is entirely up to you. If it were not for the fitted midriff, you could start with the waist dart block. However, since the waist is closely fitted, there will be less work to be done if you use the shoulder dart block.

In working with slash and spread, always select the block that most closely resembles the design you have in mind.

GATHERED NECKLINE: SIDE DARTS

Still another problem presents itself in this style. In adding the fullness for the neckline gathers, make the side dart shallower by half. This will improve the fit of the garment, since the dart need not be quite so deep when there is additional fullness elsewhere in the bodice.

Swing the waist dart to the armscye and slash your pattern as shown in Diagram A.

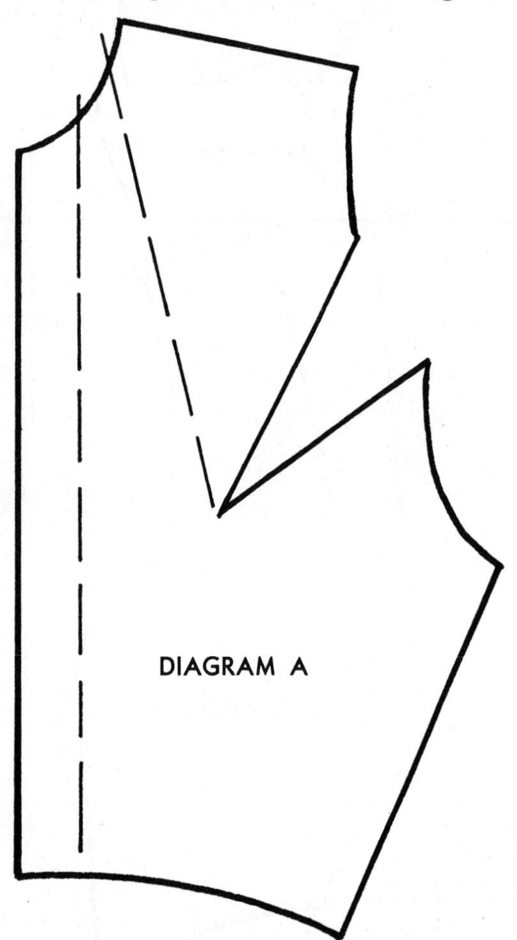

Make the slash which ends in the dart go clear through the dart point so that you have two pattern pieces. In spreading these out for fullness, close up the dart until it is only half as wide as it was originally. See Diagram B.

The broken line indicates the new neckline. You do not need to add seam allowance since the seam is already allowed at the neckline of the block.

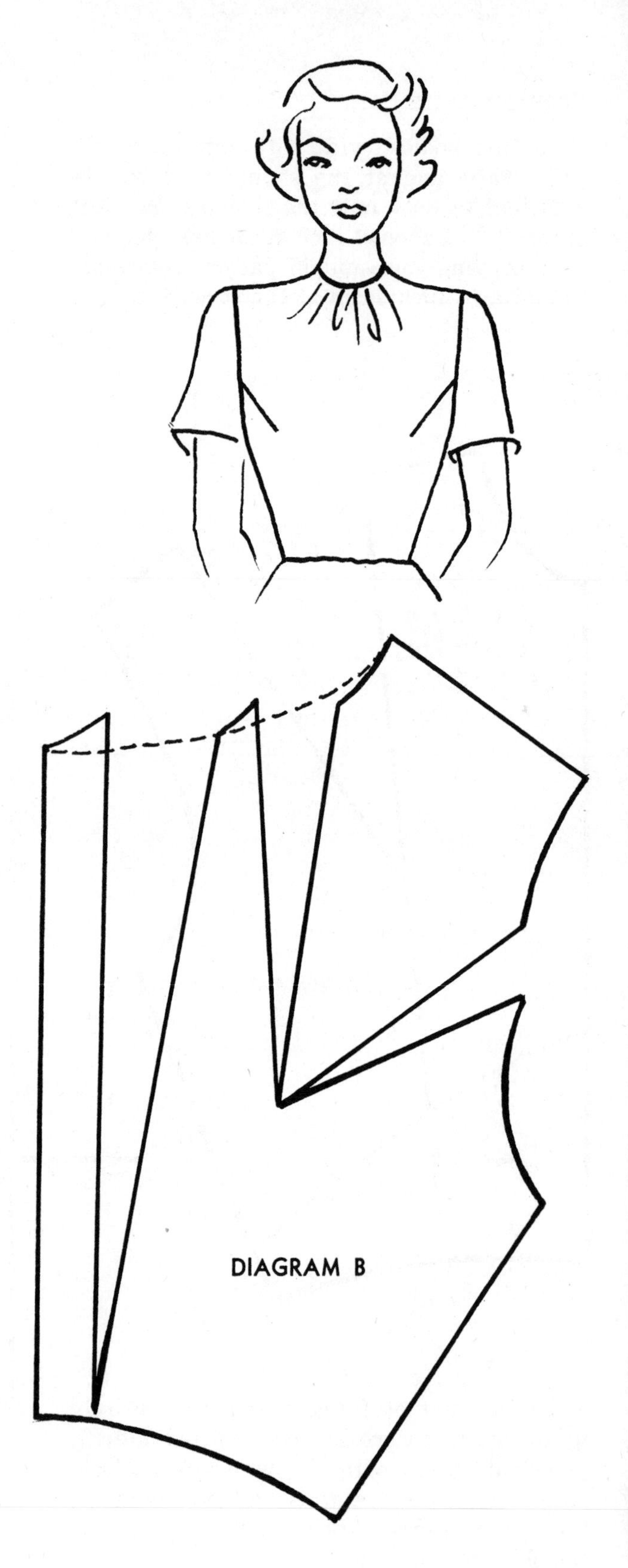

Chapter Four
Yokes

Thus far the slash-and-spread method has been concerned only with adding fullness for gathering. In this chapter, you will take up the problem of *yokes*.

The definition of a yoke is as follows: "Part of a dress fitting over the shoulders or hips to support the lower part of the garment."

The primary thing to learn about yokes is that, when you cut a pattern apart in order to make a yoke style, you must add seam allowance so that in sewing the garment together you will not lose any of its length. Ordinarily ½ inch is allowed for seaming a yoke to the garment. Some designers prefer to use only a ¼-in seam. In this book, ½-inch seams will be allowed at all yokelines.

Actually, slash and spread, pleats, gathers, yokes, and darts all work together so closely that it is very difficult to separate them into different lessons. You will find that in the lesson on yokes, both gathering and pleating will be included to some extent. And when you get to the lesson on pleats, you will still be much concerned with yokes. However, in order to simplify the problems as much as possible, they will be divided according to their major classifications.

STRAIGHT YOKE ON FULL GATHERED BODICE

The bodice shown here is a very flattering style, particularly for a person who is inclined to be too slim. The soft, blousy front gives added fullness to the figure. It is a simple pattern to make, and a simple garment to sew. The yoke should be cut double unless the material is quite heavy, in which case it can be merely faced.

In this problem, it will not be necessary to use the slash-and-spread method of obtaining extra fullness. This is one time when you can add all the fullness you need right to the center front. There are two reasons for this: One is because the entire neckline is cut away as part of the yoke. The other reason is that the bodice is to be gathered at both the yoke and the waistline.

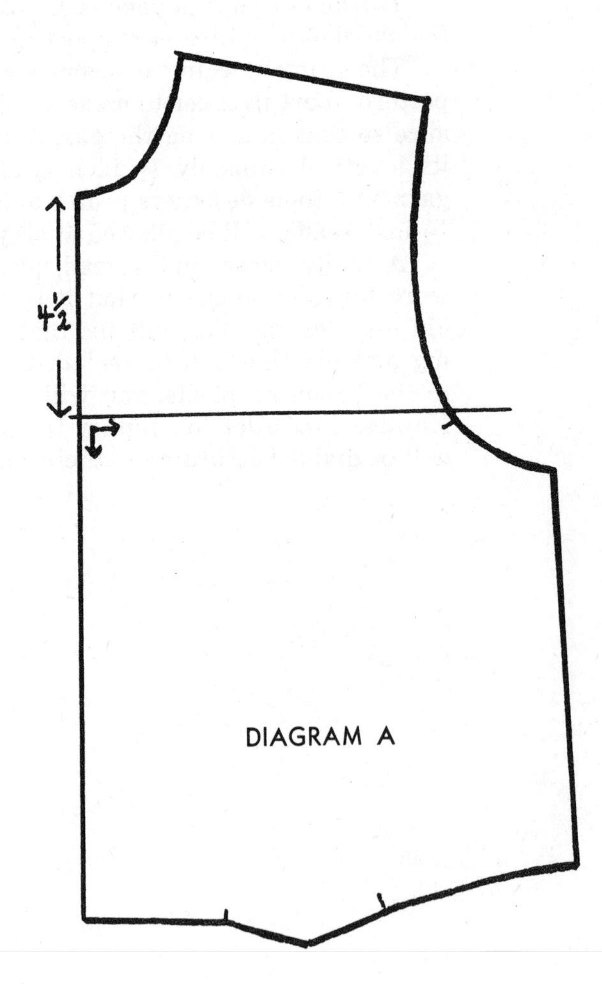

Directions

1. Trace your front block.
2. Measure down 4½ inches from the neckline on the center front. Make a mark.
3. Using a right angle, as indicated in the diagram, draw a line across the block, starting at the mark you just made. Cut apart.

Straight Yoke on Full Gathered Bodice *(cont.)*

4. Trace the yoke piece onto fresh paper. Add $\frac{1}{2}$-inch seam to the yoke line. Notch the pattern for placement of gathers. It is better for the gathers not to begin at the armscye, as that would tend to add bulk under the arm; so set your notch in $1\frac{1}{2}$ inches from the armscye.

5. To the large pattern piece you must now add the necessary fullness for the gathers. It is not necessary to eliminate the dart in this pattern, as the material in the dart will simply be added to the gathers. However, you will need to trim off the dart extension at the waistline. Place the pattern 4 inches in from the edge of the paper on which you are tracing it. This will give you plenty of fullness. Add a $\frac{1}{2}$-inch seam to the yokeline.

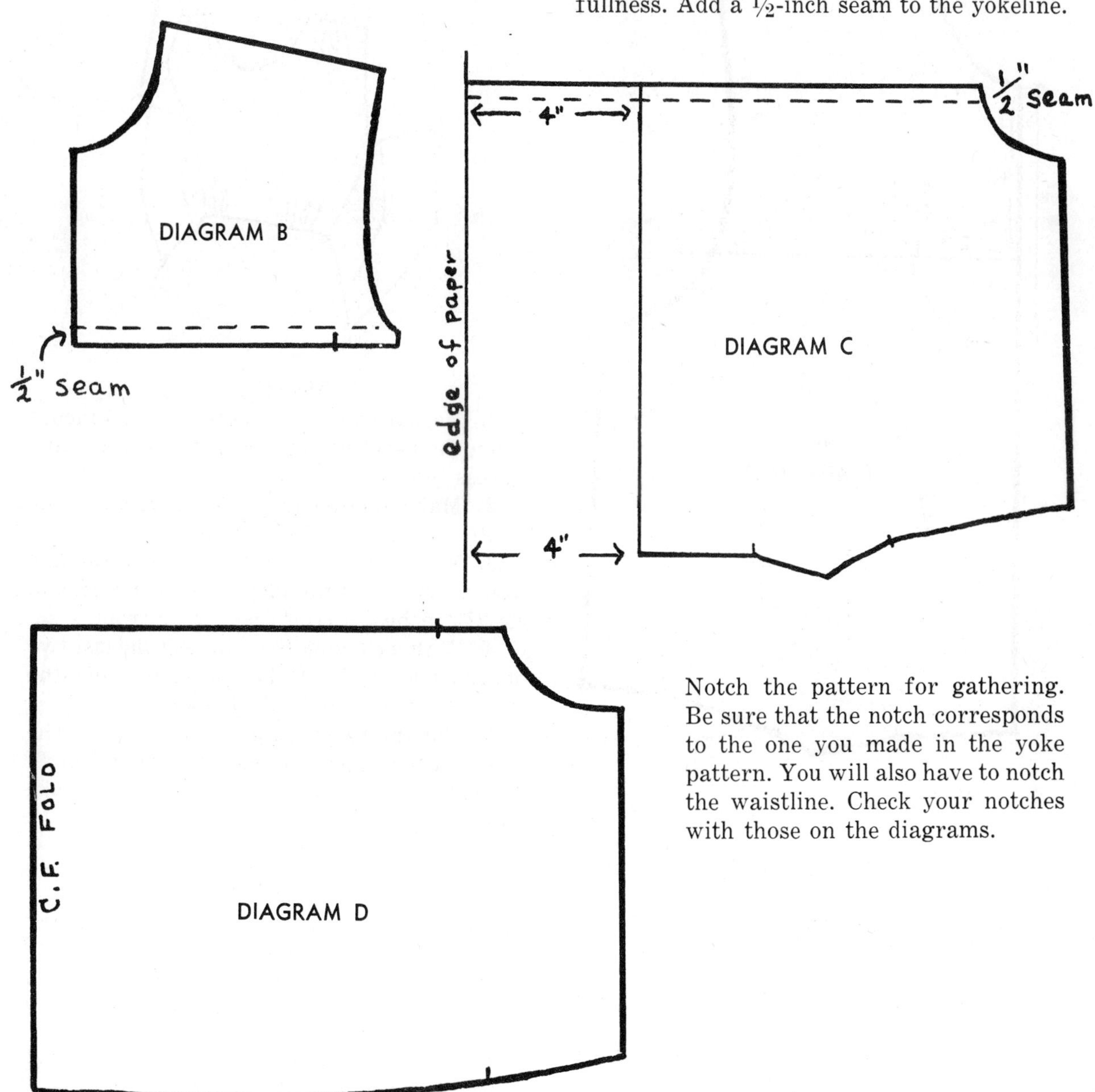

Notch the pattern for gathering. Be sure that the notch corresponds to the one you made in the yoke pattern. You will also have to notch the waistline. Check your notches with those on the diagrams.

FRONT CURVED YOKE

In this yoke style, you again need to use the slash-and-spread method of obtaining fullness. Since this yoke style is considerably more complicated than the other two which you have done, it will pay you to follow directions as closely as possible.

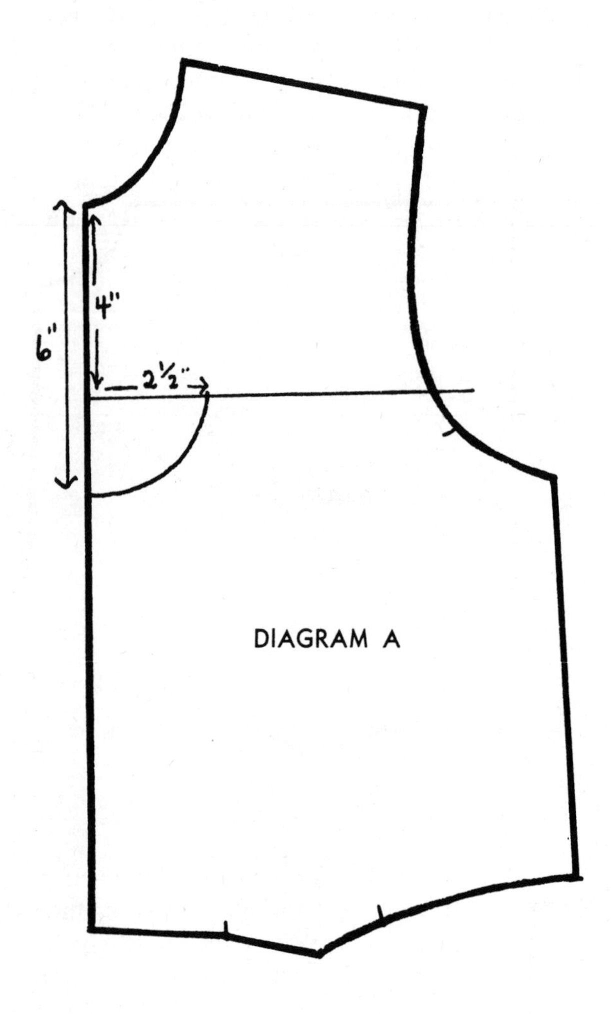

Directions

1. Measure down the center front, 4 inches from the neckline. At that point, draw a line across the block.
2. Make another mark, 6 inches down the center front from the neckline.
3. Make a third mark, this one on the line you drew across the block. The mark should be 2½ inches in from the center front.
4. With a curving line, connect the last two marks you made. Make the curve just the way you want the finished yoke to look.
5. Cut the pattern apart on this line. The yoke pattern piece is shown in Diagram B. Be sure to add a ½-inch seam at the yoke line.

FRONT CURVED YOKE *(cont.)*

This is the finished yoke pattern notched for placement of gathers.

In order to complete the pattern, you must eliminate the dart and add fullness for gathering. Cut the pattern on the slashed line. You must cut clear through, and then overlap the two pieces so that the dart is closed at the waistline. A spread of 4 inches has been allowed for gathering into the yoke. But since this is a matter of style, add as much fullness as you like.

DIAGRAM B

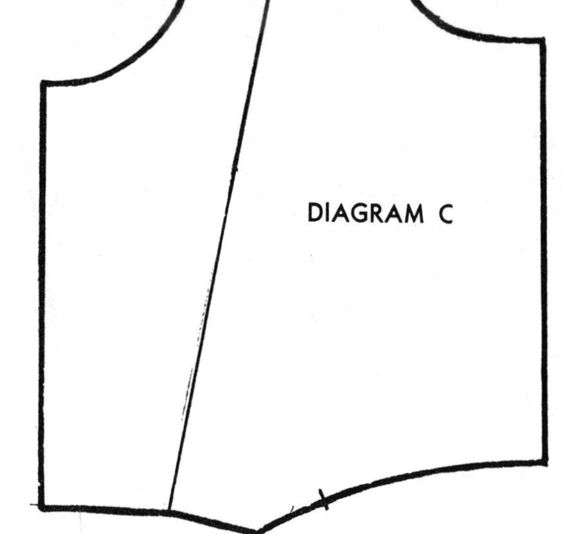

This is the slashed pattern overlapped to close the dart.

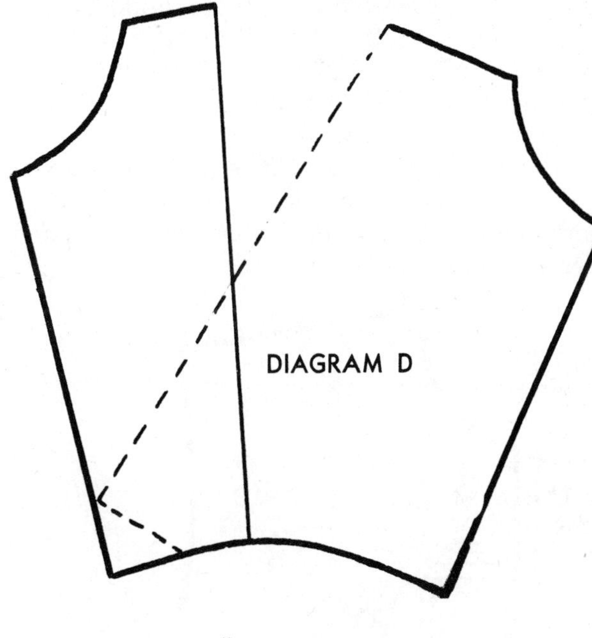

Diagram E shows the finished bodice pattern with a ½-inch seam allowed at the yoke line.

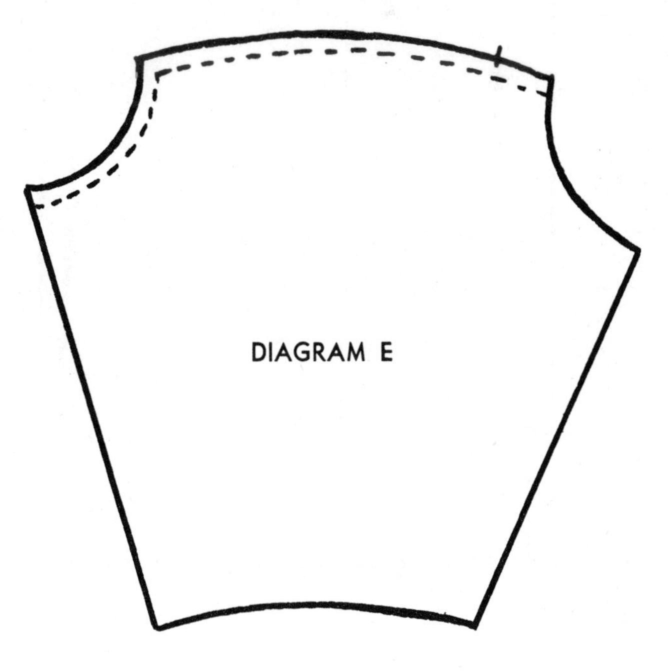

Square Yoke With a Gathered Bodice

This yoke style presents the same problems as the one in the last lesson; however, it is a good plan to work out a few more. Follow the diagrams carefully. Use the right angle wherever it is indicated. A square-cut style such as this would look very bad if it were not cut perfectly true.

These diagrams are a little more complex — but you should be able to decipher almost any diagram by this time. Remember to add seam allowance.

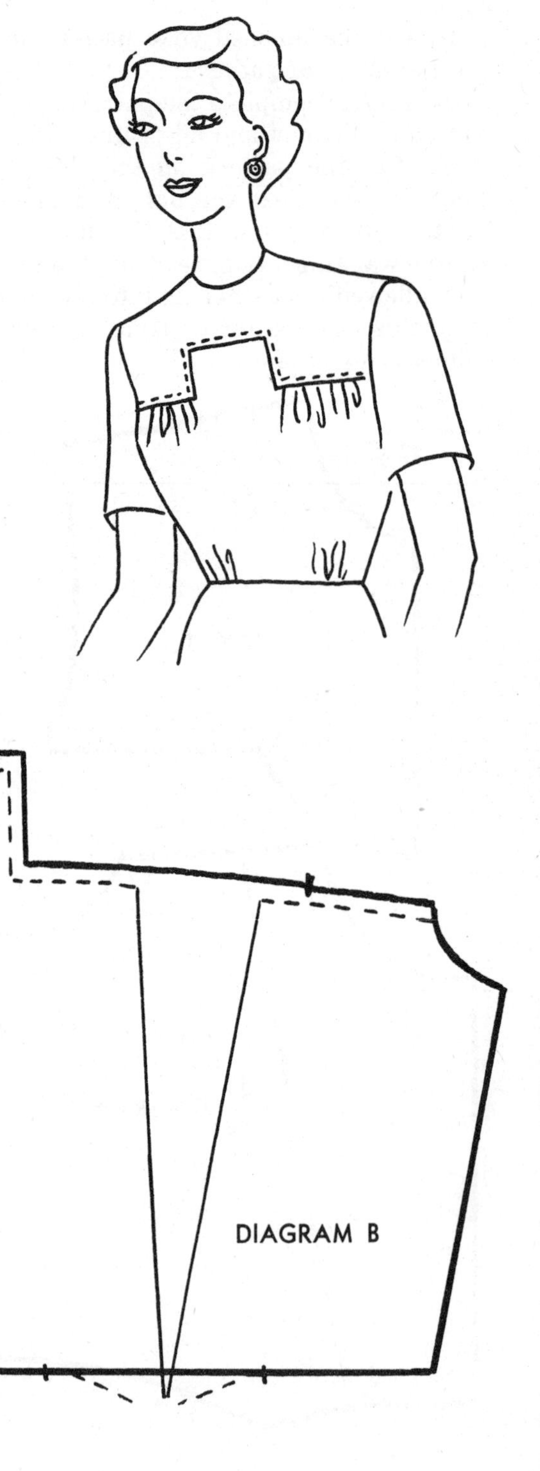

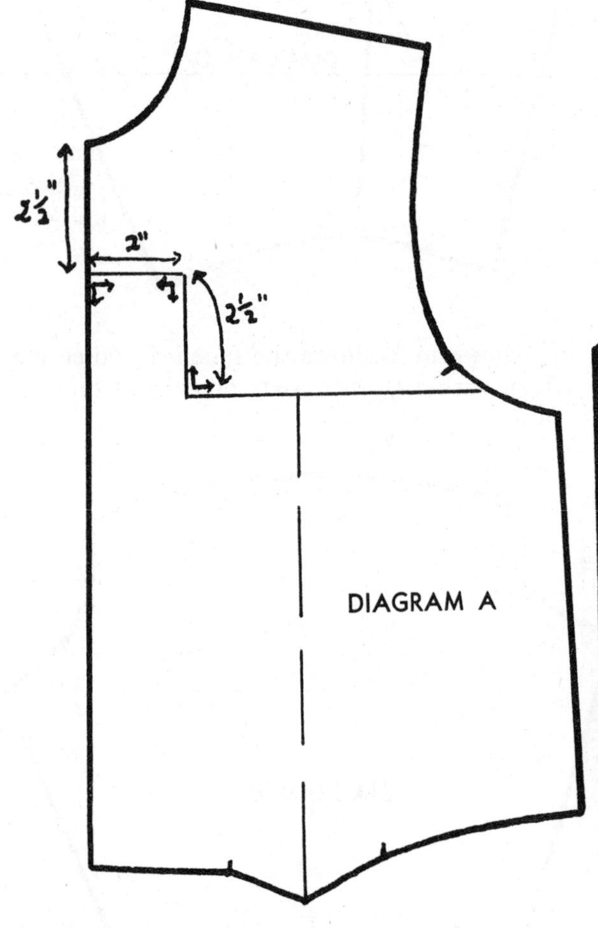

Check the measurements carefully. Trim off the dart extension as shown in Diagram B. Notch both the yoke line and the waist for gathers.

CURVED YOKE WITH PLEATED BODICE

In a yoke of this type, exact measurements cannot be given. You simply have to draw in a line that is pleasing to your own eye. Cut the yoke away from the bodice. Trace the yoke onto fresh paper, adding seam allowance.

Slash the body of the pattern and spread, to allow fullness for the pleats and to close up the dart.

You will find that much time and trouble will be saved if you add the ½-inch seam to the yoke line before you slash and spread. This may seem to be a lot of extra work, since you will have to copy the pattern. However. it will save work in the long run.

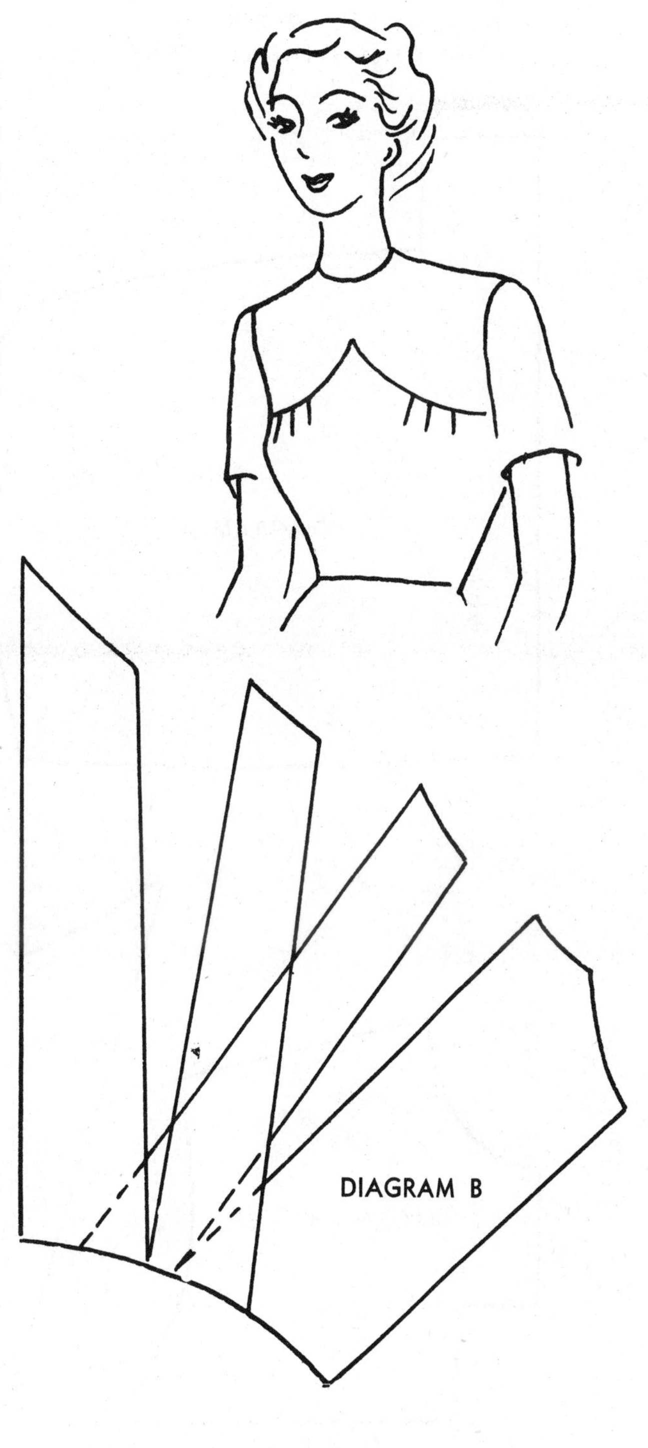

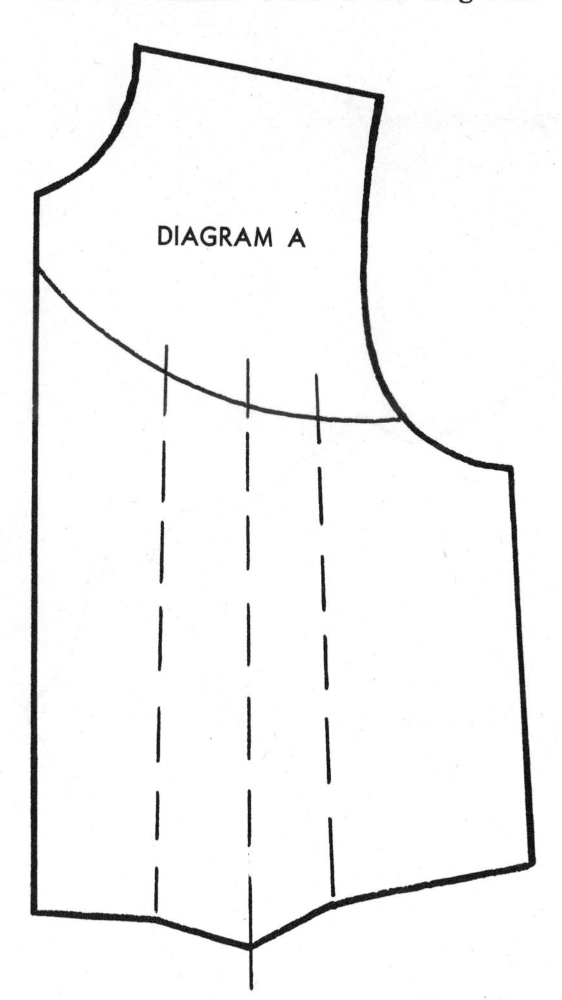

It is essential in this case to fold in the pleats before cutting the yoke line. Check your finished pattern with the one shown on the next page.

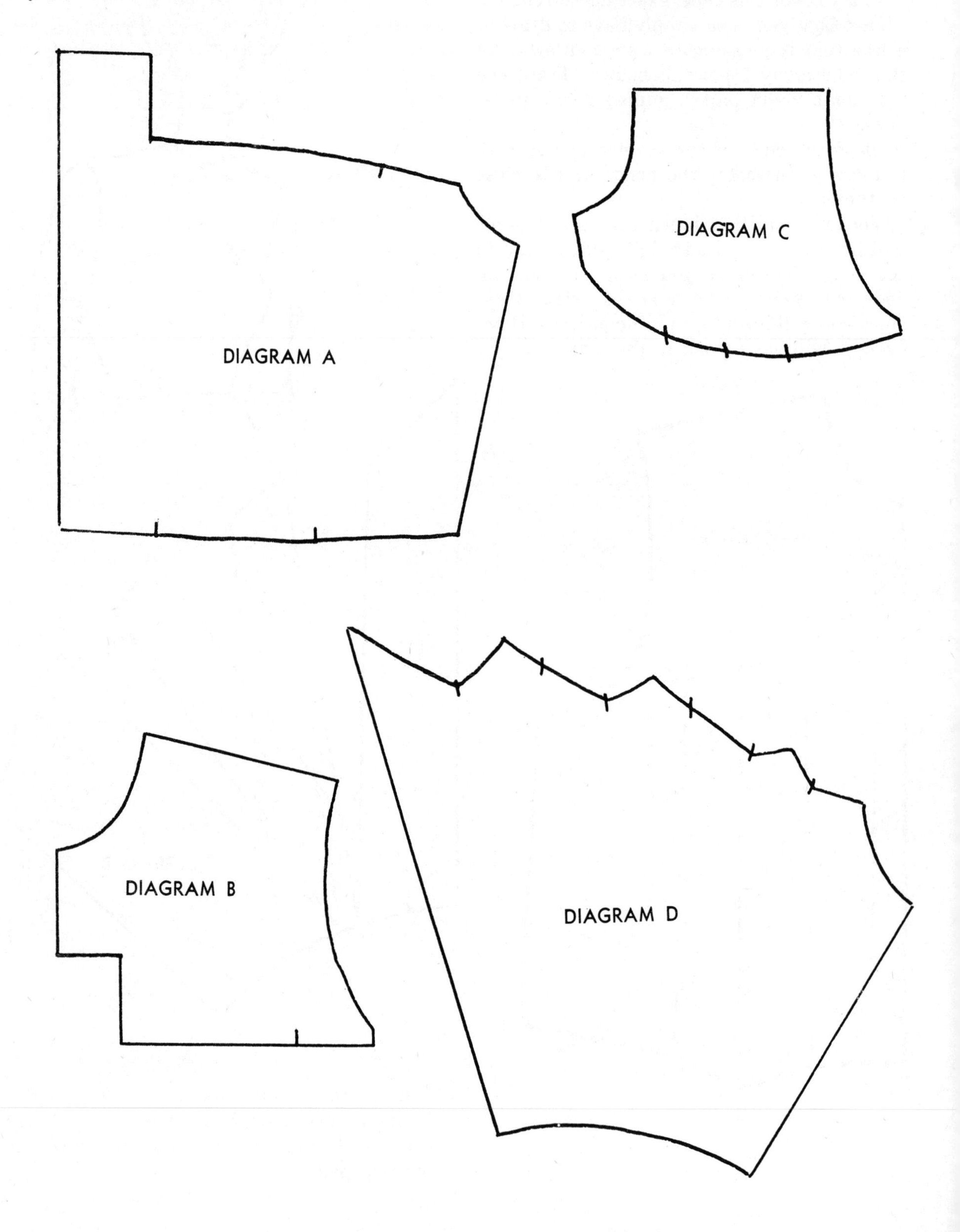
FINISHED PATTERN PIECES FOR
SQUARE YOKE WITH GATHERED BODICE
FINISHED PATTERN PIECES FOR
CURVED YOKE WITH PLEATED BODICE
DIAGRAM A
DIAGRAM C
DIAGRAM B
DIAGRAM D

Simplified Method of Adding Seam Allowance to a Yoke Pattern

In order to avoid unnecessary confusion while working out the yoke patterns, the simpler method of adding seam allowance was not discussed. It will be explained here.

Take a bodice with a perfectly straight yoke. First draw in the yoke line as shown in Diagram A with a broken line. Next, make another line parallel to the first one, ½ inch lower down on the pattern.

The lower line is the one on which you cut the pattern apart. The added ½ inch is the seam allowance for the yoke. In adding this seam you have stolen ½ inch from the lower bodice. This has to be replaced or the garment will come out too short. So, instead of adding the customary ½ inch to the lower pattern piece, you will have to add a full inch. This will provide for the seam allowance and for replacing the stolen ½ inch.

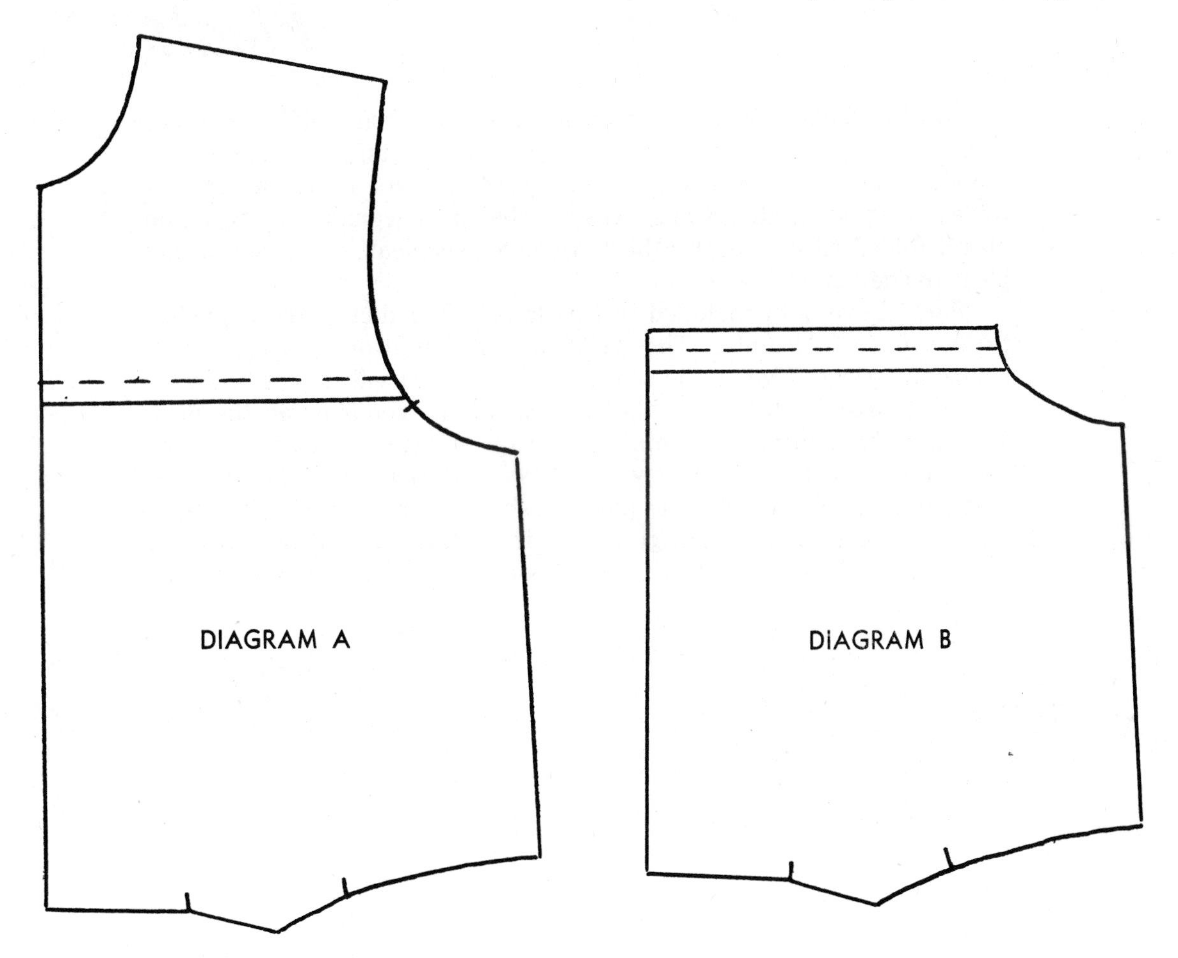

Chapter Five

Pleats

To *pleat* means to fold or lap over. There are many different types of pleats. Side pleats, sometimes called knife pleats, are pleats which are all folded in one direction. A box pleat consists of two side pleats folded in opposite directions. An inverted pleat consists of two side pleats folded to face each other. An inverted pleat is actually a box pleat inside out.

Tucks have been included in this lesson. The dictionary says that to tuck is to fold under. The writer's own definition of a tuck is: a horizontal pleat. That is the sense in which it is used in this book.

Pleats may be folded on the straight of the goods or on the bias. The important thing is to make accurate measurements so that the pleat in the finished garment will not twist. In the case of an inverted pleat, it will help to keep the pleat in shape if the fold is stitched on the inside as close to the edge as possible. Pleating will be discussed again in the lesson on *skirts*. This lesson covers only pleats as they are used in a bodice.

Knife-Pleated Bodice

Even though the bodice is pleated, you have to have another control for the fullness over the bust. If there were no other fullness, the contour of the bust would pull the pleat open all the time.

Since a pleat has to be folded right on the straight grain of the goods (except for bias pleats) you cannot hide the dart under a pleat. The only alternative is to place a dart elsewhere, in the least conspicuous place.

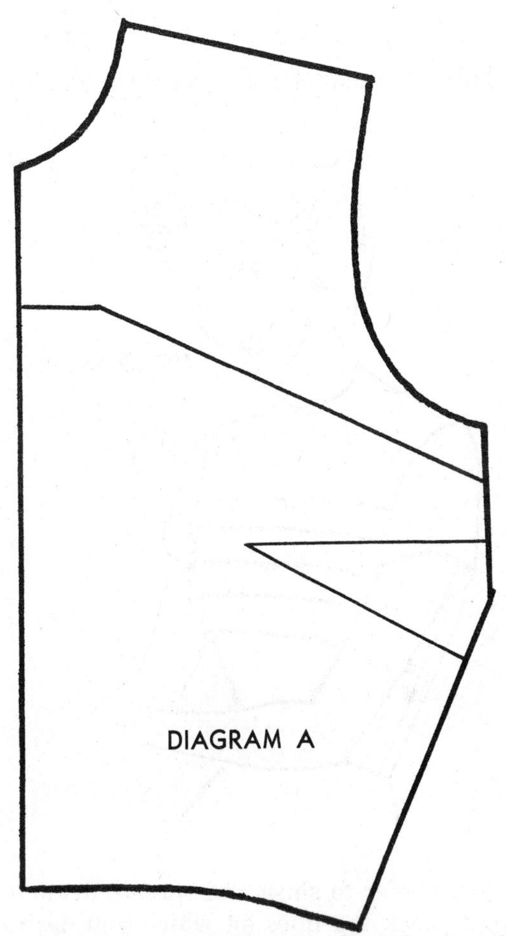

In case you put in your pleats by the slash-and-spread method, you will find it necessary to draw a line across the block, and also across the paper on which you are working. Otherwise, you will have no guide to follow in laying out the slashed pattern pieces.

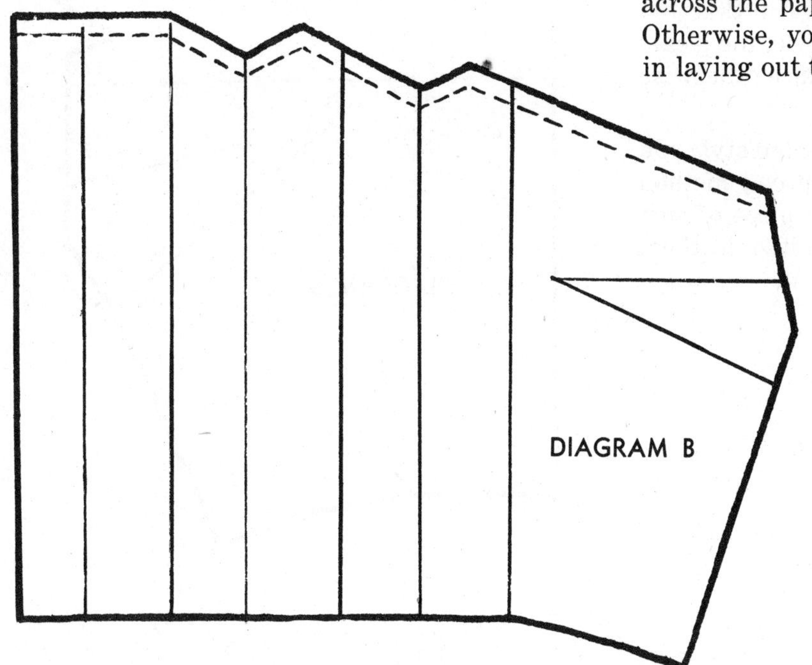

BODICE WITH HORIZONTAL PLEATS (or Tucks)

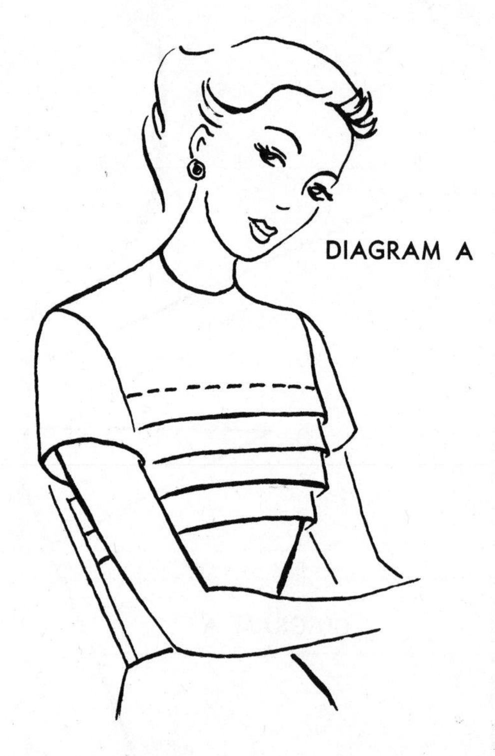

If you prefer to slash and spread, draw in on your block the lines on which you desire pleats. Cut the block apart on the lines and spread the pieces out. If you want the pleats 2 inches in depth, spread the pattern pieces out 2 inches apart. Be very careful that you lay them out straight. In this style, the pleats will have to be stitched shut, since otherwise they would pull open.

In making a pattern for a pleated style you can use either the slash-and-spread method or you can simply take a large piece of soft paper, measure your pleats on it, fold them in, and then put your block on top of the pleated paper and trace. In general, this is the simplest method. Be sure that you use a ruler to draw in the lines to fold; and be sure that your measurements are accurate.

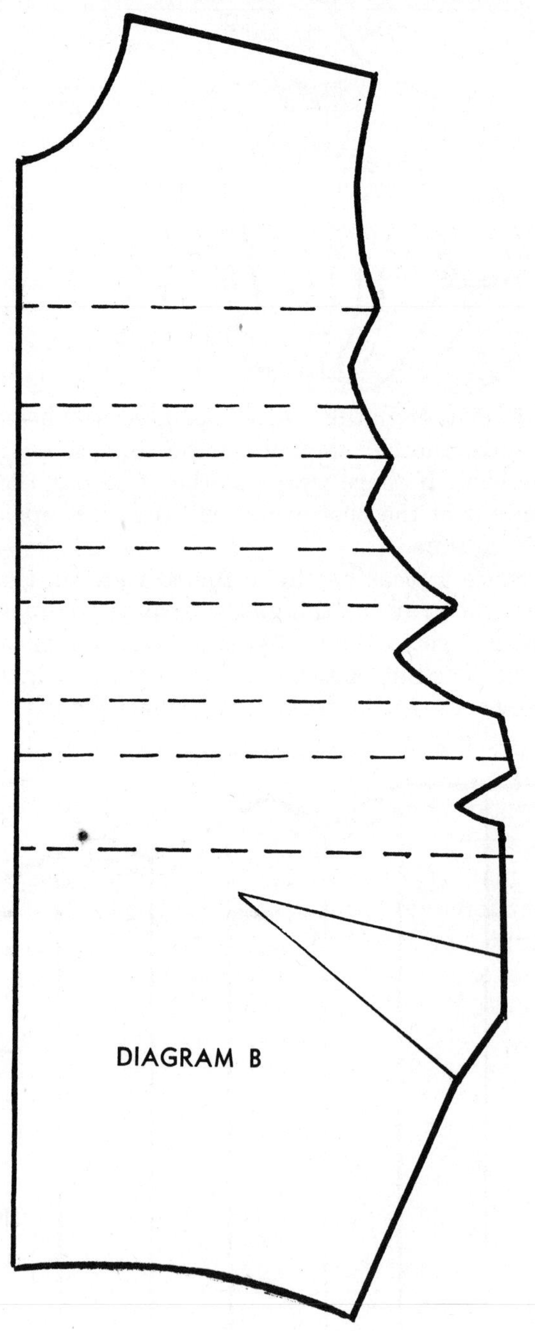

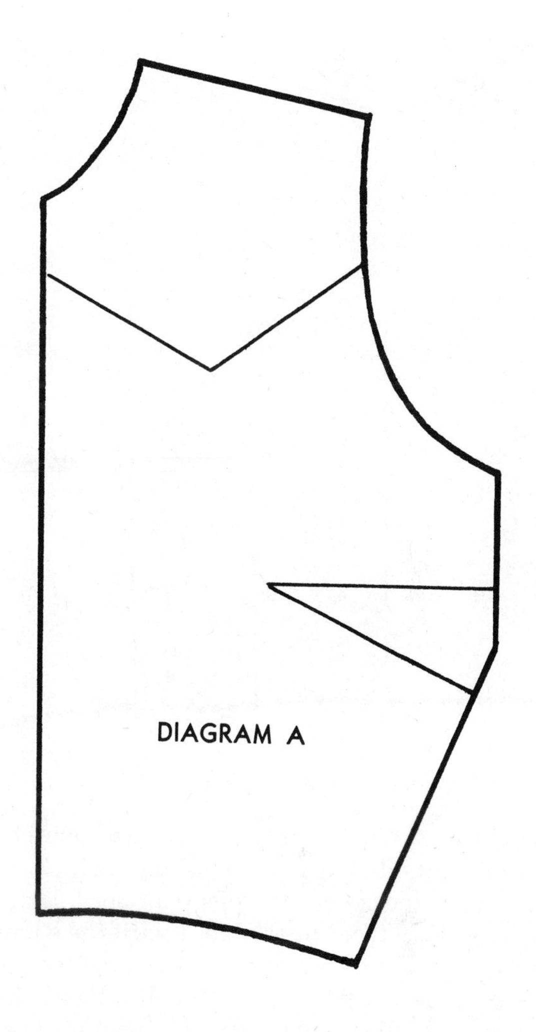

Up to now, since you have been doing the work almost entirely in quarter-size patterns, it has not been necessary for you to attempt to use the tracing wheel. However, in making full-size patterns, you will find that it is indispensable. This style is a very simple one to make a pattern for, and a good one on which to begin using the tracing wheel; so make this pattern full size.

Take a large piece of soft paper. It must be large enough for the block after the paper is pleated. The box pleat is 6 inches in depth. You will need to draw three parallel lines on the paper 3 inches apart. The first line should be placed 3½ inches in from the edge of the paper. Be sure that your measurements are accurate. Nothing is more important than accuracy in pattern making.

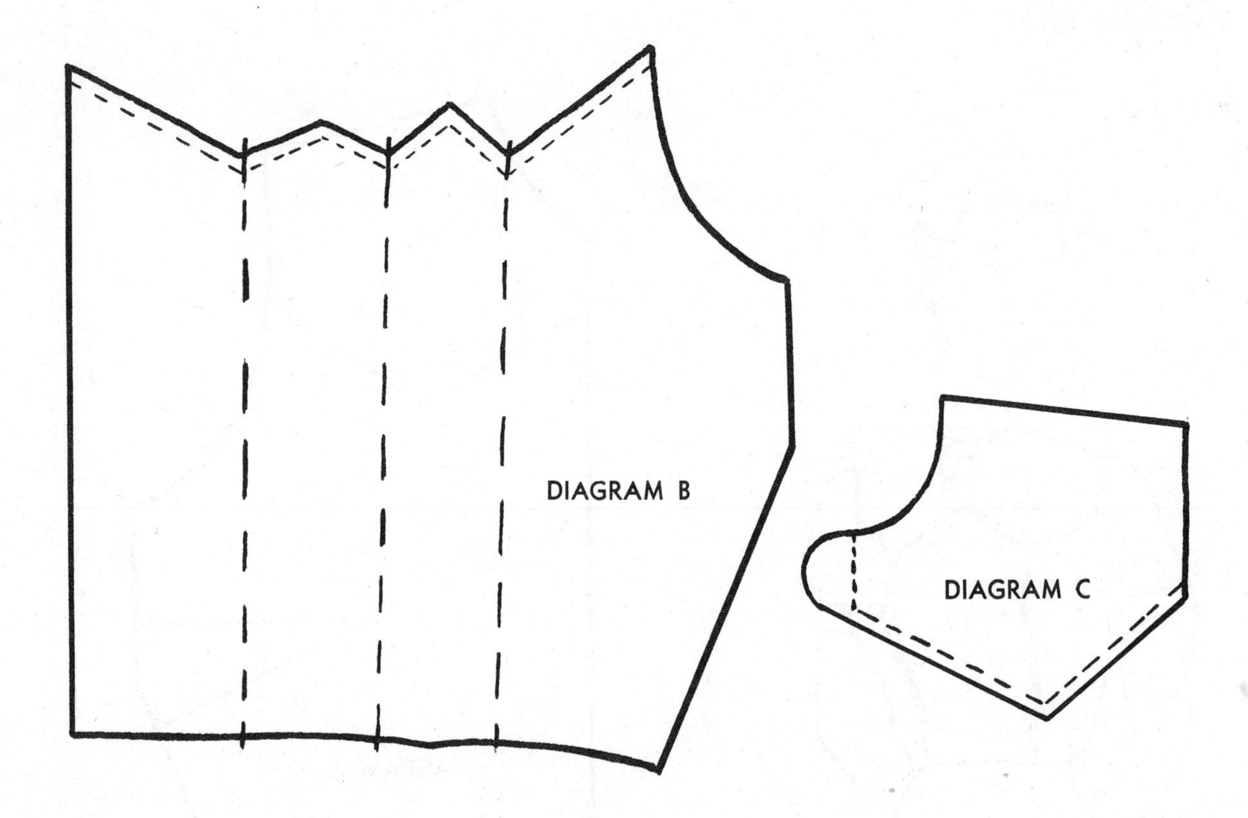

Fold in the pleat; be sure that you match the two outside lines to the center line. Now place your block over the pleated paper. Line up the center front of the block with the edge of the paper, making sure that the center of the pleat is set in from the center front of the bodice 3½ inches. Draw around the block. Draw the yoke on the block and trace the yoke line with the tracing wheel. This line will show up as a perforated line on the underneath paper and also on the table; so use a bread board or other protection.

Remove the block; add a ½-inch seam to the perforated line. Cut the pattern out while the pleat is still folded in place. Be sure that you cut on the seam line and not on the perforated line.

Next, copy the upper part of the block. Trace the yoke line with the tracing wheel. Remove the block. Add the button extension and the seam allowance to the yoke. The tracing wheel saved you the extra work of copying the block in order to cut it into pieces to recopy. You will find it increasingly useful as you become accustomed to working with it. Use it wherever you can. You will find it as important as your pencil.

Pleated Bodice With Curved Yoke

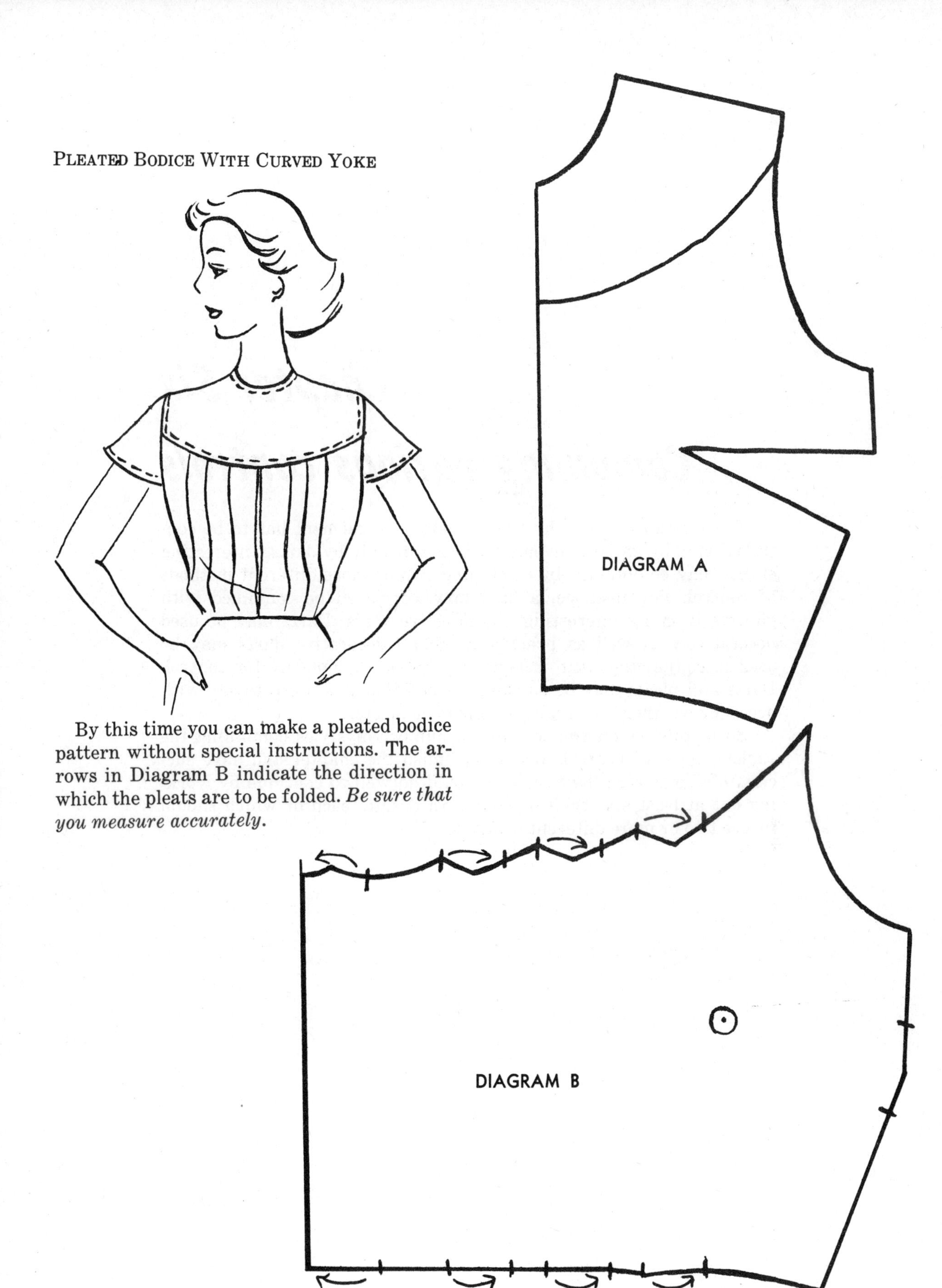

By this time you can make a pleated bodice pattern without special instructions. The arrows in Diagram B indicate the direction in which the pleats are to be folded. *Be sure that you measure accurately.*

Chapter Six
Combining various controls

There is no reason why the fullness in a garment has to be controlled only by gathers or only by pleats or only by darts. Interesting effects may be obtained by combining two or more different methods of control. For instance, a dart may very well be combined with gathers in many interesting and effective ways. Darts may be used decoratively as well as practically. Small decorative darts may be used in conjunction with a dart which is used primarily for control. Darts and pleats may be so closely allied that it is hard to say with accuracy whether they really are darts or pleats.

So in this lesson you will find a number of styles combining the various types of control. When you finish the chapter and have successfully completed the test, you would do well to continue by working out at least six styles of your own design, each of which should utilize two or more different controls.

HORIZONTAL SLASH WITH GATHERS

Thus far we have added fullness for gathering at the waistline, the bustline, the shoulder, and at various yoke lines.

This time the bodice will simply be slashed to allow the spread. In sewing up such a style, start with a ½-inch seam at the armscye and taper it off to nothing at the inner edges. Keep that in mind when adding seam allowance to the pattern. Diagram A shows the slash line.

As shown in Diagram B, the dart has been closed by overlapping the pattern pieces. Add the ½-inch seam as far as you are able. Trim ¹⁄₁₆ inch of paper out of the remainder of the slash — just enough so that it is obviously a slash and not an error.

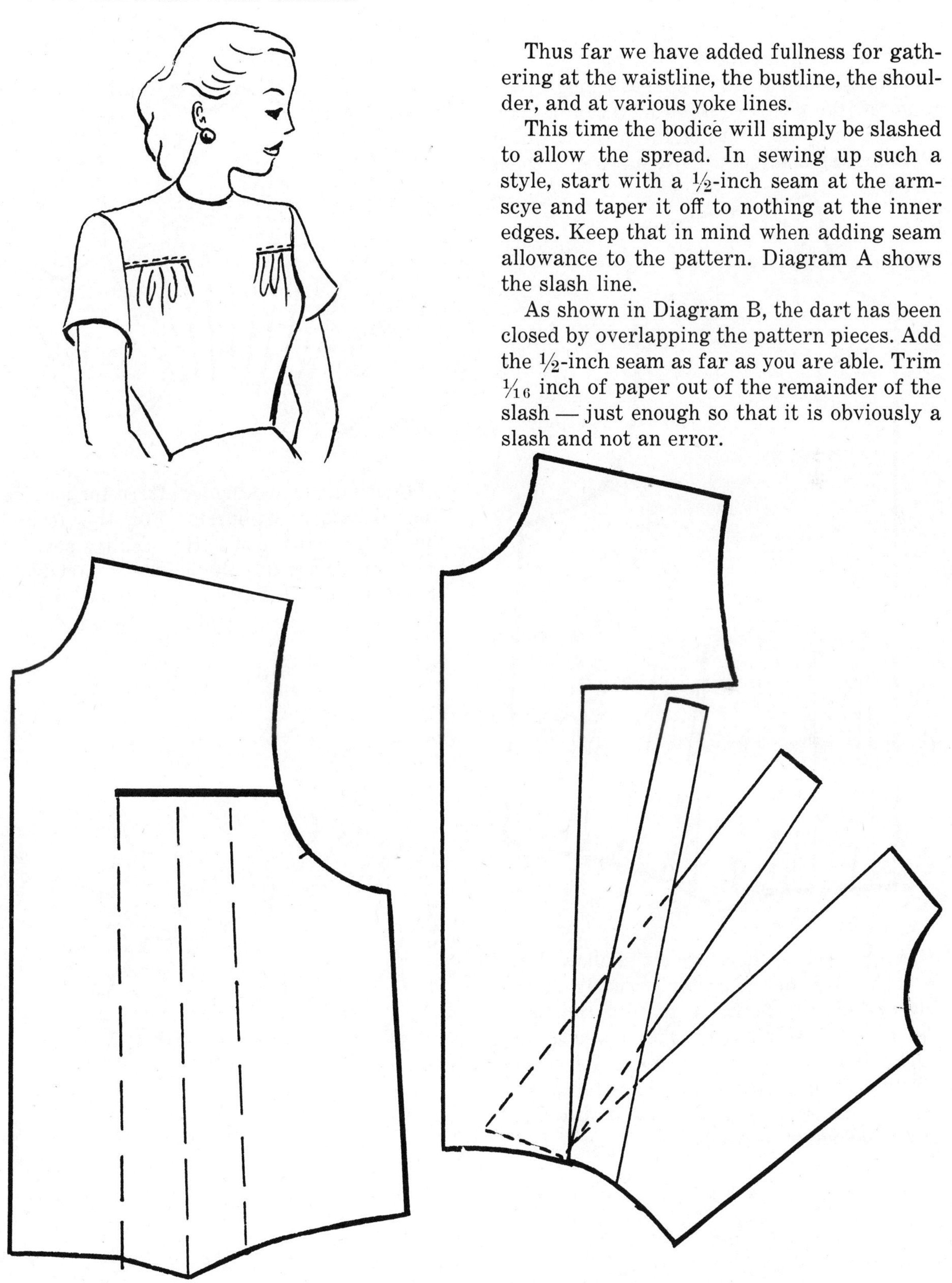

MIDRIFF STYLE WITH SHALLOW DARTS

With darts as shallow as these, it is not necessary to add fullness. The problem here is merely one of careful measuring. First, trim off the dart extension at the waistline. Next, divide the width of the present single dart into as many new darts as your pattern needs.

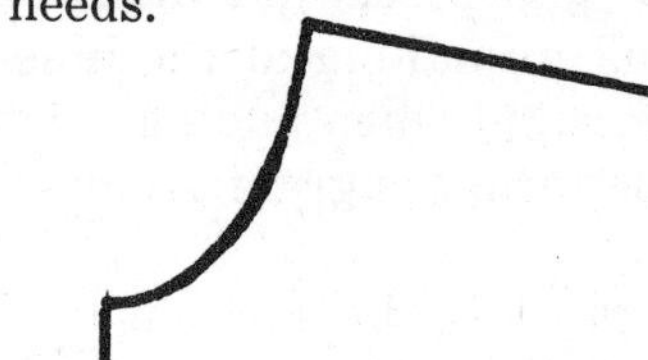

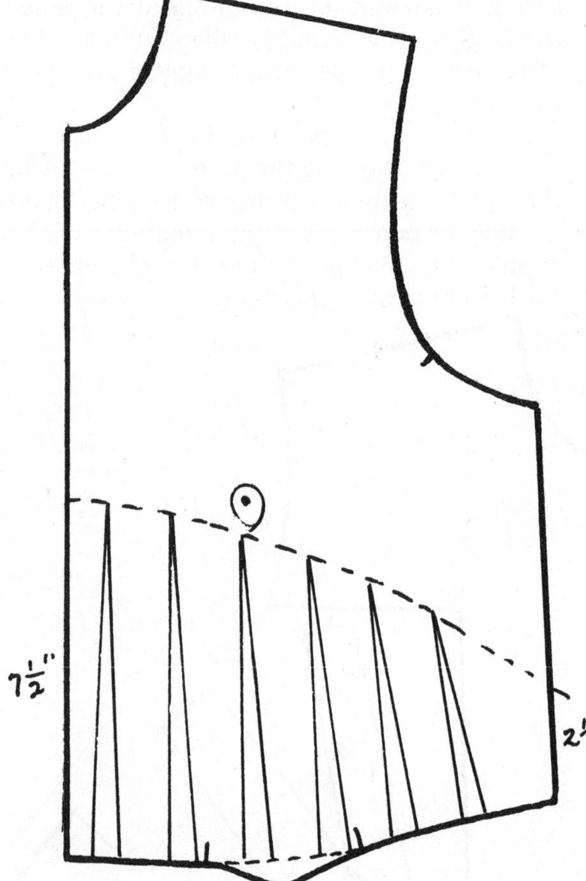

In this bodice, there are six shallow darts on either side of the center front. The curving dotted line shown on the diagram is to aid in establishing the length of each new dart. This type of dart control is sometimes referred to as a "sunburst." It makes a very interesting neckline detail and is also good as a shoulder or sleeve treatment.

Continue by making a pattern for neckline and shoulder sunbursts. For the former, swing the waist dart to the neckline position. For the latter, use the shoulder dart block. Be sure that all darts are an equal distance apart, or the results will be unfortunate.

Square Neck Bodice With Decorative Darts

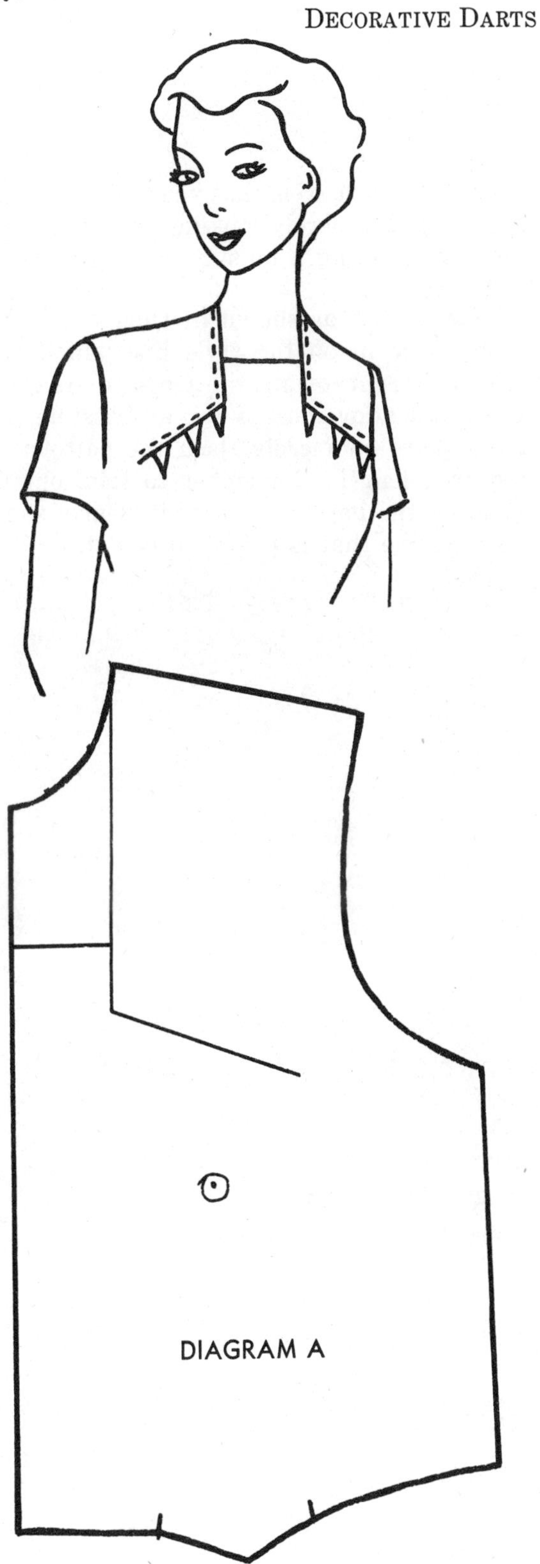

Here, you could begin with either the shoulder or the waist dart block. The latter has been used because, in closing the waist dart by overlapping the two slashed pieces, you automatically get the right amount of fullness.

Directions

1. Draw in the square neckline and the style line. Cut out the square neck.
2. Slash the block into two pieces, cutting right through the center of the waist dart.
3. Overlap the two pieces so that the dart is completely closed. Now you have obtained a spread of about 4 inches at the style line. One inch of this will be used for seaming the garment back together. Measure the remainder of the fullness and divide the amount into three. Use the resulting meas-

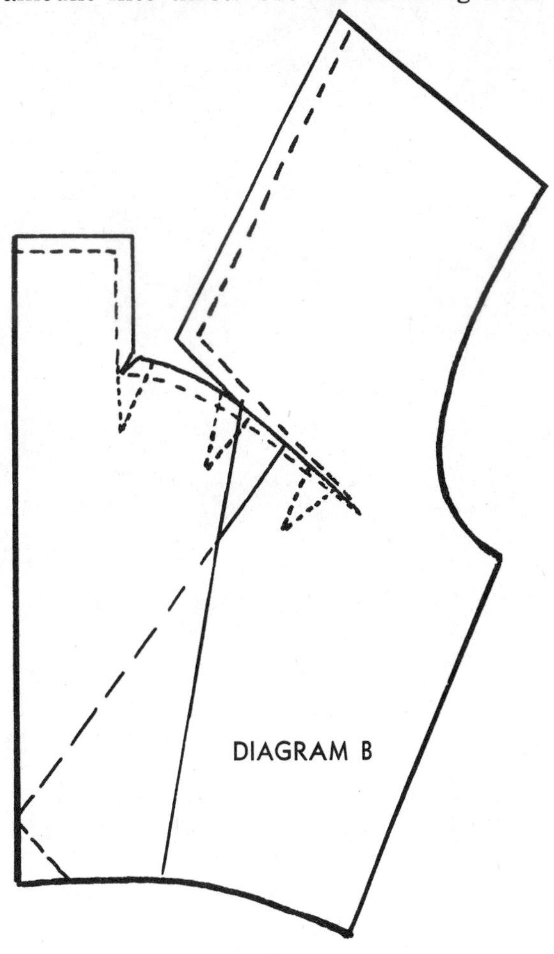

urement as the total width of *each* of the new darts. Draw in the three new darts. Be very careful in measuring so that the darts are evenly spaced. These darts will be folded and stitched on the outside of the garment.

It may seem contradictory that with these shallow darts there is no longer dart elsewhere to help control the fullness. The reason is that these darts are placed low enough on the bodice so that they end fairly near the natural bust point. This is a matter to decide upon with each style that you do. If you cannot judge by merely looking at your sketch, then try pinning a muslin or tissue directly to the form.

This bodice, as shown in Diagram B, has a stolen seam on the style line which goes from the front toward the armscye. As usual, add seam allowance as far as possible, and from there on merely slash the pattern the required length. Remember to trim out the slash on the pattern so that it clearly shows up as a line that is meant to be cut.

CURVED YOKE WITH DECORATIVE DARTS

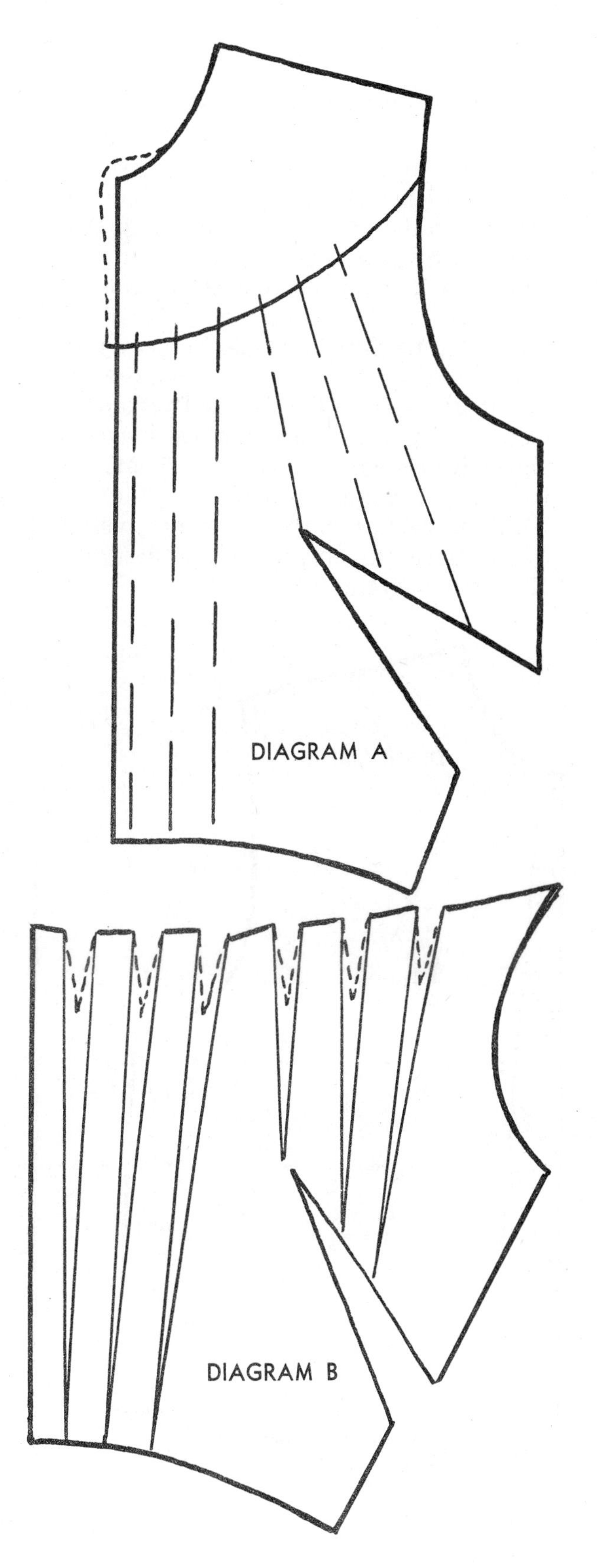

Since the decorative darts are so short and do not end close to the bust point, you must control the fullness partially by another dart. A side dart has been used in this style.

Directions

1. Draw in the curving yoke line.
2. Round the neckline and add ½-inch seam to the center front opening.
3. Decide how far apart you want the darts. Make a mark for each dart on the yoke line. Slash at each mark and spread the pieces out 1 inch apart. This will make the depth of the darts 1 inch.
4. Make a mark in the exact center of each spread piece 2 inches below the yoke line. These will be the dart points. Draw in the darts. These are shown with dotted lines on Diagram B.
5. As shown in Diagram B, the side dart is now much shallower, as it has been partly closed by the spread. Remember the seam allowance on both pieces.

Darts With Released Fullness

This special type of dart is left open for part of its length, which gives a soft effect similar to gathering. The dotted line in Diagram A helps you judge the length of your darts. Draw this line on your traced copy of the block. Carefully measure in the dart lines. Be sure that they are an equal distance apart. Slash from the neckline to the waist. Cut the block apart on one of the slashes. Overlap the two pattern pieces so that the waist dart is completely closed. The pieces should be spread 1¾ inches apart at the neckline.

Draw in the new darts, using the greatest care to have the measurements accurate. Follow the diagrams closely.

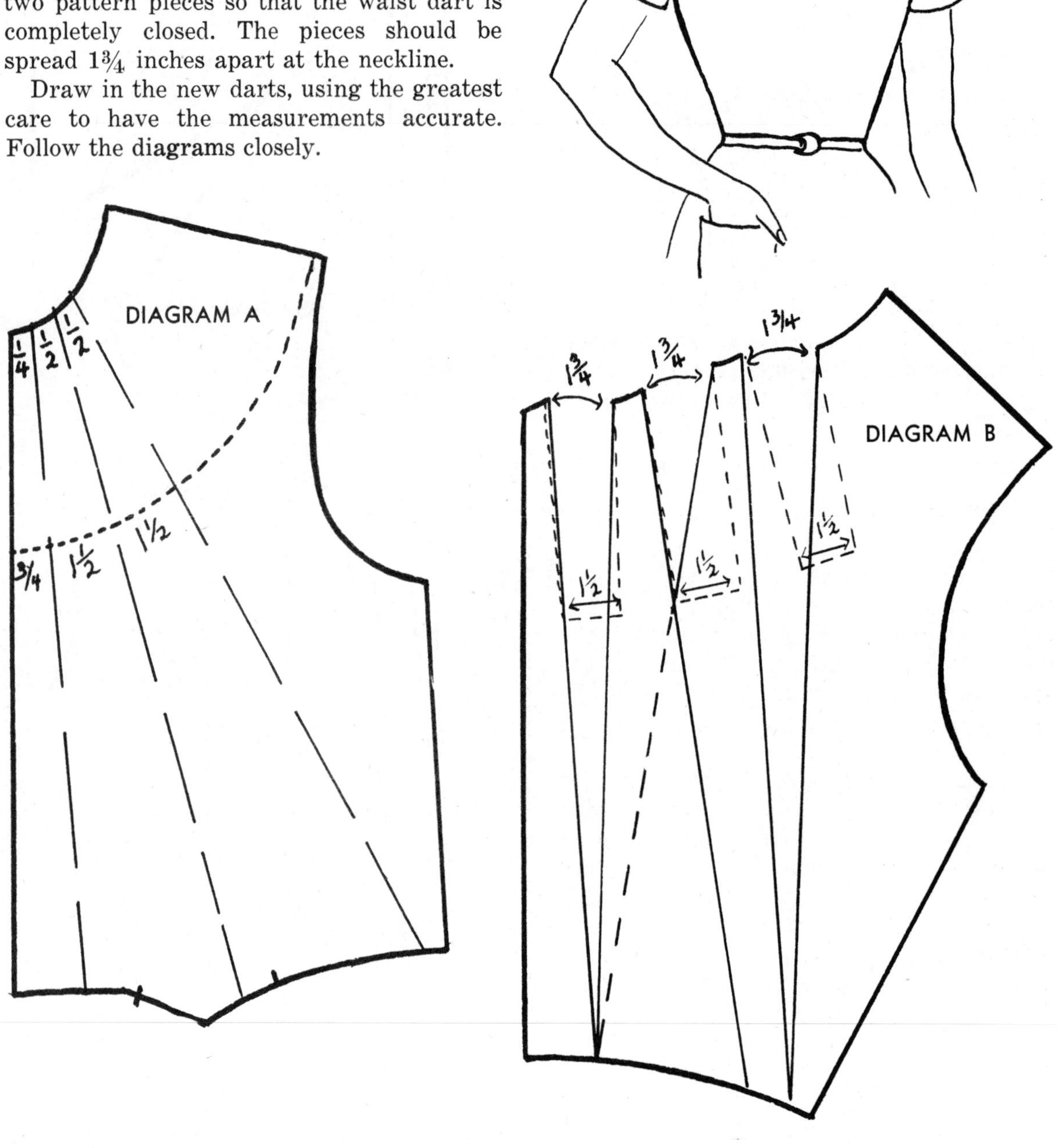

Decorative Darts With Gathers

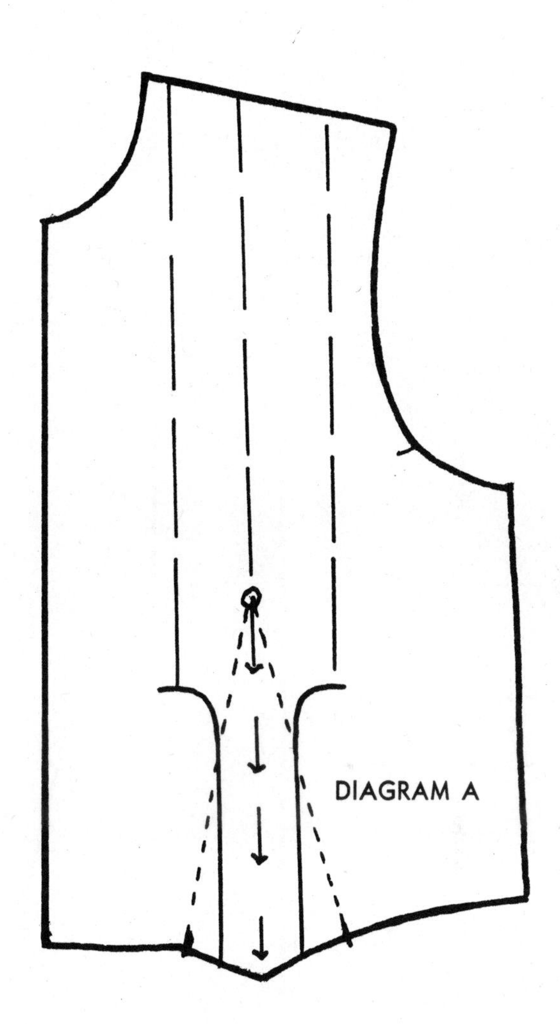

This style is a little more complicated than any of the previous ones, but if you study the diagrams closely you should not have any trouble.

Directions

1. Draw in the decorative waist dart; shown with a heavy solid line in Diagram A.
2. Slash the block almost to the shoulder as indicated with the broken lines on Diagram A.

3. Spread for fullness. Since you cannot add additional length at the bust line to compensate for the snug fit of the bodice, add the length at the shoulder.

4. The horizontal seams are almost entirely stolen. Add seam allowance as far as possible.

5. You do not need to add seam allowance for the vertical style lines. The fullness from the original dart is utilized for this purpose. Leave the dart extension on, as it forms a body onto which you sew the edges of the new dart. The line of arrows indicates the center where the edges are brought together.

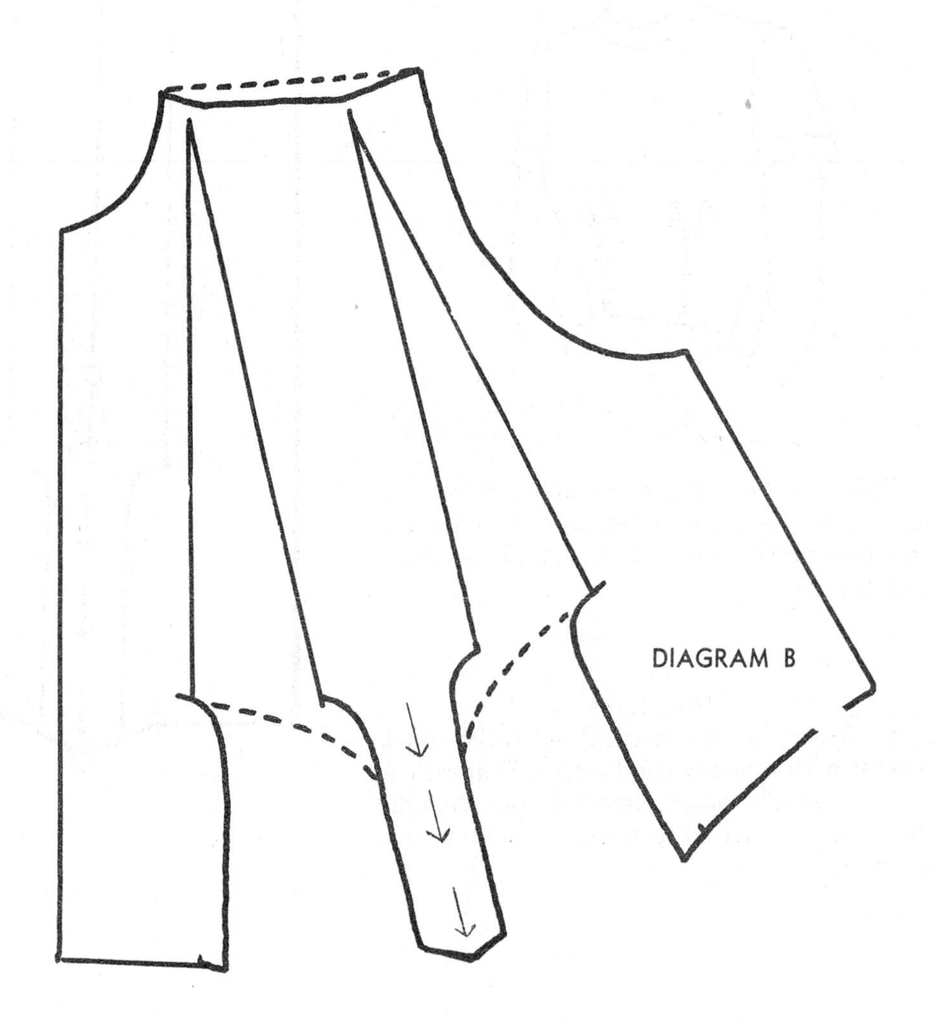

Slash and Spread Combined With a Side Dart

For adding gathers directly to a dart, see the style shown here. To do this, proceed as for any other slash-and-spread operation, the only difference being that you begin the slashes at the dart. Diagram A shows the bodice marked for slashing. Cut to the shoulder but not through it. When swinging in the side dart, lower the bust point about $1\frac{1}{2}$ inches.

This pattern, Diagram B, needs a little extra length to go over the bust contour. Allow $1\frac{1}{2}$ inches. The seam allowance is $\frac{1}{2}$ inch at the side seam and tapers to nothing at the inside point of the dart. The seam has been allowed while drawing in the bust line.

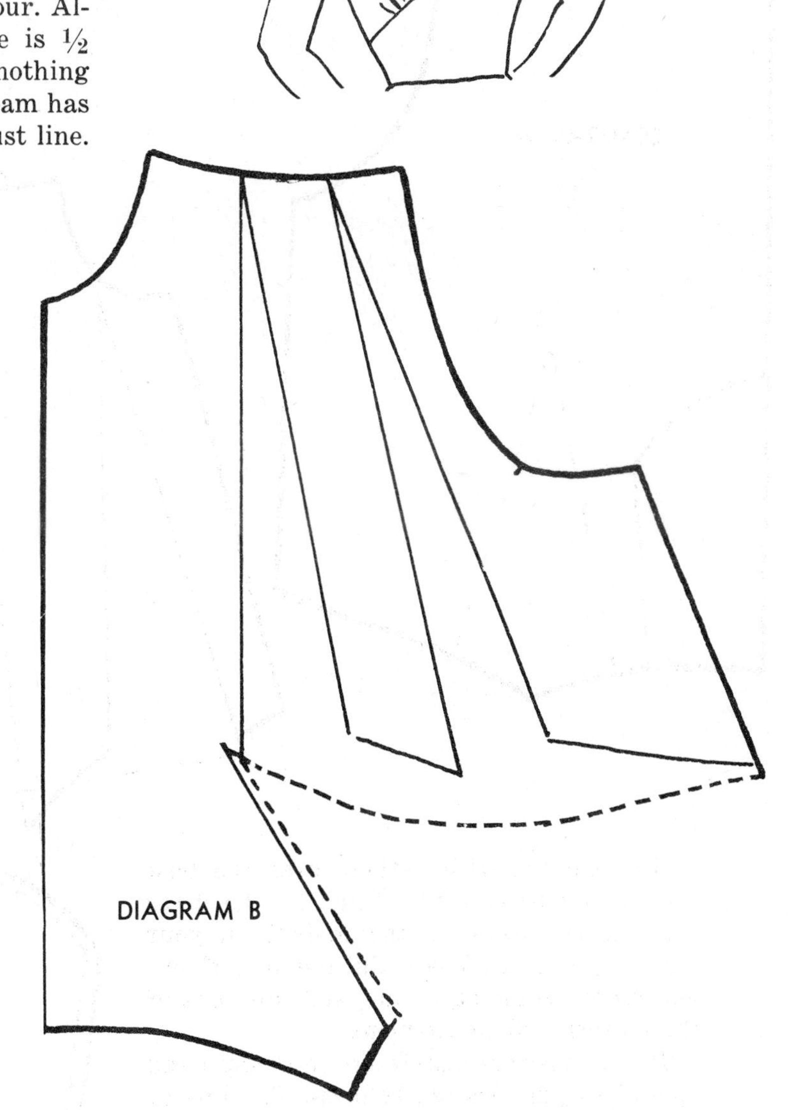

DIAGRAM A

SET-IN FRONT MIDRIFF

This style presents another problem in combining slash and spread with darts. Move the dart closer to the center front to make it conform to the style line of the midriff.

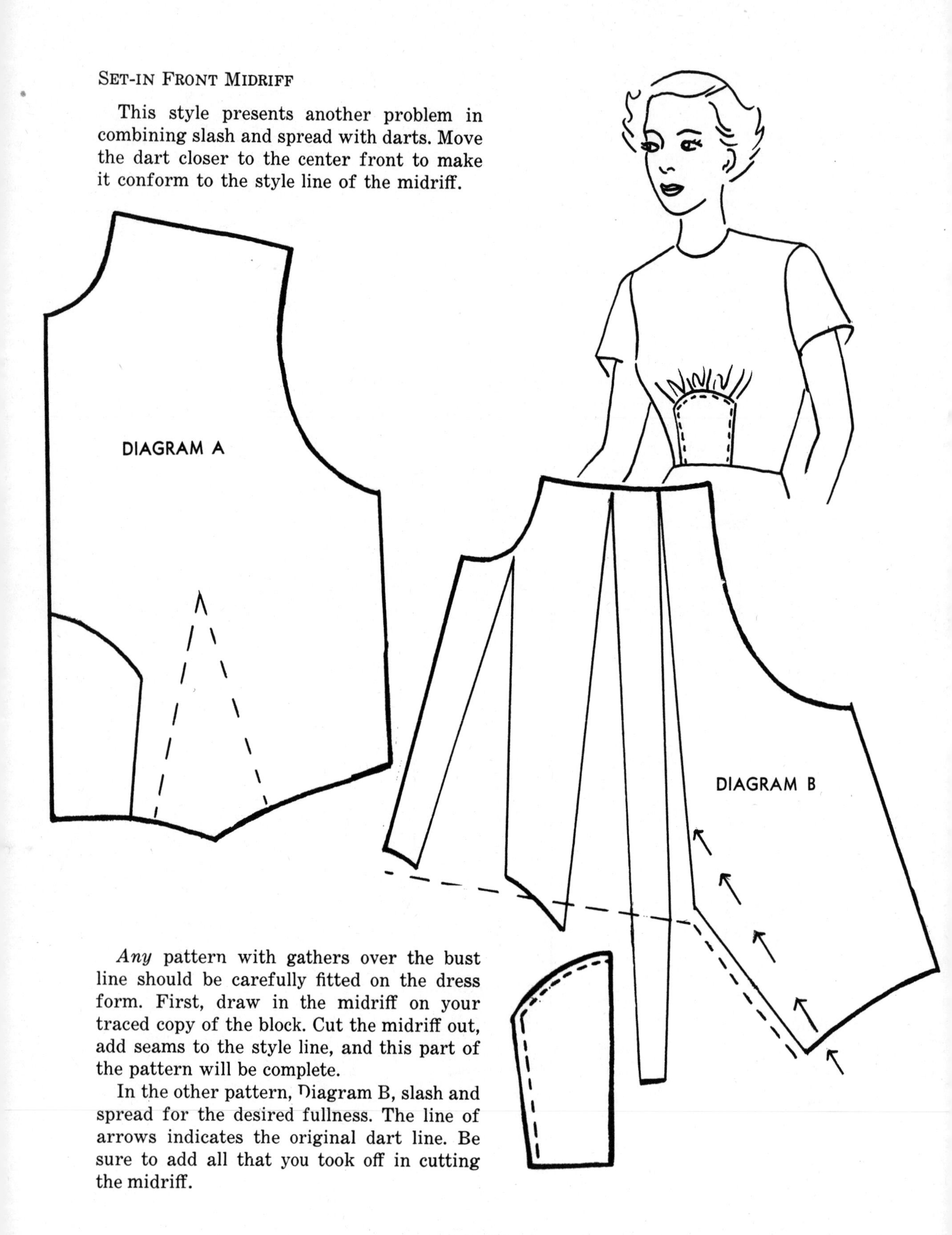

Any pattern with gathers over the bust line should be carefully fitted on the dress form. First, draw in the midriff on your traced copy of the block. Cut the midriff out, add seams to the style line, and this part of the pattern will be complete.

In the other pattern, Diagram B, slash and spread for the desired fullness. The line of arrows indicates the original dart line. Be sure to add all that you took off in cutting the midriff.

Test

Slash and Spread

You may find this test more difficult than the test on darts. Working diagrams are included so that you may check your results. Only one diagram is shown of each style, but you should be able to decipher them all after making your own attempt.

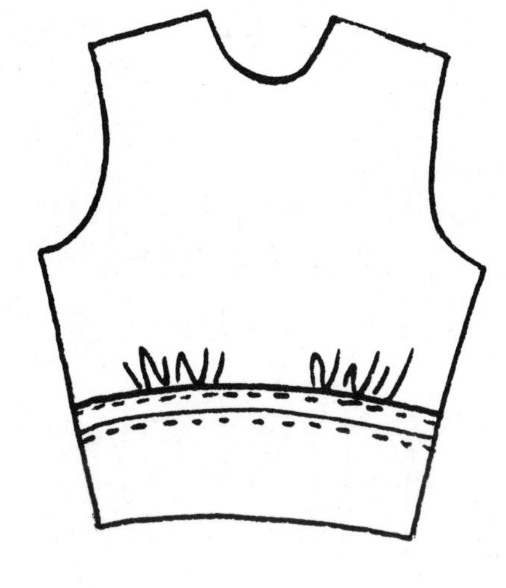

2.

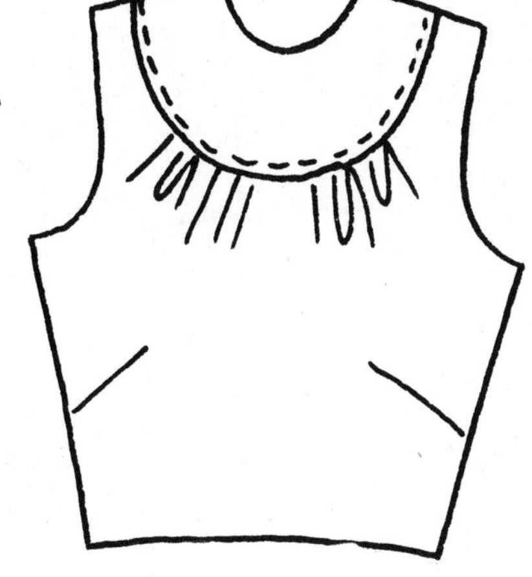

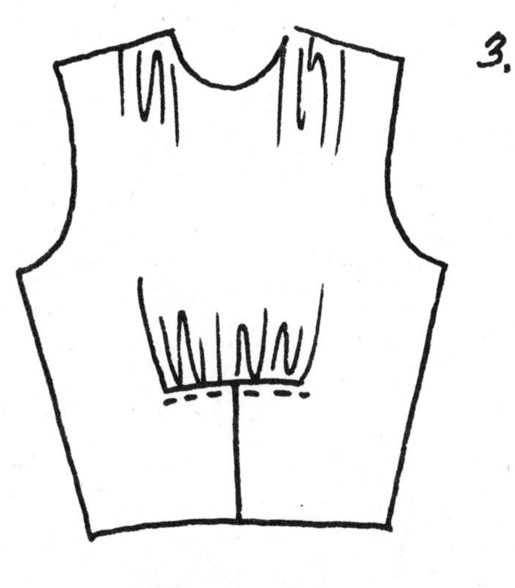

4.

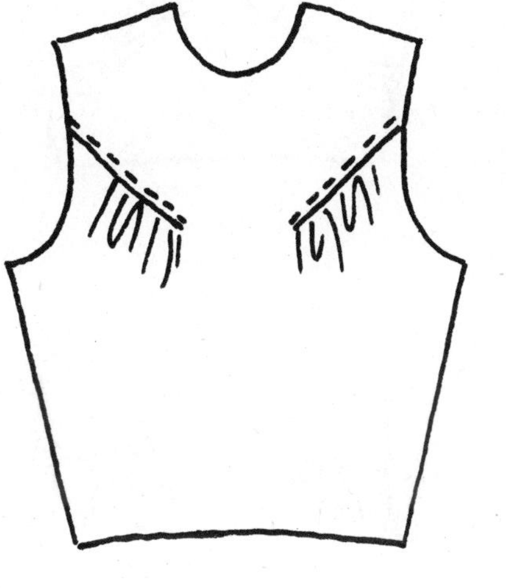

6.

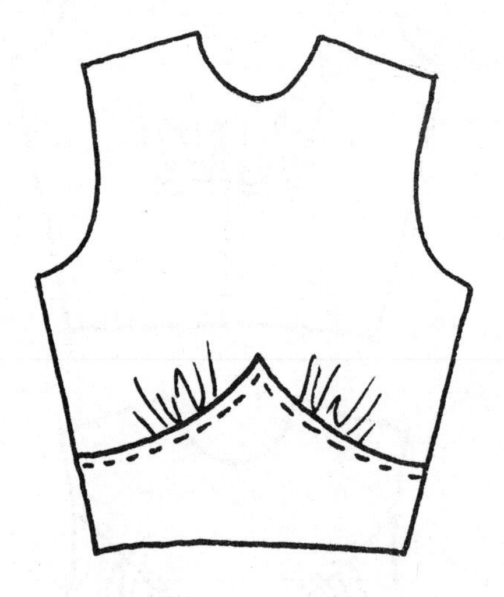

8.

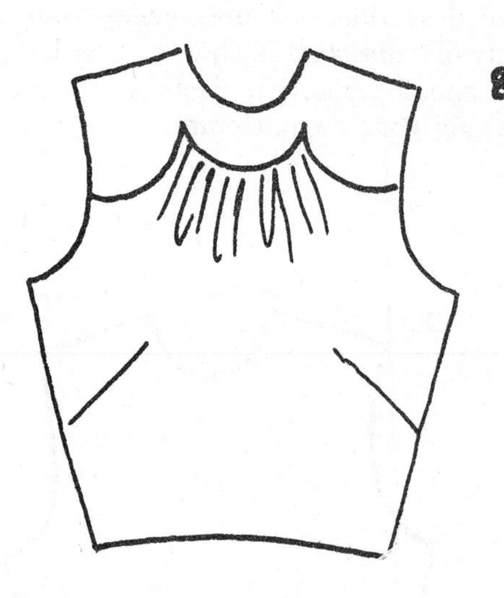

7.

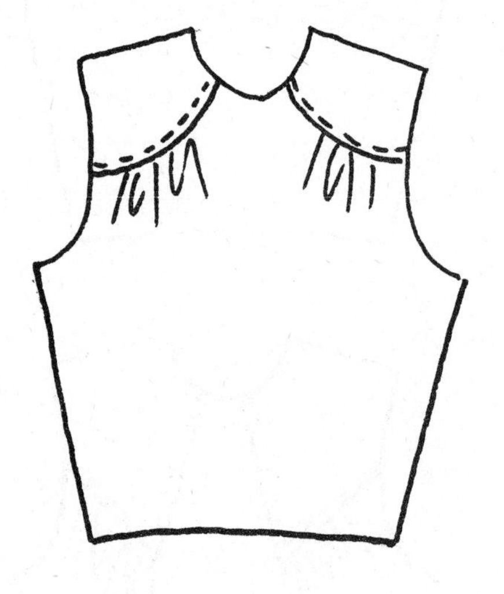

9.

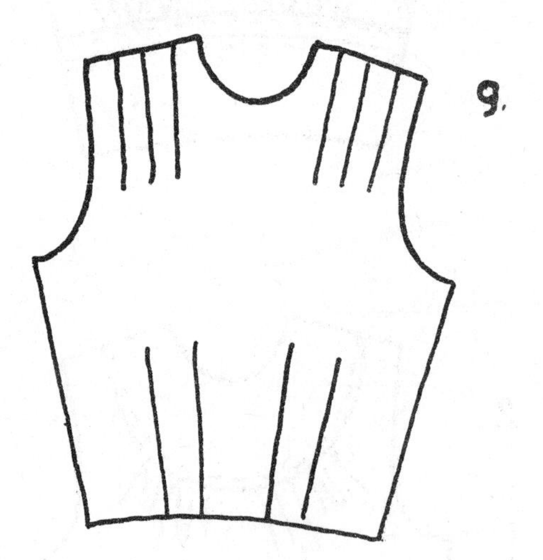

Working Diagrams

In all working diagrams that follow, seam allowance has been added to the style lines. Check all of your results with these diagrams. If any differ too much, you had better do it over.

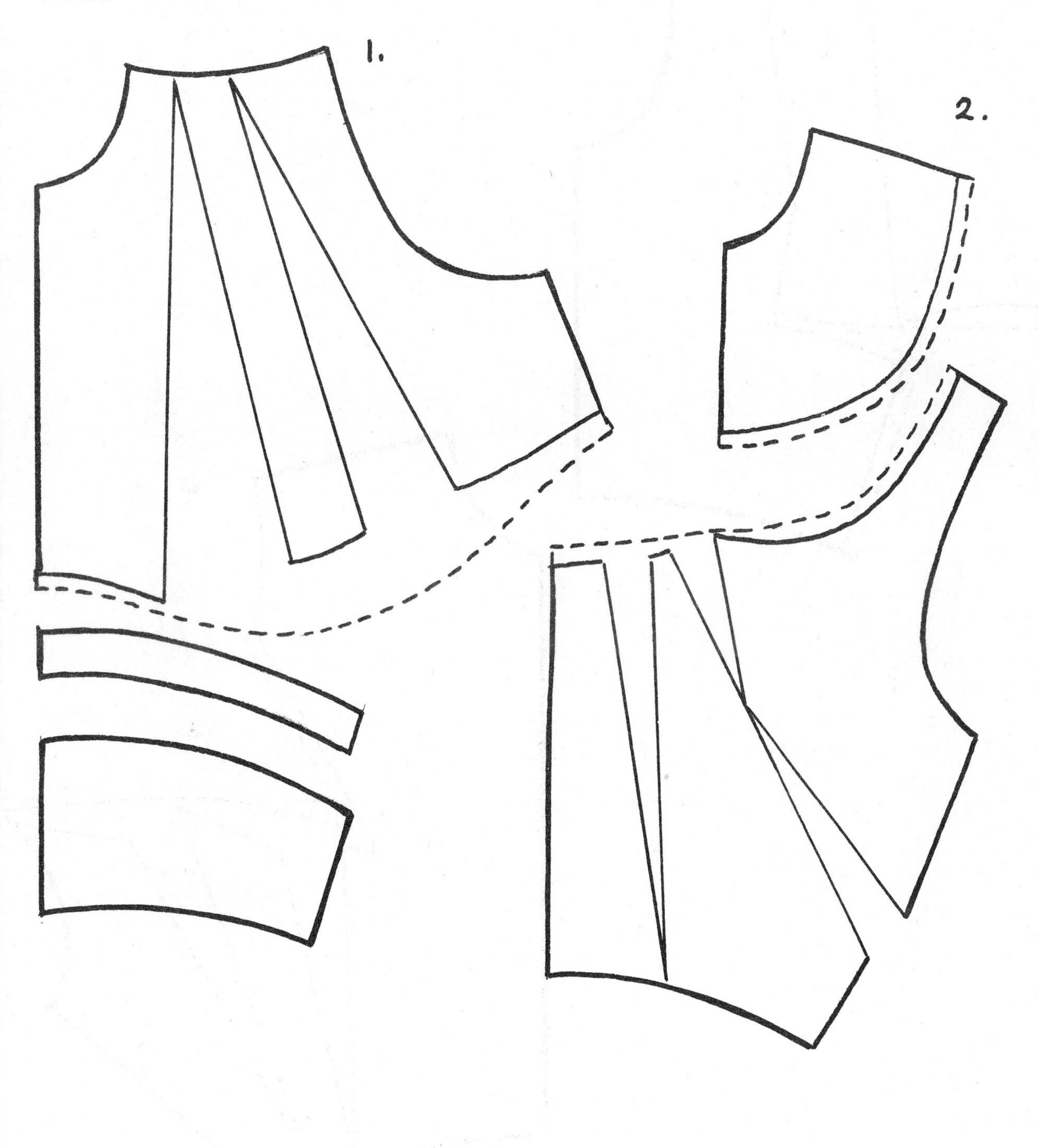

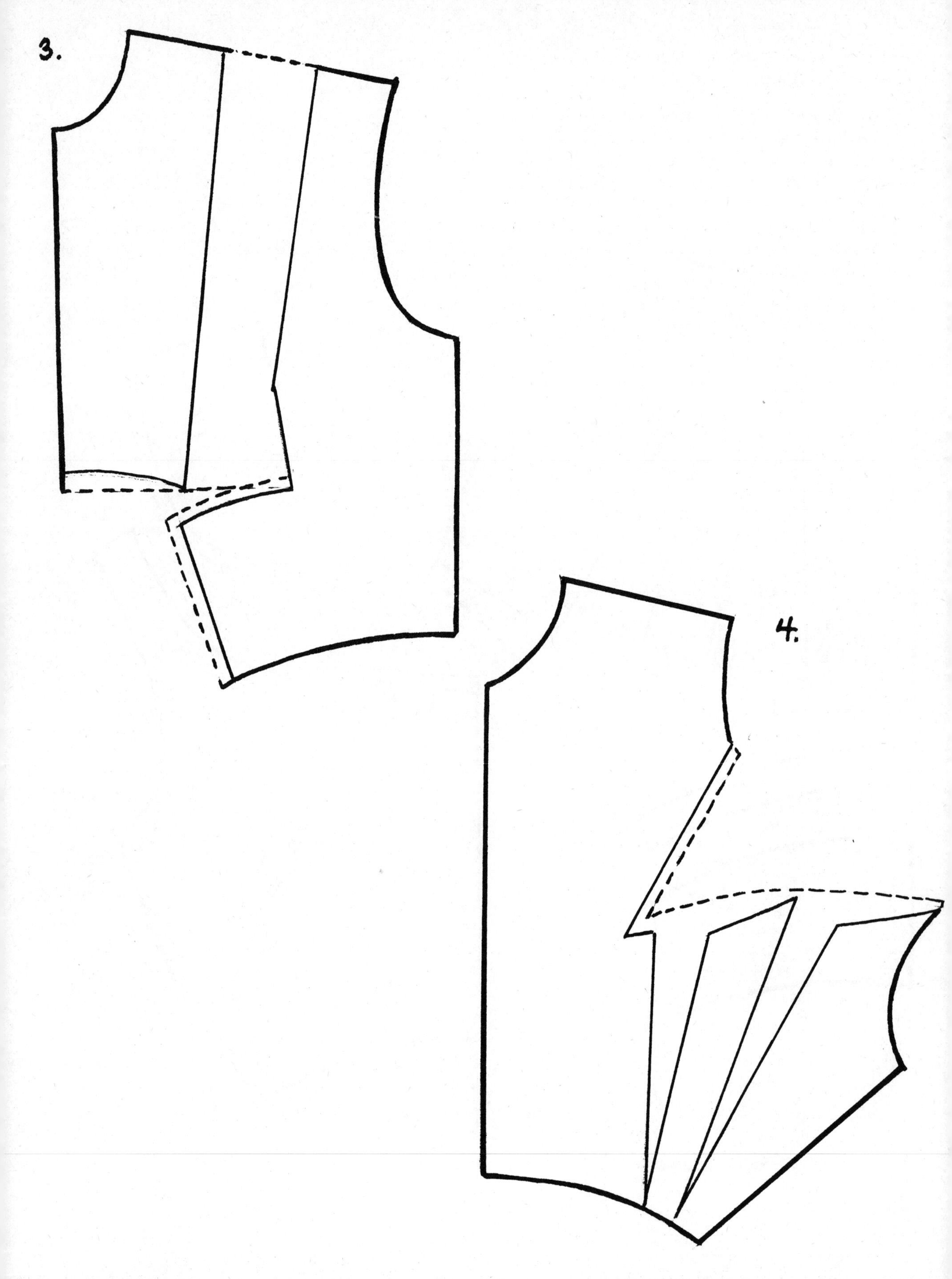
3.
4.

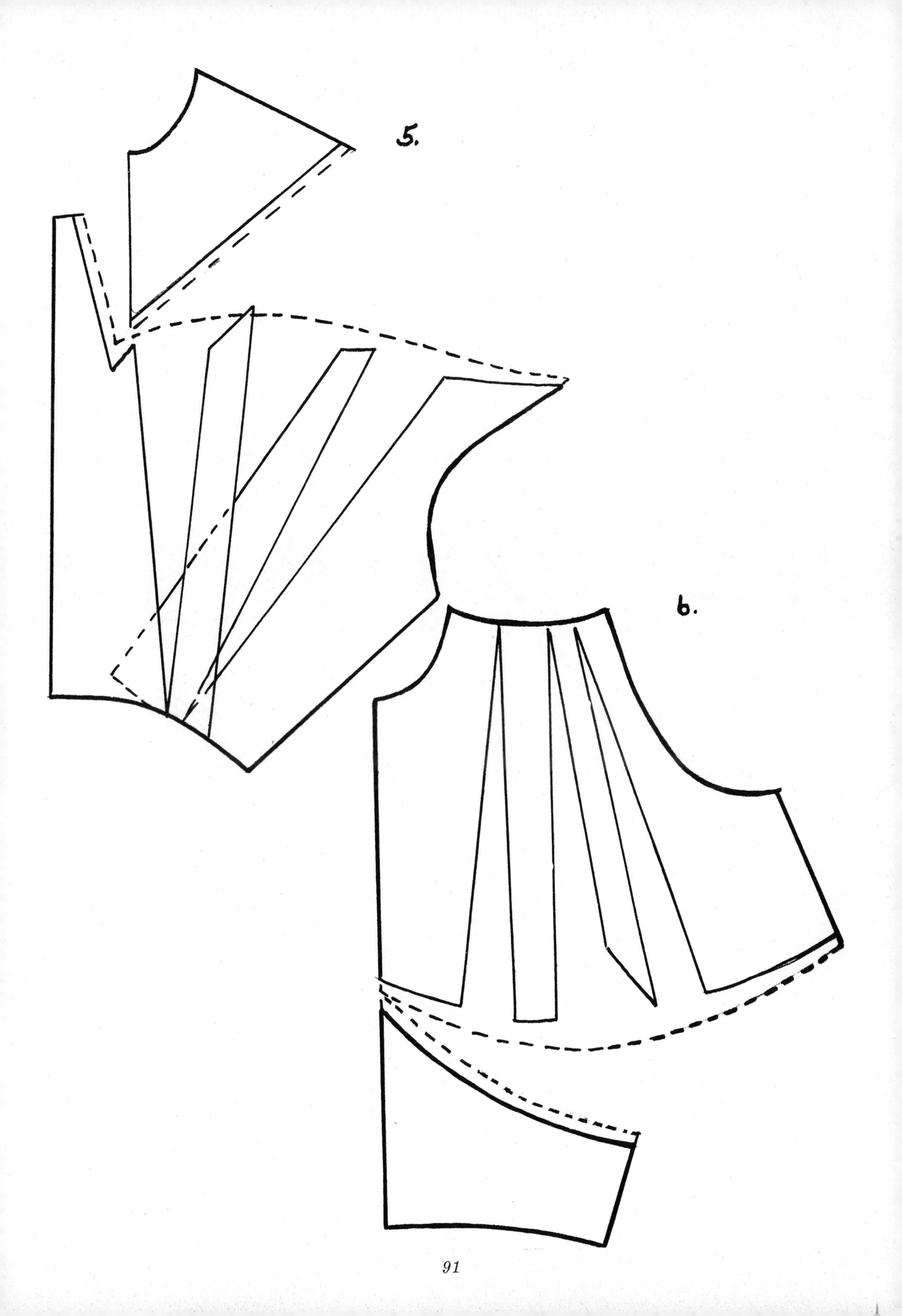
5.
6.

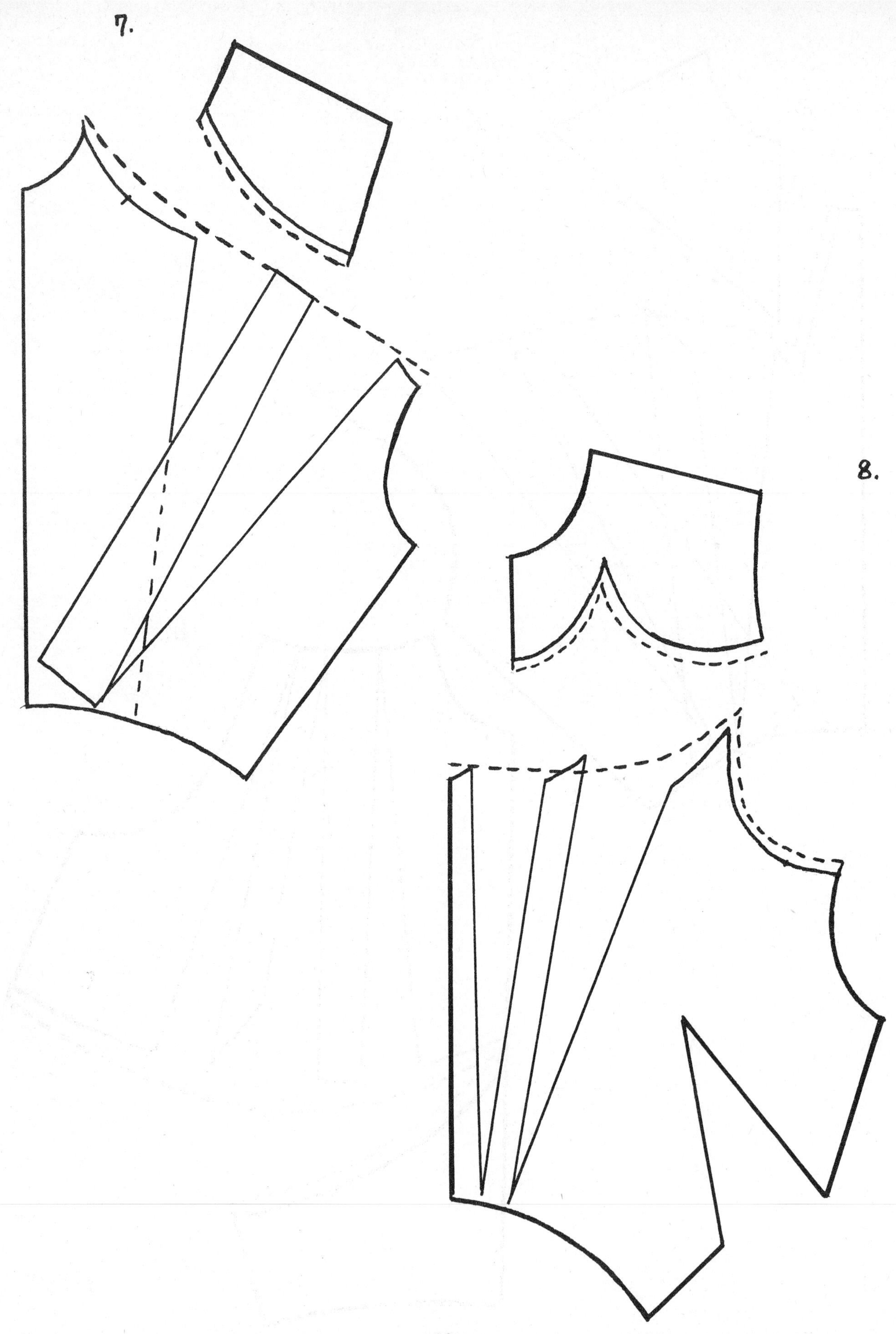
7.
8.

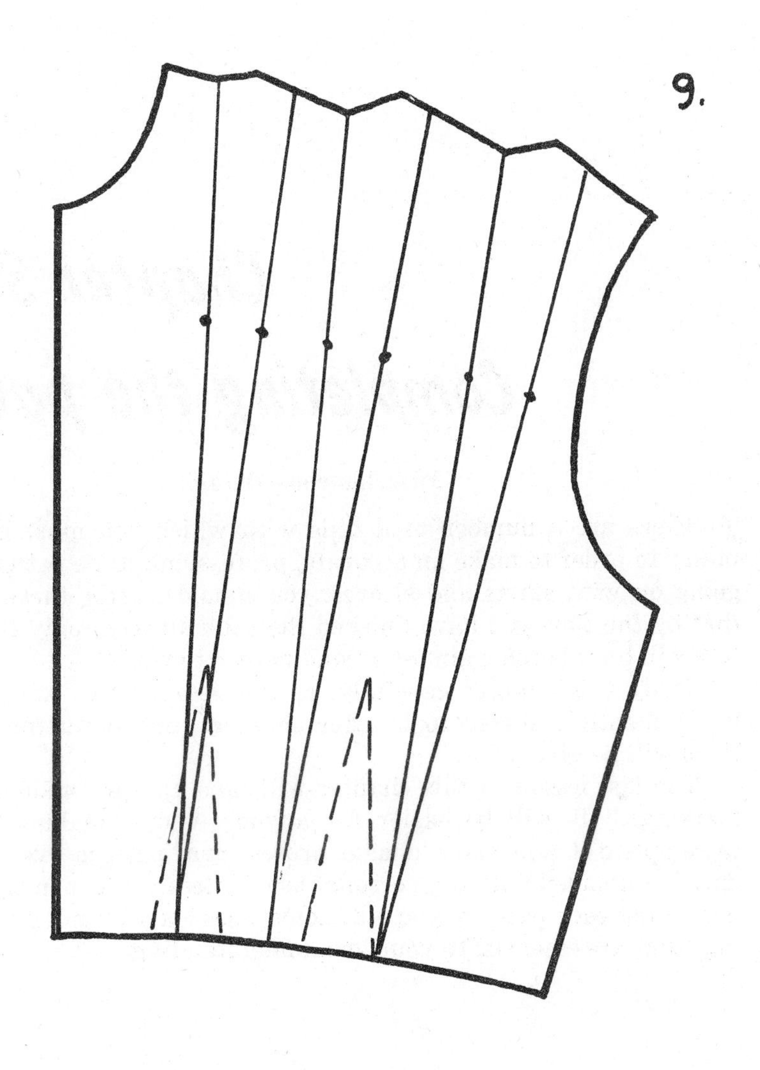
9.

Chapter Seven

Completing the pattern

Miscellaneous Details

There are a number of details with which you must become familiar in order to make an accurate, professional-type pattern. Before going on with skirts and sleeves, you should master these details so that by the time you have finished the book all seemingly trivial matters will have become almost second nature to you.

Study this chapter carefully, as the details dealt with here will be frequently referred to in later chapters, but no further explanations will be given.

The last lesson in this chapter will take up "professional pattern markings." It will be easier for anyone who is making a pattern to complete it and mark it as a professional pattern even though it may be intended only for personal use. Unless you get in the habit of perfecting each pattern, you may sometimes leave off notches or markings that are essential to your own understanding.

Cutting a Back Yoke

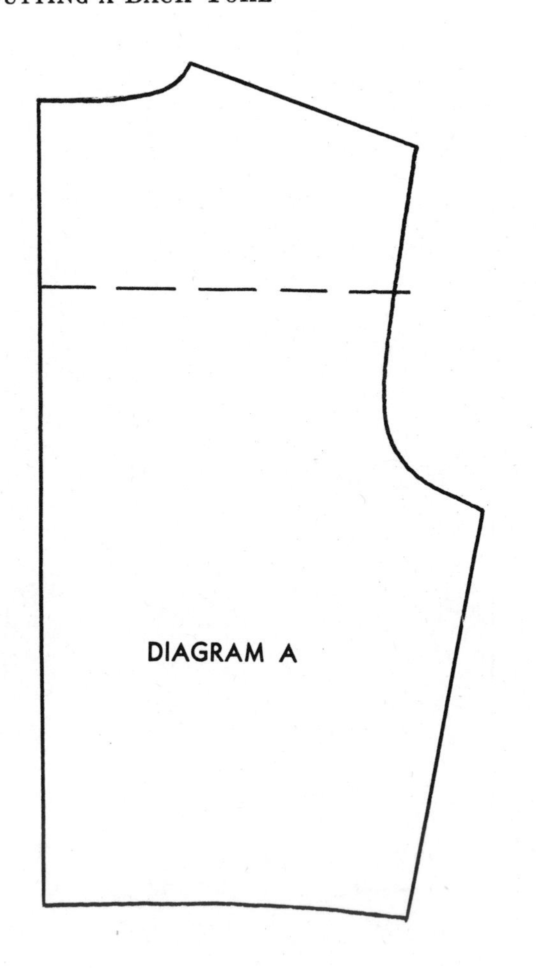

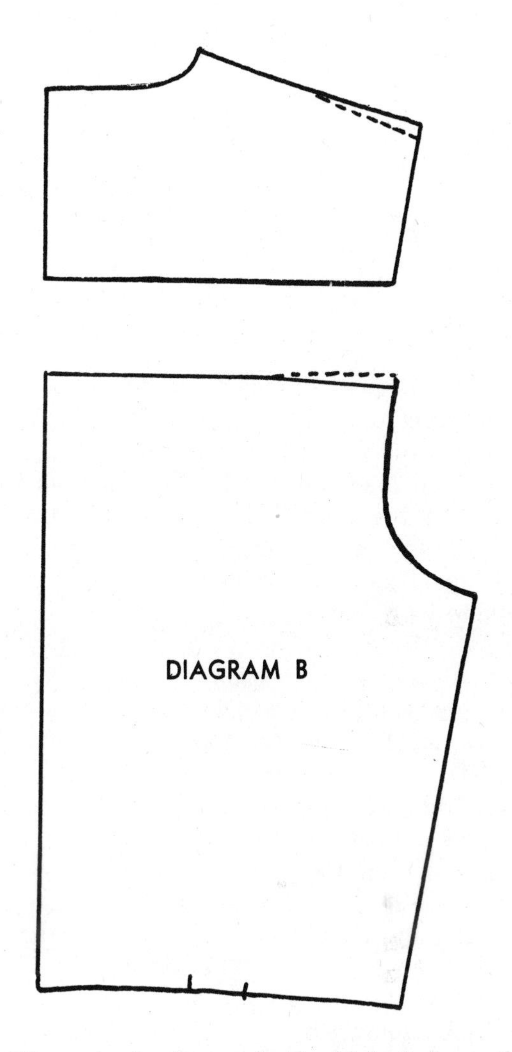

There is a little trick in cutting a back yoke so that the fit of the garment is smooth over the shoulder blade. Good pattern makers take the little extra trouble it requires in order to achieve a better fit.

A garment which has a back yoke tends to develop a slight bulge at the yoke seamline near the armscye. To prevent this, make a short, shallow dart at that point. Trim off 1/4 inch from the lower bodice piece and add the same amount to the shoulder seam of the yoke. The original shape of the two pieces is indicated by the dotted lines in the diagrams.

If you took off merely the 1/4 inch from the lower piece you would find that the armscye would be 1/4 inch too small. For that reason you need to add the 1/4 inch at the shoulder or at the side seam. It does not matter to which of the two places you add the 1/4 inch. In either case, as long as you take off the 1/4 inch from the yoke line, your result will be the same as though you had taken a small dart at that point.

Button Lap

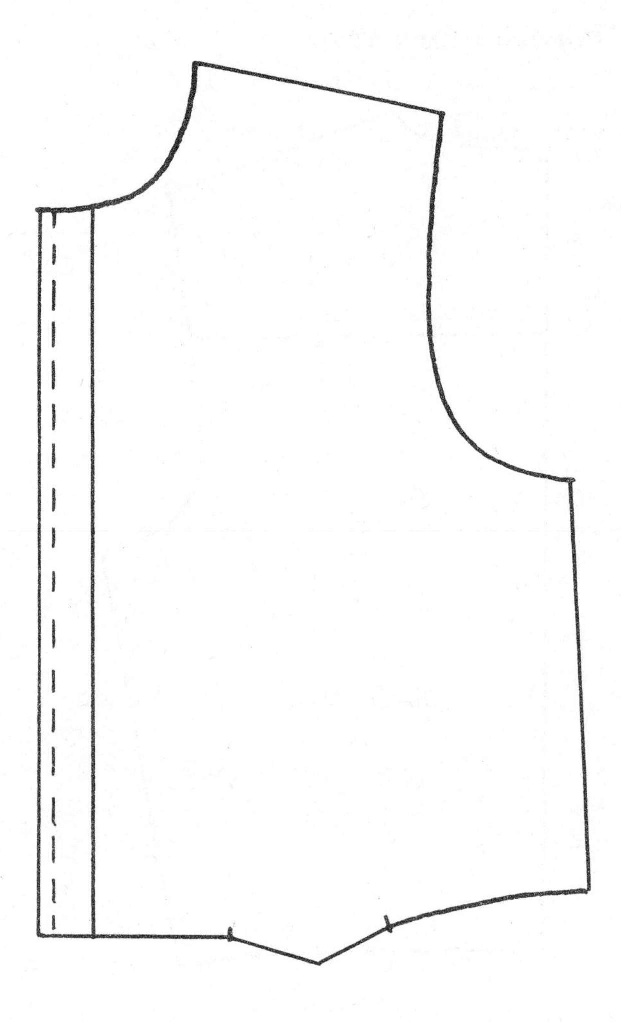

Your garment cannot fit properly unless the correct amount of button lap has been added to the pattern. The button lap should be $\frac{1}{2}$ the diameter of the button, plus the seam. In the case of a very small button, allow a little more than the above amount for the lap. This is a problem which you will have to work out.

Directions

In general, if you add $\frac{3}{4}$ inch or 1 inch to the center front of the garment for button lap, it works out well. If the button is extremely large, follow the rule given above: half the diameter of the button, plus seam.

In marking the garment or pattern for buttonholes, the distance from the edge of the garment should be half the diameter of the button, plus seam. The buttonhole itself should be $\frac{1}{16}$ inch longer than the diameter of the button used.

In marking for placement of buttons, be sure that the center of the button is in the exact center front of the garment.

Be sure to notch the pattern at the center front. This is necessary in order to lap the two fronts correctly, to place a collar correctly, and to fit the facing. Notch both top and bottom.

PIECED BUTTON EXTENSION

When you want the button lap to be accented as part of the design of the garment, piece the button lap as shown in the sketch. When the button lap is pieced, put in the buttonholes *vertically* in order to keep the buttons centered.

You cannot add material to the front for a button extension without removing the same amount from the original pattern piece. If you do, the garment will come out much too large. Take off 3/4 inch from the center front. This amount, plus the seam, which will also come off in sewing, is equal to half the width of the button extension.

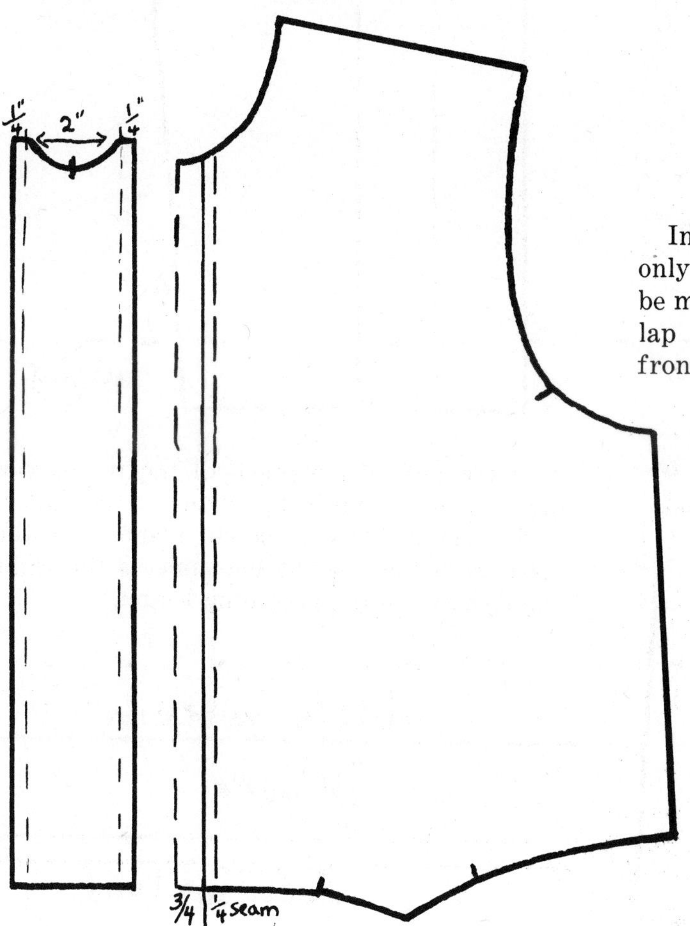

In a pattern of this kind it is better to have only the *left* side pieced. The *right* side can be made with a 1 1/4 inch extension for button lap (not pieced). Always notch for center front.

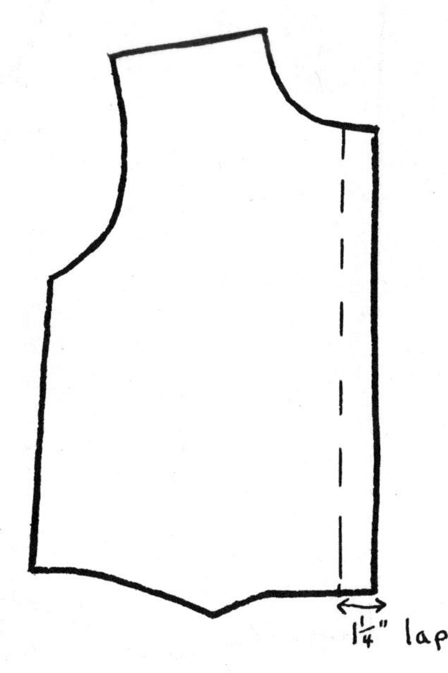

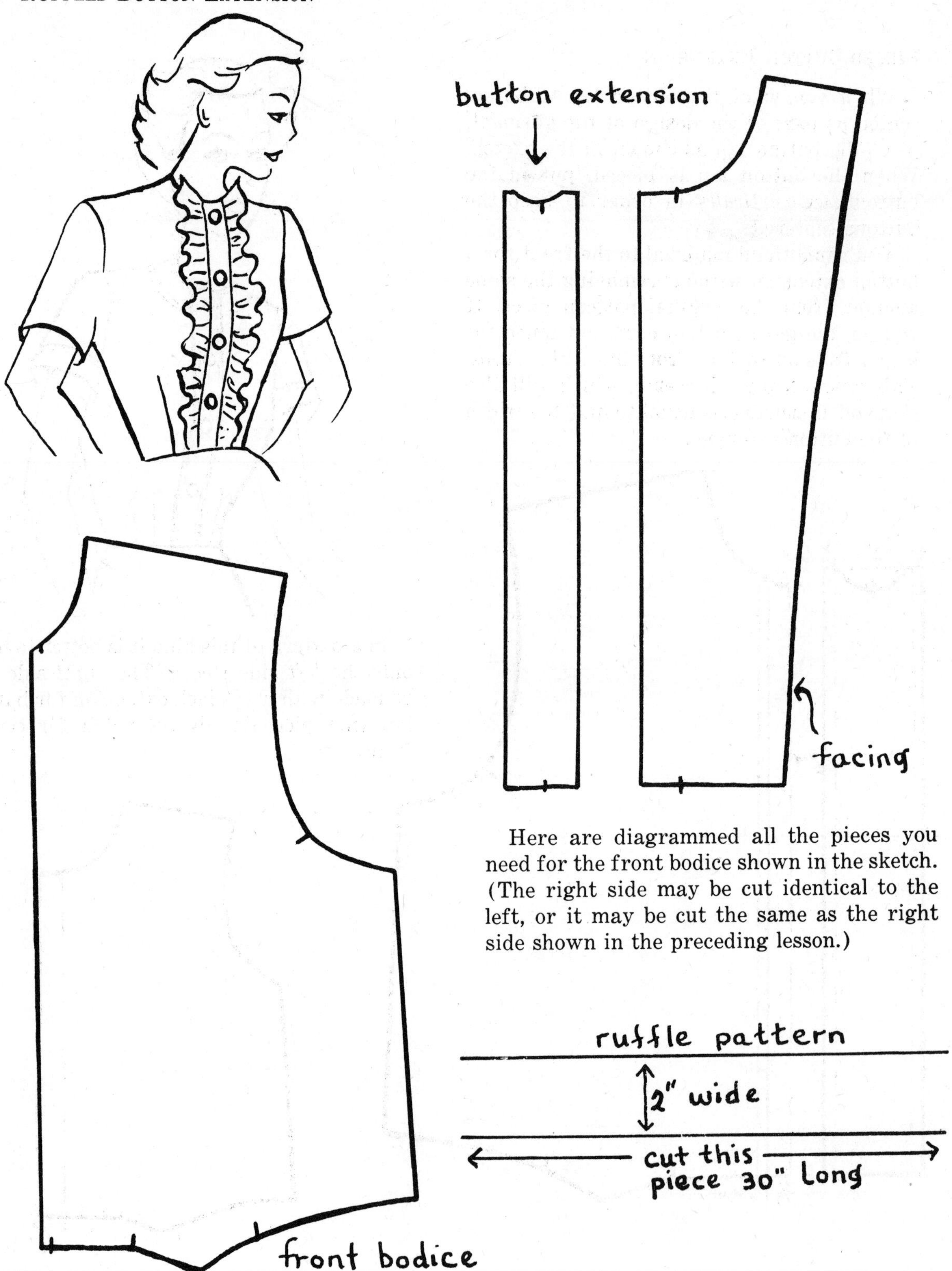

Here are diagrammed all the pieces you need for the front bodice shown in the sketch. (The right side may be cut identical to the left, or it may be cut the same as the right side shown in the preceding lesson.)

ruffle pattern

2" wide

cut this piece 30" long

FACINGS

All openings of a garment have to be finished so as to prevent the material from fraying on the cut edges. This lesson takes up facing the raw edges.

A facing is usually cut about 2½ inches in width at the shoulder and about 3 inches in width at the bottom. These measurements can be varied to fit more economically into the yardage lay.

The facing is usually sewed to the garment with a ¼-inch seam, which gives the least bulk when turned and is easier to turn than a ½-inch seam would be.

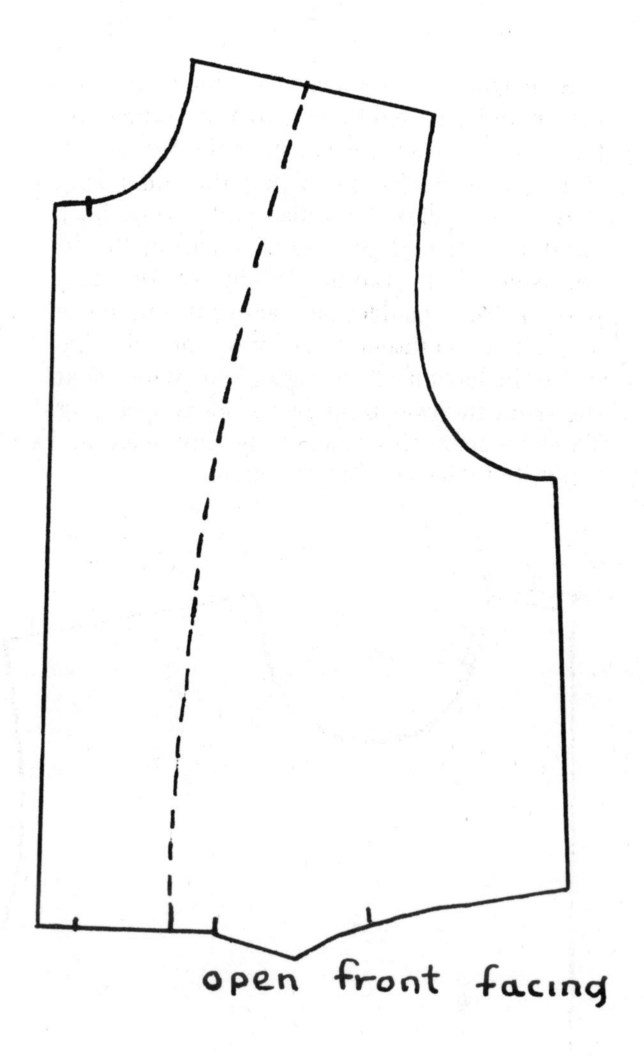

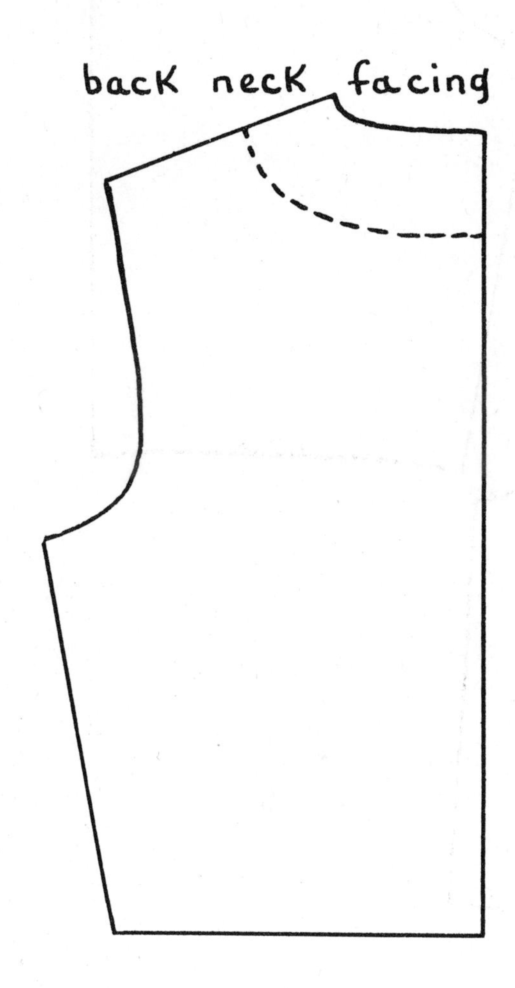

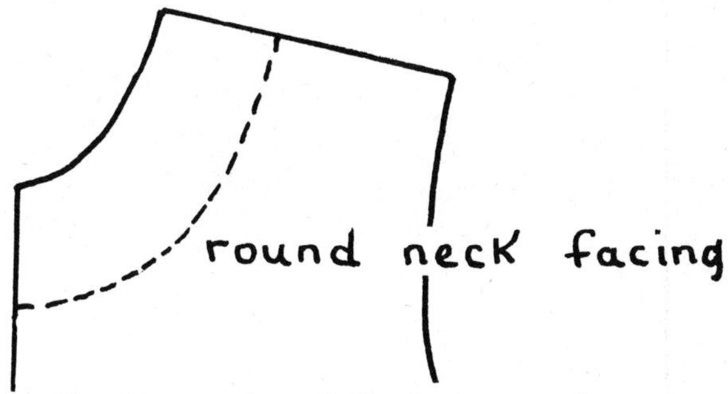

The inner edge of the facing can be overcast by hand, bound, overlocked on a special machine, pinked, or clean-seamed. The back neck has to have a facing corresponding to that used in front. Be sure that the width of both facings is exactly the same at the shoulder where they are joined together.

Sometimes it is more convenient to have the facing cut together with the bodice pattern, but it is not always suitable. When possible, place the facing so that the inner edge is on a selvedge. This also saves time as it eliminates the necessity for finishing the inner edge of the facing. When you do cut a pattern for a bodice and facing in one piece, and when you intend to cut it on the selvedge, make the back neck facing ¼ inch wider than the front in order to allow for clean-seaming. To clean-seam, turn under the raw edge and top-stitch very close to the edge.

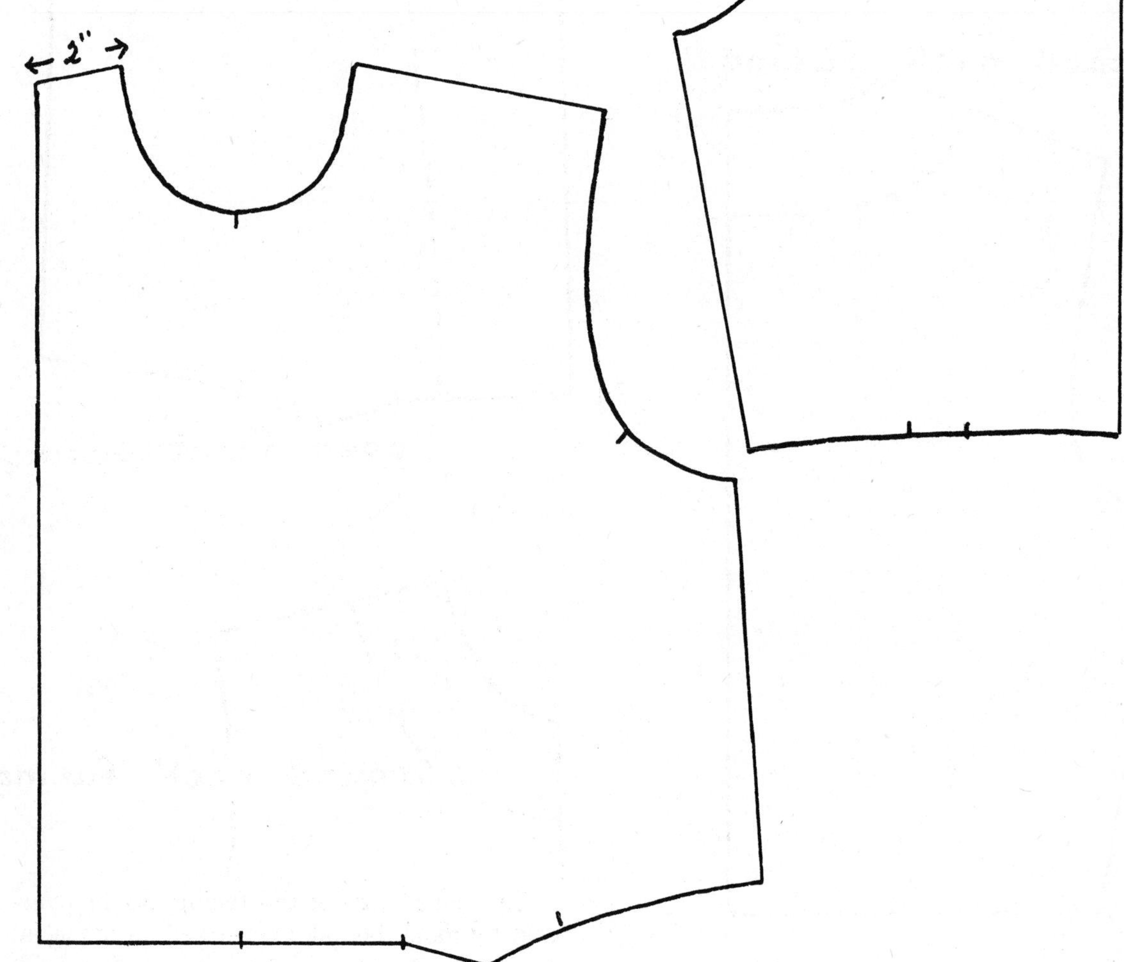

Shirt Blocks

The regular bodice blocks may simply be extended to blouse length to provide a basic shirt pattern. Since a shirt or blouse should fit rather loosely around the waist, make the darts shallower than they are on the basic blocks. The back dart is not very deep to begin with, so for the back it is better to add an inch of ease at the side seam. Follow the diagrams.

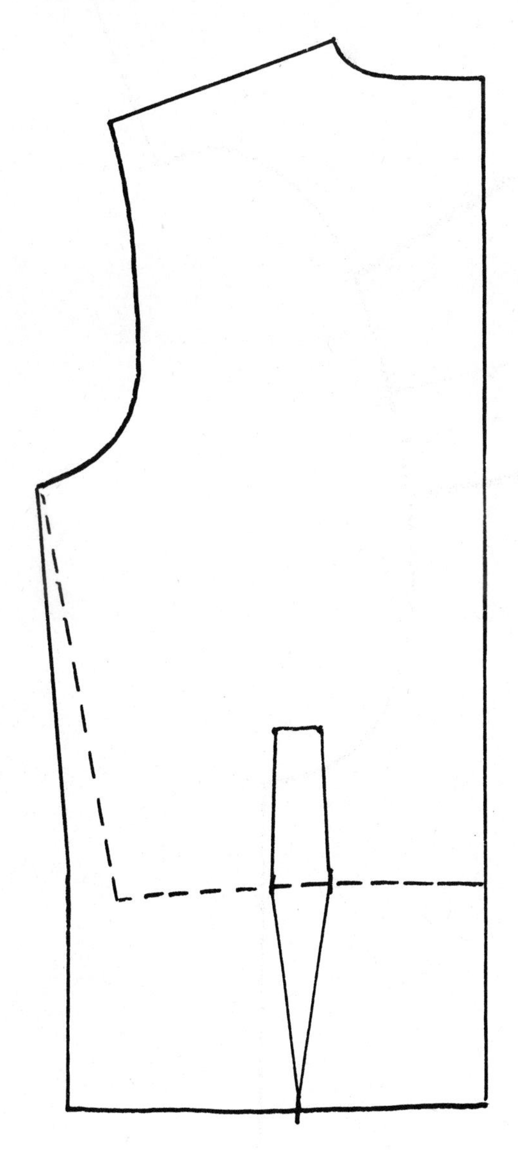

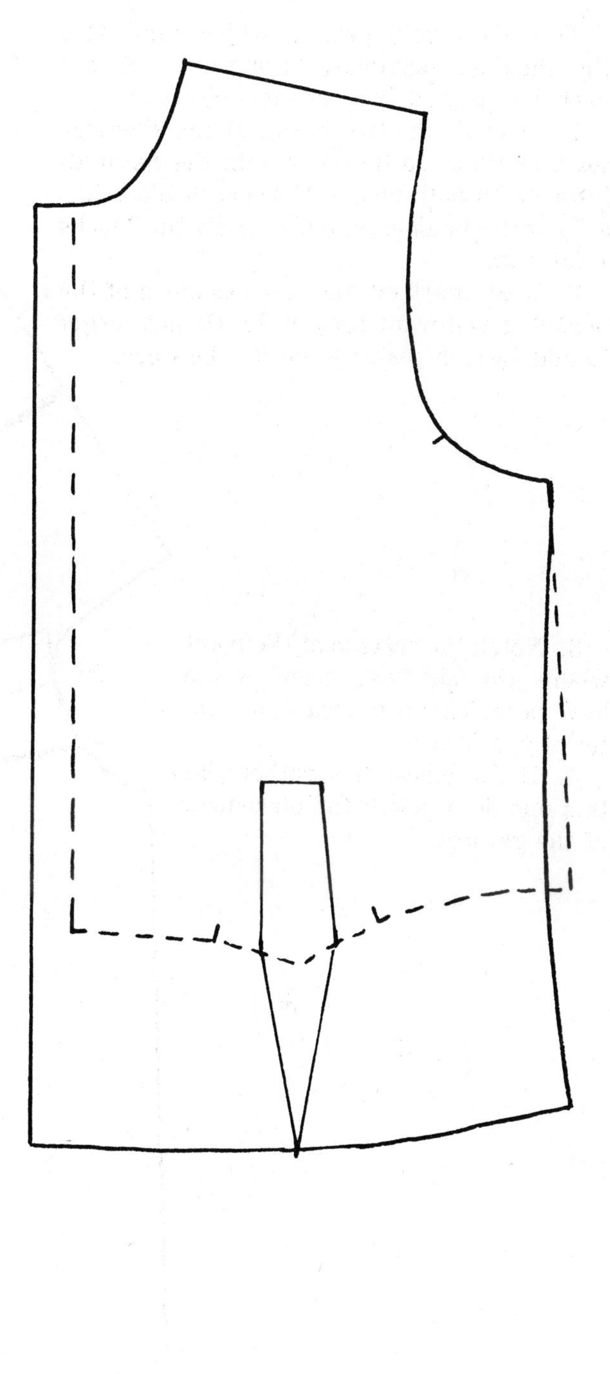

Combined Back and Shoulder Yoke

To make a yoke pattern which eliminates the shoulder seam, use both the front and back blocks and proceed as follows:

1. Overlap the two blocks at the shoulder seam so that you do away with the seam allowance on both blocks. Since each block has a ½ inch shoulder seam, overlap the blocks 1 full inch.
2. Next, mark off and trace as much of the blocks as you want for a yoke. Do not forget to add ½-inch seams to both yoke lines.

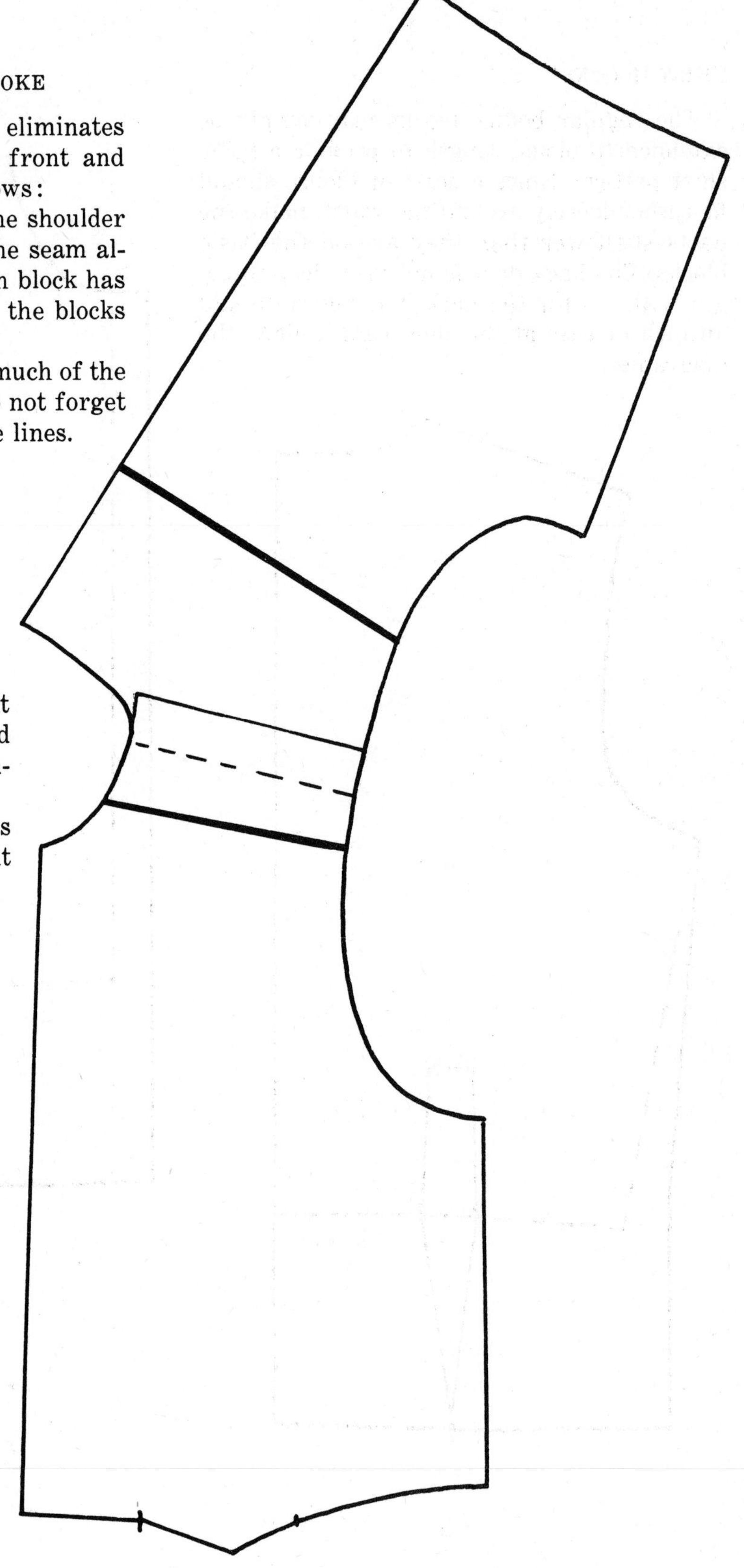

3. Notch the pattern at the point where the shoulder seam would have been. This is to locate the center of your sleeve.
4. If the blouse has gathers, as this one does, notch for placement of the gathers.

COMBINED BACK AND SHOULDER YOKE *(cont.)*

In order to prevent a bulge at the back yoke line, again make the small dart at the back armscye. In this case, you have no choice as to the location of the replaced 1/4 inch. It will have to be added to the side seam, as there no longer is any shoulder seam.

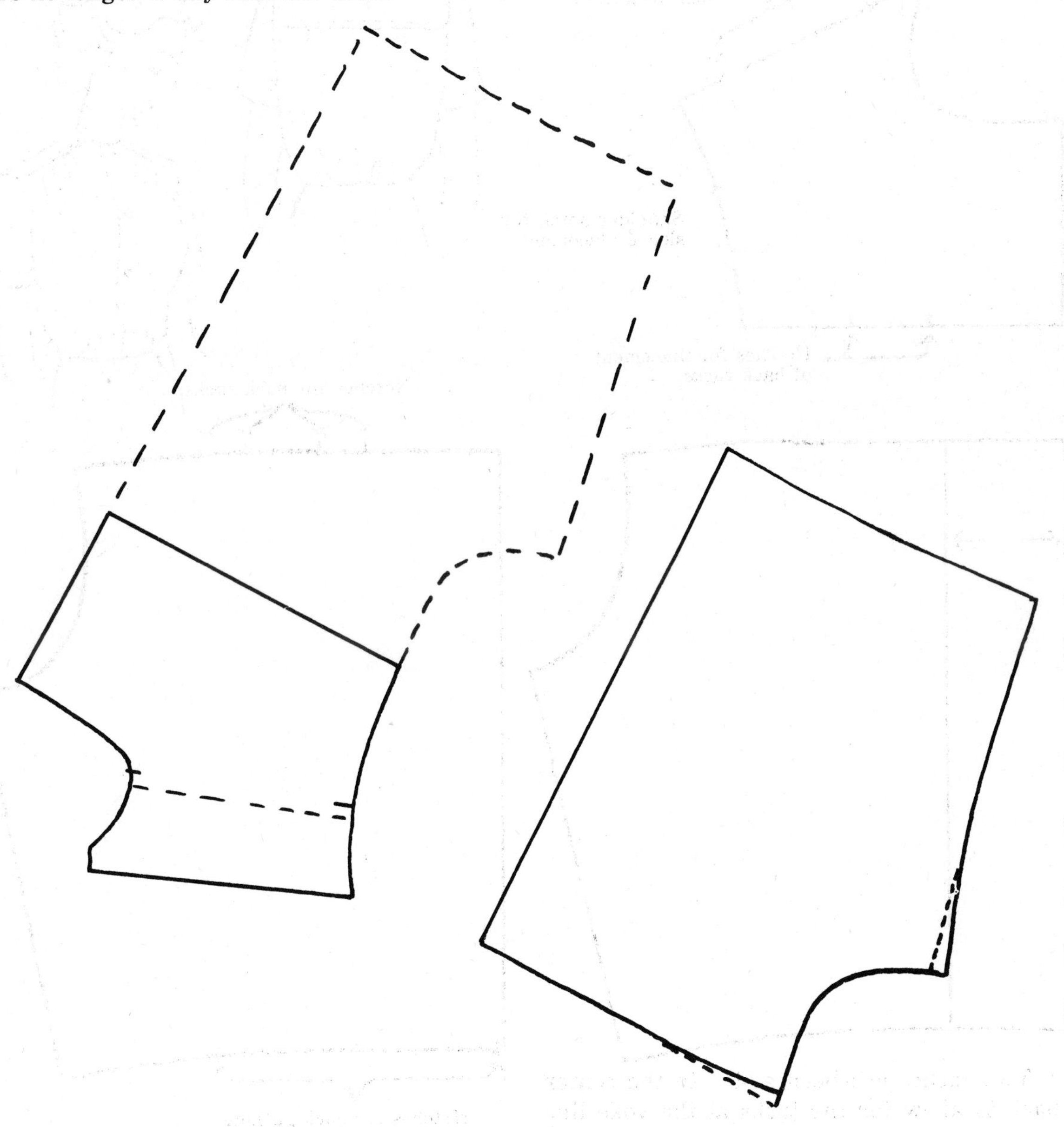

COMBINED BACK AND SHOULDER YOKE *(cont.)*

More on the shirt waist pattern. It is so important to learn to notch correctly that the notching will be covered in detail.

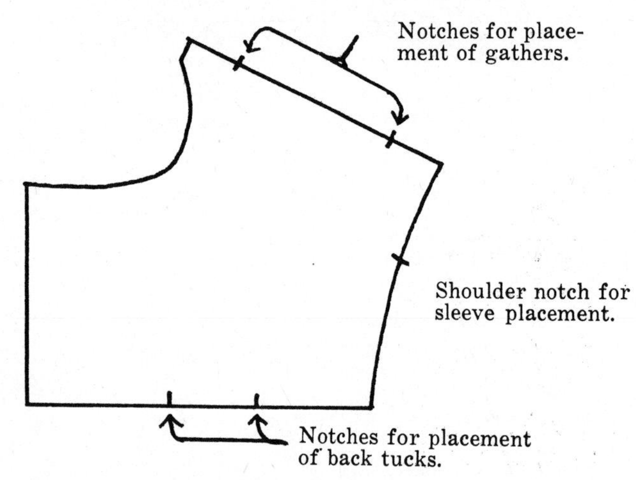

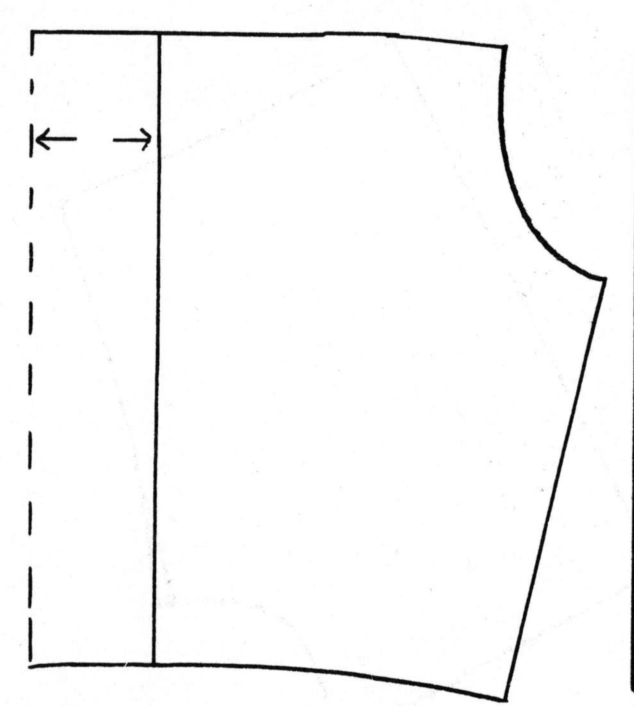

Two inches has been added to the center back to allow for the tucks at the yoke line and the gathers at the waistline.

Notches for back tucks.

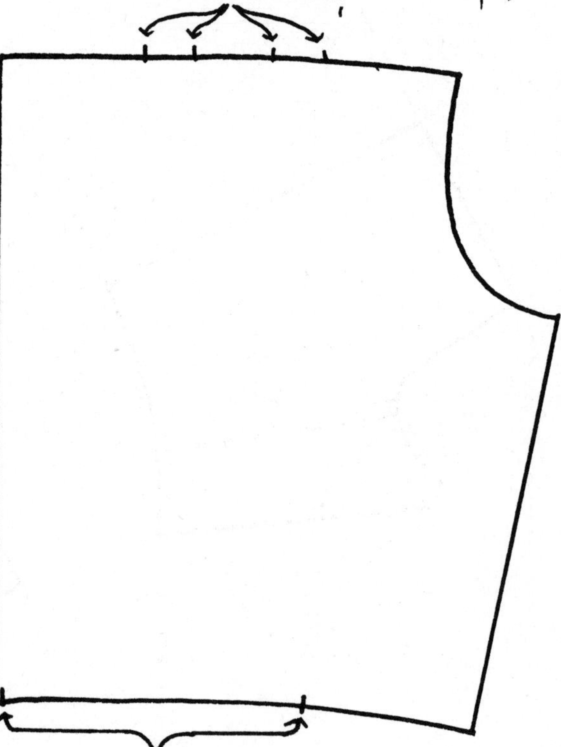

Notches for back gathers.

COMBINED BACK AND SHOULDER YOKE *(cont.)*

To finish this pattern, trace the front block, cutting off the shoulder yoke. Slash to the waist and spread out about 3 inches for the soft gathers at the yoke line. Do not close the dart, for this style is gathered softly at the waist as well as at the shoulder. Eliminate the punch hole, as there will be no dart. Be absolutely certain that the notches in all the pattern pieces match up correctly.

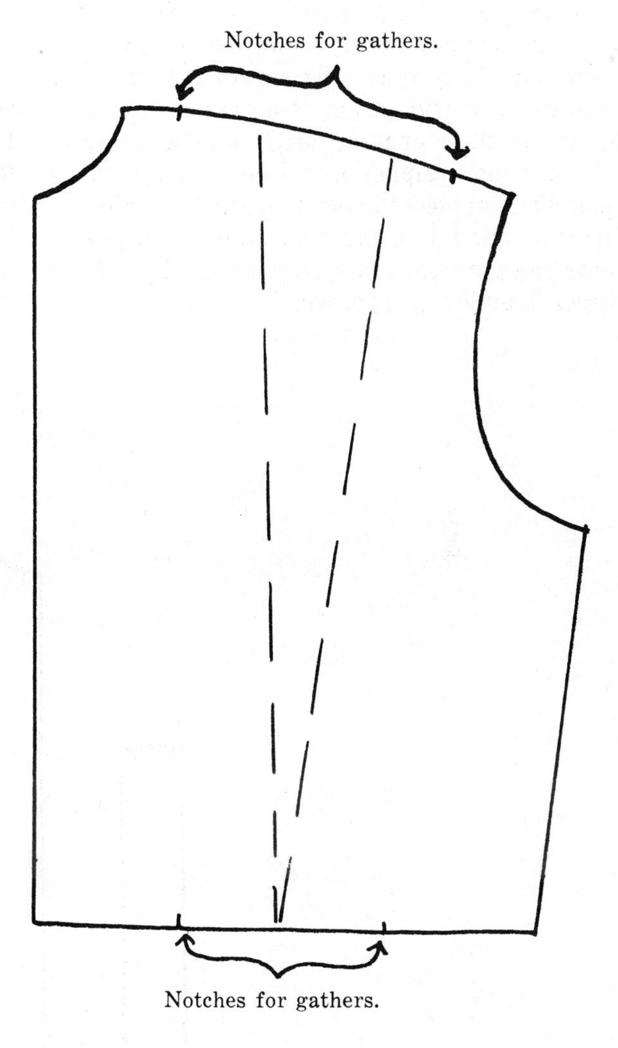

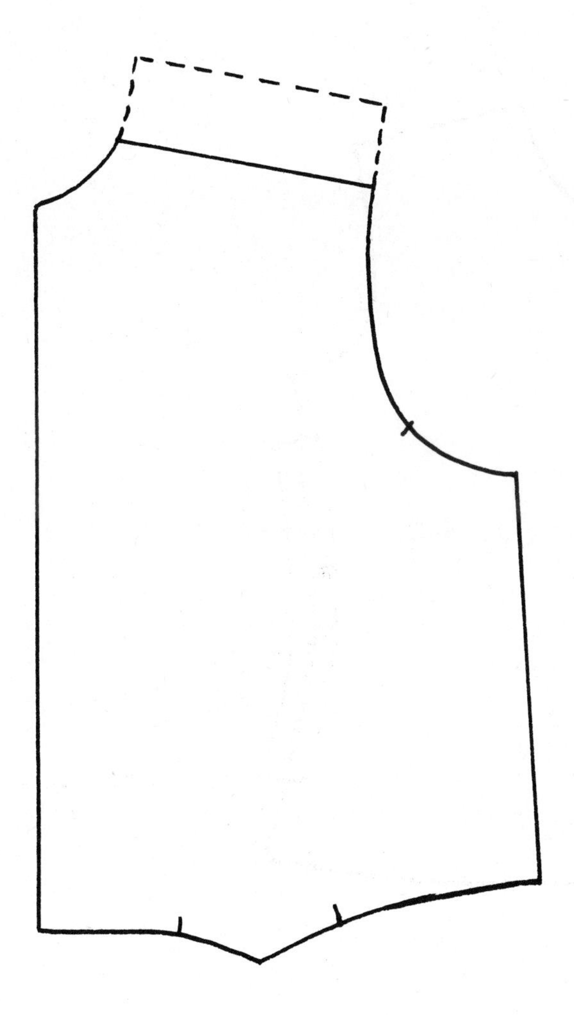

The simplest way to check your pattern to see that the notches match up is to fit the pieces together just as if you were going to sew them. See that the notches are exactly the same distance from a given point. First, the armscye; then shift the yoke over so that the two pattern pieces fit together at the neckline. Check again. Do this with both the back and the front.

ZIPPER OPENING

In setting in the zipper down the front of a bodice, leave a 1-inch seam, but a ¾-inch seam will do if it can be cut to better advantage. The wide seam is necessary in order to set the zipper in neatly and securely.

In putting a zipper in a side opening, cut an additional piece to your pattern. This piece forms a foundation for your zipper and prevents the garment from stretching when the zipper is pulled up or down.

Cut the piece parallel to the selvedge 1 inch longer than the zipper and 1½ inches wide. The right side of the zipper will be sewed in between this piece and the body of the garment. The piece extends out under the other side of the zipper as in any placket or fly opening. The reason for cutting the extension piece on the selvedge is to have a finished edge for the extension. The raw edge is sewed into the seam.

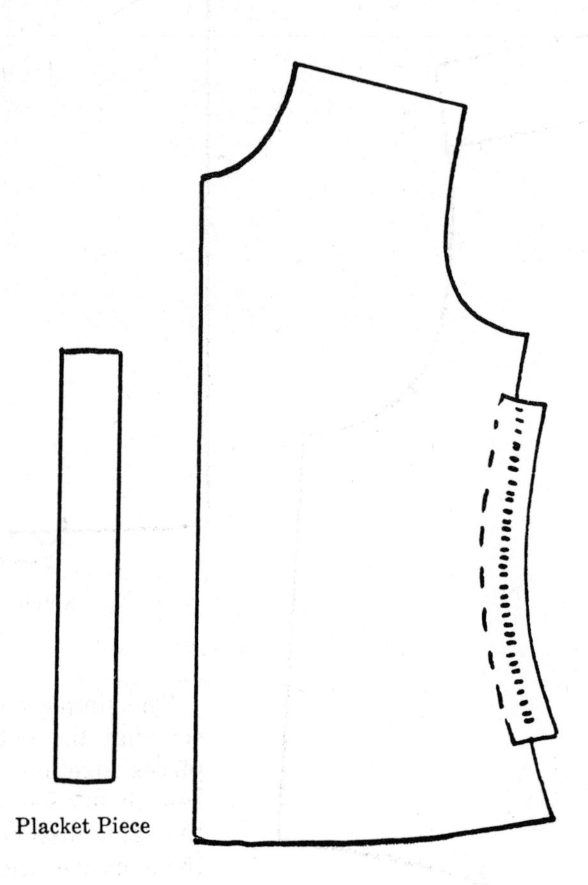

Pockets

For a single pocket, mark your pattern as in Diagram A. A standard shirt pocket measures about 4½″ x 5¼″. This is large enough to accommodate a package of cigarets. The size of any pocket is up to the designer, but it should be large enough for use.

In the case of an odd-shaped pocket, mark the entire shape of the pocket on the bodice. Use a tracing wheel for this and then when marking the material chalk over the perforations.

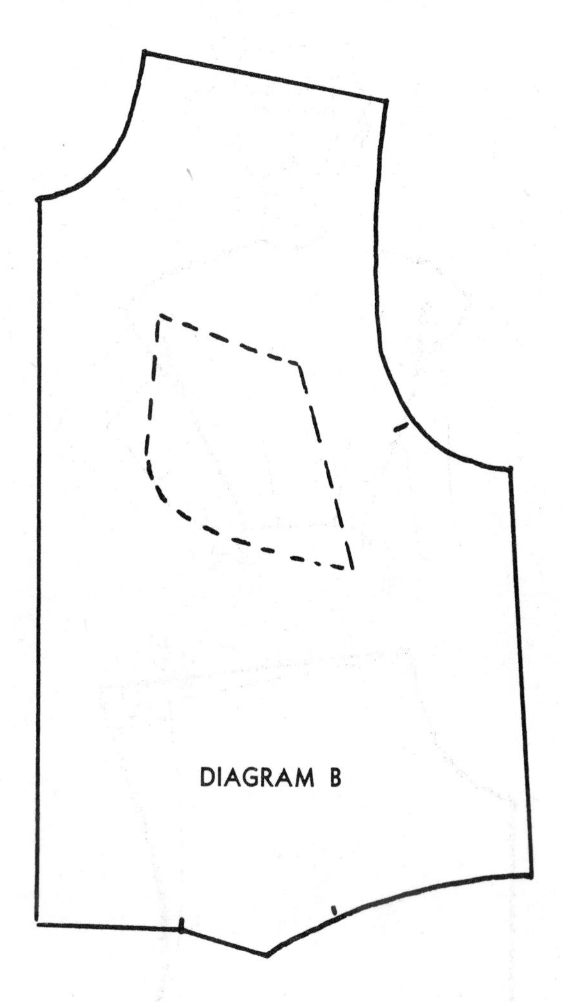

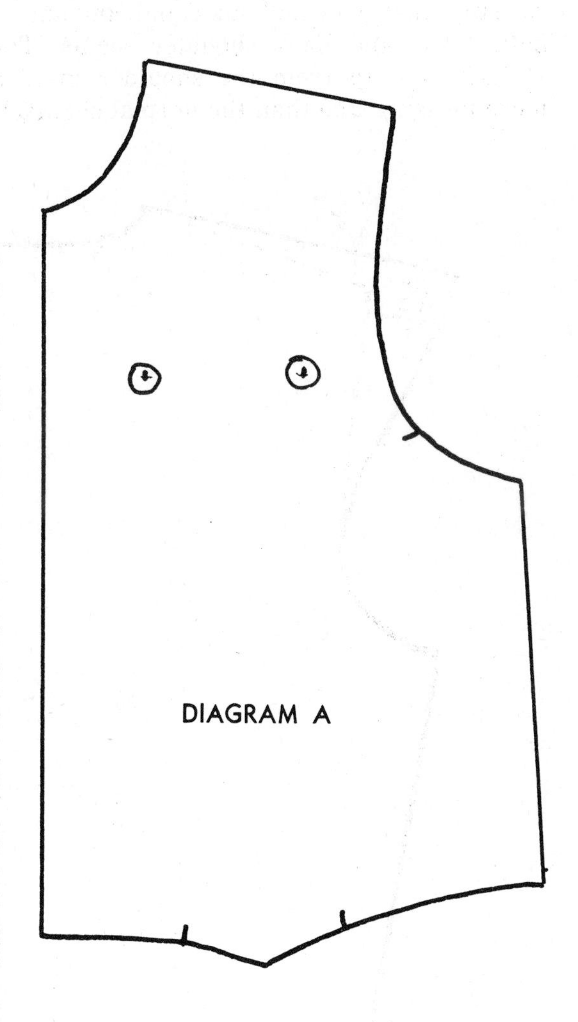

If the bodice fits snugly, place the pocket to allow for about a ½-inch gape at the top. Otherwise you cannot put anything in the pocket. This means that your punch marks should be ½ inch closer together than the finished width of the top of the pocket.

Extended Shoulder Blocks

How much extension you add to your original blocks depends on how much of a drop you wish to have in the finished garment. The bodice shown in the sketch here has only a slight drop — hardly more than a very wide shoulder.

Follow the diagrams for measurements. Be sure that you add an equal amount to both front and back shoulder seams. The ½-inch rise up from the shoulder gives a more pleasing line than the normal shoulder.

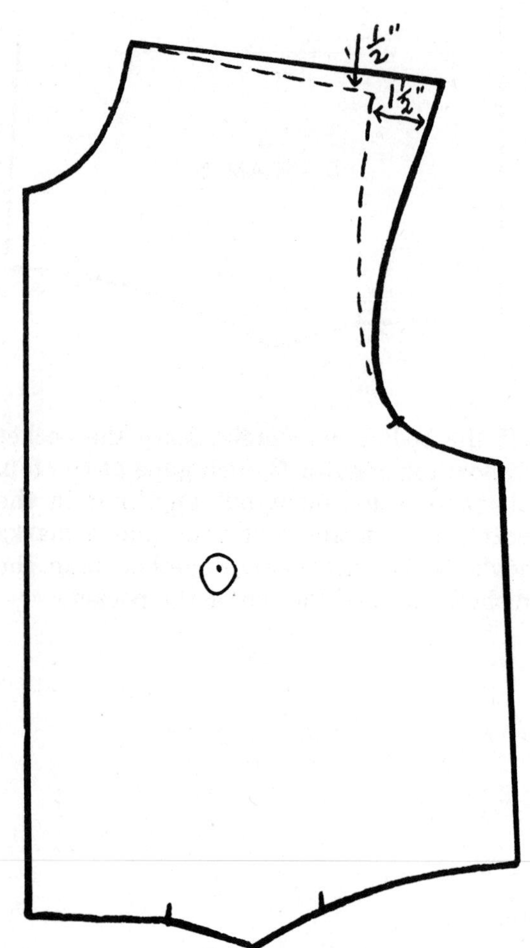

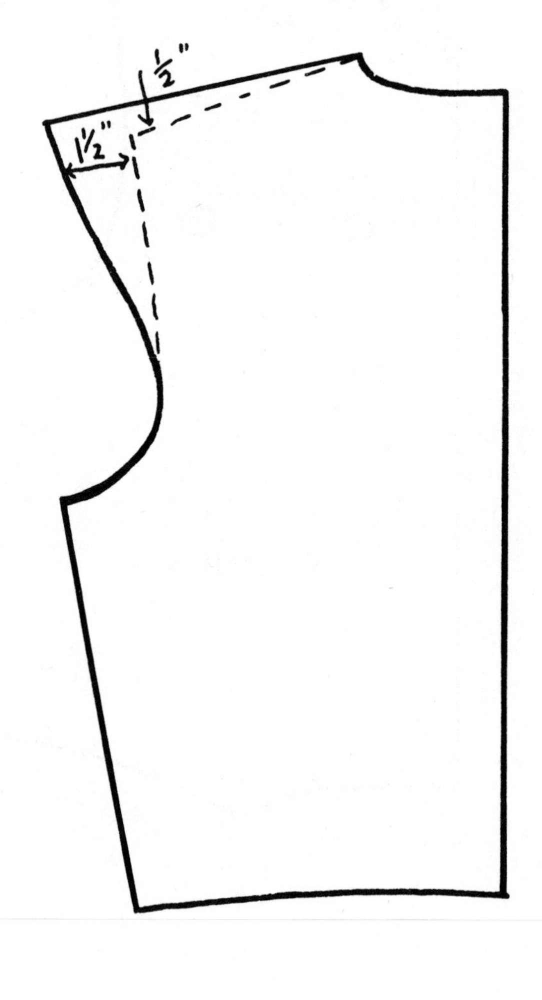

EXTENDED SHOULDER BLOCKS: #2

This bodice has a wider extension, which acts as a dropped shoulder. The garment may be sleeveless, or sleeves may be attached at the dropped shoulderline.

This is a pattern that you had best make up full size in tissue paper and pin on yourself or the dress form. It is the only way to tell exactly what proportions are the most pleasing.

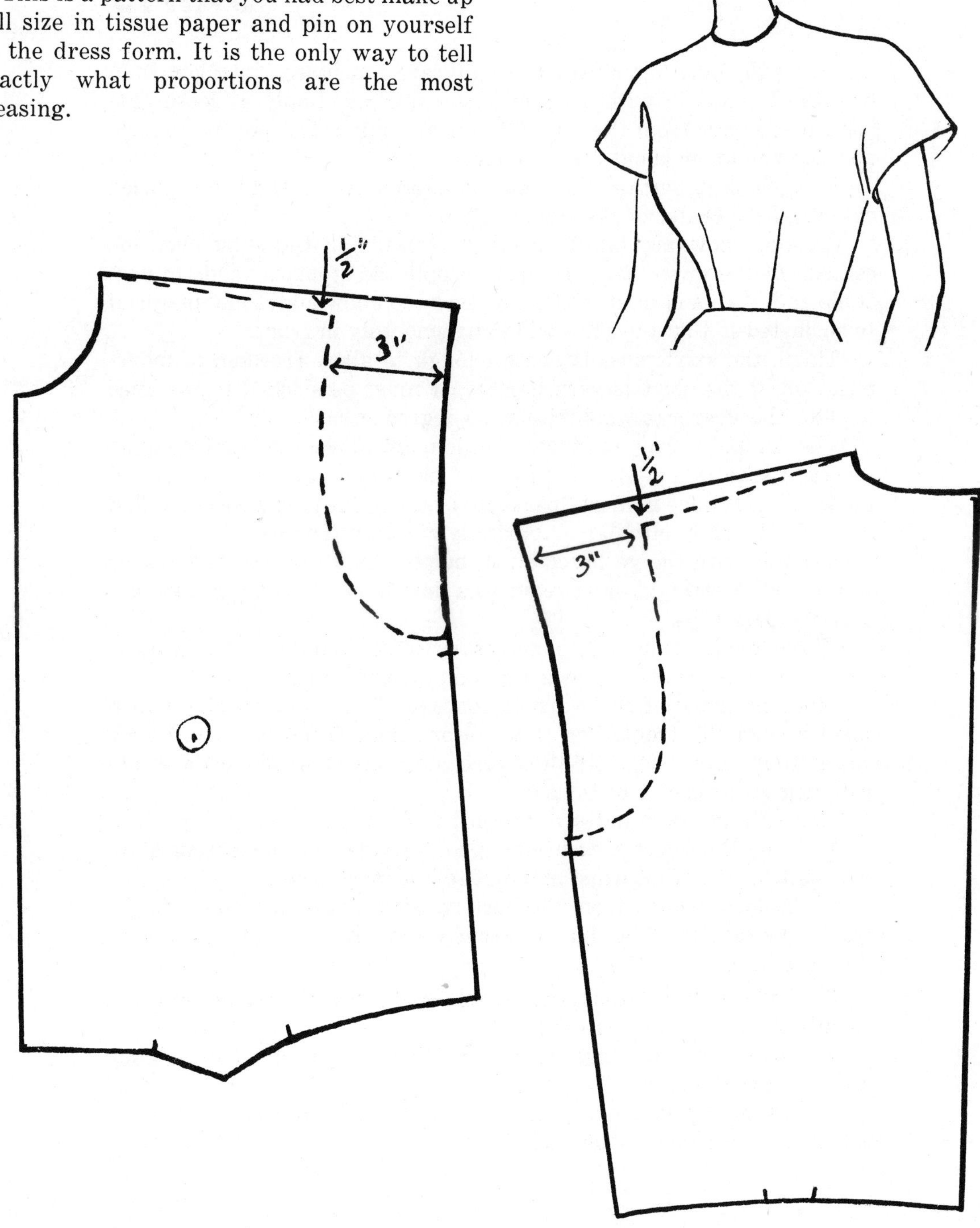

Chapter Eight
Skirts

You will find that skirts generally are much less involved than bodices. To explain with a definition, a skirt is simply a "loose garment that hangs from the hips." There are only a few points that are necessary to know about fitting a skirt.

First, it is important that the side seams are straight and placed exactly at the center of the side.

Second, allowance has to be made for fitting the skirt over the contour of the lower back. In some people the stomach tends to protrude and, if this is so, it is also necessary to allow additional material to be darted so that the skirt will hang smoothly in front.

Third, the skirt must be loose enough to allow freedom of movement, or, if the skirt is very narrow, it must be slashed to the knee to allow the wearer to walk with some degree of ease.

The simplest way to allow freedom of movement and contour coverage is to take a straight piece of cloth and gather it all around the waist as is done in most "peasant" clothes. The next easiest method is to cut the skirt circular or partially circular. The same effects are achieved as with the gathered skirt, but the bulk around the waist is eliminated. A straight skirt requires a dart in order to hang smoothly over the back hips.

Three measurements are necessary in making a skirt pattern: the waist measure, the hip measure, and the skirt length.

Since the back of the waist is concave, it is usually about 1 inch smaller than the front. For this reason, skirt fronts are cut 1 inch larger than skirt backs. If this were not done, the side seam would not hang at the center of the side.

In drafting a skirt pattern, proceed as follows:

1. Take the waist measurement and divide this measurement in two, half for the front waist and half for the back waist.

2. Deduct ½ inch from the back waist measure and add it to the front. The result will be that the front waist will measure 1 inch more than the back.

3. Take the hip measurement, 9 inches below the waist, which is usually the widest part of the hips.

4. Divide the hip measure in two. Deduct ½ inch from the back and add it to the front.

5. To the hip measurement you will have to add ease — 1 inch to the front, and 1 inch to the back.

To have the skirt fit smoothly over the back contour, you will also have to allow material for a dart. The dart should be 1½ inches in depth and should extend from the waistline to the widest part of the hips. In working with the bodice you found that two shallow darts generally gave a smoother fit than one wide dart. This also applies to skirt patterns. If the person for whom the pattern is made has a protruding stomach, a shallow dart in the front will improve the fit of the skirt. For the front dart, a depth of ½ inch is enough, and the length of the dart should be 3 or 3½ inches.

For the foundation blocks with which you will work out the lessons, only the single back dart has been included.

The waist measure of a size 14 pattern is usually 27 inches, so we can use it here as an example. This will give you 13½ inches for the front and 13½ inches for the back. However, since the front of a skirt pattern is always made 1 inch larger than the back, subtract ½ inch from the back and add it to the front.

When you have done this, your front skirt will measure 14 inches and the back 13 inches.

The back block has a dart to allow for hip fullness. The dart is necessary only in straight skirts. In flared, gathered, or circular skirts the dart is eliminated.

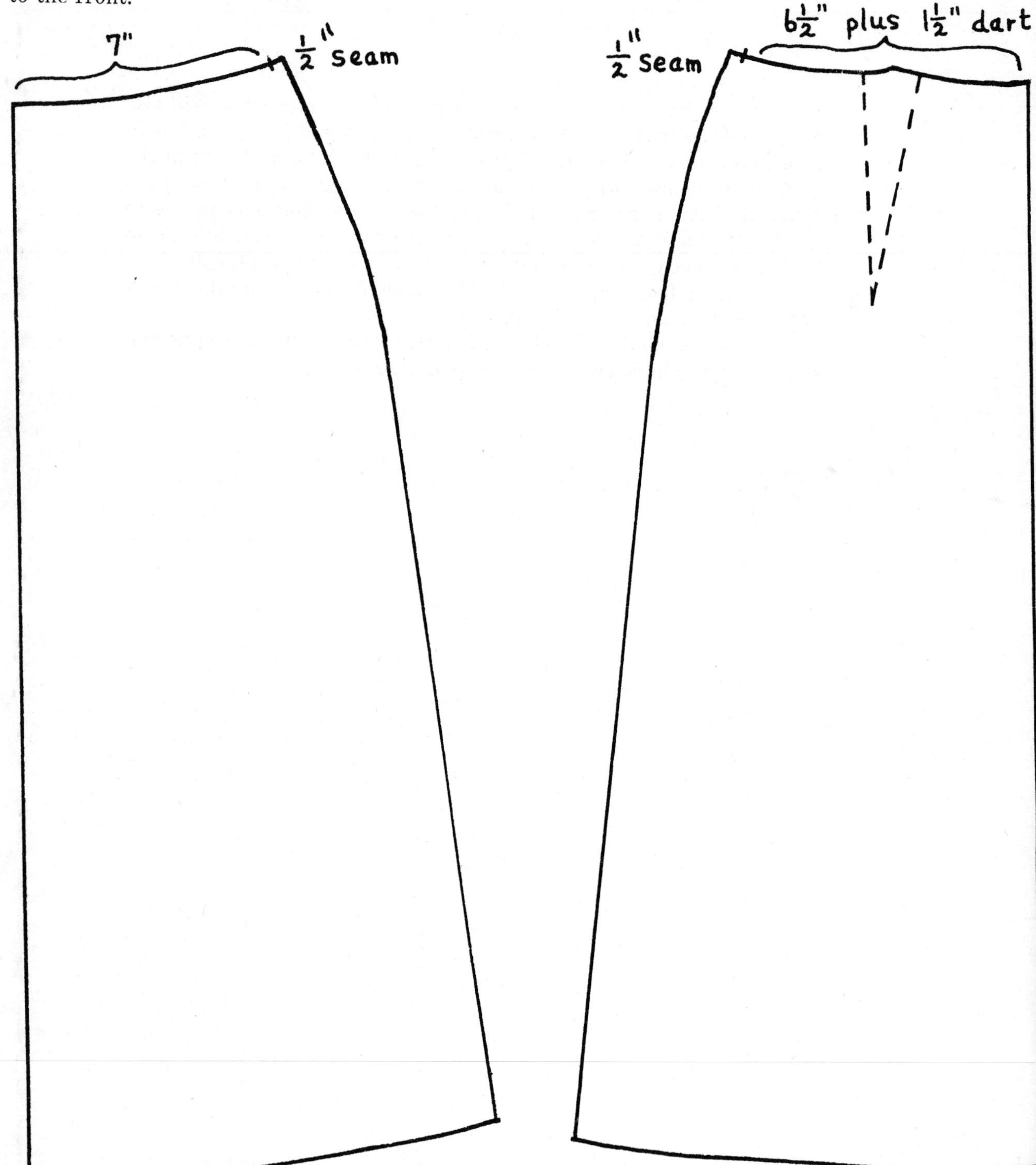

FOUR-GORE SKIRT:
FRONT

Trace your front block as indicated by the broken lines. Swing the block upward about 1 inch and continue tracing. This second step is indicated by a dotted line.

Third, add 2 inches more flare to the side seam and 1 inch more flare to the center front. A solid line is used for the final outline of the skirt pattern. Add ½-inch seam to the center front. The side seam has already been allowed for on the block itself. As shown on the diagram, additional flare is measured at the hem line.

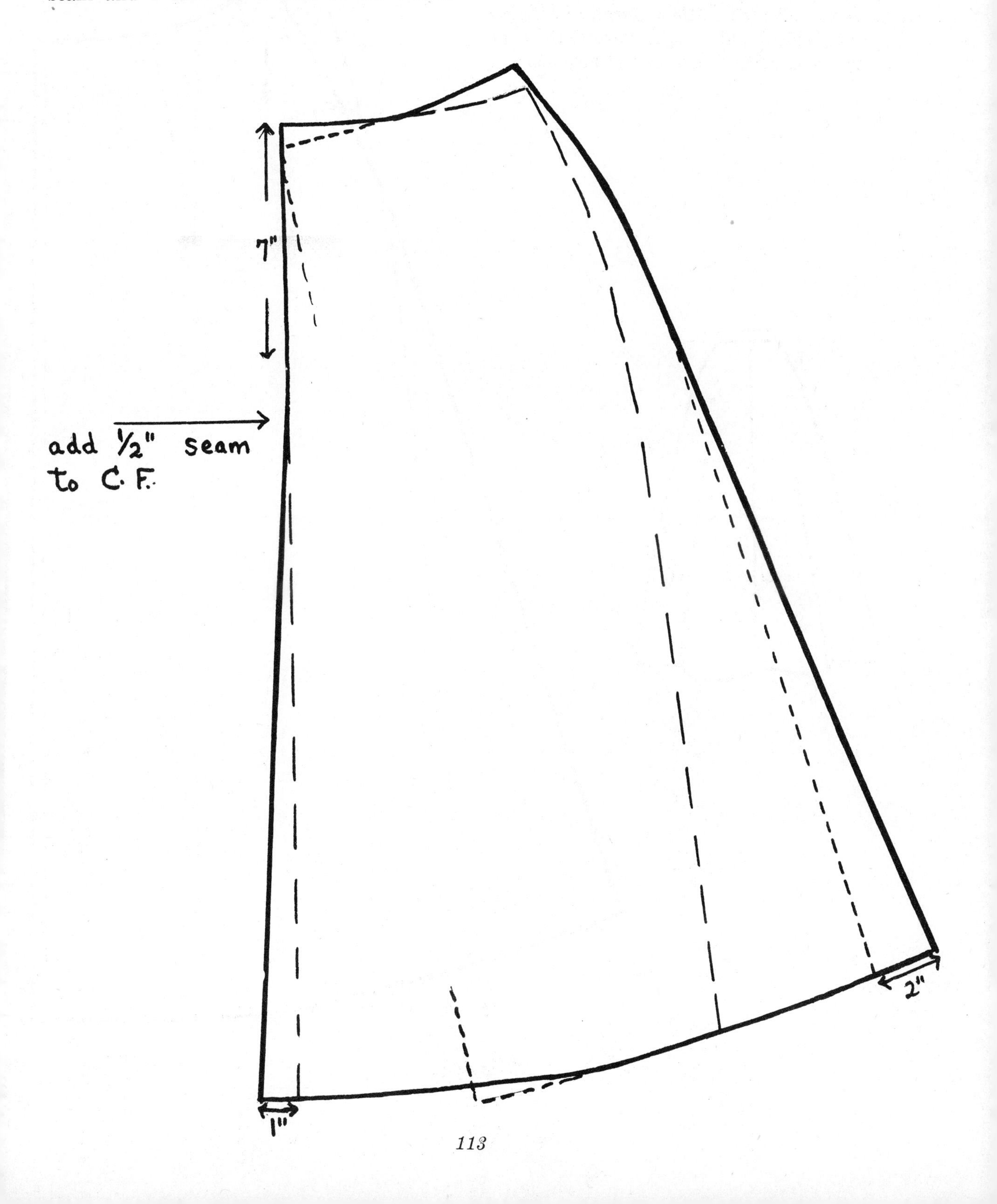

Four-Gore Skirt: Back

Trace the back block. Swing the dart closed. Add seam to center back and notch twice as indicated on the diagram. Swinging the dart closed adds enough flare to the back so that you do not have to add any more.

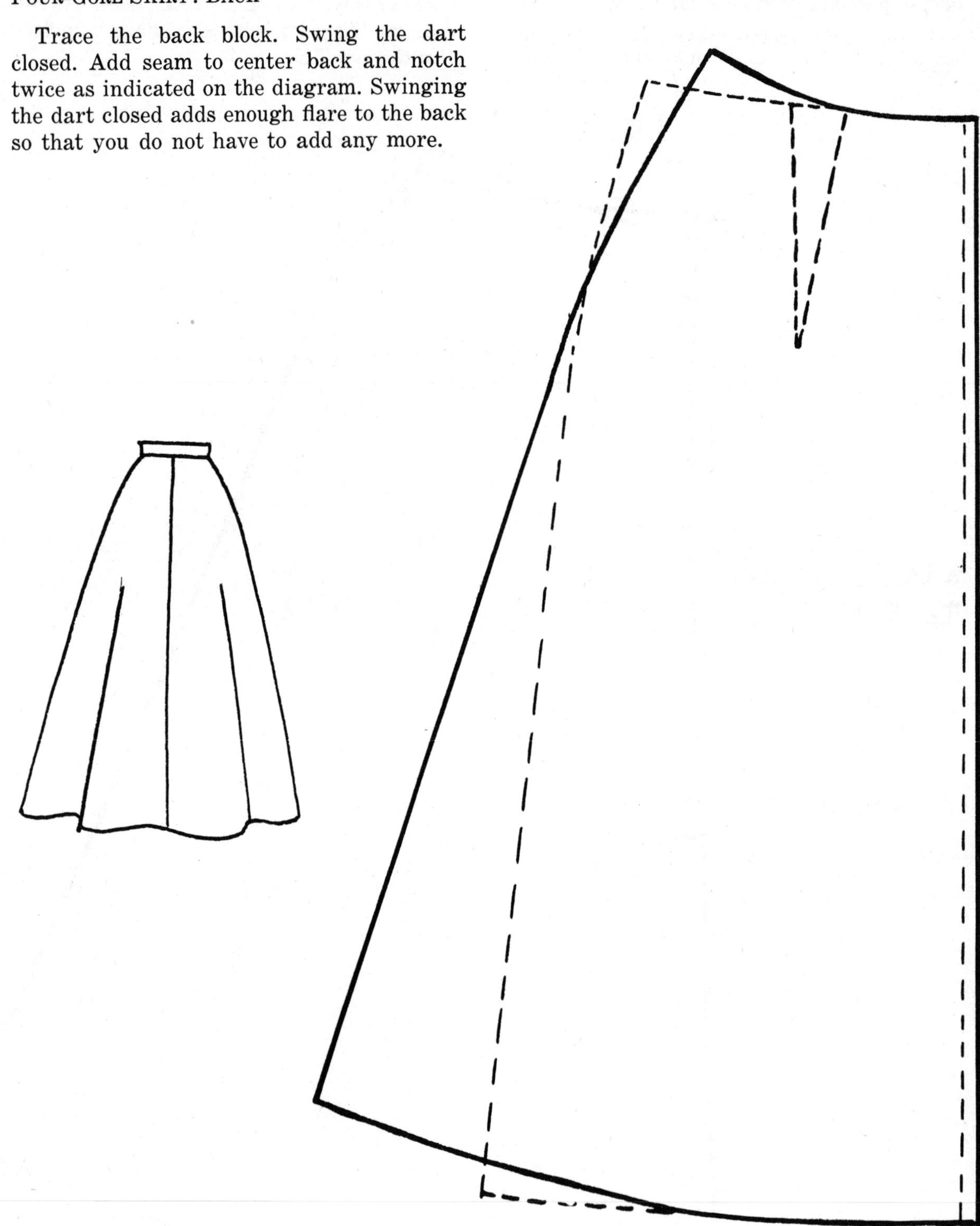

TWENTY-GORE SKIRT

Waist — 27

Hip — 36

Length — optional

Make the waist measure of the gore a shade more than $1\frac{1}{3}$ inches, plus $\frac{1}{2}$-inch seam on each side.

Make the hip measure $1\frac{4}{5}$ inches, plus seams.

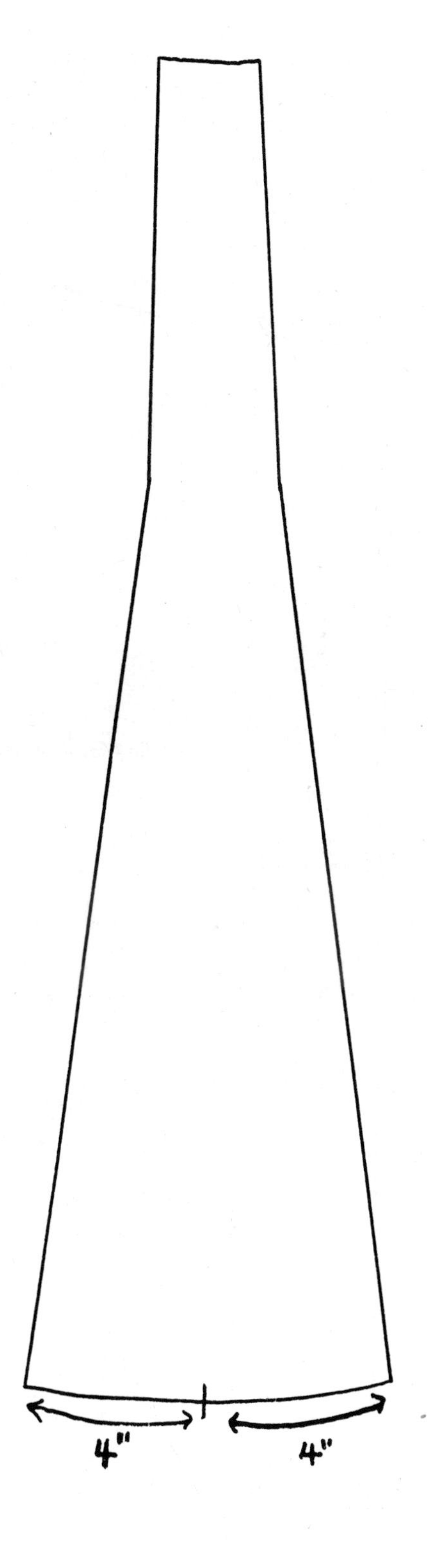

To get more swish, add more flare at the bottom and taper it to a point 7 or 9 inches below the waistline. This will give you a very swirly skirt with snug-fitting hips.

To make a twelve- or sixteen-gore skirt, divide the waist measure and hip measure into as many parts as you want gores and proceed as for the twenty-gore skirt.

Six-Gore Skirt: Front

Start by tracing your front skirt block; cut a vertical panel 3 inches wide off the c.f. as shown in Diagram A with a broken line.

Next, trace the front piece onto fresh paper and add 2 inches of flare at the bottom. Connect this added 2 inches to the mark 9 inches below the waist. Use a ruler in drawing in the line. Check the length with the original pattern piece. You may have to curve the hem line slightly.

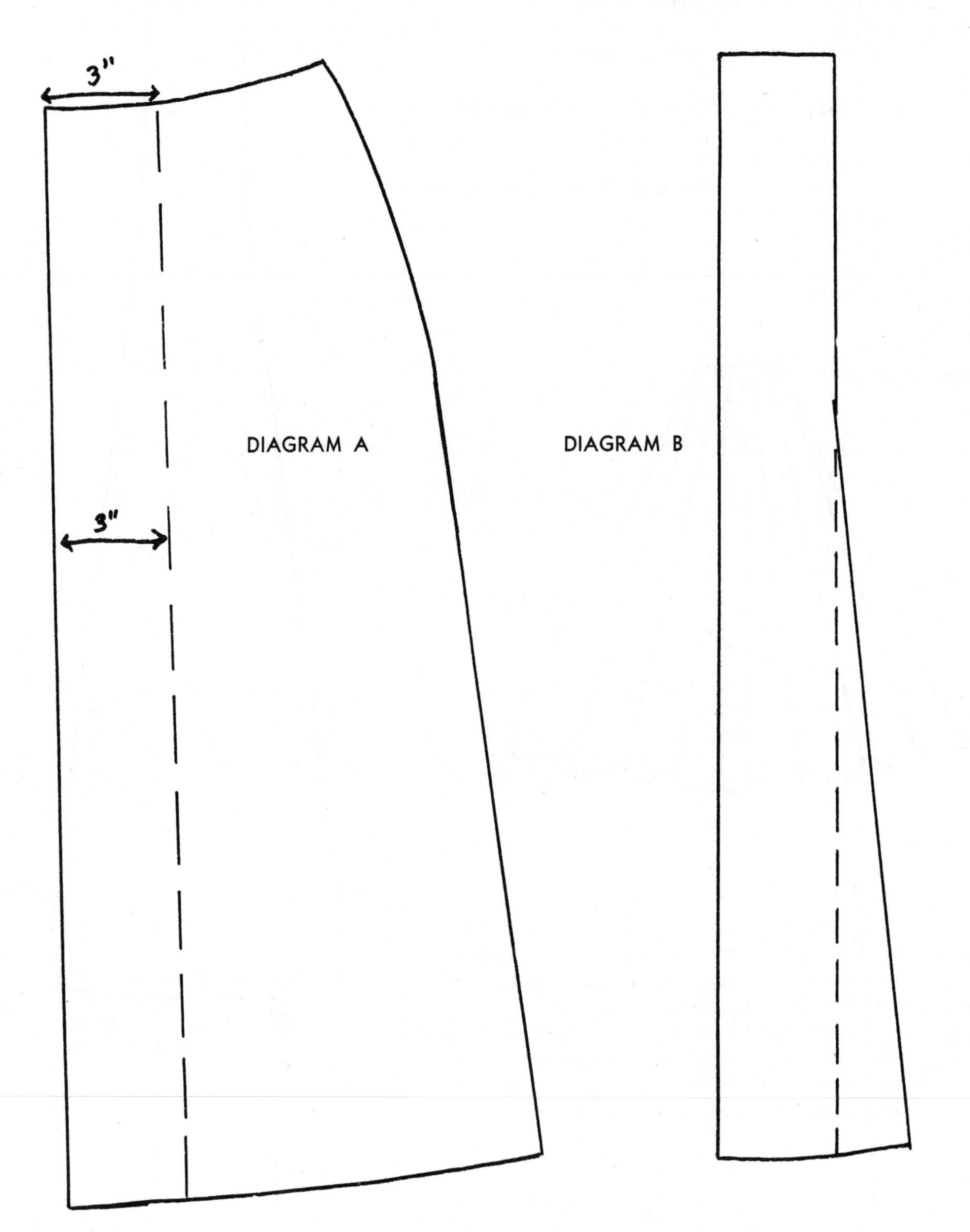

SIX-GORE SKIRT: FRONT *(cont.)*

Next, take the other piece of the skirt pattern, the side-front panel, and proceed just as you did with the center-front panel. First add 2 inches of flare to the side-center seam line and connect to the notch. Then add 2 inches of flare to the side seam. Add ½-inch seam allowance to the side-center line on both pieces. Check the length to be sure that the pattern pieces fit together perfectly.

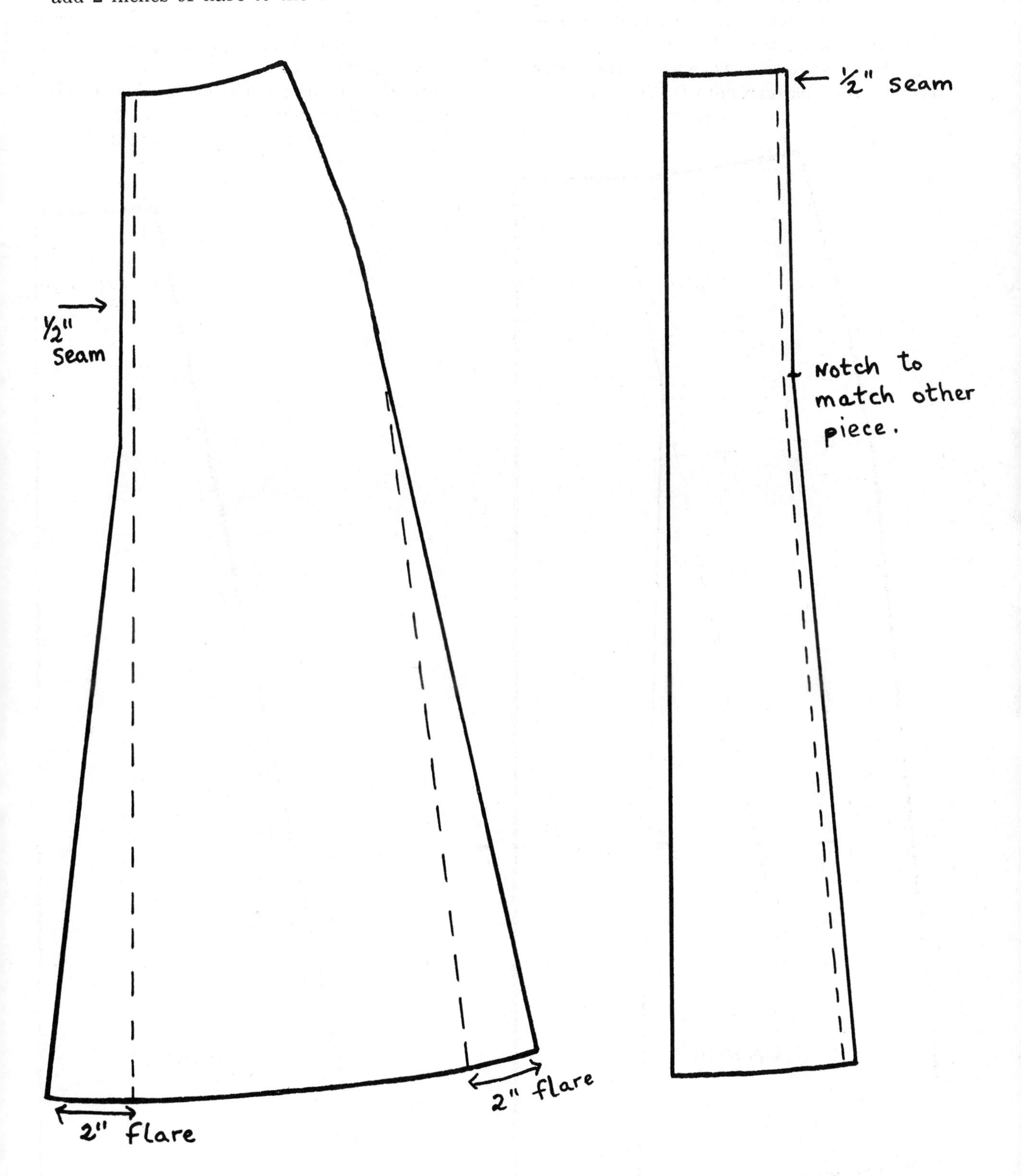

SIX-GORE SKIRT: BACK

For back gores, proceed as follows:

1. Draw straight down the dart lines to the hem. (Use a ruler.)
2. With your tracing wheel, trace each piece of your pattern onto fresh paper.
3. The center back gore already has enough flare, so all you do is add the center back seam, ½ inch. There will be no dart in the gored pattern.

Be sure to notch the pieces. Two notches close together indicate a back pattern piece. Don't forget to check the hem length.

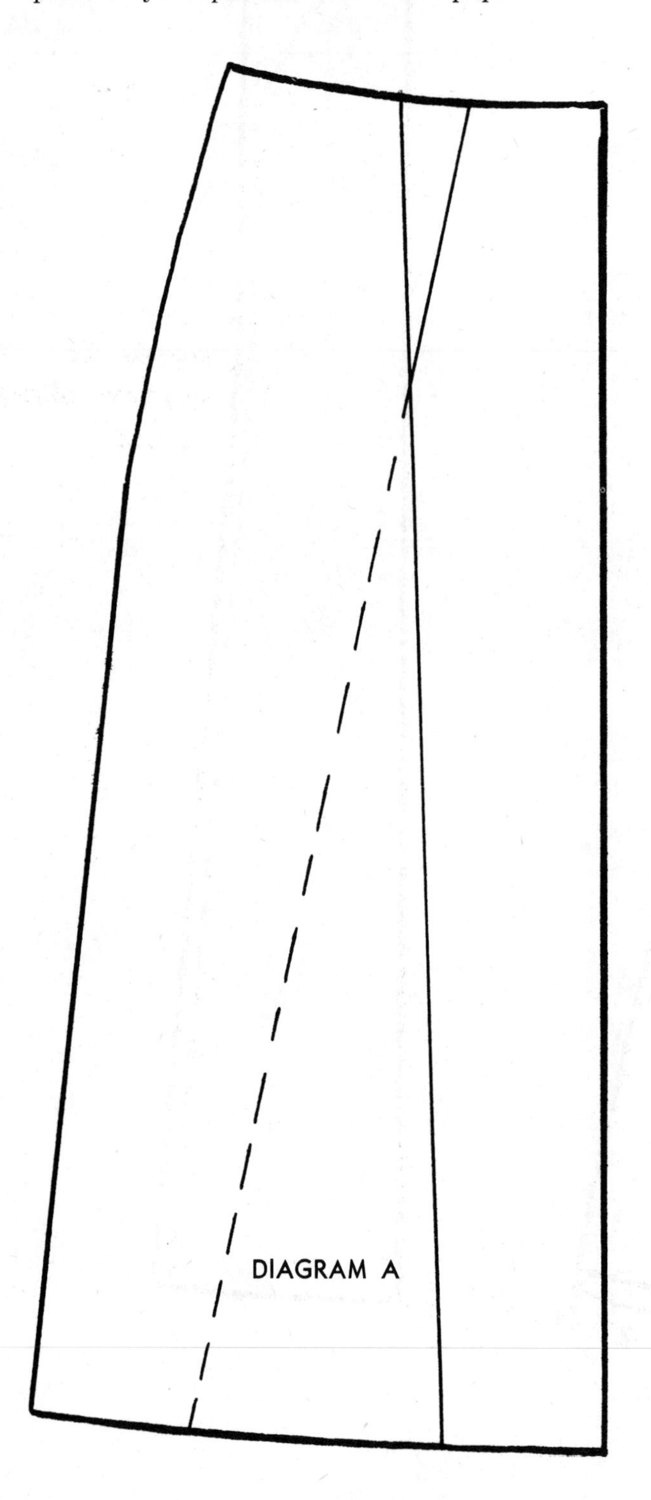

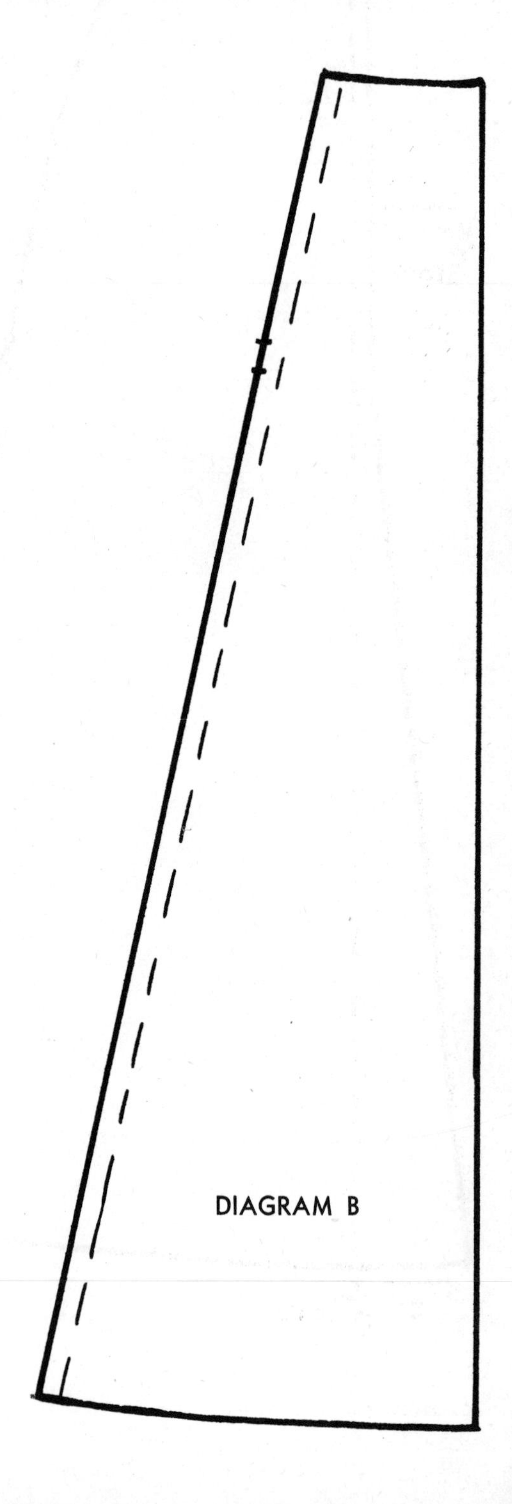

SIX-GORE SKIRT: BACK *(cont.)*

Add 2 inches of flare to both sides of the side-back panel. Add seam allowance and notch to match the center back.

The silhouette is naturally up to the designer; so if you wish to have more flare in your gored skirt pattern, simply add as much as you like rather than following the measurements given here. Try out your pattern in muslin or tissue paper to achieve a shape that really pleases you.

Since a good gored skirt pattern can be used almost forever, make a copy of this pattern in stiff paper.

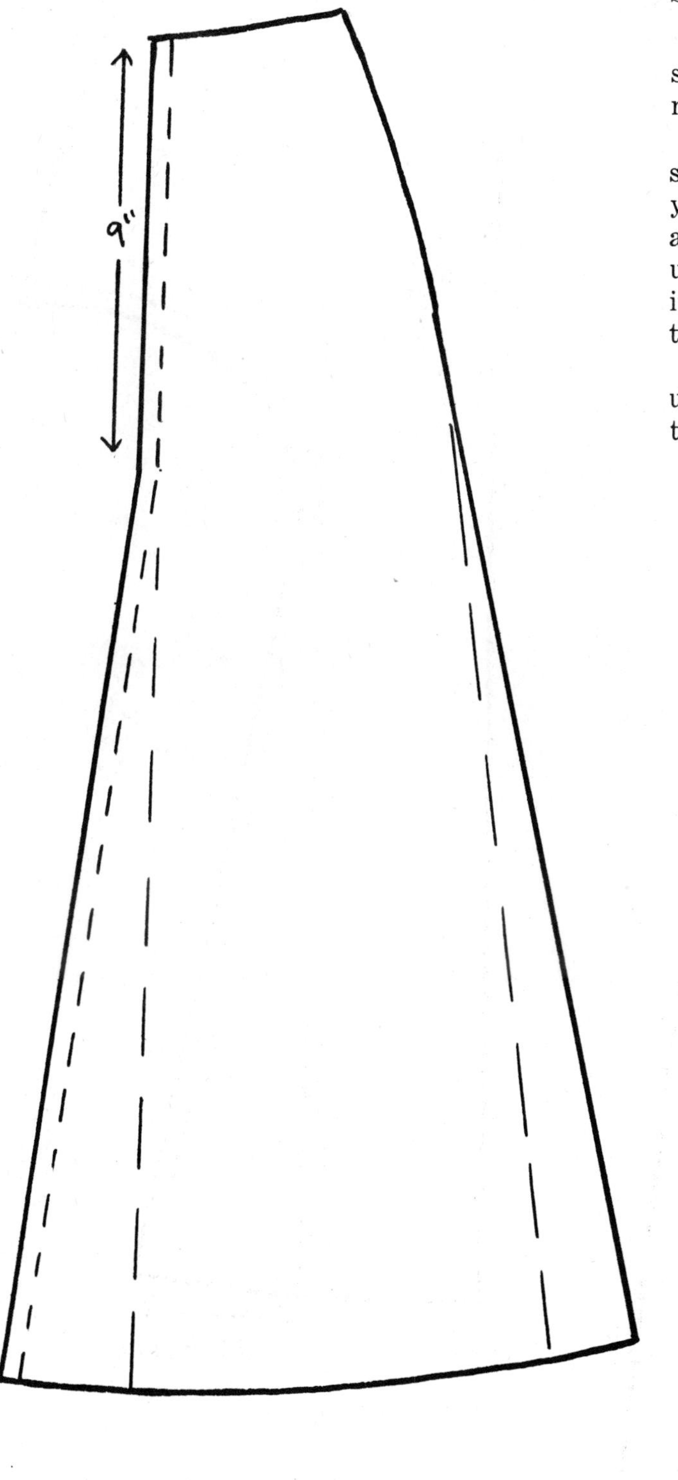

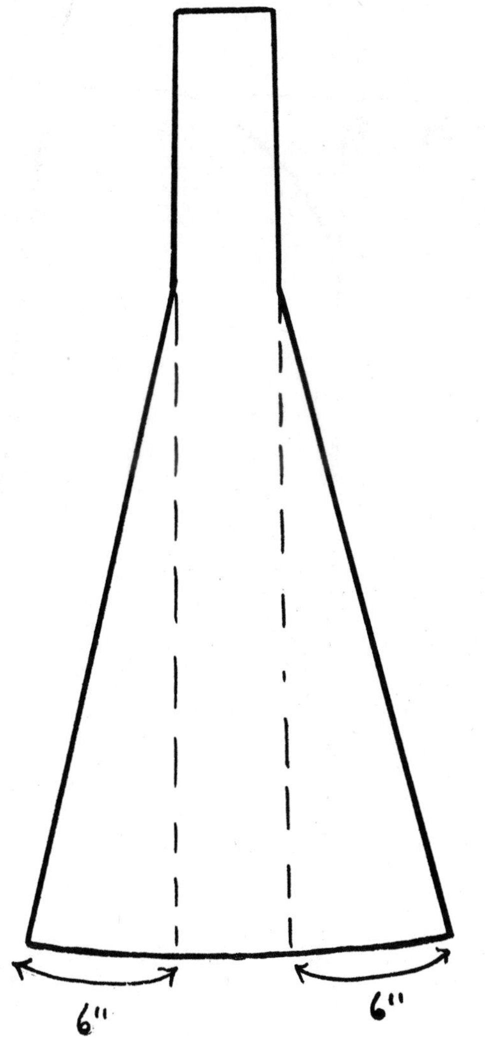

Hip Yoke and Front Panel

Cut your skirt block into two pieces as shown in Diagram A. Use the measurements given or use your own. However, always keep in mind the body lines as they are shown on a dress form. These are the most desirable lines on which to dissect the pattern.

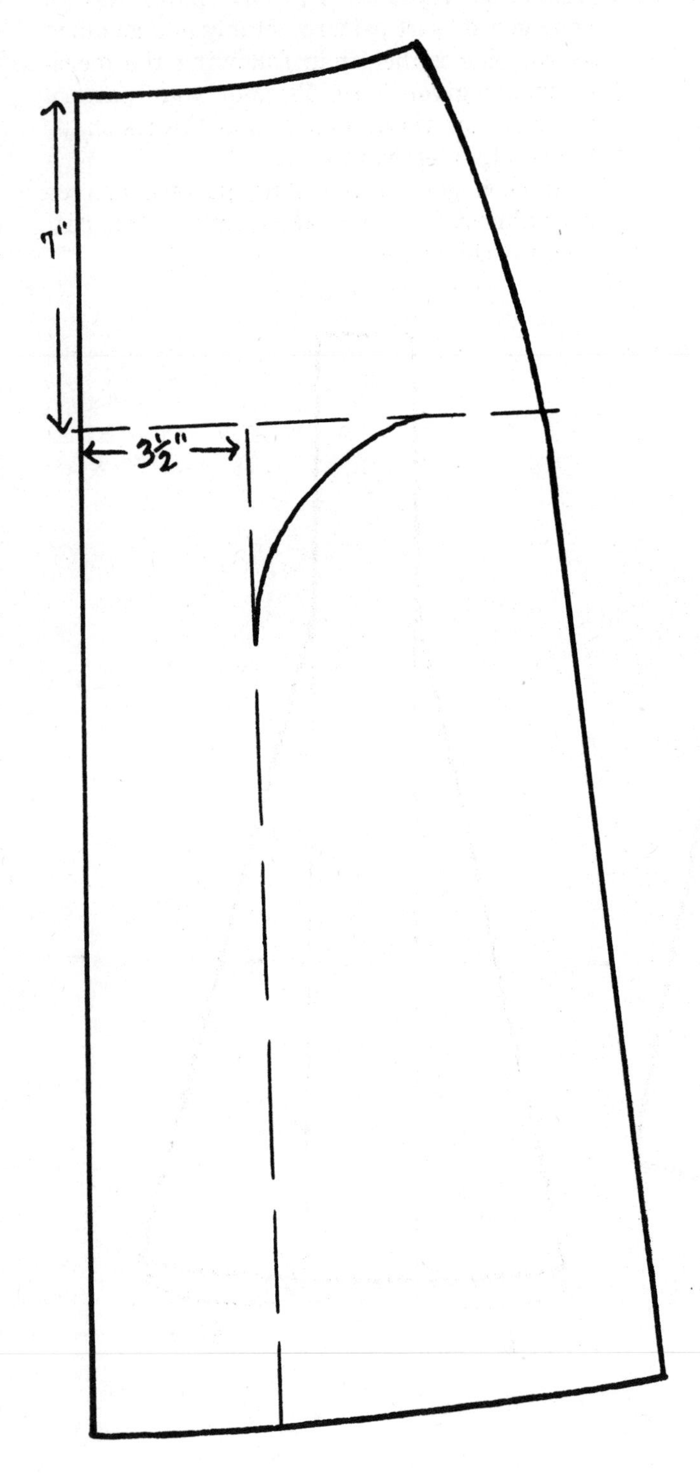

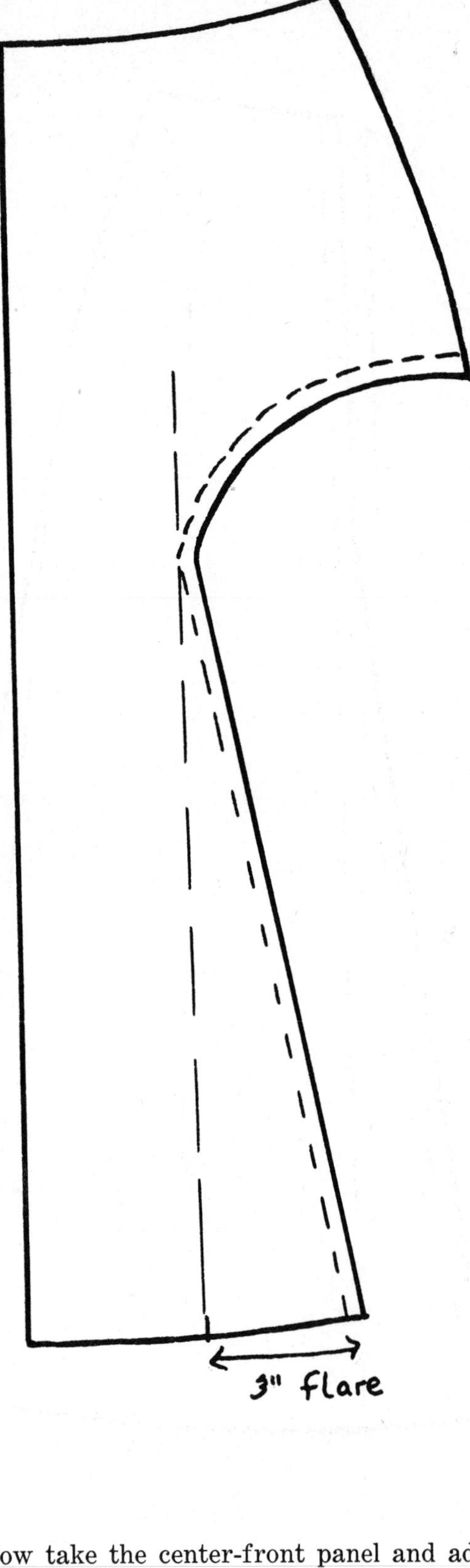

Now take the center-front panel and add flare, any amount that you think will look good. Don't forget to add ½-inch seam allowance, and notch.

Use the slash-and-spread method to get flare into the side-front panel. Be sure to add ½-inch seam to the style line, and notch this piece correctly so that it will fit onto the center-front panel.

Flared Skirt With Hip Yoke

Trace your front skirt block and draw in the style line. Cut apart on that line and add seam allowance to the yoke pattern. Slash the lower pattern piece and spread for desired flare.

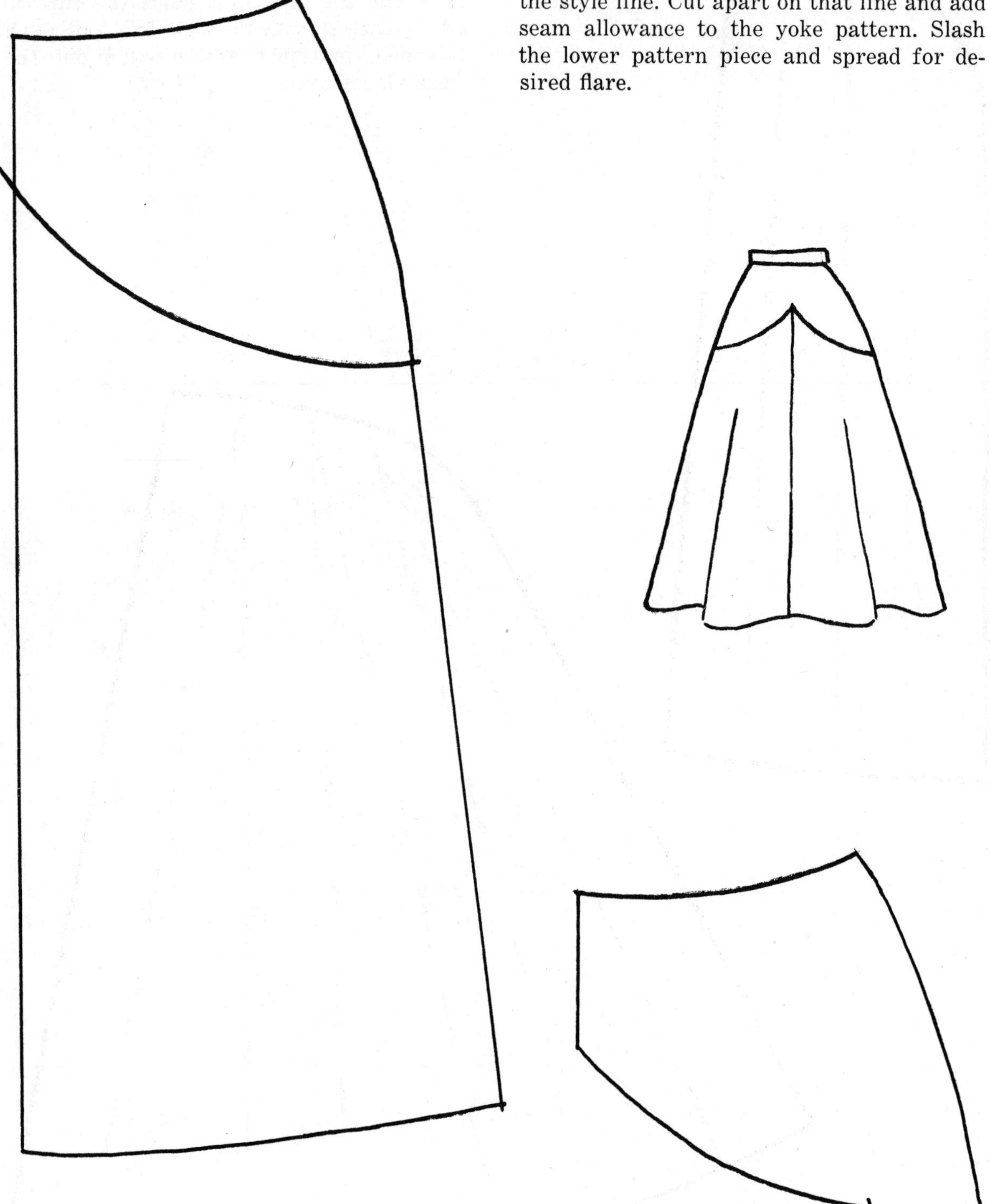

Flared Skirt With Hip Yoke *(cont.)*

Slash and spread the lower front pattern piece. If you want a seam at the center-front, add seam allowance. Be sure to notch the yoke and the skirt, and add seam allowance to the style line of the lower skirt.

Do the back skirt the same as the front. The yoke can be made either with or without the dart. If you do not want the dart, then swing it out as you make the back yoke pattern. This piece should be fitted on the dress form in tissue paper or muslin.

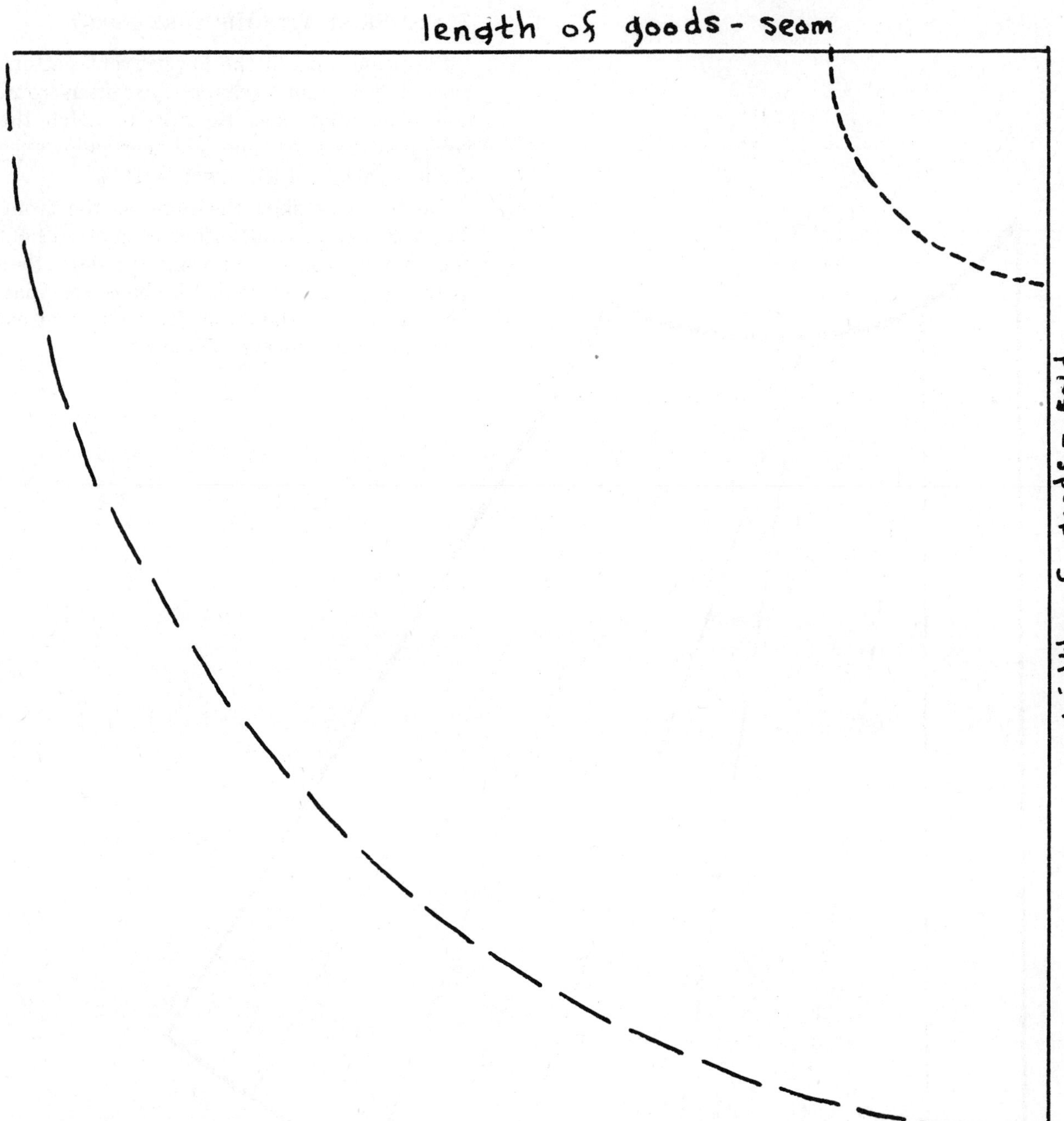

Draw in the waistline so that it is a true quarter circle with the correct measurement for 1/4 of the waist. In a standard size 14 it would be 6 3/4 inches. However, there is so much bias in cutting this skirt that you will have to make your measurement about 1/2 inch smaller, as it will stretch quite a lot. So make your waistline 6 1/4 inches instead of 6 3/4 inches. Measure down from the waistline to establish the hem line.

For a semicircular skirt, proceed exactly the same except make the waistline 13 1/2 inches (half the full waist measure). The skirt will have to be pieced near the hem for either the circular or semicircular skirt, unless it is a very short skating or bathing dress. Most material is not woven wide enough to do otherwise.

FULL FLARED SKIRT WITH HIP YOKE

For this pattern, you need the block only in making the yoke pattern. In this case, the dart should be eliminated. The measurements are entirely a matter of style, so decide for yourself what the proportions are to be.

Make the skirt in four gores, each one as full as the width of the material will allow. For a skirt of this kind it is not necessary to cut the back gores smaller than the front. There is so much bias that it can be worked into the yoke to fit correctly.

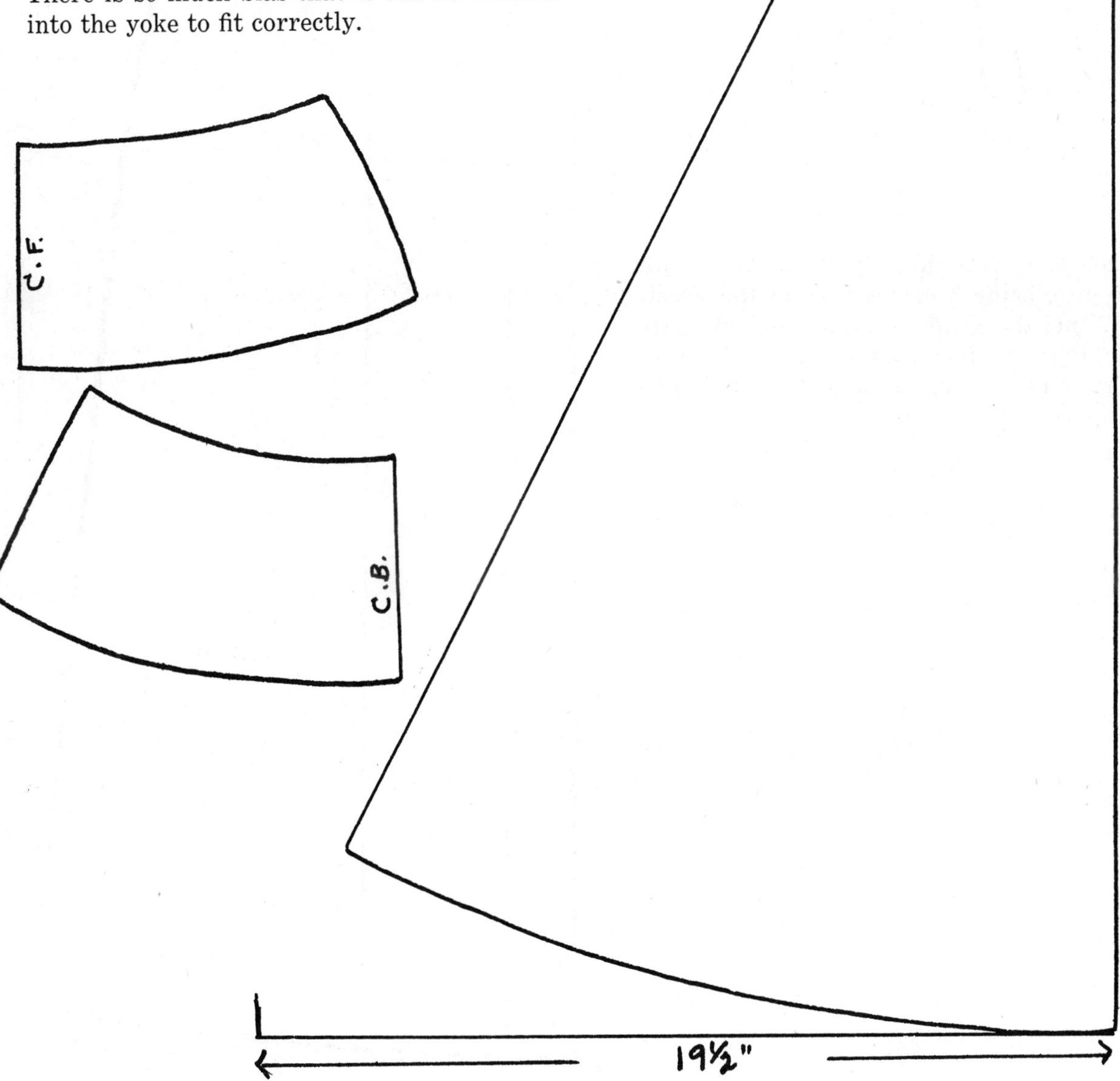

UNPRESSED PLEATS

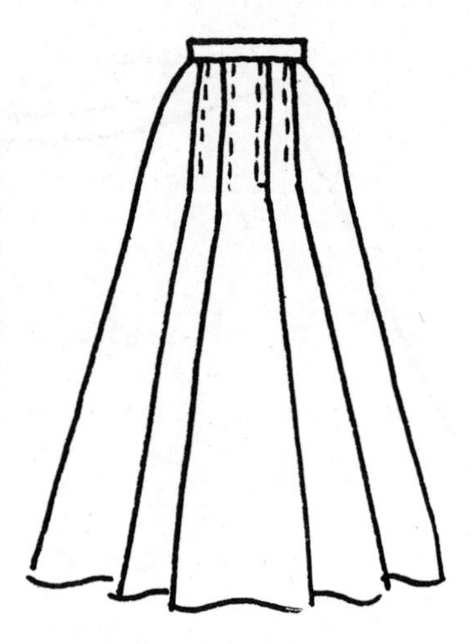

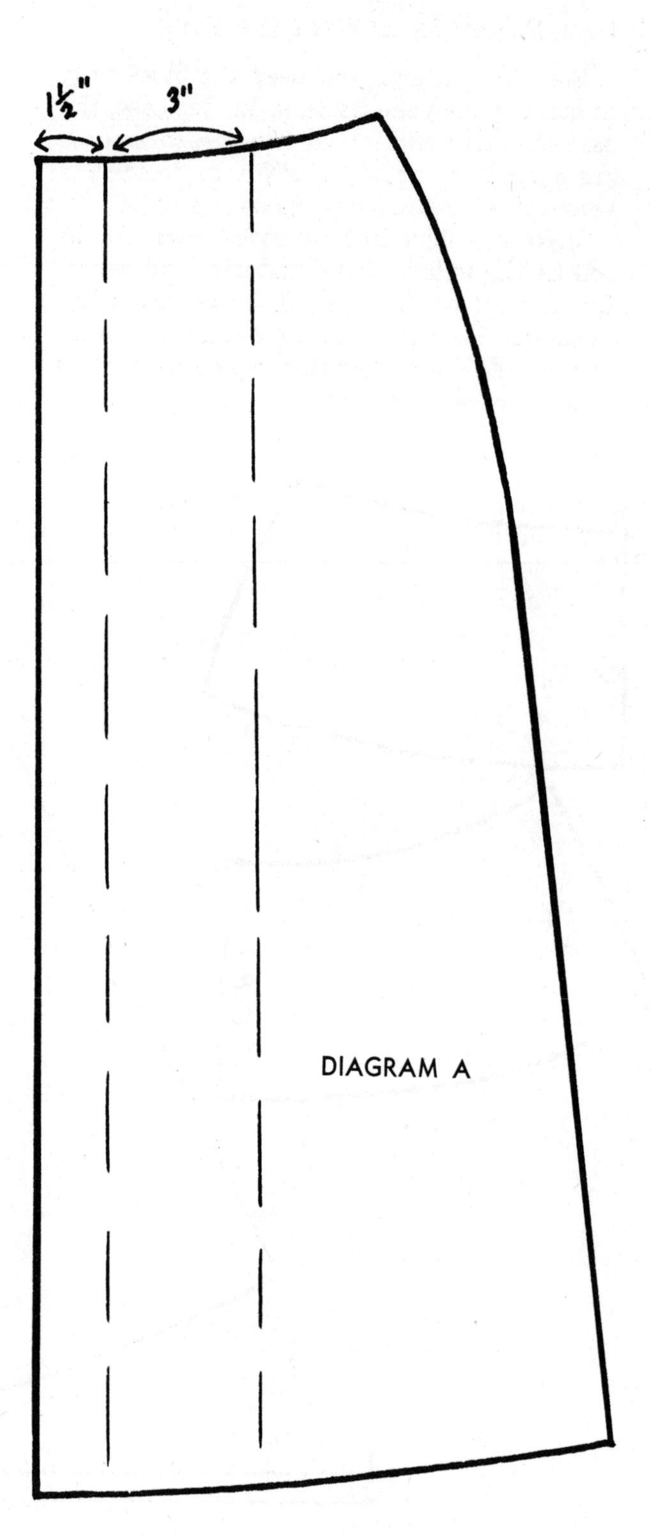

This skirt has three gores in the front, each gore being 3 inches wide at the waistline. Since the center front is a fold, measure only 1½ inches for that gore.

Trace the block, mark as directed, and cut apart.

UNPRESSED PLEATS *(cont.)*

Measure down 7 inches from the waistline, as shown, and then with your square draw a right angle 1 inch out. Add 3 inches of flare to the hem and with a ruler draw in the seam line. Since this gore is identical to the other two, simply mark it to cut three pieces. You may then discard the other narrow piece which you cut.

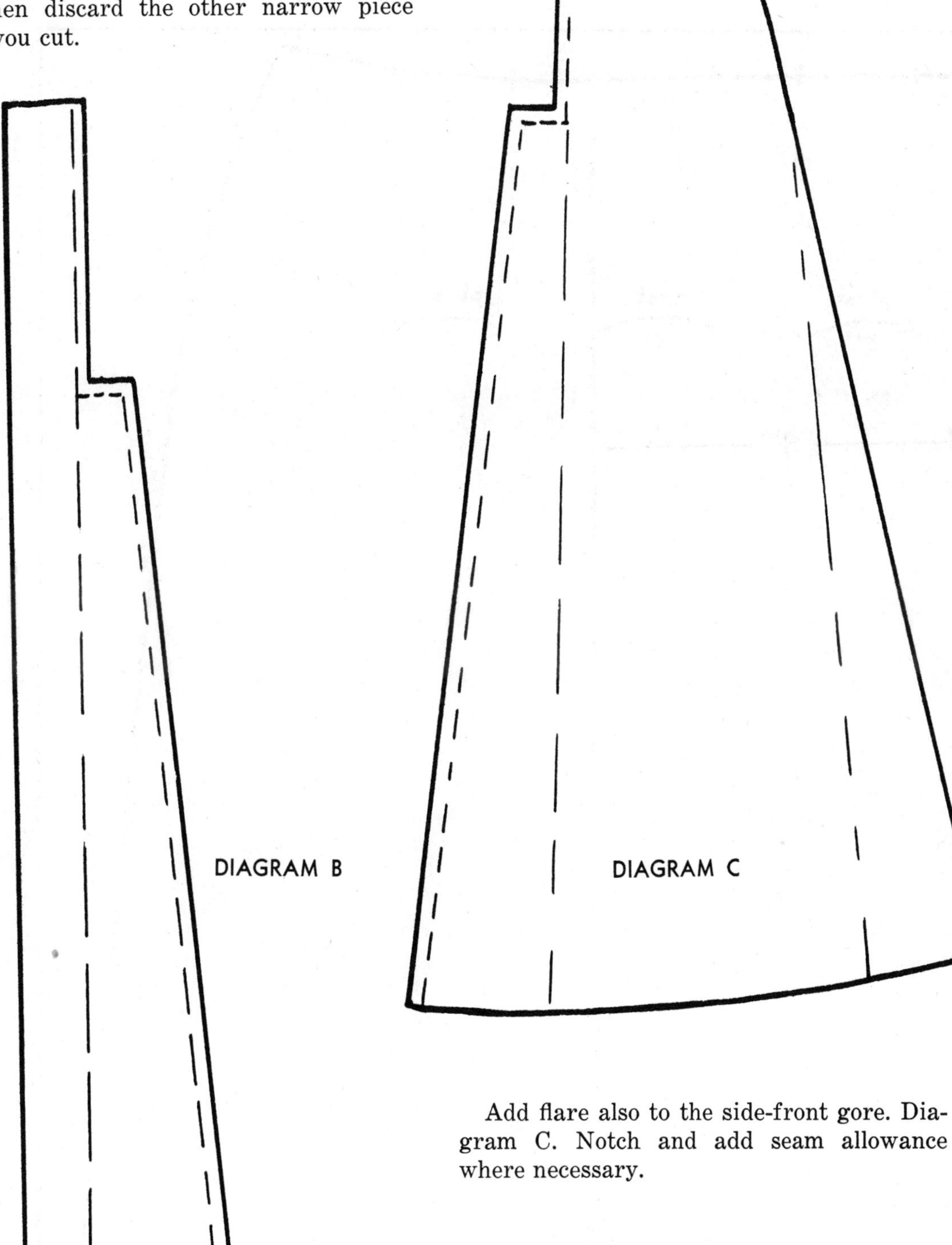

Add flare also to the side-front gore. Diagram C. Notch and add seam allowance where necessary.

PLEATED SKIRT

The simplest way to make a pleated skirt is to fold a piece of lightweight paper into the desired pleats, then lay your block over the folded paper and trace around it. Cut, unfold, then notch and punch on the fold lines.

Or, if you want three knife pleats, each 3 inches in depth, measure in 9 inches from the edge of your pattern paper, lay down the block, and trace. Then measure and mark the pleats as indicated in the diagram.

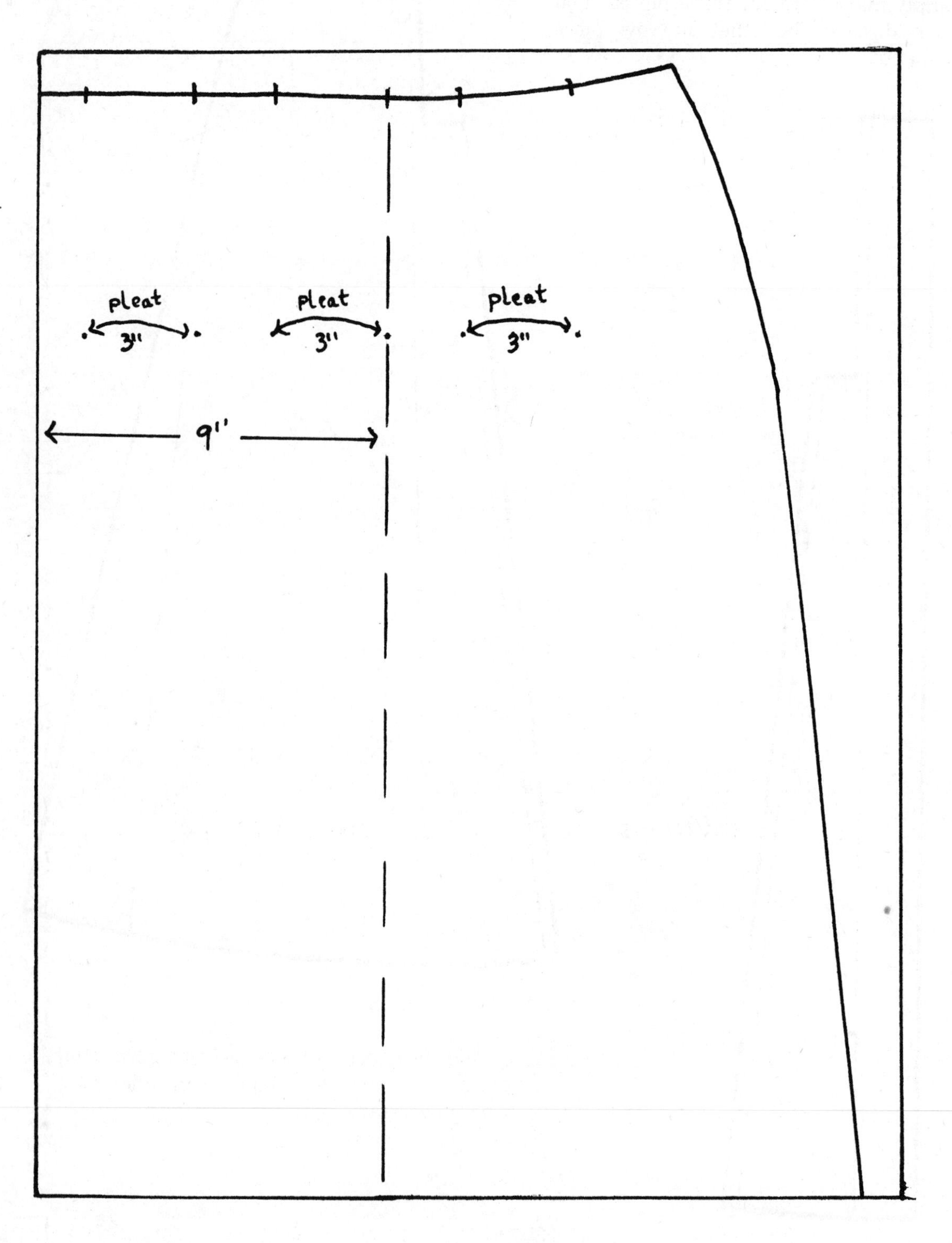

Skirts with all-around knife pleats or accordion pleats are sent out to a pleater. For the knife-pleated skirt, provide the pleater with two skirt lengths of the goods, if it is 54-inch material. If the material is narrower, include an additional panel to make up the difference. In pleating, it is always best to consult with the pleater. He will probably have many novelty styles of pleating that can be worked into your styling.

For an accordion-pleated skirt, provide the pleater with two skirt sections cut on the quarter circle. Have the waist about 3 inches larger than normal.

For a dirndl or straight gathered skirt, take two or three skirt lengths of goods, seam them together, and gather at the top to fit the waistband. A more attractive dirndl can be made by cutting four or six flared panels which are tightly gathered into the waistband. This takes a lot more material but is so much more flattering that it is worth the additional expense.

Chapter Nine

Sleeves

Sleeves lend themselves readily to various decorative effects, and all through the ages they have been used in this way to add style and flare to the garments of both men and women, as well as for their primary purpose — to cover and protect the arm.

The *Chinese kimona* sleeve is probably the simplest of all sleeves to cut, fit, and sew. The only problem is to cut it wide enough for maximum comfort. There are many adaptations of the kimona sleeve, some of which will be explained in this chapter.

The *set-in* sleeve is the other important basic sleeve from which many variations may be made.

It is important that all sleeves be cut and set-in in such a way that the straight grain of the goods falls directly from the center of the shoulder to the center of the second finger. This will give you a true center line for the entire length of the sleeve.

A long sleeve should be cut long enough to extend about 3/4 inch past the wrist bone. A long, loose sleeve that is gathered into a wristband should be cut long enough to blouse slightly so that when the arm is extended the sleeve will not pull taut.

A short sleeve should end about halfway between the elbow and the shoulder. A bracelet sleeve should end about halfway between the wrist and the elbow. Your own eye is the best judge in determining sleeve lengths, but since it is very easy to get a sleeve length that simply does not look smart, you must use great care in judging your proportions.

Basic Sleeve Block

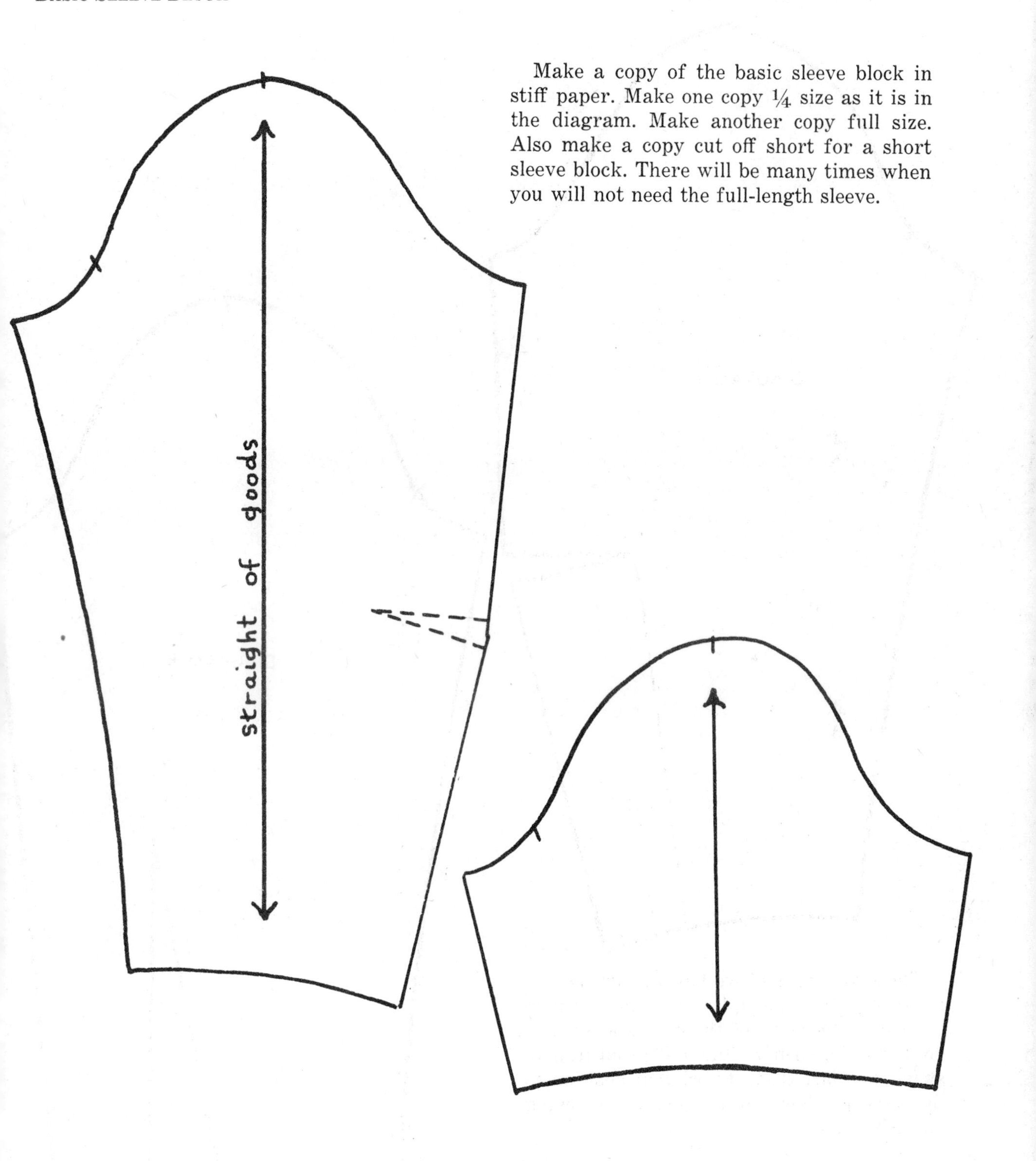

Make a copy of the basic sleeve block in stiff paper. Make one copy ¼ size as it is in the diagram. Make another copy full size. Also make a copy cut off short for a short sleeve block. There will be many times when you will not need the full-length sleeve.

SWINGING THE SLEEVE DART

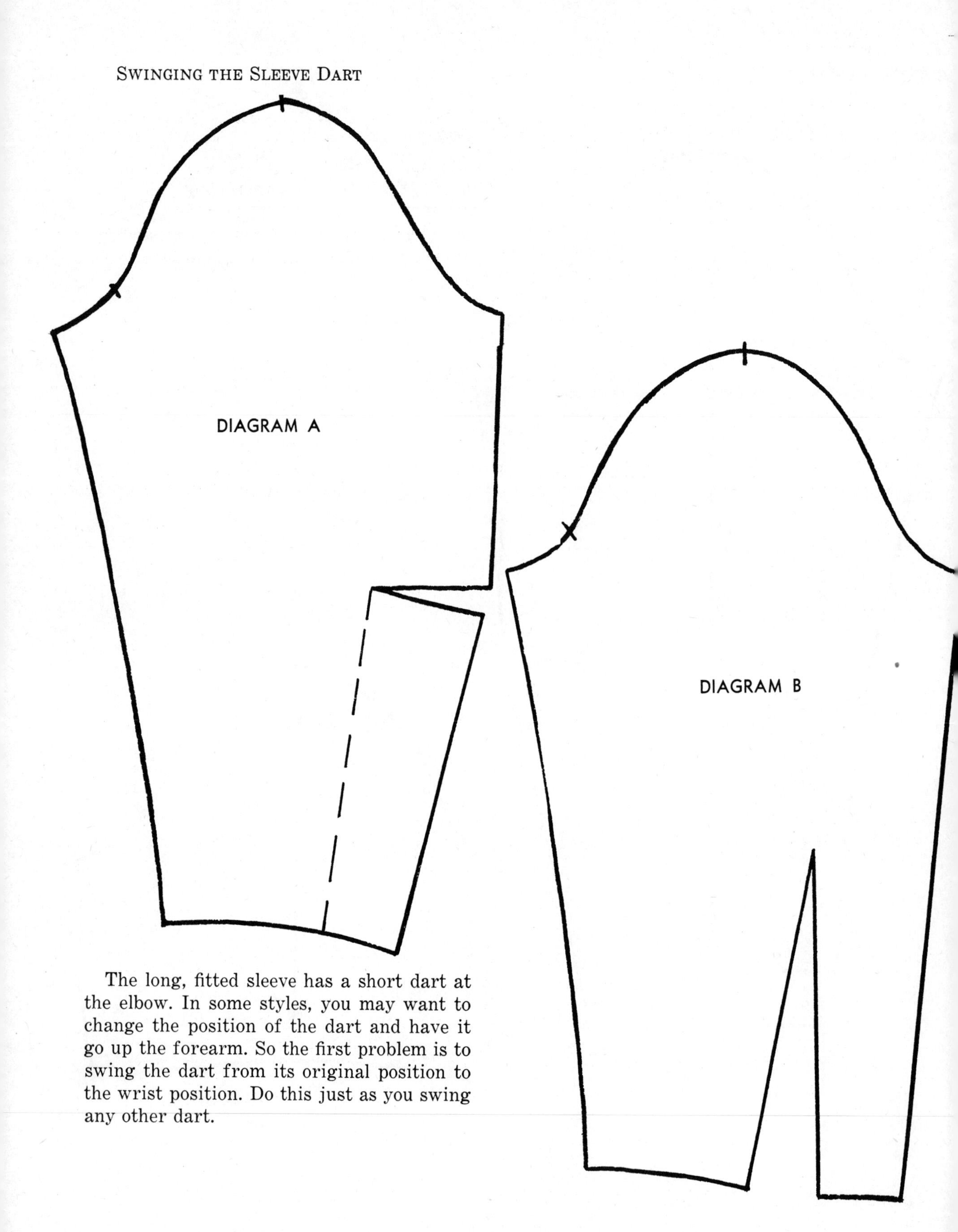

The long, fitted sleeve has a short dart at the elbow. In some styles, you may want to change the position of the dart and have it go up the forearm. So the first problem is to swing the dart from its original position to the wrist position. Do this just as you swing any other dart.

Long Gathered Sleeve

When the sleeve is gathered at the wrist, you will not need a dart. In this case, swing the dart to the wrist position and simply leave the excess space there to include in the gathers.

Add 2 inches to the width of the wrist at the front, and 1 inch to the width of the wrist at the back. Draw in the new sleeve shape, using a ruler for the underarm seam lines. Make a gentle slope for the wristline, dropping the length 1 inch near the back as shown in the diagram. Make a cuff pattern as shown.

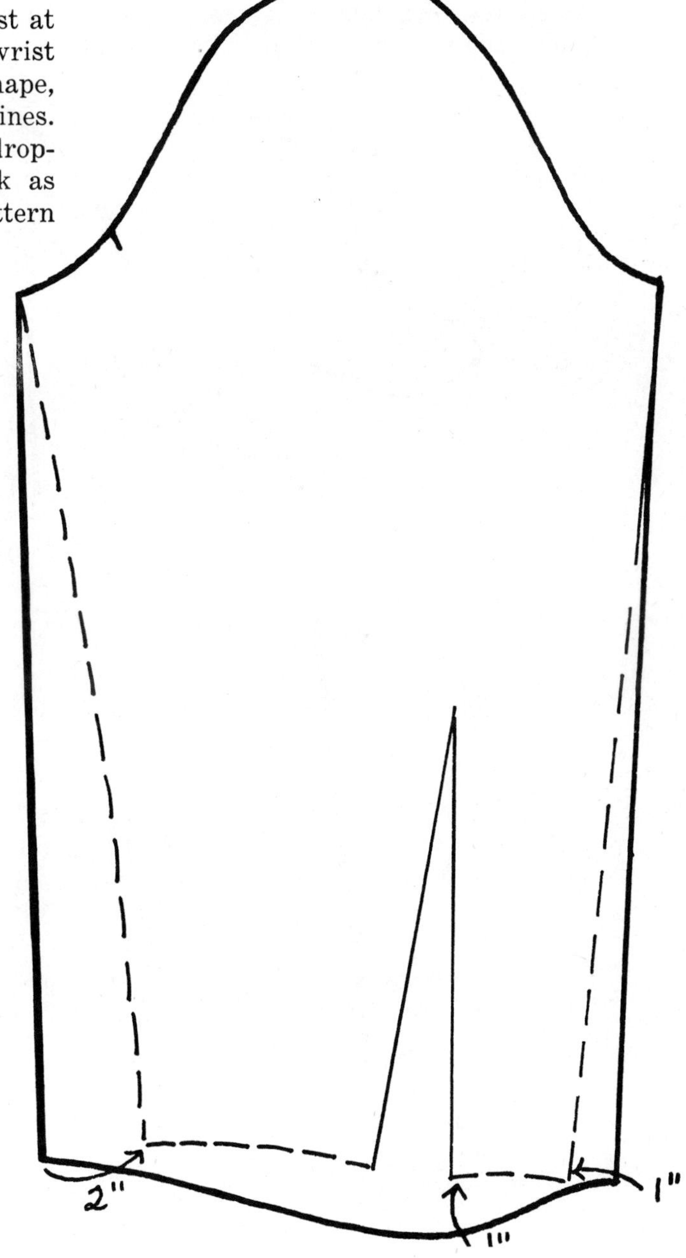

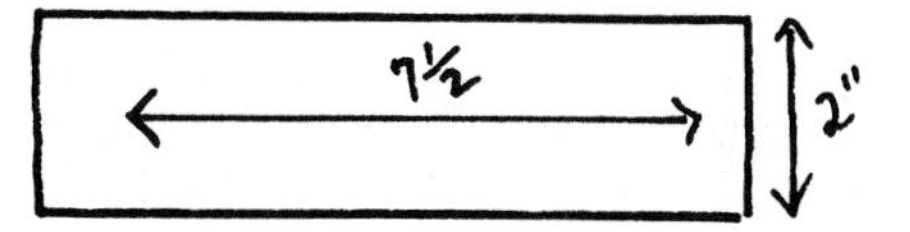

Bishop Sleeve

The "bishop" sleeve is a full, gathered sleeve such as that used in some ecclesiastical robes. The sleeve should be very wide and should be gathered at the shoulder as well as at the wrist. Use your own measurements for this style. Raise the sleeve cap about $1\frac{1}{2}$ inches at the center shoulder, and draw in the new shoulder line. Follow the diagram carefully here. After you have made a few high-capped sleeves, you will be able to draw in the shape with ease; meanwhile, follow the diagram.

BELL SLEEVE

A bell sleeve can be gathered at the shoulder or left with a smooth shoulder, as you desire. In this instance the shoulder has been left smooth. Make a copy of the sleeve block and slash it several times to the shoulder. Spread the pieces out for as much fullness as you think will look best. This is usually made in a $^3/_4$ length, but that too is up to the stylist.

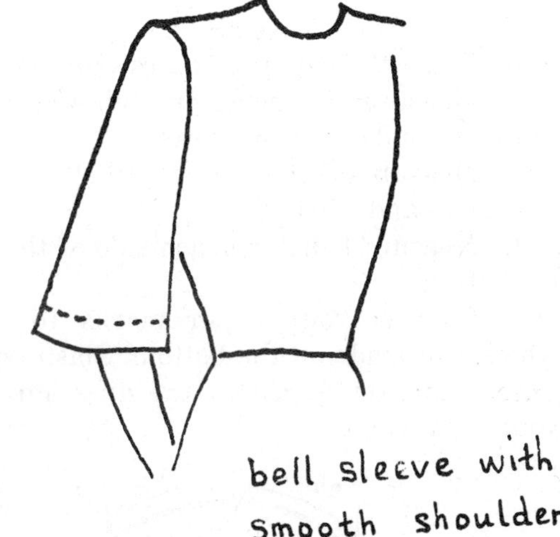

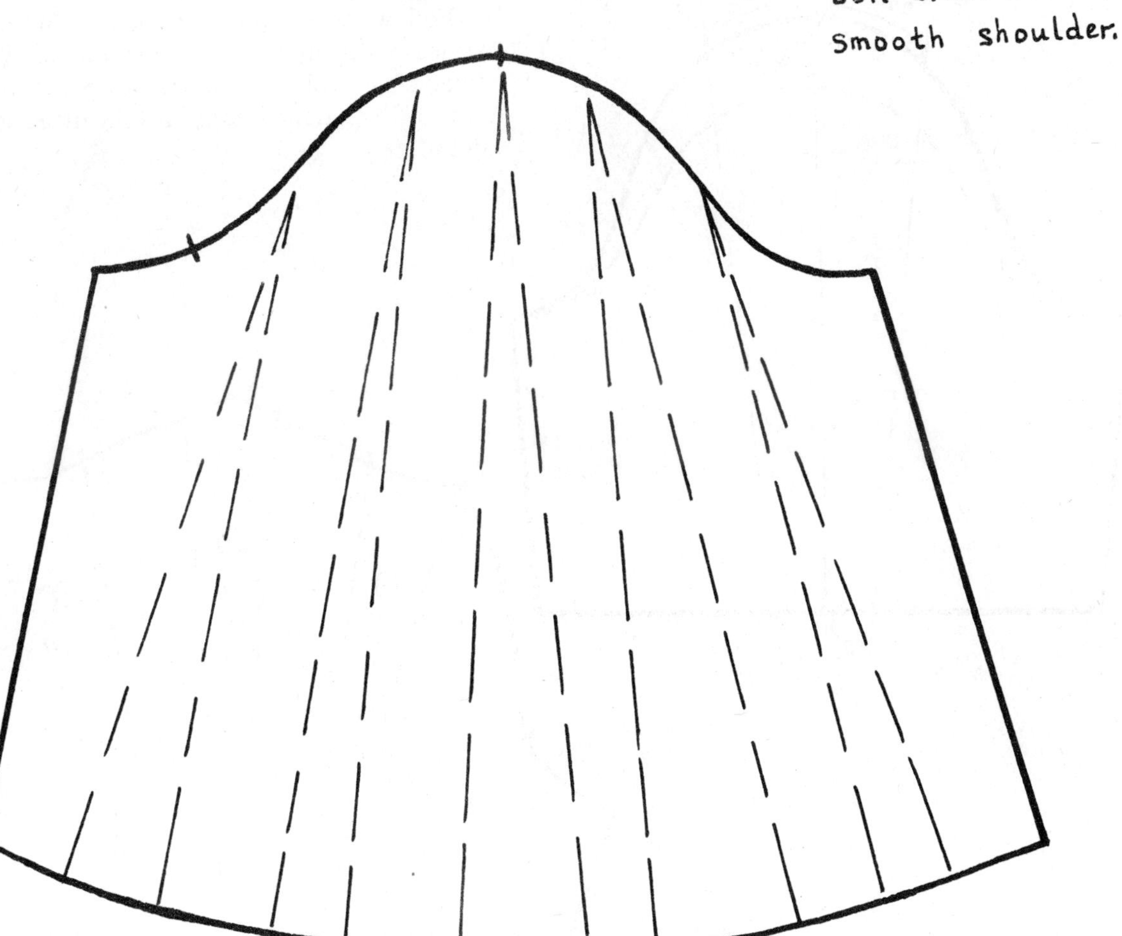

Sleeve With Shoulder Darts

Use the short sleeve block.

1. Raise the cap 1½ inches. Diagram A.
2. Measure 2½ inches on each side of the center shoulder. Make marks.
3. Measure off the center of the bottom of the sleeve and mark.
4. Measure 1 inch on each side of the center bottom.
5. Connect your upper marks to those which you made on the bottom. Slash on the lines. Diagram A. Check the diagram with your own work.
6. Spread the slashed pieces out about 2 inches apart.
7. Make a mark 2½ inches down in the exact center of each of the spread sections. These will be the dart points. Notch and punch the darts.
8. The bottom will be curved from spreading the pieces apart. Either leave it curved or straighten it out. Diagram B. Drawing a straight line across the bottom will add to the height of the sleeve cap — makes the shoulder look square.

Follow this same procedure for darted styles with more or fewer darts. Ten or twelve very shallow darts sewn on the outside of the garment make a very nice shoulder detail.

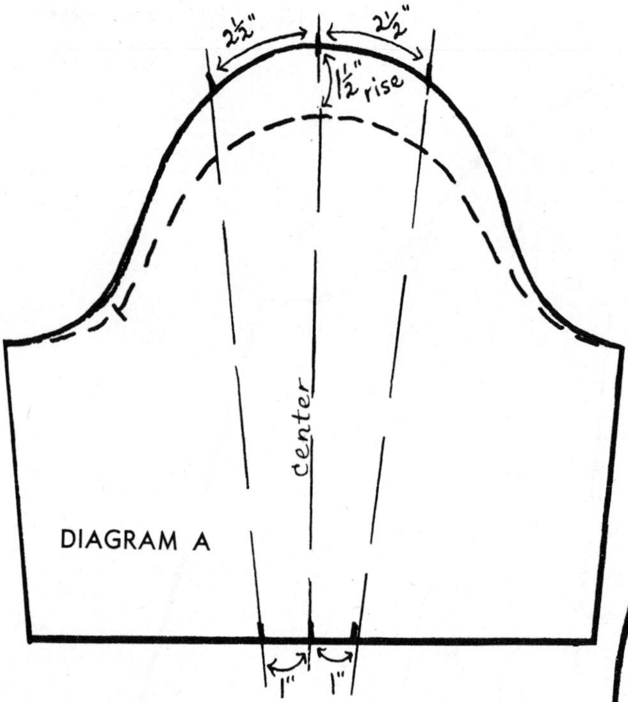

DIAGRAM A

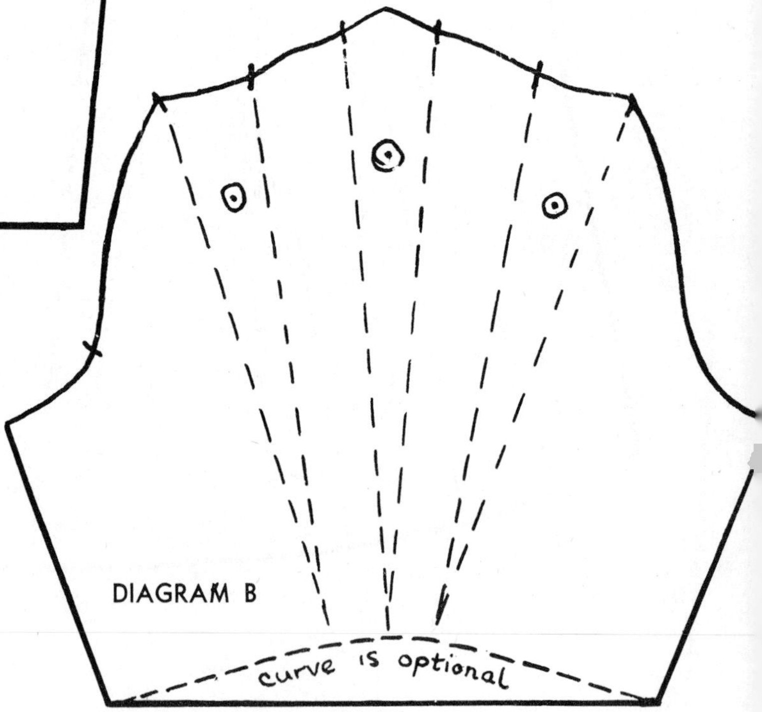

DIAGRAM B

Raglan Sleeve

1. Put the back and front bodice blocks together with the shoulder seams overlapped. Use no seam or the neck will come out too large.
2. Measure down the center back ½ inch. Make a mark.
3. Measure down the center front 1 inch. Make a mark.
4. Draw in the yoke. Diagram A.
5. Add the cut-out yoke to the sleeve. Diagram B.
6. Add seam allowance where needed (at the dart).

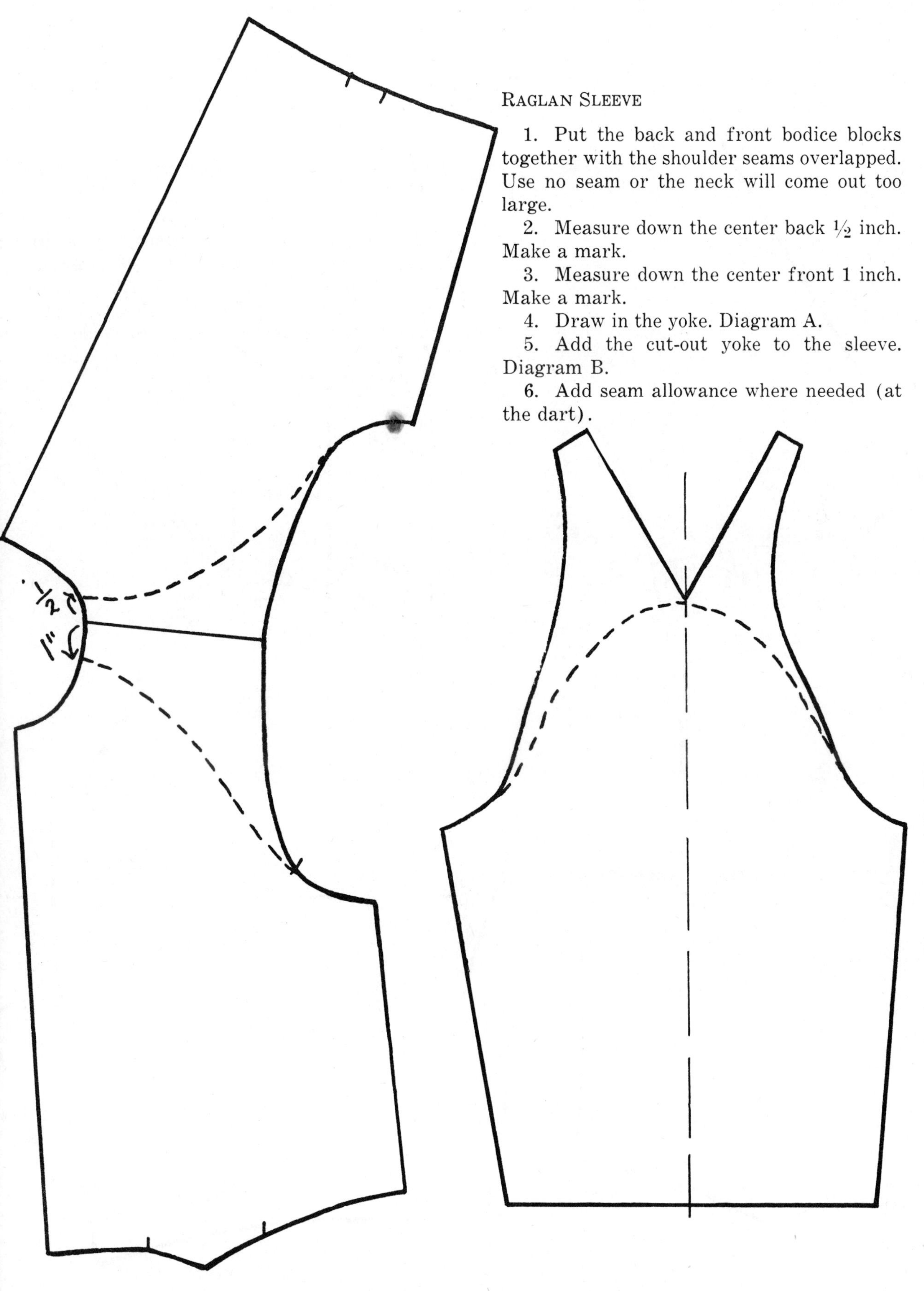

Saddle Sleeve

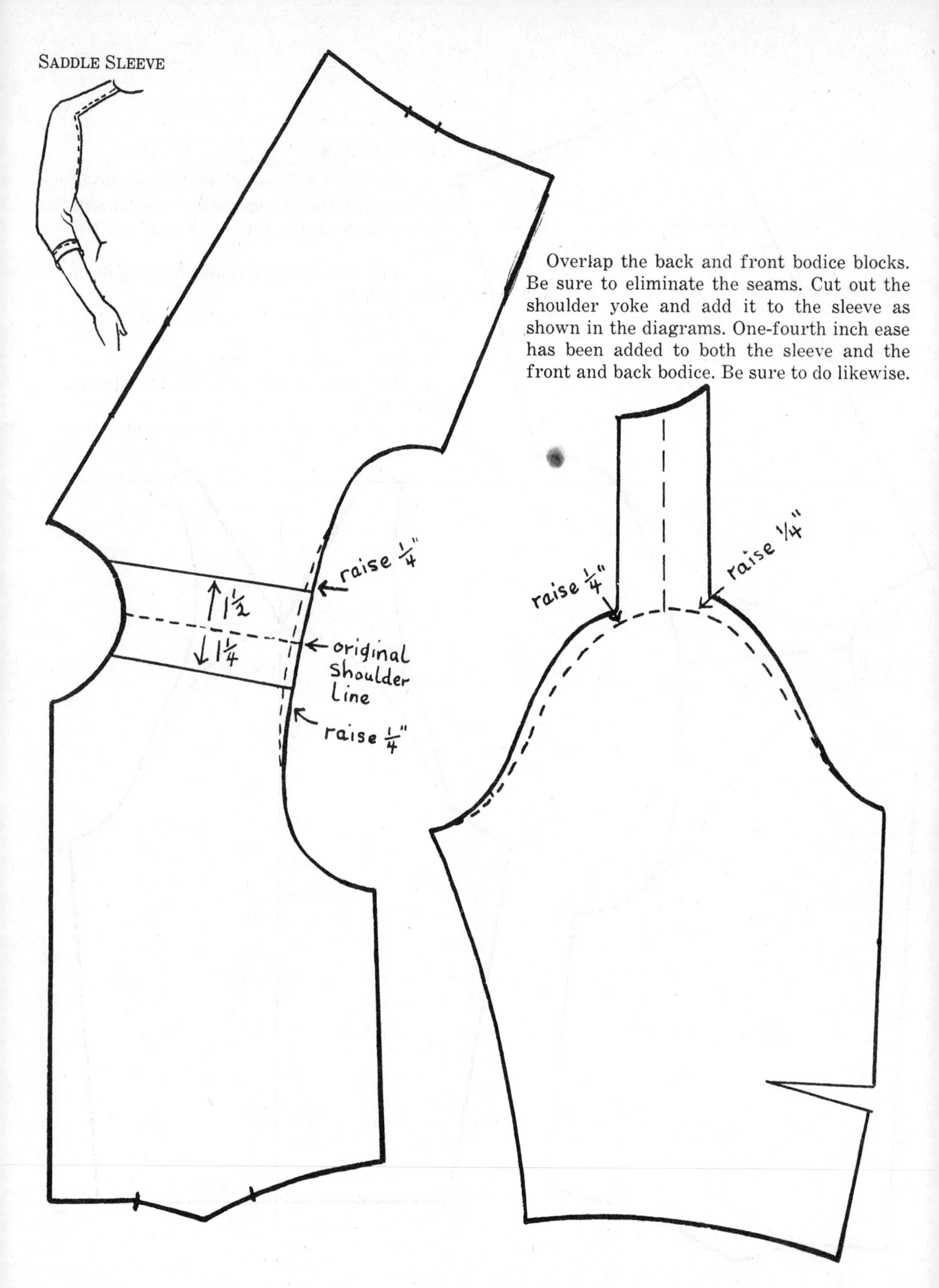

Overlap the back and front bodice blocks. Be sure to eliminate the seams. Cut out the shoulder yoke and add it to the sleeve as shown in the diagrams. One-fourth inch ease has been added to both the sleeve and the front and back bodice. Be sure to do likewise.

Darted Saddle Sleeve

The dotted line shows the original shoulder cap. Use the plain saddle sleeve pattern for a block. Fold in the two darts and cut out with the dart folded. The dart itself appears to be an odd shape, but it gives you something to sew into the shoulder line in order to hold the dart in place. This dart looks best if folded rather than sewed.

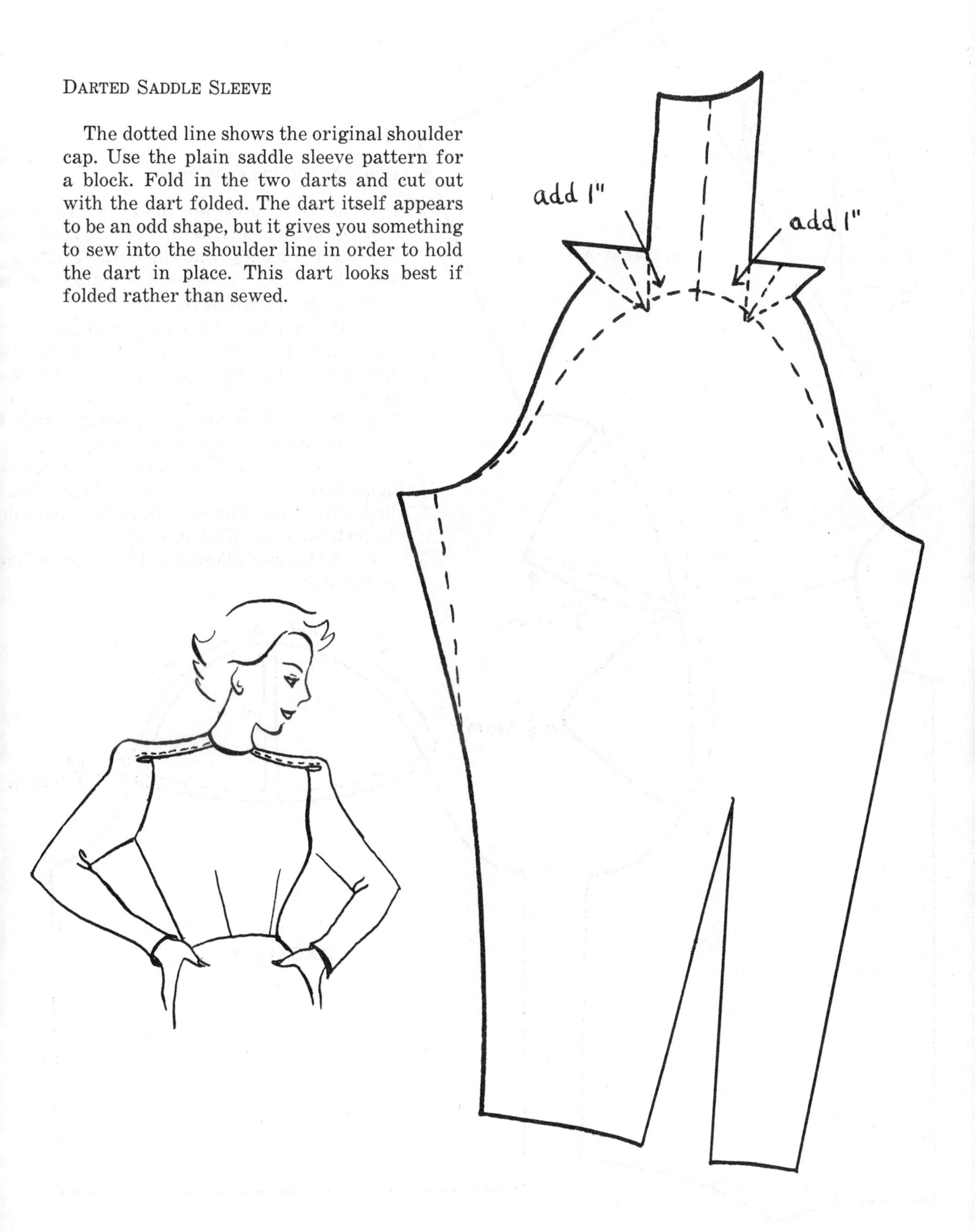

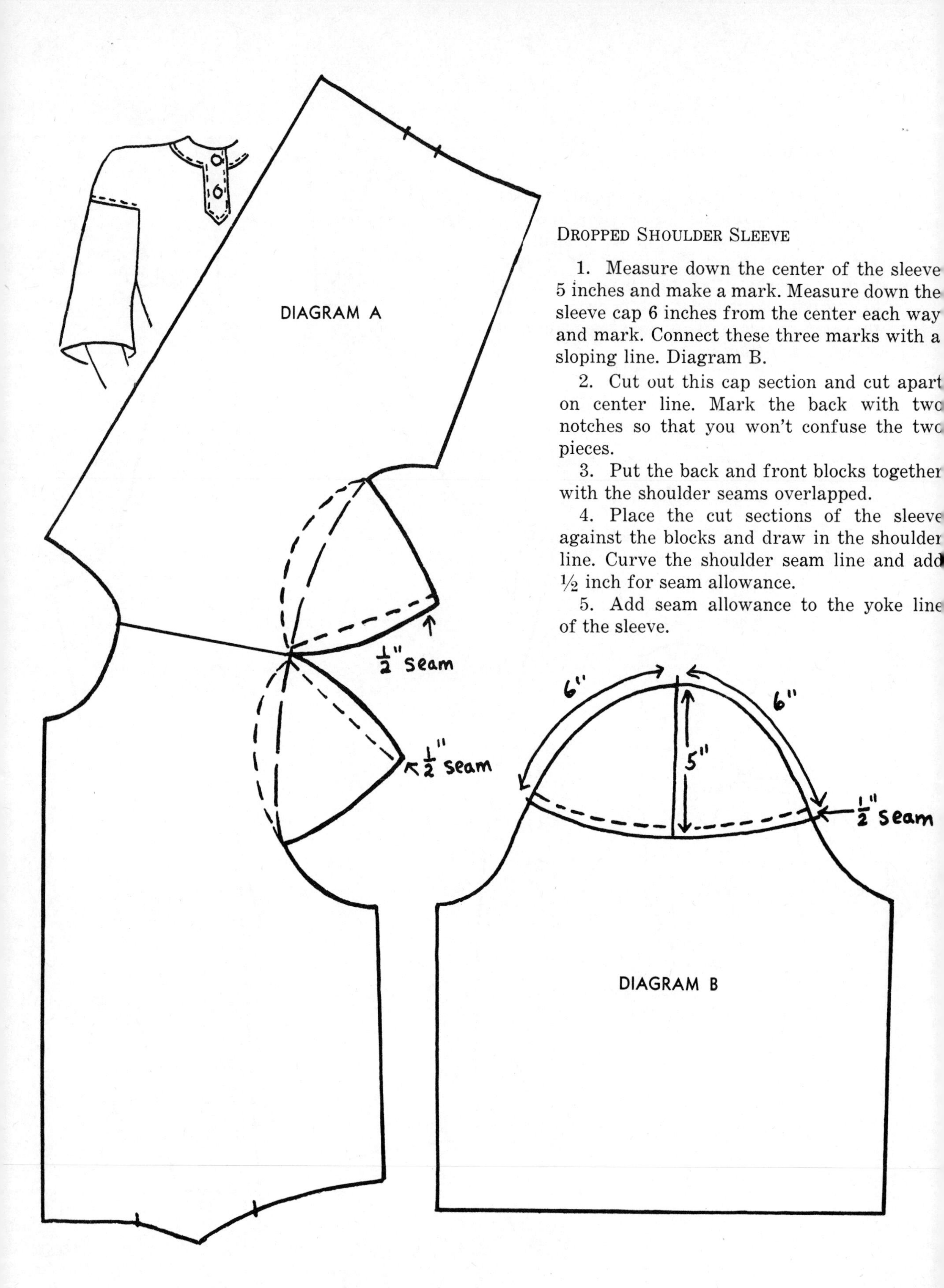

DROPPED SHOULDER SLEEVE

1. Measure down the center of the sleeve 5 inches and make a mark. Measure down the sleeve cap 6 inches from the center each way and mark. Connect these three marks with a sloping line. Diagram B.

2. Cut out this cap section and cut apart on center line. Mark the back with two notches so that you won't confuse the two pieces.

3. Put the back and front blocks together with the shoulder seams overlapped.

4. Place the cut sections of the sleeve against the blocks and draw in the shoulder line. Curve the shoulder seam line and add ½ inch for seam allowance.

5. Add seam allowance to the yoke line of the sleeve.

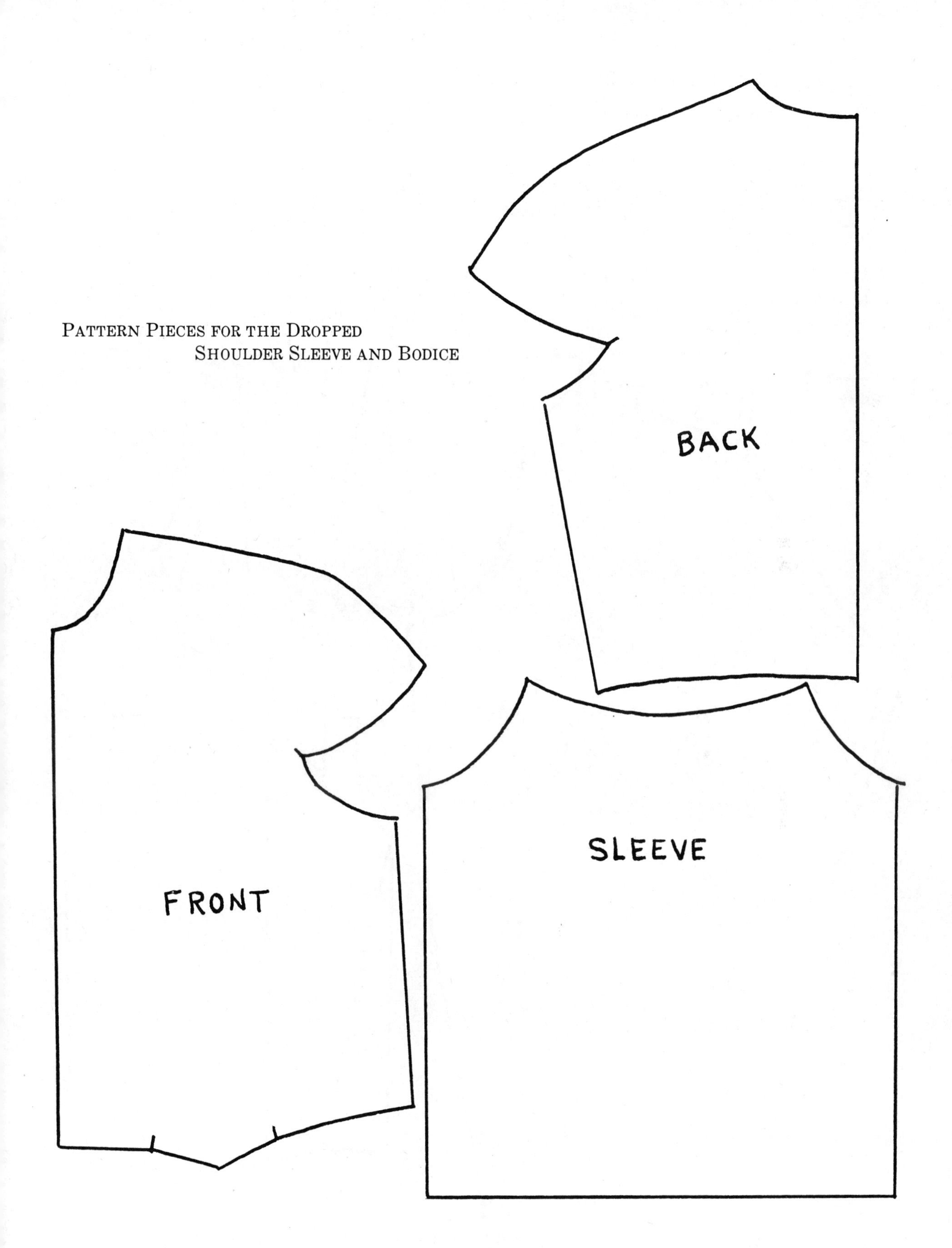

Pattern Pieces for the Dropped Shoulder Sleeve and Bodice

Square-Shoulder Sleeve Style

This interesting sleeve lends itself to several variations. The shoulder can fit into the straight yoke section either smoothly or gathered, or with pleats or darts. Try some variations. The notches at the top indicate that those two pieces are to be seamed together. The seam line sets right at the center of the shoulder when placed in the armscye of the garment.

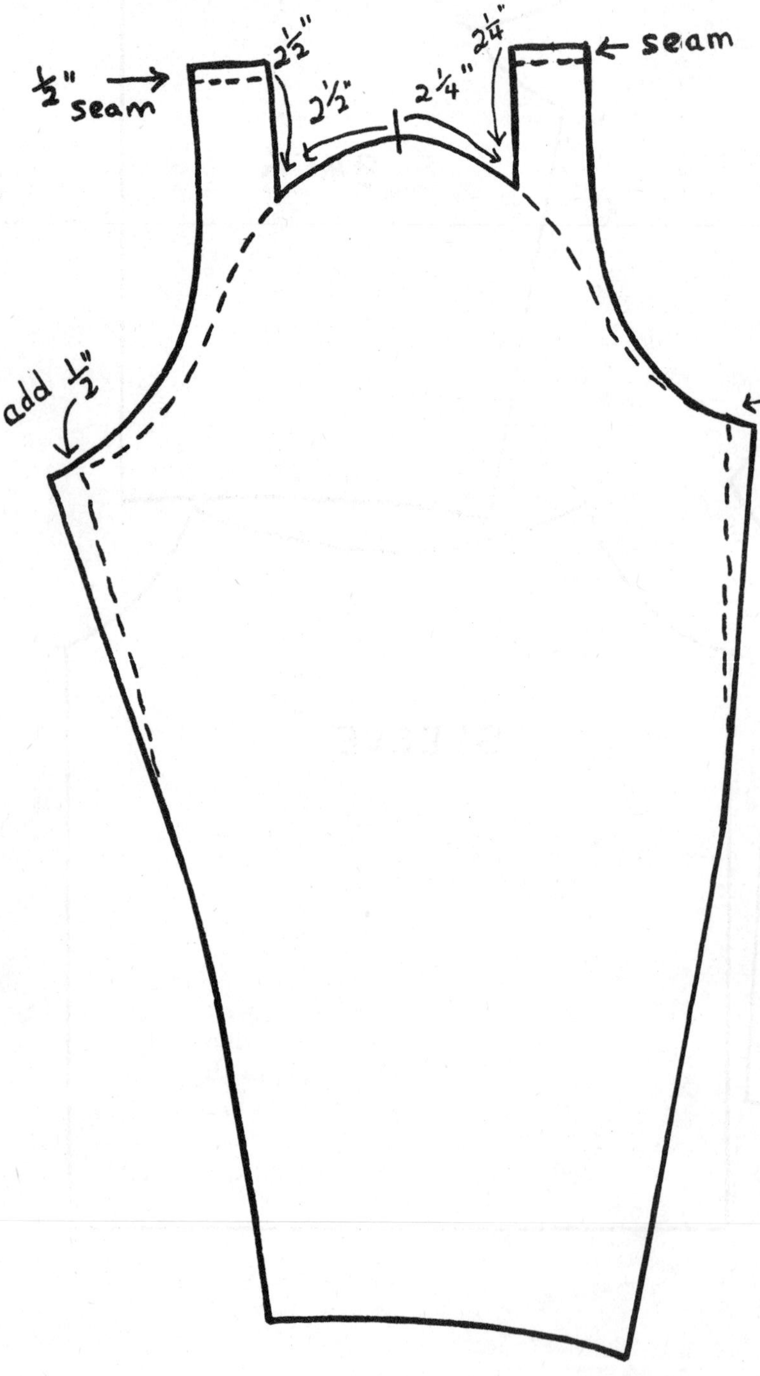

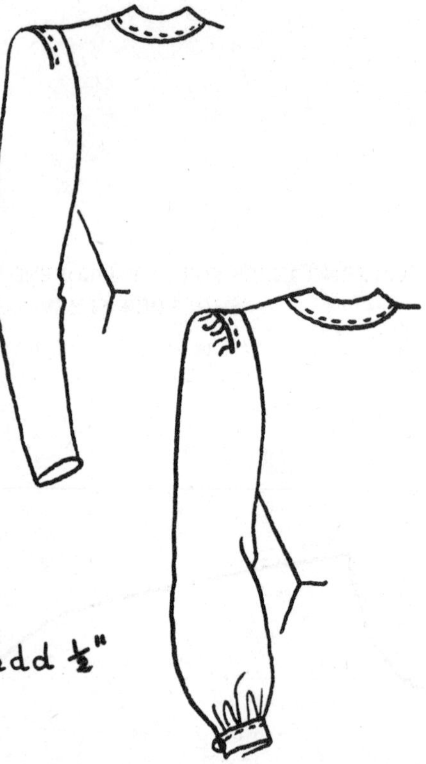

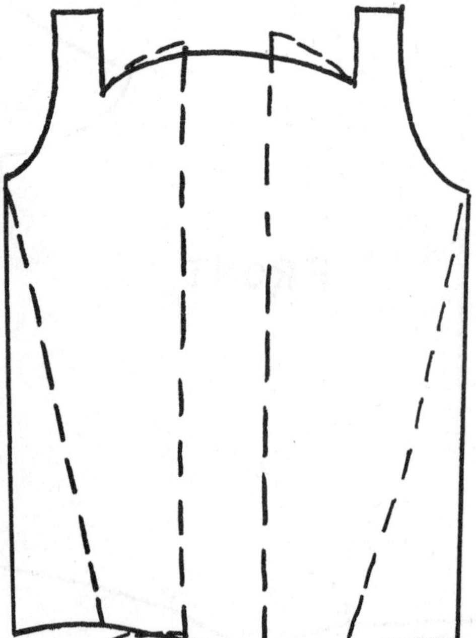

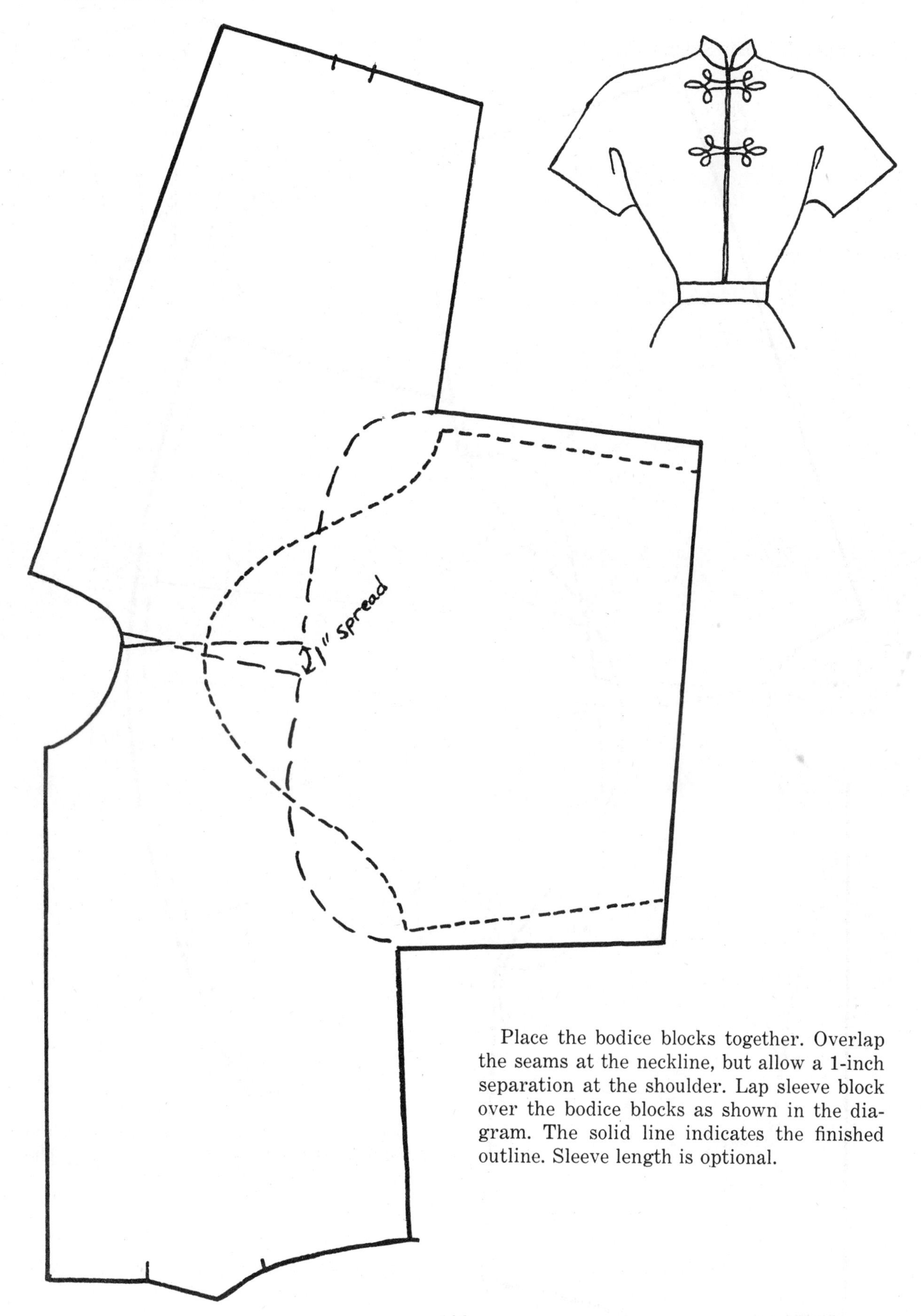

Place the bodice blocks together. Overlap the seams at the neckline, but allow a 1-inch separation at the shoulder. Lap sleeve block over the bodice blocks as shown in the diagram. The solid line indicates the finished outline. Sleeve length is optional.

Full Kimona Sleeve

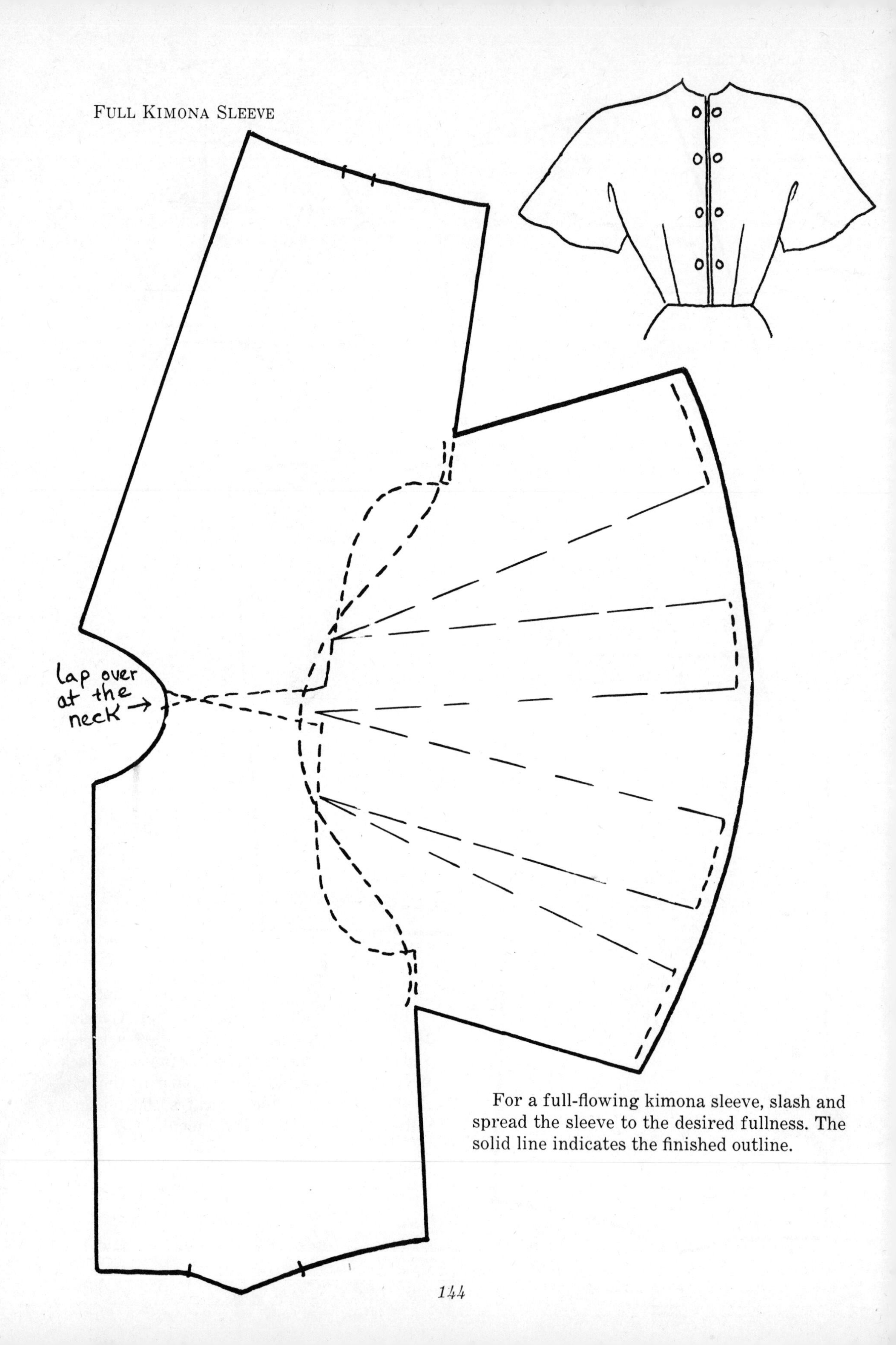

For a full-flowing kimona sleeve, slash and spread the sleeve to the desired fullness. The solid line indicates the finished outline.

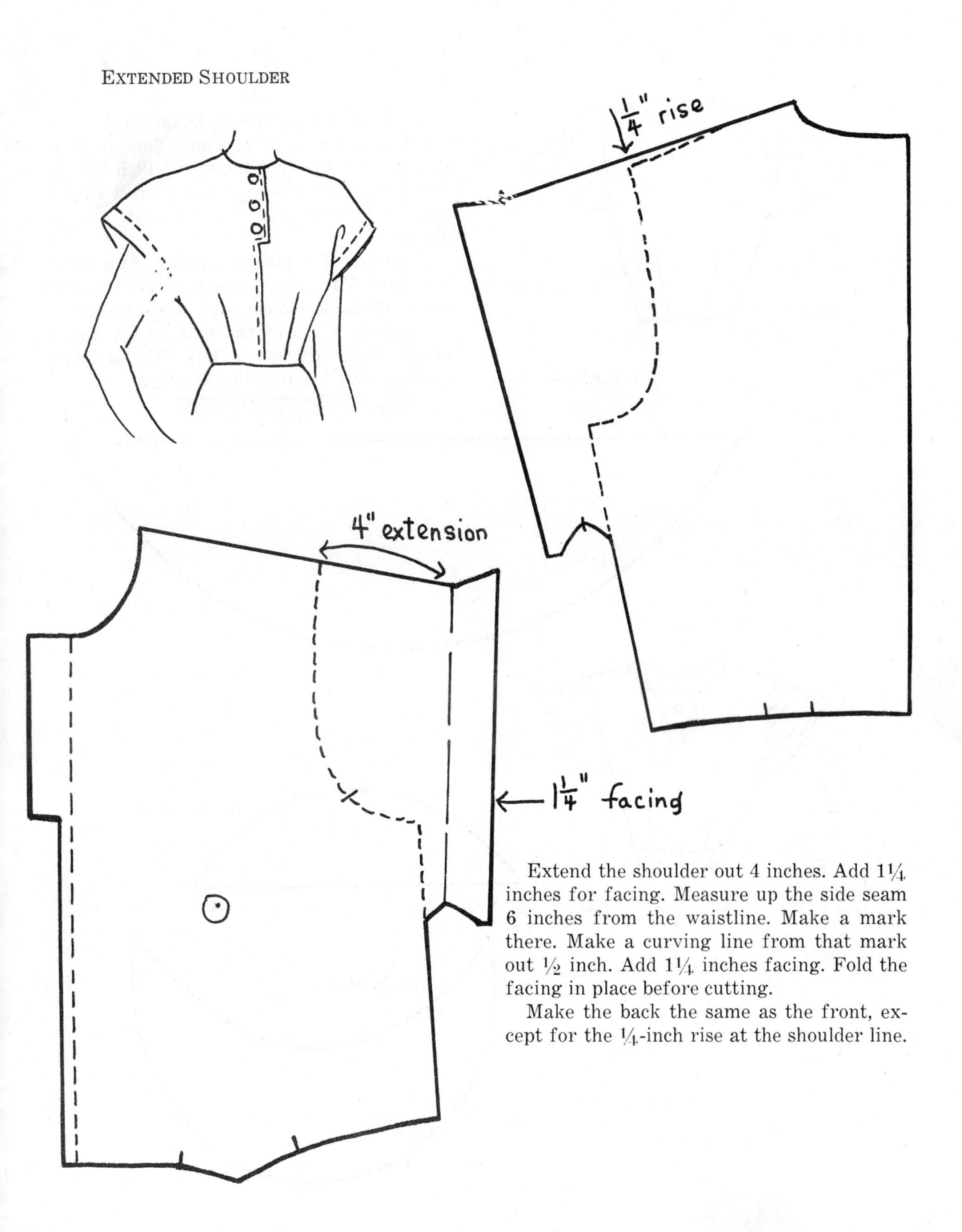

Extend the shoulder out 4 inches. Add 1¼ inches for facing. Measure up the side seam 6 inches from the waistline. Make a mark there. Make a curving line from that mark out ½ inch. Add 1¼ inches facing. Fold the facing in place before cutting.

Make the back the same as the front, except for the ¼-inch rise at the shoulder line.

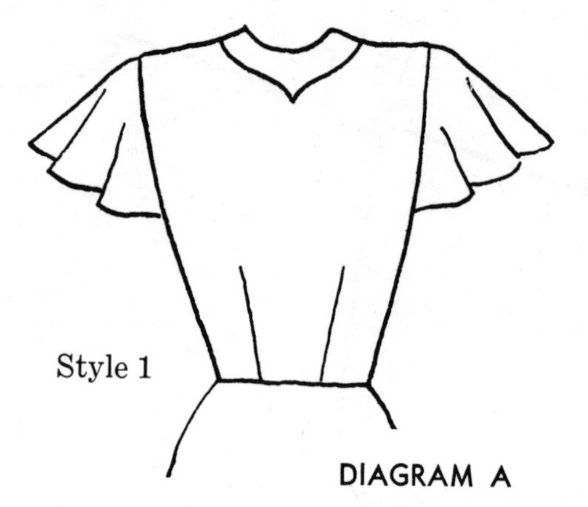

To make a cape sleeve, Diagram A, cut a circular shape with as much flare in it as desired. Be sure that the part which is to be fitted into the armscye is the correct length, and be sure to notch for the center of the shoulder.

Diagram B shows a pattern with much less flare. The curved line goes into the armscye to make the lower edge quite straight.

Diagram C shows the pattern for a cape sleeve with still more flare. The notched, curving line fits into the armscye.

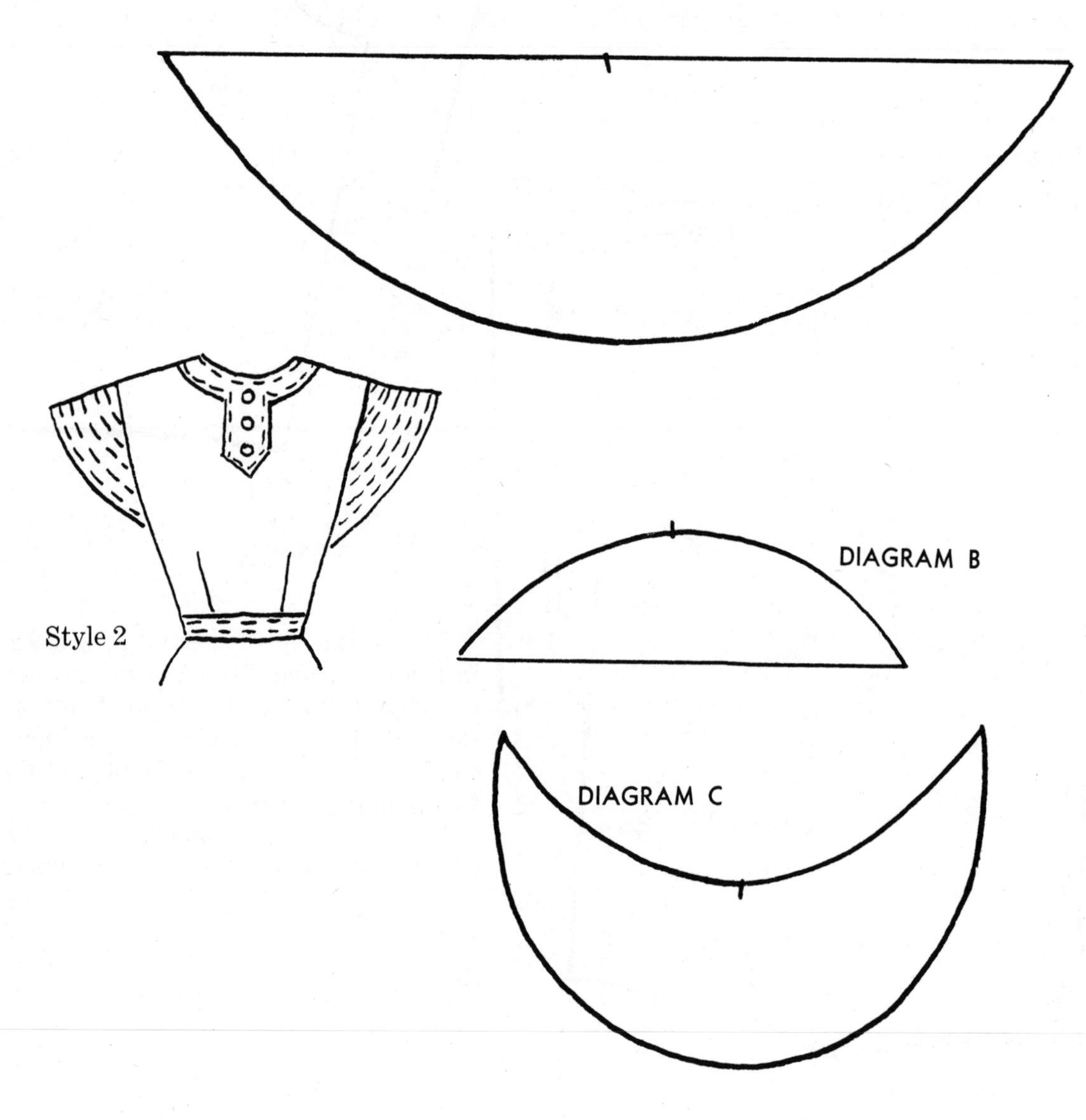

Cape Sleeve Style

1. Extend the shoulder out 12 inches.
2. Use the right angle to start the curving line. Connect the shoulder to a point 1 inch below the armscye at the side seam.
3. Fold the pattern on the long, broken line indicated on the diagrams. While it is folded, trace the armscye with your tracing wheel. The lower part of this cape sleeve is sewn into the armscye like any other sleeve.
4. Seam allowance has to be added to both the bodice pieces and the cape sections.

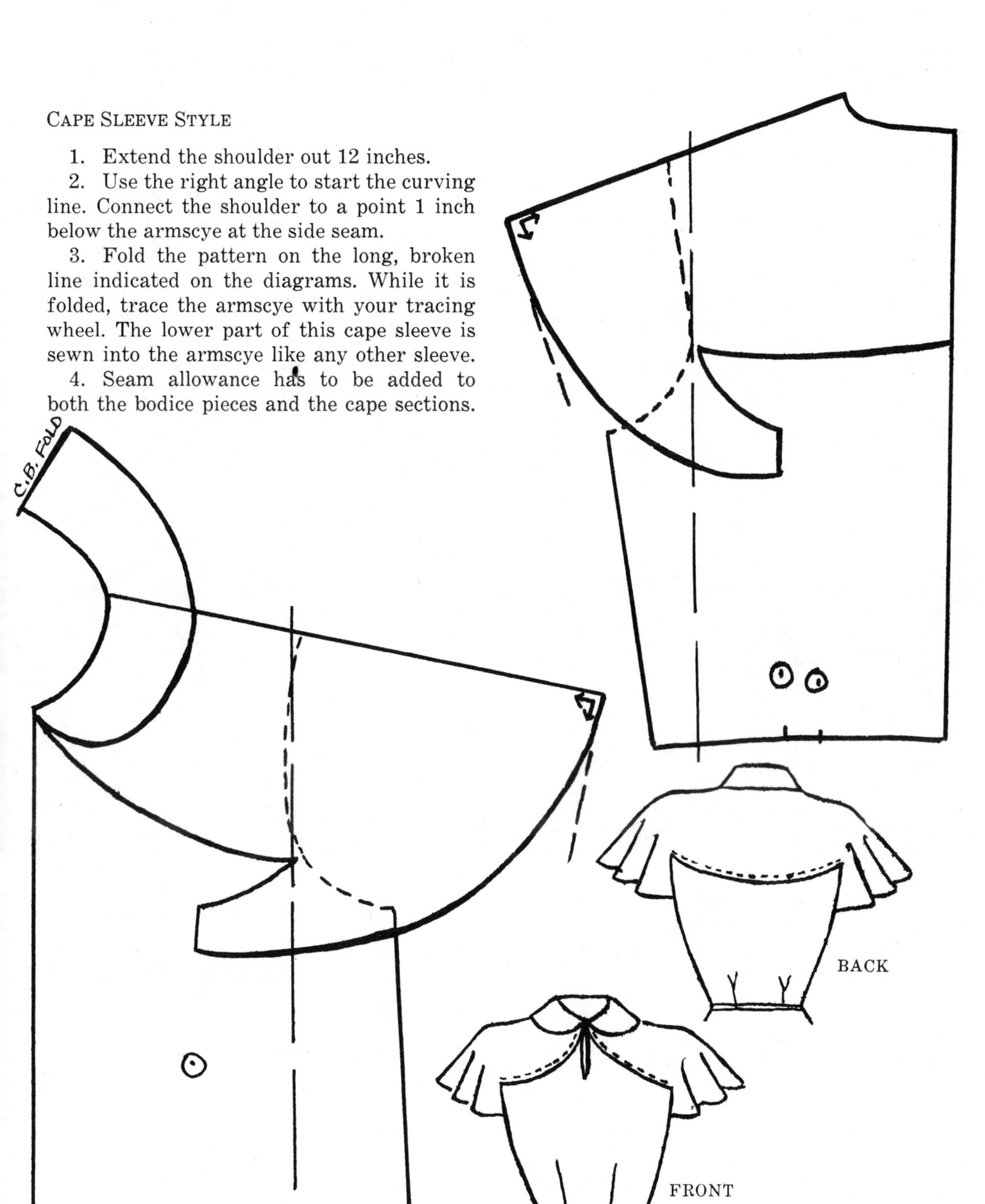

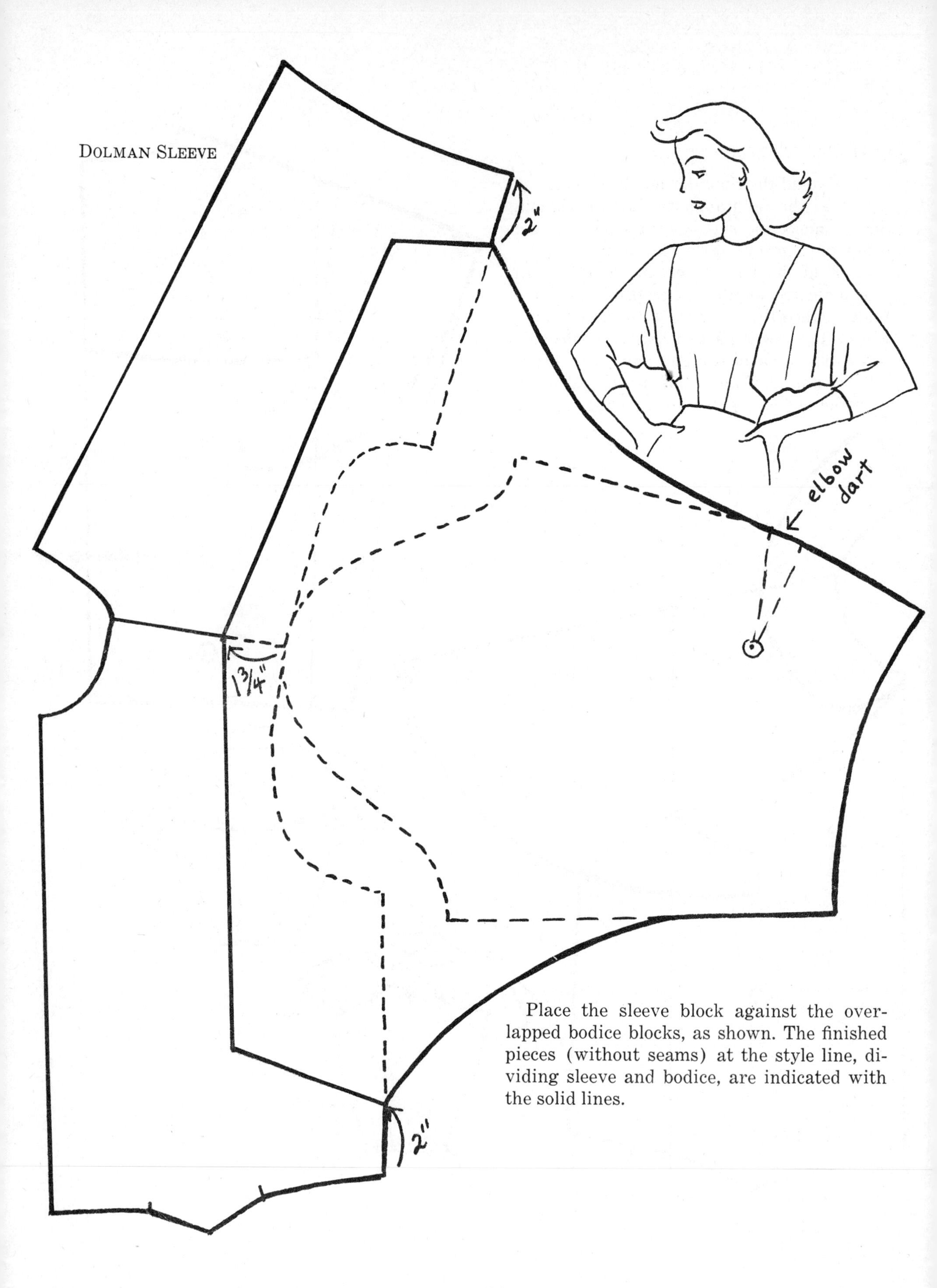

Place the sleeve block against the overlapped bodice blocks, as shown. The finished pieces (without seams) at the style line, dividing sleeve and bodice, are indicated with the solid lines.

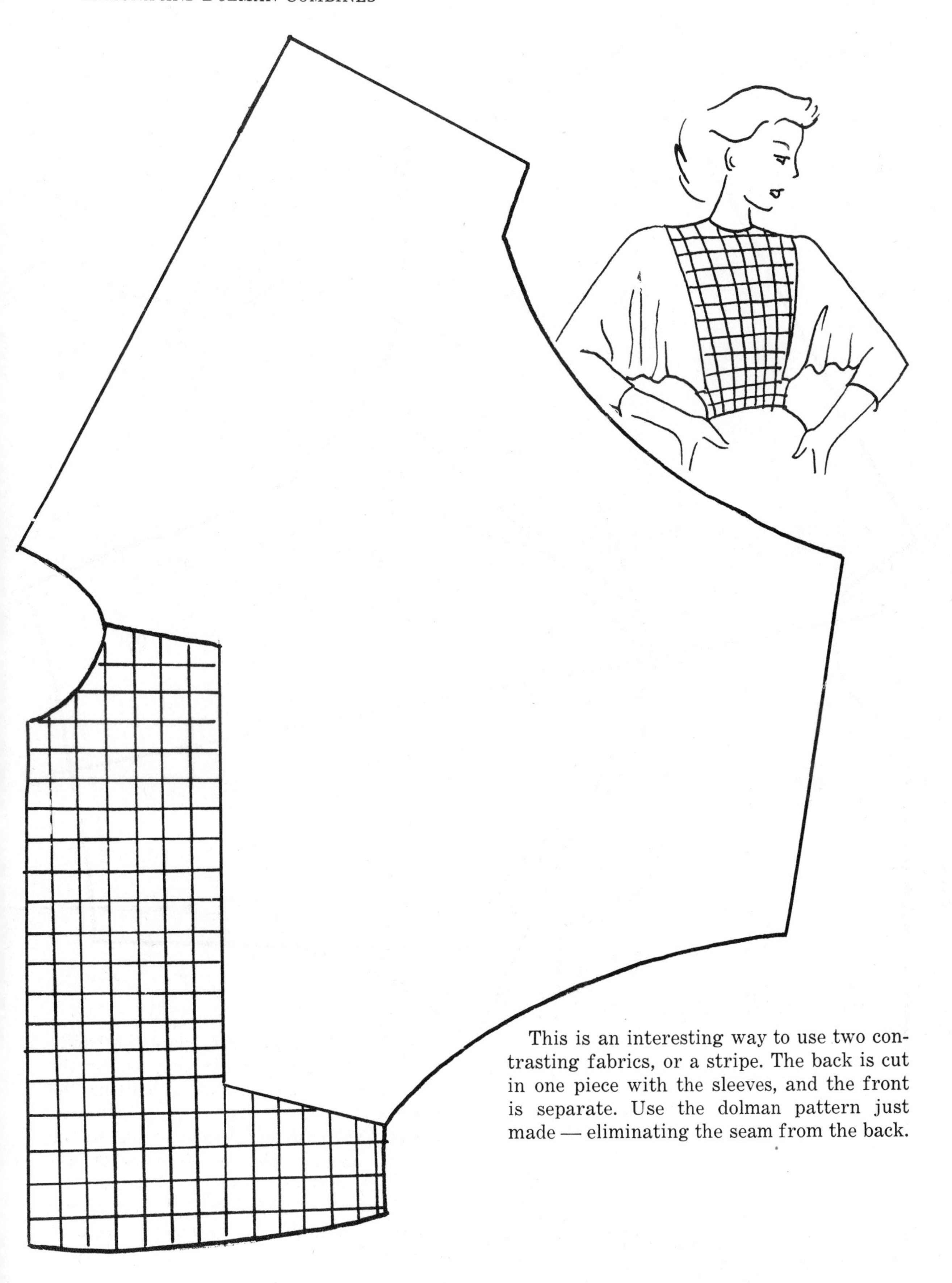

This is an interesting way to use two contrasting fabrics, or a stripe. The back is cut in one piece with the sleeves, and the front is separate. Use the dolman pattern just made — eliminating the seam from the back.

Bat-Wing Sleeve

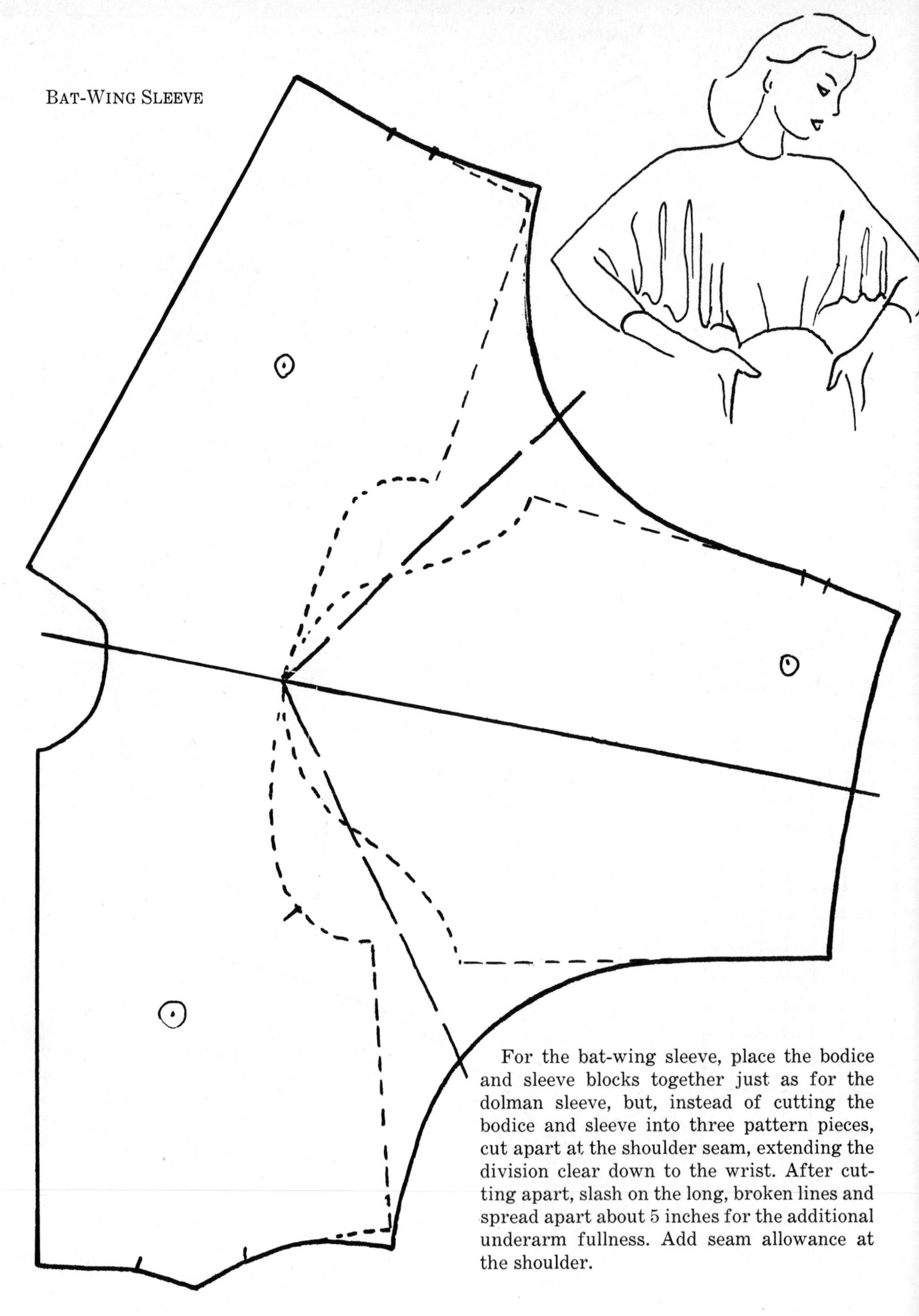

For the bat-wing sleeve, place the bodice and sleeve blocks together just as for the dolman sleeve, but, instead of cutting the bodice and sleeve into three pattern pieces, cut apart at the shoulder seam, extending the division clear down to the wrist. After cutting apart, slash on the long, broken lines and spread apart about 5 inches for the additional underarm fullness. Add seam allowance at the shoulder.

BURNOOSE SLEEVE

This sleeve style is made just the same as the extended shoulder bodice except that here you must slash the underarm and spread for as much fullness as you wish.

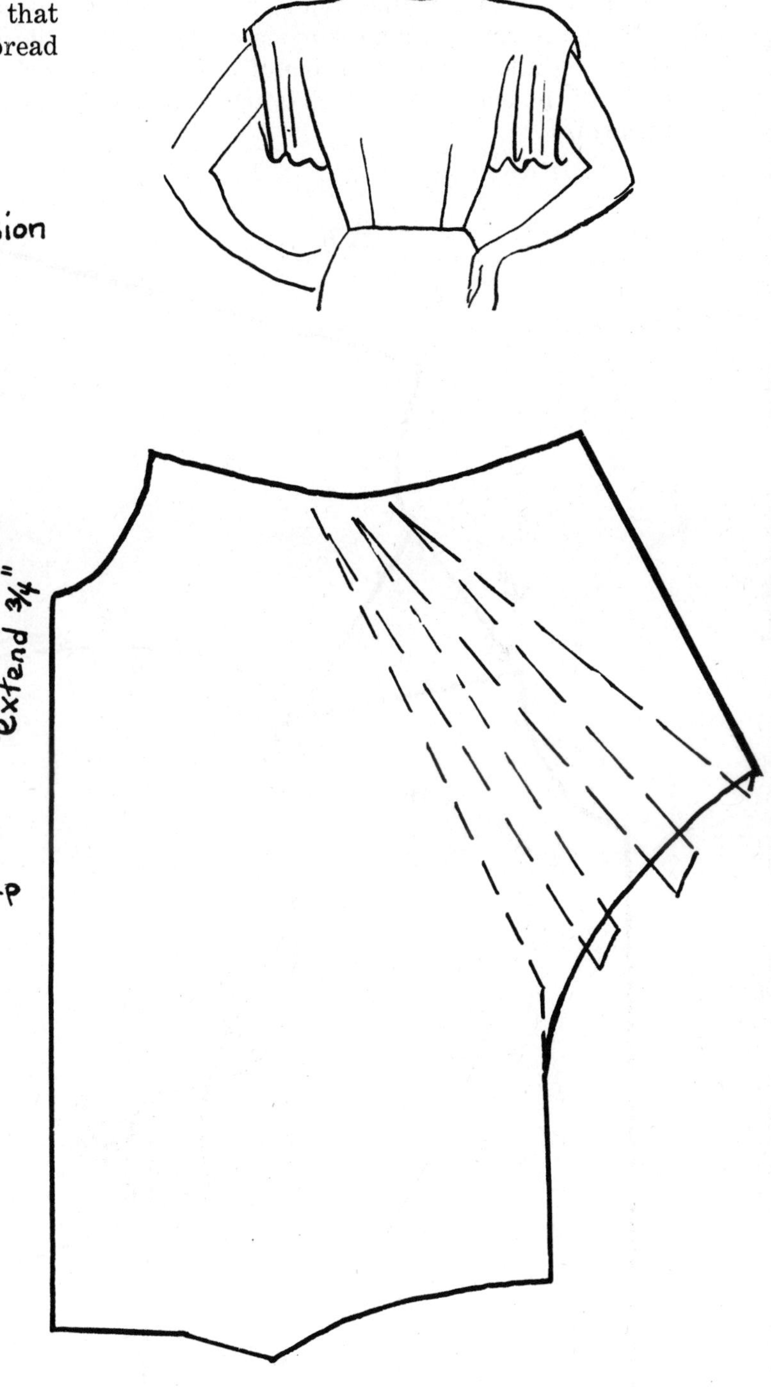

GUSSET SLEEVE

This is a particularly nice sleeve to use when a rounded, seamless shoulder is desired. It fits more snugly than a kimona or dolman sleeve yet allows more freedom of action because of the bias gusset which is set-in under the arm.

Place the blocks together as shown, with a 4-inch spread at the neckline. Lap the sleeve block over as it is on the diagram and trace off your pattern. The gusset pattern is shown next.

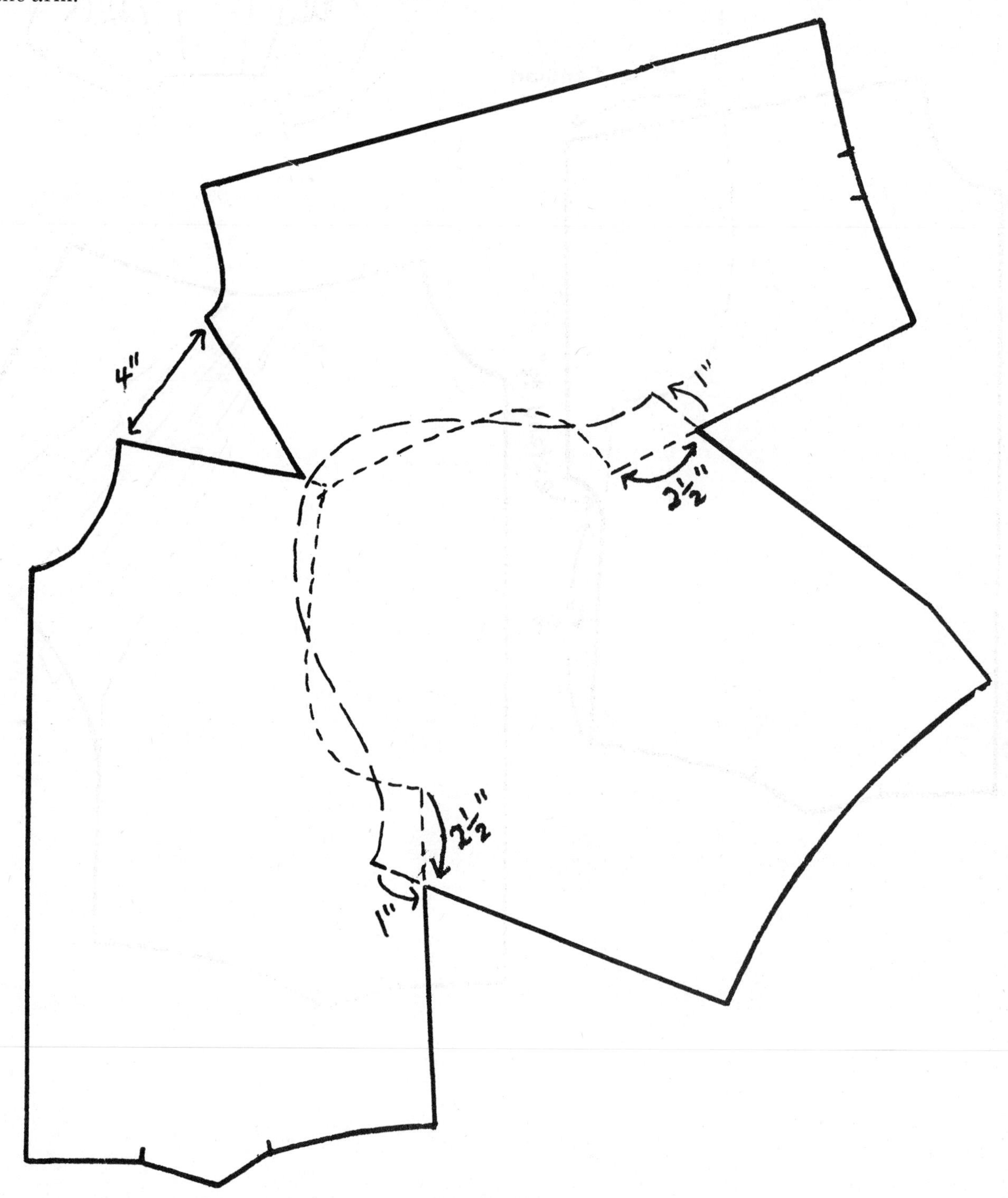

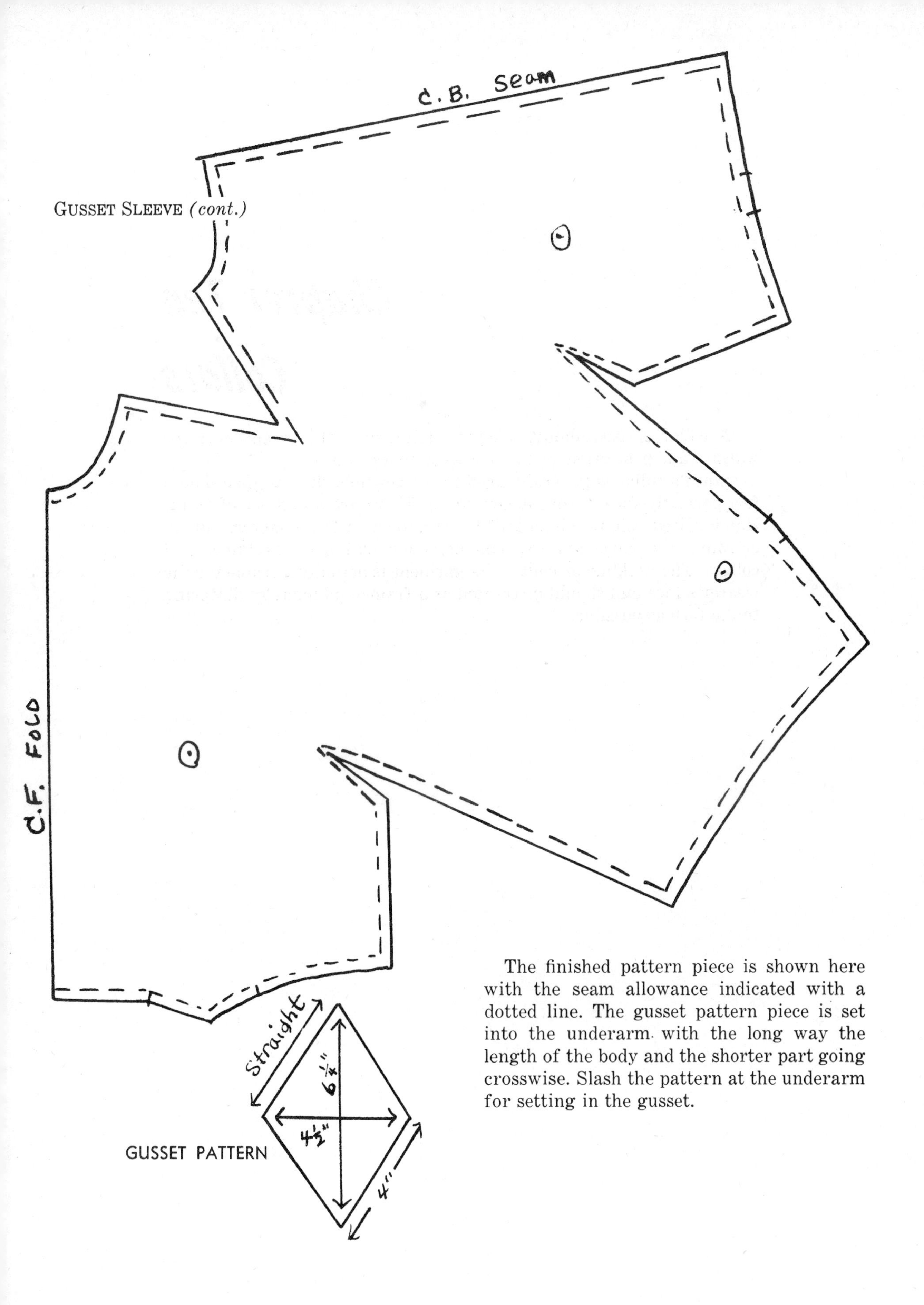

The finished pattern piece is shown here with the seam allowance indicated with a dotted line. The gusset pattern piece is set into the underarm with the long way the length of the body and the shorter part going crosswise. Slash the pattern at the underarm for setting in the gusset.

Chapter Ten
Collars

A collar is used almost solely as decoration; the exception is for warmth and protection, as in the case of coat collars.

Since a collar is generally used for decoration, the designer should feel perfectly free to invent new ideas. There are a number of fairly standardized collars which will be explained in this chapter, but, in creating new garments, experiment freely with your necklines and collars. The neckline or collar of a garment is actually a frame for the wearer's face and should be treated as a frame and made as flattering to the face as possible.

PETER PAN COLLAR

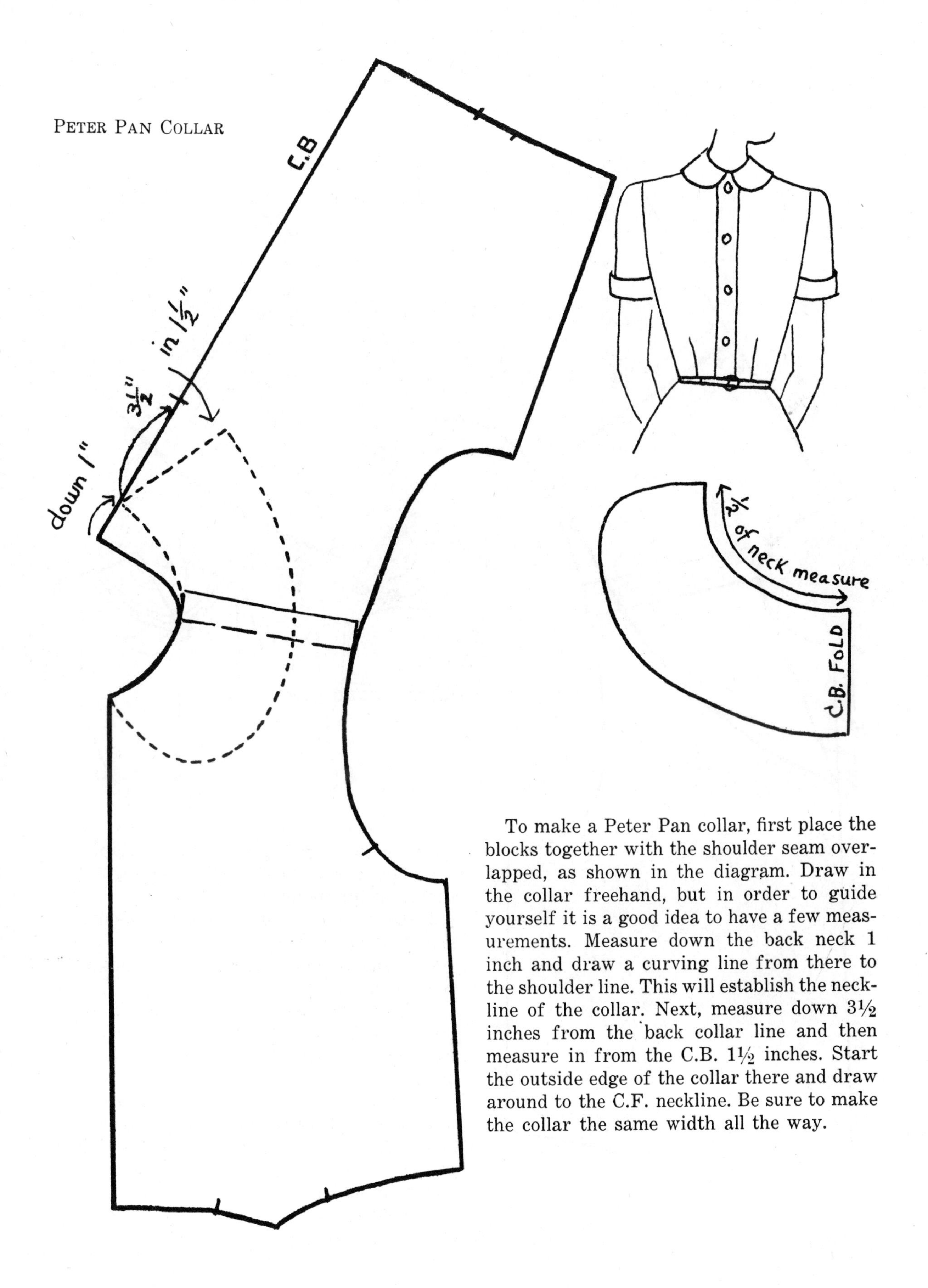

To make a Peter Pan collar, first place the blocks together with the shoulder seam overlapped, as shown in the diagram. Draw in the collar freehand, but in order to guide yourself it is a good idea to have a few measurements. Measure down the back neck 1 inch and draw a curving line from there to the shoulder line. This will establish the neckline of the collar. Next, measure down 3½ inches from the back collar line and then measure in from the C.B. 1½ inches. Start the outside edge of the collar there and draw around to the C.F. neckline. Be sure to make the collar the same width all the way.

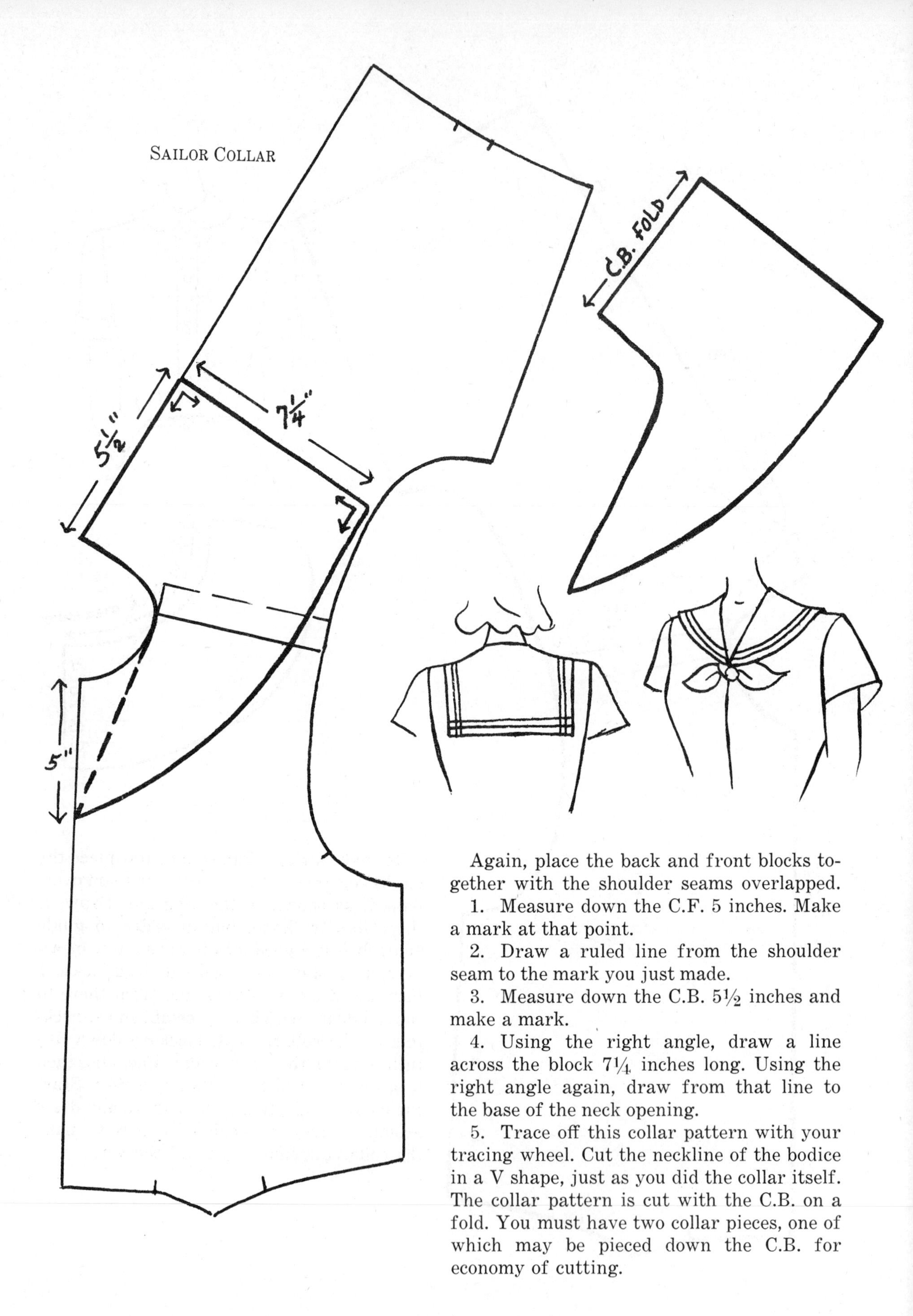

Again, place the back and front blocks together with the shoulder seams overlapped.

1. Measure down the C.F. 5 inches. Make a mark at that point.
2. Draw a ruled line from the shoulder seam to the mark you just made.
3. Measure down the C.B. 5½ inches and make a mark.
4. Using the right angle, draw a line across the block 7¼ inches long. Using the right angle again, draw from that line to the base of the neck opening.
5. Trace off this collar pattern with your tracing wheel. Cut the neckline of the bodice in a V shape, just as you did the collar itself. The collar pattern is cut with the C.B. on a fold. You must have two collar pieces, one of which may be pieced down the C.B. for economy of cutting.

High Standing Collar

This neckline is extremely simple to cut, yet is a flattering style to most people. Draw in the neckline freehand, using the measurements given in the diagrams as a guide. Do not fail to raise the shoulder as indicated or the collar will draw, in an unpleasing manner. The dotted lines indicate the shape of the facing pieces.

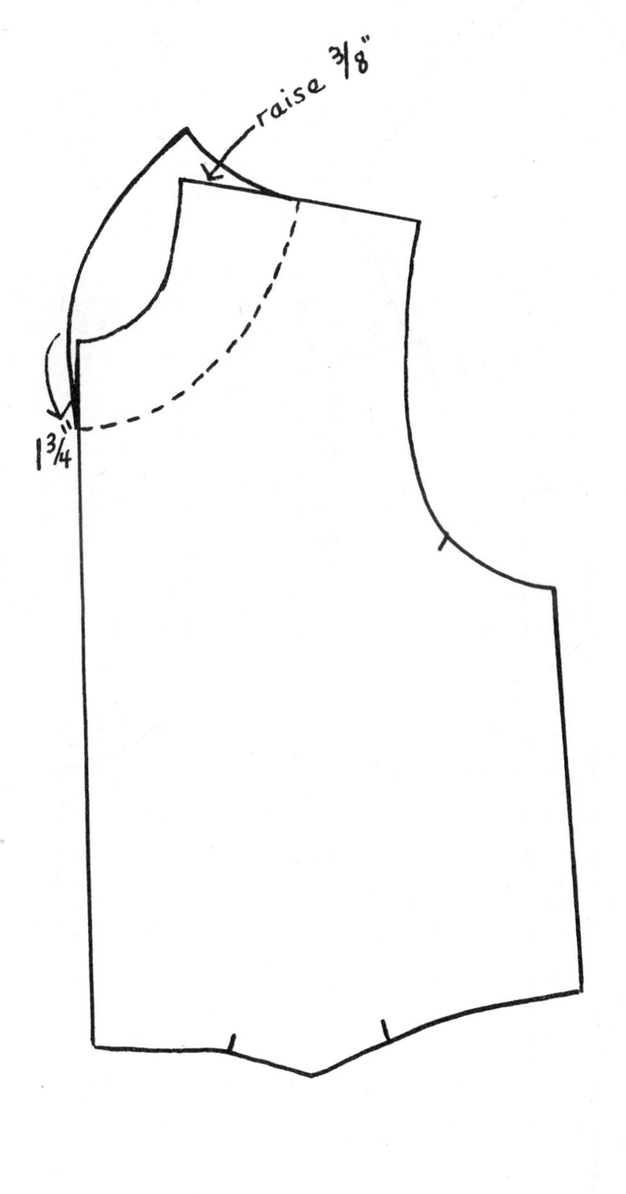

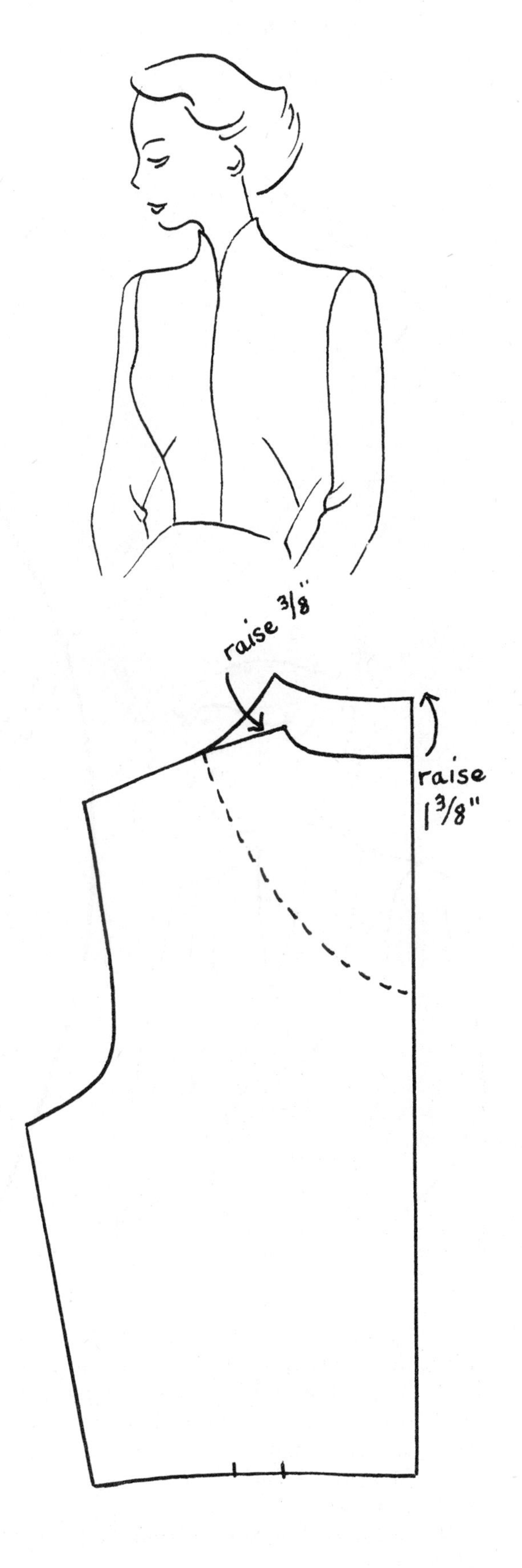

Shawl Collar

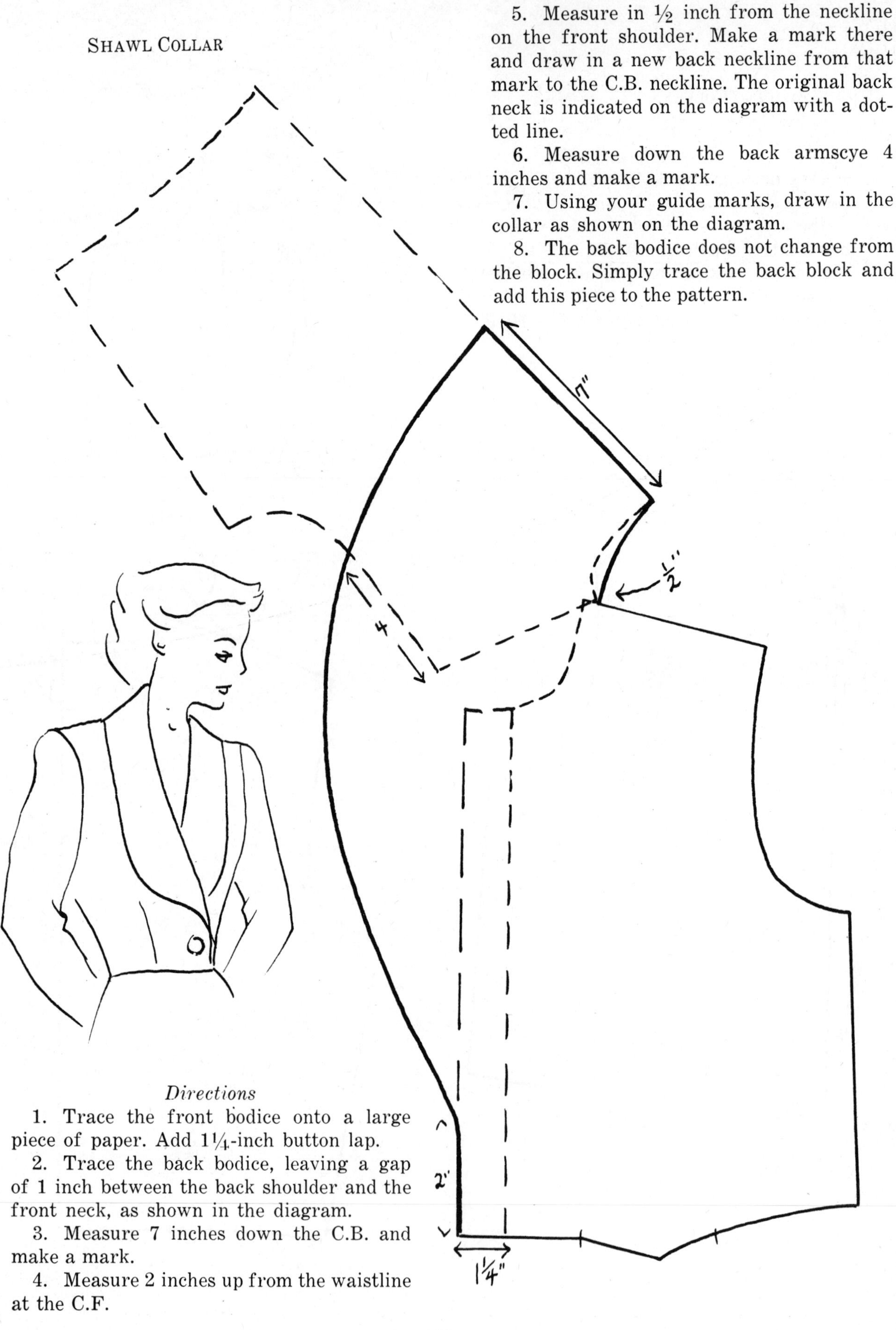

Directions

1. Trace the front bodice onto a large piece of paper. Add 1¼-inch button lap.
2. Trace the back bodice, leaving a gap of 1 inch between the back shoulder and the front neck, as shown in the diagram.
3. Measure 7 inches down the C.B. and make a mark.
4. Measure 2 inches up from the waistline at the C.F.
5. Measure in ½ inch from the neckline on the front shoulder. Make a mark there and draw in a new back neckline from that mark to the C.B. neckline. The original back neck is indicated on the diagram with a dotted line.
6. Measure down the back armscye 4 inches and make a mark.
7. Using your guide marks, draw in the collar as shown on the diagram.
8. The back bodice does not change from the block. Simply trace the back block and add this piece to the pattern.

Shawl Collar *(cont.)*

These diagrams are of the finished pattern pieces for the shawl collar bodice. Diagram A shows the collar facing. The outline of this piece is shown with a solid line. The dotted lines indicate the front bodice.

Diagram B shows the finished pattern for the bodice front.

Diagram C shows the under-collar pattern.

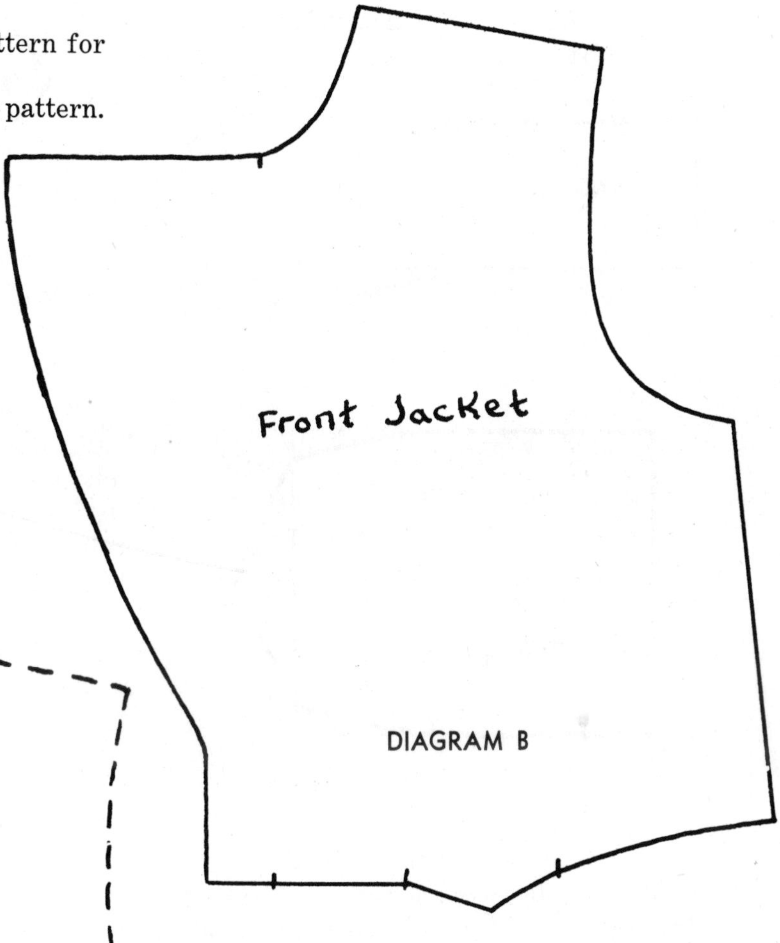

Front Jacket

DIAGRAM B

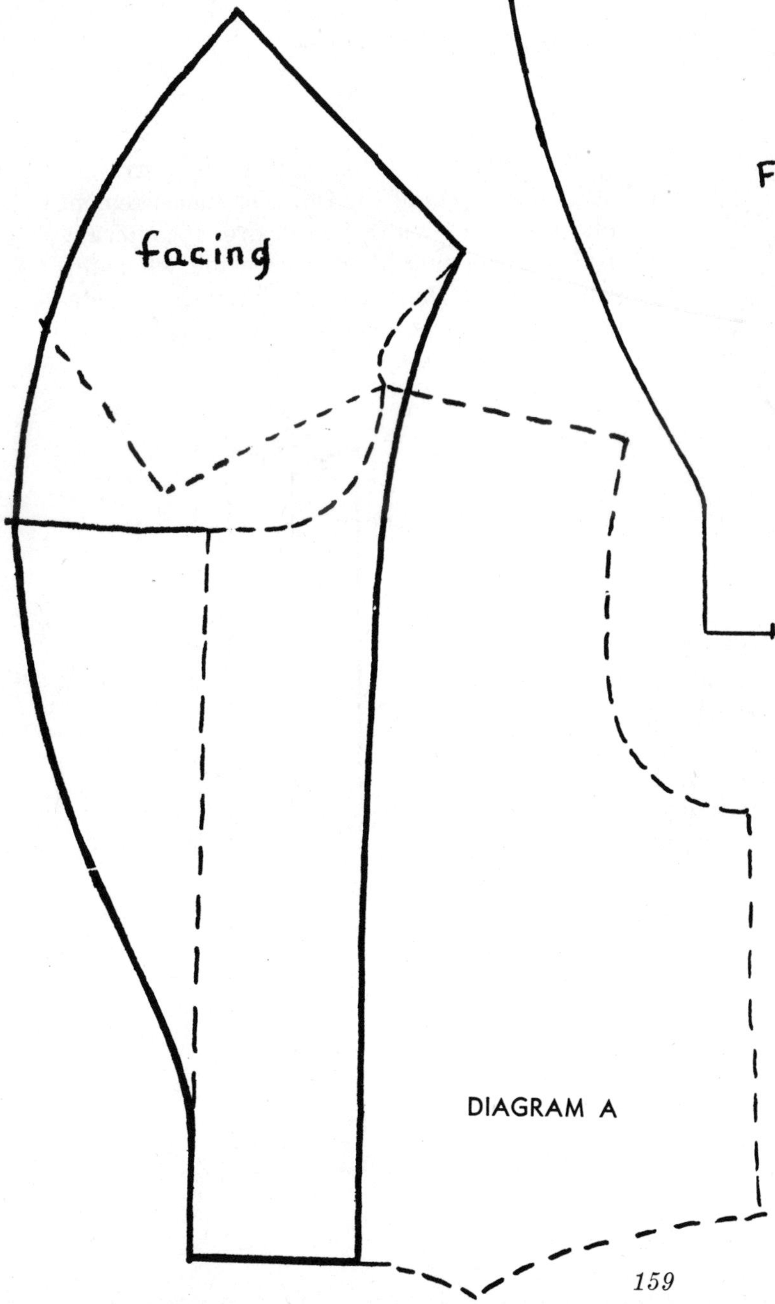

facing

DIAGRAM A

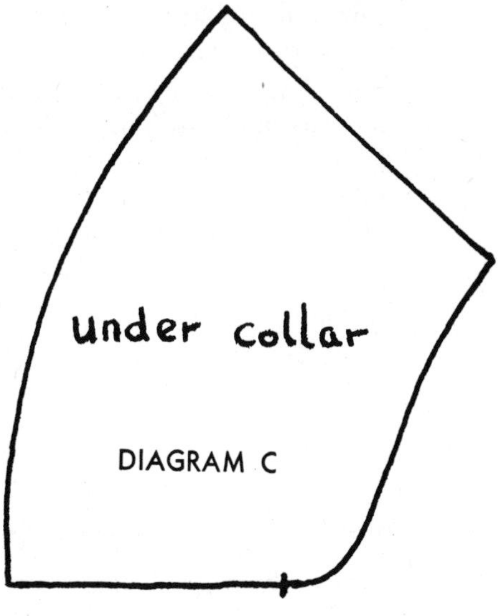

under collar

DIAGRAM C

SHIRT COLLARS

Diagram A shows a shirt collar with deep points. This collar has to be cut into two pieces. First, make a rectangle ½ the neck measurement in length, and 3½ inches in width. Using the rectangle as a guide, draw in the shirt collar pattern.

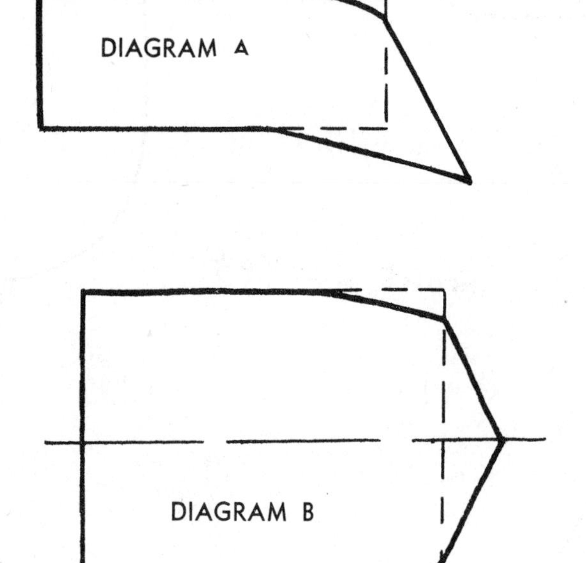

Diagram B shows a 1-piece shirt collar. This collar is not as pointed but is easier to sew, since a seam is eliminated. Start with a rectangle twice as wide as the previous one but the same length; that is, ½ the neck measurement in length, by 7 inches in width. In completing these patterns, make a seam allowance wherever they are to be sewed.

MANDARIN COLLAR

The mandarin collar pattern is a straight strip the length of the full neck measurement and whatever width you desire. It generally is a band about 1¼ inches wide when finished. Curve the edges as shown in the diagram unless you wish to have the collar perfectly straight where it opens.

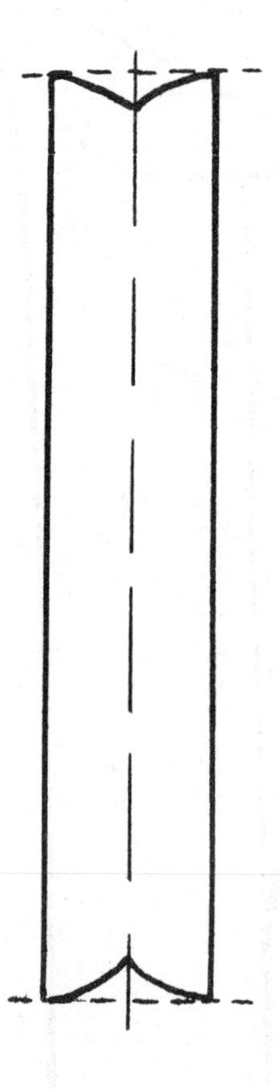

Draped Cowl Neckline

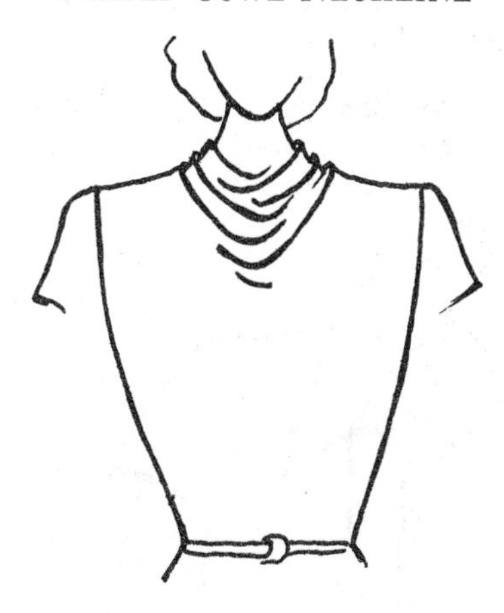

For this style, start with the shoulder dart block. Since the drape is quite full, you can eliminate the dart completely and throw the dart material into the cowl drape. The bodice must be cut on the bias as indicated by the arrows.

High Cowl Neckline

For the high cowl, add height to the C.F. and curve the shoulder seam as shown. Both necklines are very flattering. They work out to the best advantage in soft material.

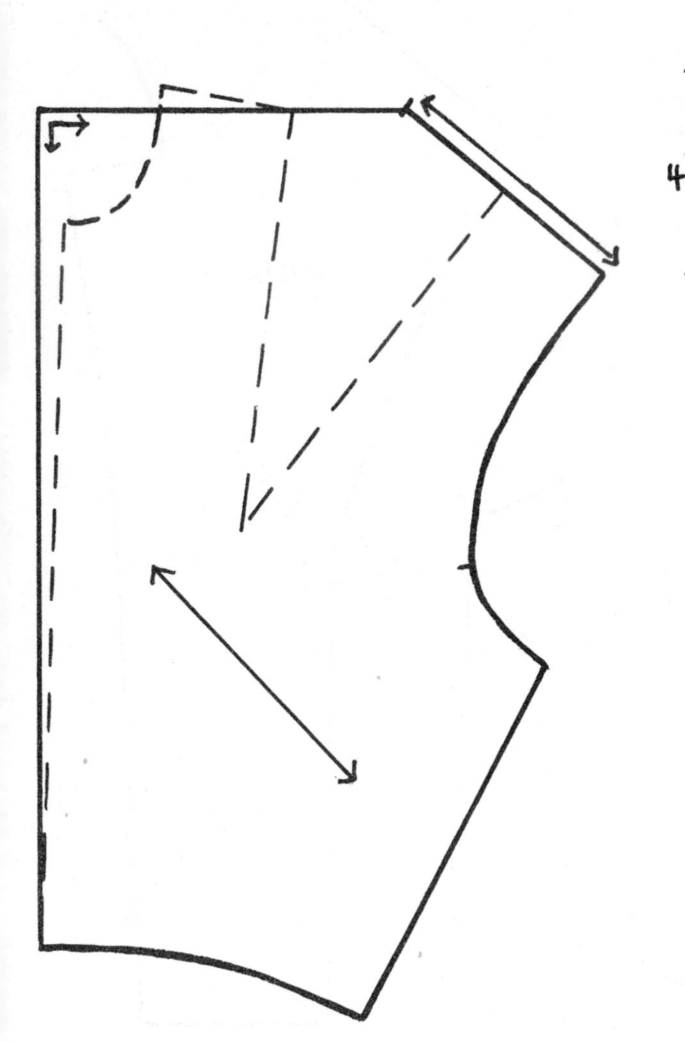

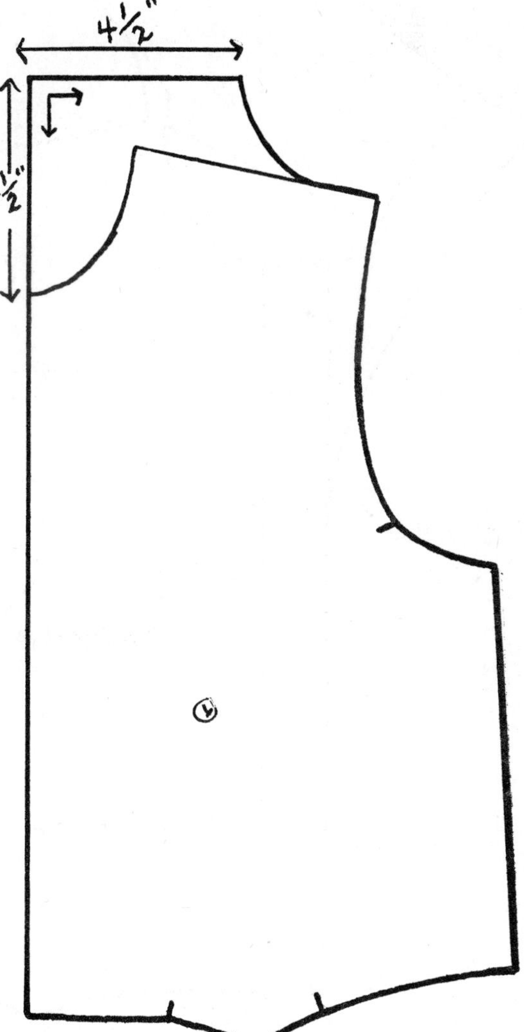

Bodice With Built-in Collar

There are many ways to vary this kind of collar. Do some experimenting with it. Be sure that the back neck is accurately measured, and that the center back of the collar is right-angled at both corners. The width and shape of the collar itself is up to you. Diagram B shows the pattern for the facing. Allow for a C.B. seam in both pieces.

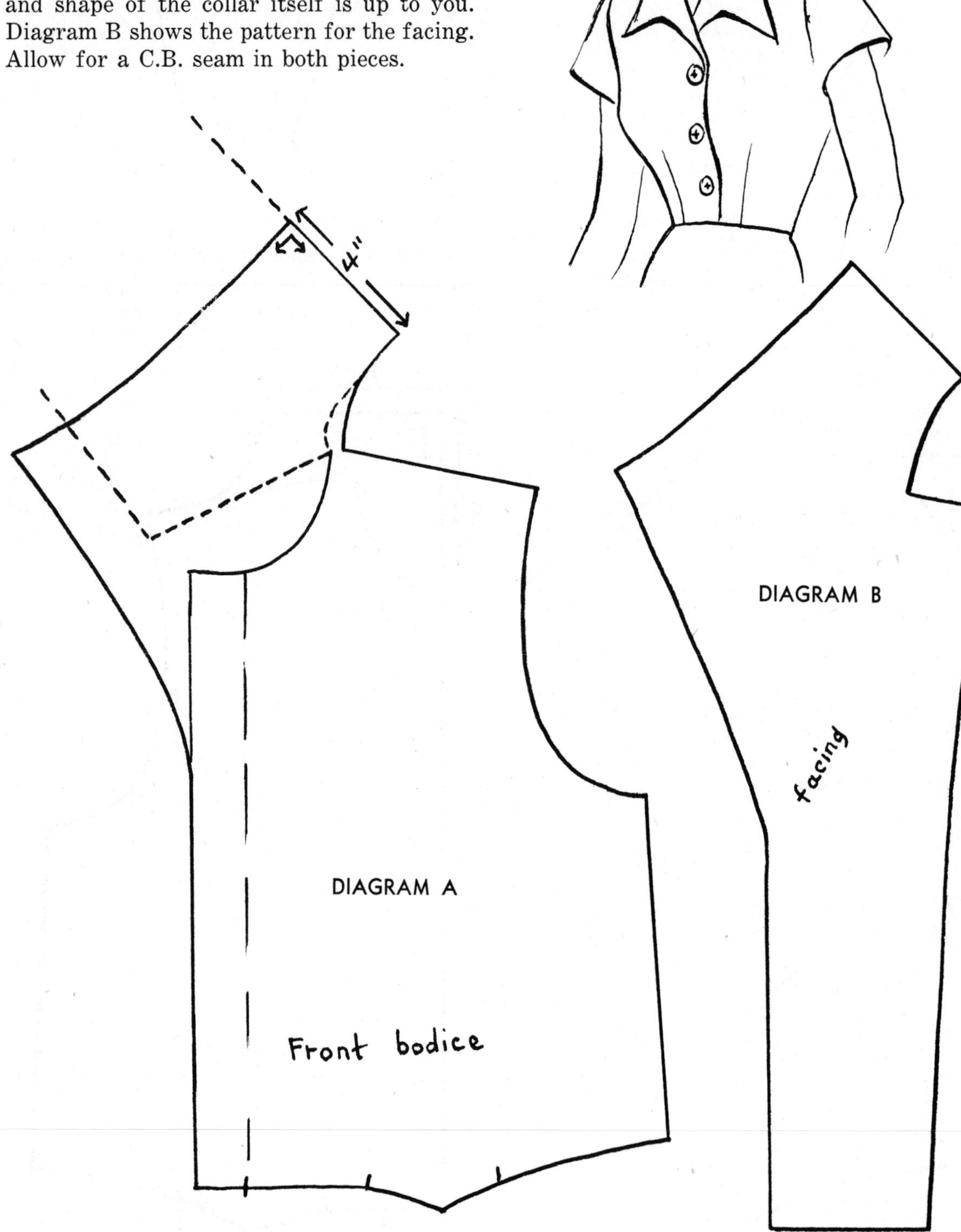

Built-in Collar Style

This built-in style is a little trickier but worth it. First, decide where you want the collar to turn over and then fold the paper on that line. Draw in the collar shape on the front bodice and trace it through to the paper underneath — the paper you folded under. Open up the folded paper. The shape should look like that in Diagram B.

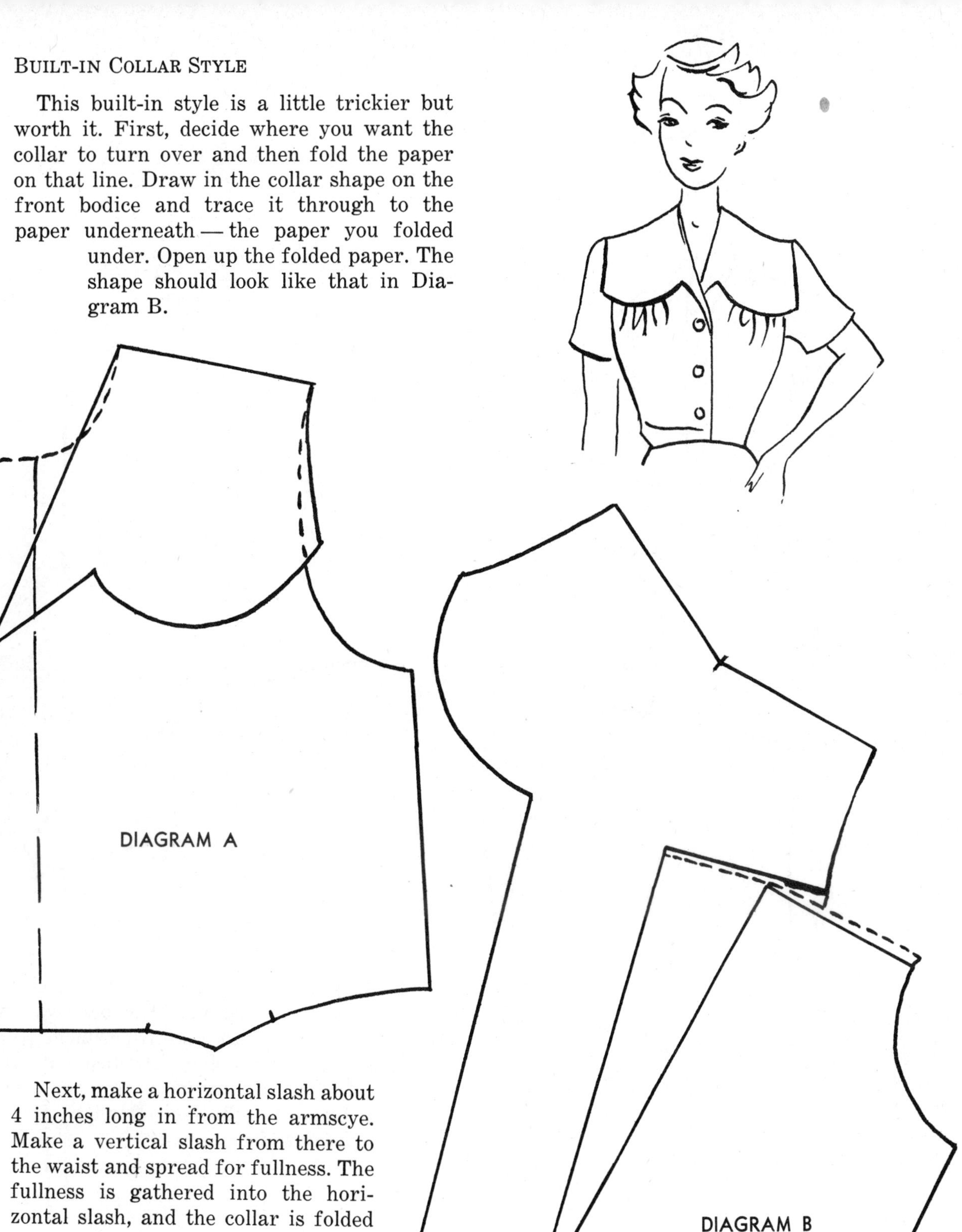

Next, make a horizontal slash about 4 inches long in from the armscye. Make a vertical slash from there to the waist and spread for fullness. The fullness is gathered into the horizontal slash, and the collar is folded over on the right side of the garment and sewed into the armscye.

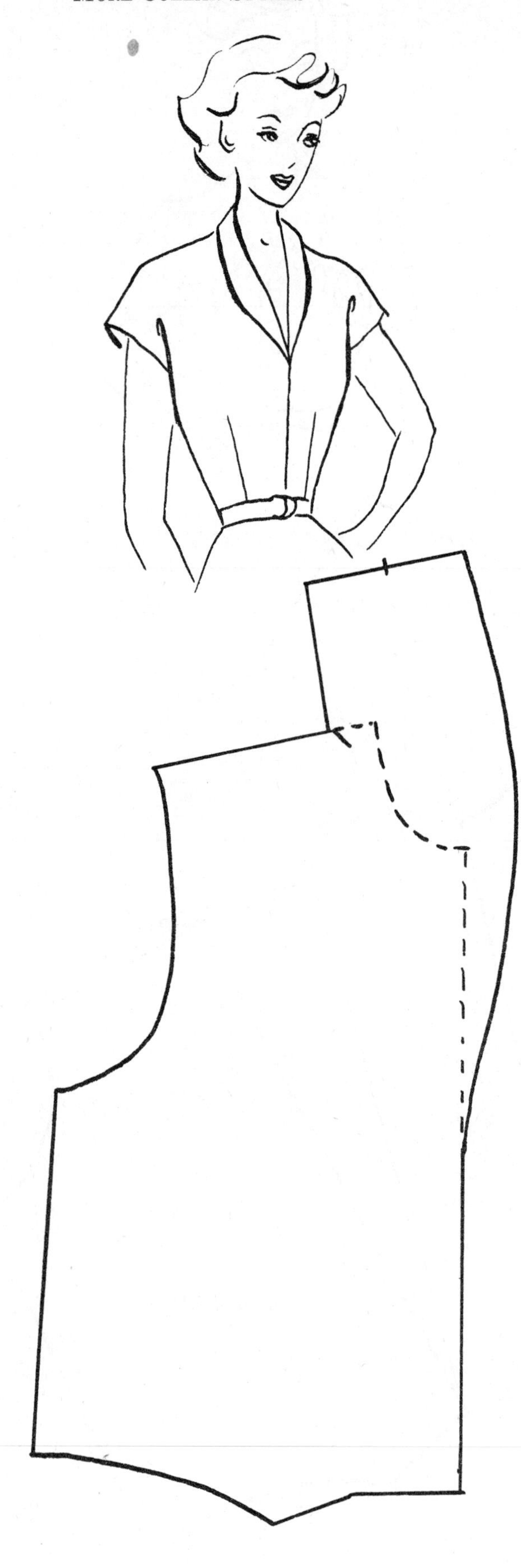

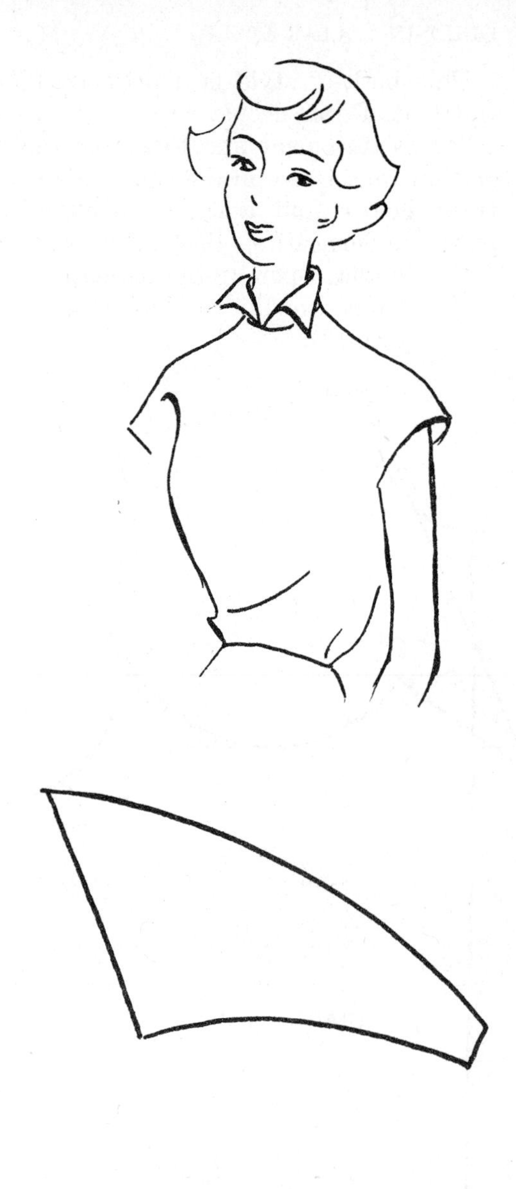

By now you can probably cut any collar which you have in mind. The best way to find out about collars is to experiment with them. There are no hard-and-fast rules to go by. The main objective is to make a becoming frame for the face. Don't be afraid to try out your ideas.

Chapter Eleven

Coats and suits

Coats and suit jackets are nearly always worn over some other garment, and for this reason they must be cut slightly larger than a dress or blouse. If both the undergarment and the overgarment were to be cut the same size in the shoulders and armscyes and worn one on top of the other, the wearer would be constricted and uncomfortable. Too, these garments are usually padded to some extent in the shoulders and room for the padding must be added to the pattern. Hence, there has to be a change in the basic blocks for coats and suits.

In making a fitted coat, you also have to consider the waist bulk of the undergarment. The coat, therefore, will not be made as small in the waist or hips as a dress of the same size. If you keep the word *comfort* in mind in making coats and suits, you should not experience any difficulty in fitting them properly.

Tailoring is an art in itself, and since this book is not intended as a sewing guide, neither sewing nor tailoring will be taken up here. However, it is suggested that, in addition to studying a good book on sewing and tailoring, the student who wishes to understand tailored garments thoroughly should rip apart an old, well-tailored garment, study it carefully, and then copy it. In doing this, it is wise to cut the garment in half up the center back, keep one half intact, and rip apart the other half. This way, you will be able to check from the part which you left whole at some stage when you may have forgotten a step in the procedure.

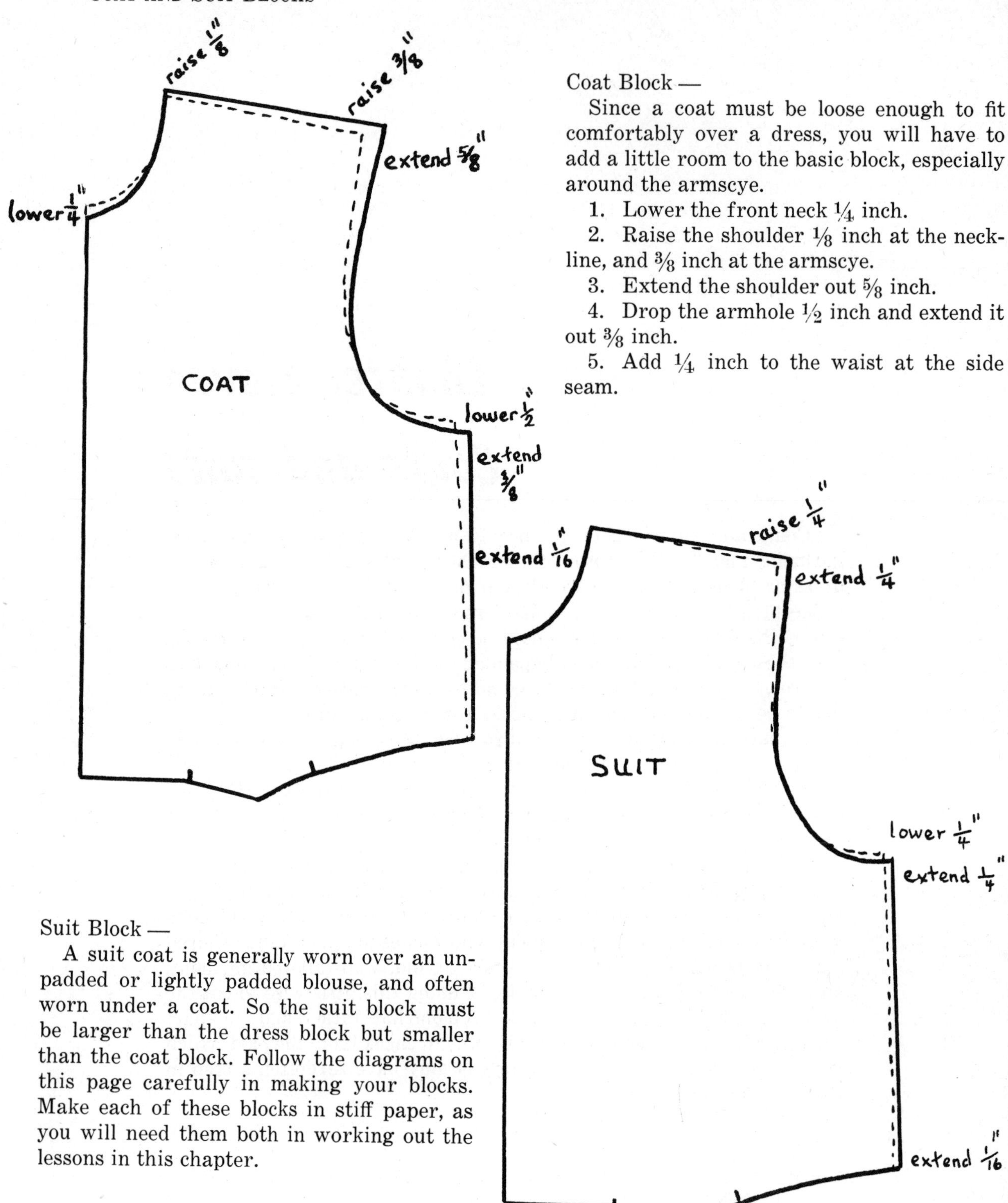

Coat Block —

Since a coat must be loose enough to fit comfortably over a dress, you will have to add a little room to the basic block, especially around the armscye.

1. Lower the front neck 1/4 inch.
2. Raise the shoulder 1/8 inch at the neckline, and 3/8 inch at the armscye.
3. Extend the shoulder out 5/8 inch.
4. Drop the armhole 1/2 inch and extend it out 3/8 inch.
5. Add 1/4 inch to the waist at the side seam.

Suit Block —

A suit coat is generally worn over an unpadded or lightly padded blouse, and often worn under a coat. So the suit block must be larger than the dress block but smaller than the coat block. Follow the diagrams on this page carefully in making your blocks. Make each of these blocks in stiff paper, as you will need them both in working out the lessons in this chapter.

Fitted Coat or Suit Foundation

Determine whether it is to be a coat or a suit and use the correct block. Make your pattern exactly as you did the princess bodice in Chapter One, but add the hip section to the bodice.

If you have not made the back block, do it now, with the same changes as in the front blocks.

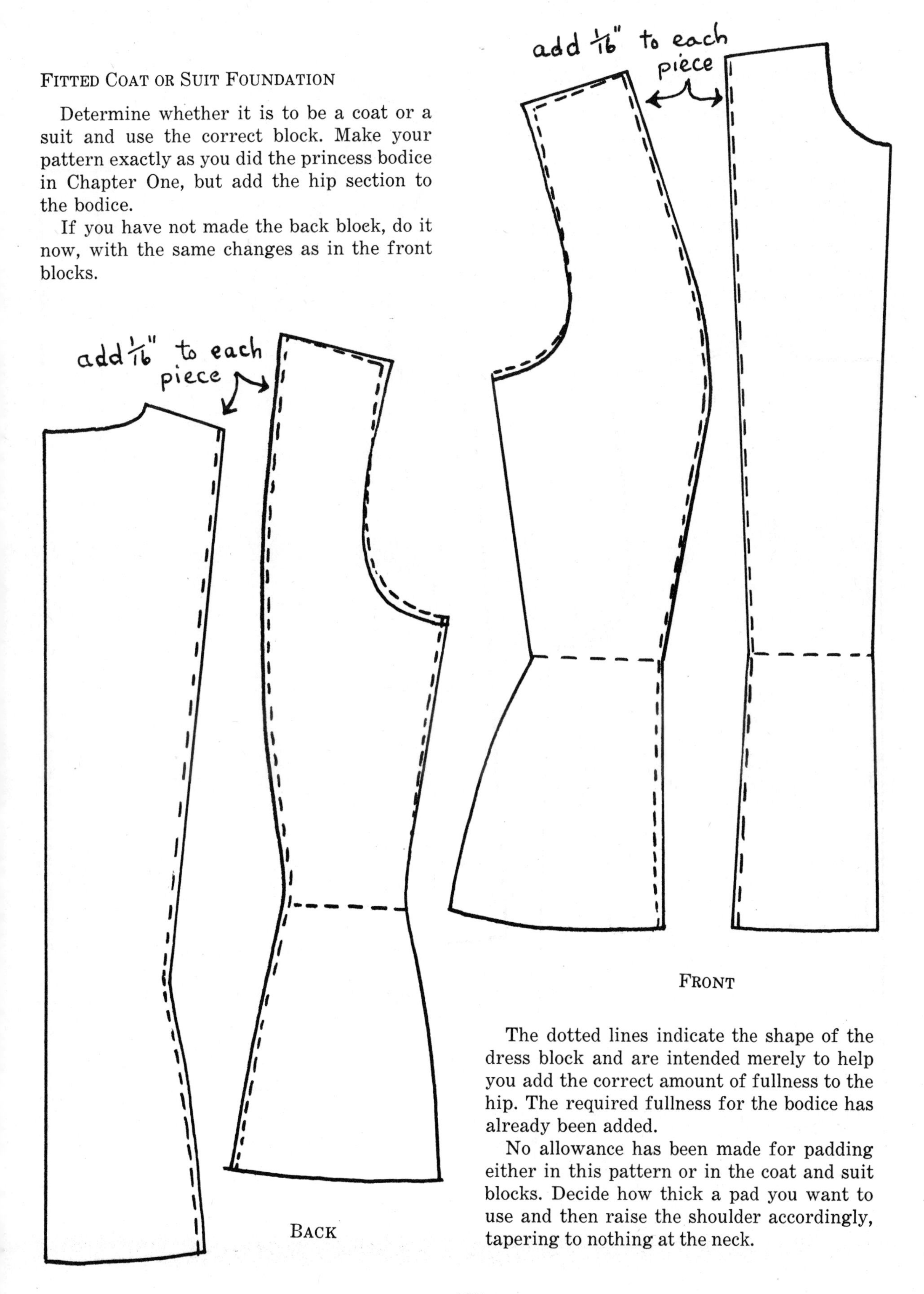

Back

Front

The dotted lines indicate the shape of the dress block and are intended merely to help you add the correct amount of fullness to the hip. The required fullness for the bodice has already been added.

No allowance has been made for padding either in this pattern or in the coat and suit blocks. Decide how thick a pad you want to use and then raise the shoulder accordingly, tapering to nothing at the neck.

SWAGGER COAT OR JACKET FOUNDATION

A swagger coat or jacket should be made with a shoulder dart, so begin this pattern by swinging the waist dart to the shoulder in your coat block.

Add a button lap of 1¼ inches; this is wider than the button lap on a dress, but on a coat you need a wider lap — for closing the garment securely for warmth and because most coat buttons are rather large.

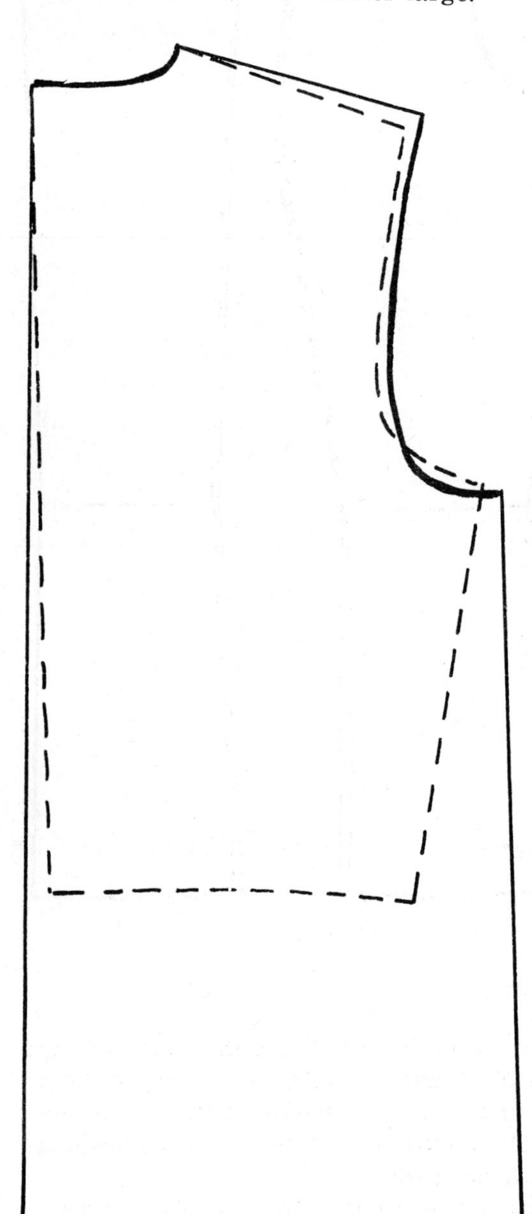

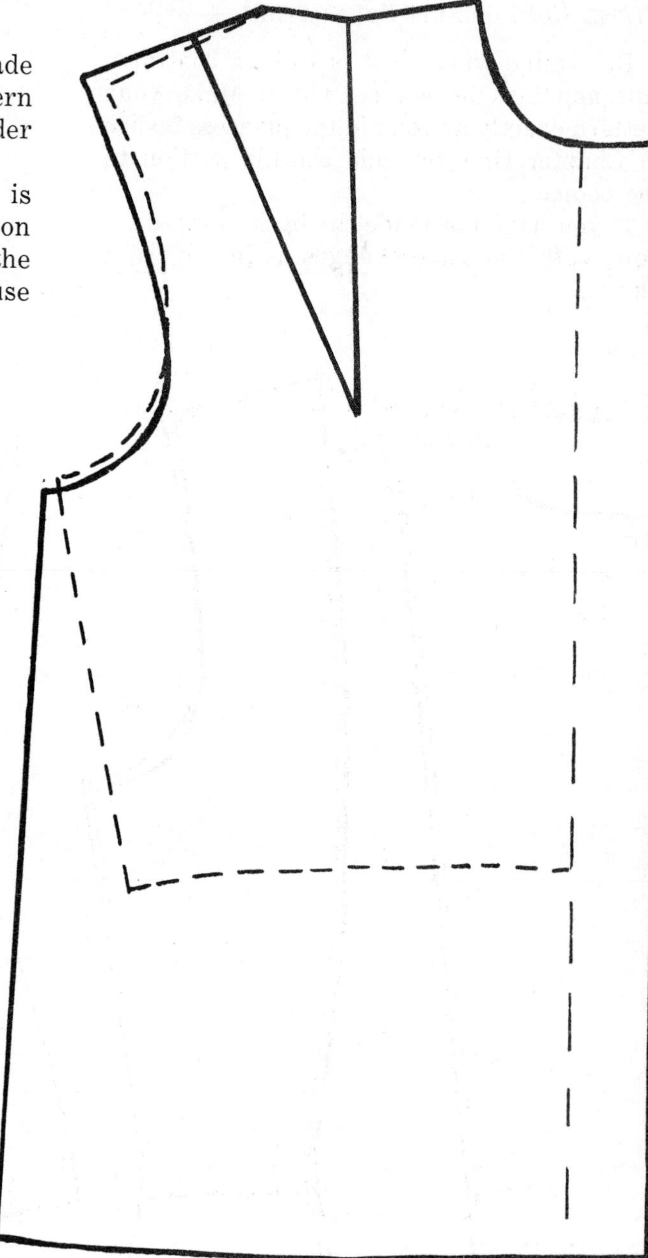

Determine the length that you want your coat or jacket and then add flare to the side seam approximately as you see it in the diagrams. In order to add more flare for a fuller coat, it is necessary to slash and spread. See Chapter Three.

Be sure that your side seams are the same length in both back and front pattern pieces.

Straight Coat With Built-in Collar

First, swing half the shoulder dart to the waist. Trace the skirt blocks onto the bodice as shown, as a guide in drawing in the side seam. Follow the diagrams carefully. Use the right angle wherever indicated.

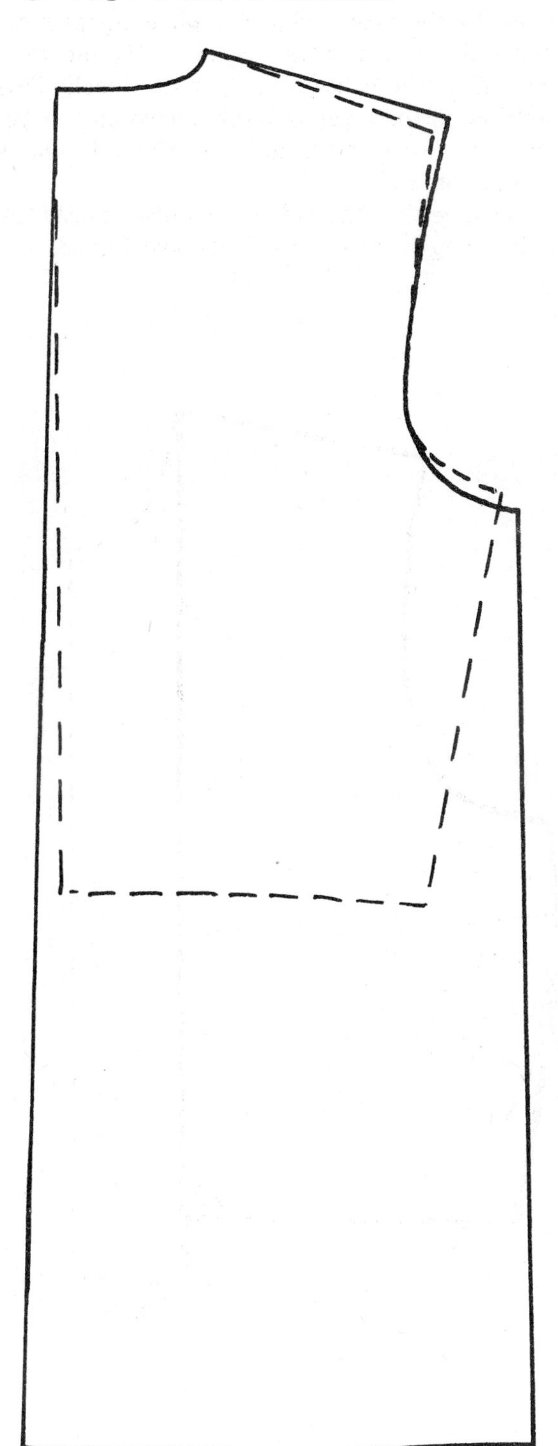

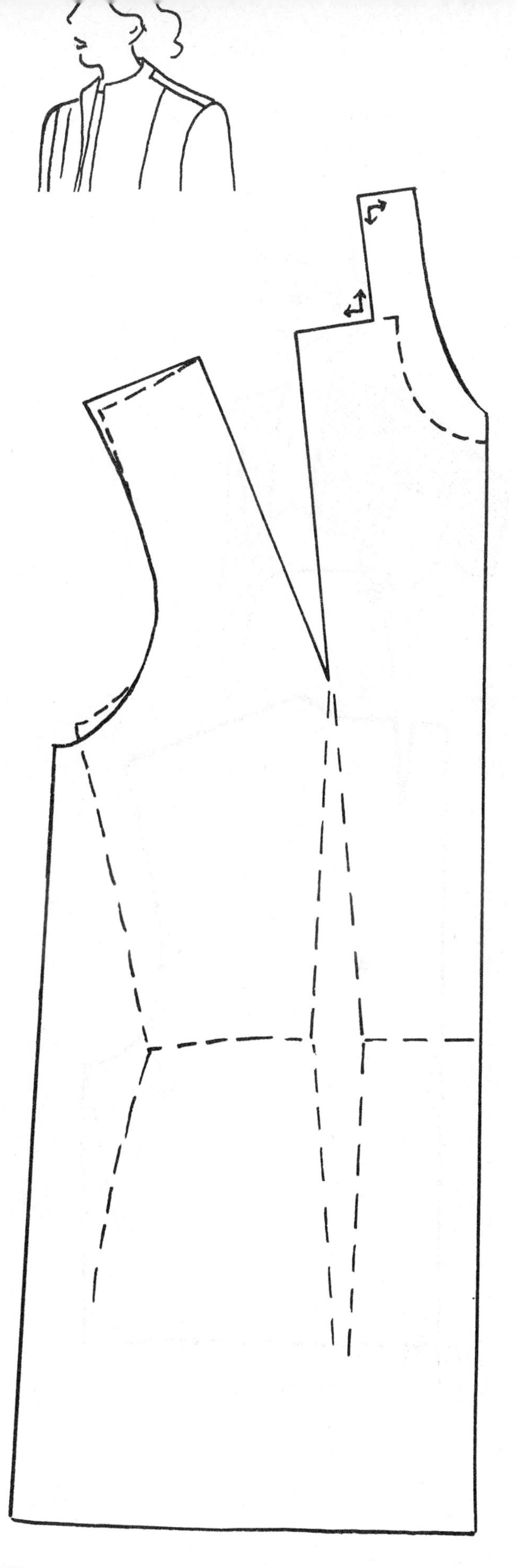

Since a bolero generally does not close in front, use a block with underarm darts rather than the waist dart block. With the waist dart block, the dart would come too close to the front edge for pleasing proportions. As shown in the diagram, 2½ inches is cut off of the center front of the block. This pattern is for a fairly boxy bolero and therefore width has been added to the side seams at the hem line.

Be sure that the side seams are exactly the same length, after the darts are folded.

BOLERO WITH BUILT-IN COLLAR

This bolero is boxy like the first one, but a built-in collar has been added. Use the under-arm darts again here, or you may use the shoulder dart. Use the suit block in working out this pattern. Be sure to right-angle as indicated.

Put the back and front bodice blocks together at the shoulder with the shoulder seams overlapped as shown in the diagram. Decide on the length of the cape and measure down the C.B. and the C.F. an equal distance. At the shoulder, add 2 inches to the measurement used for the front and back, to allow for the shoulder curve. Draw in the hemline and add the button lap.

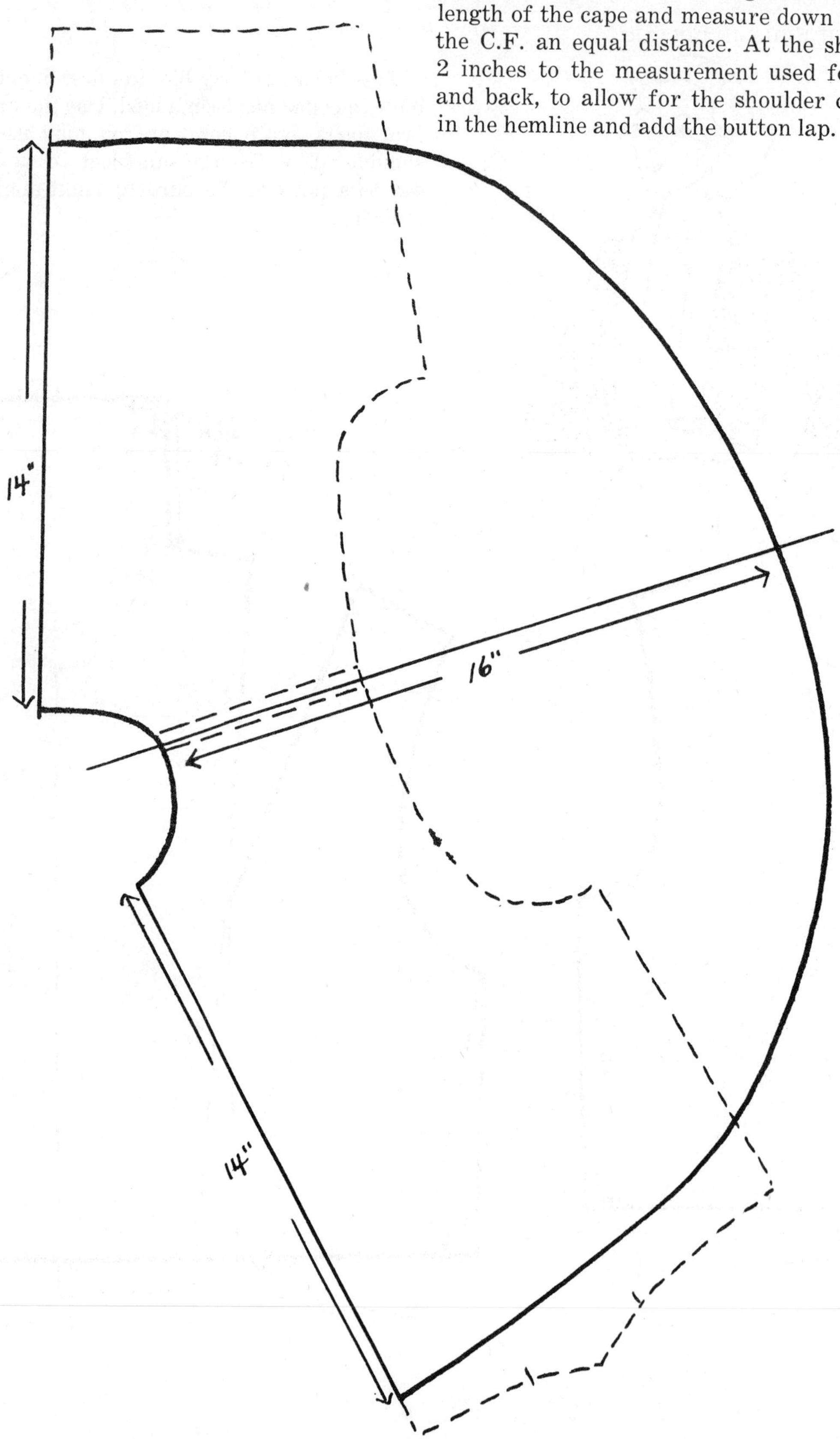

14"

16"

14"

Cape With Flared Back

To make a cape pattern with a full, flared back, take the original cape pattern which you just completed, make a tracing of it, and then slash and spread for the required amount of fullness. Plan two or three different versions and try them on in either tissue paper or muslin.

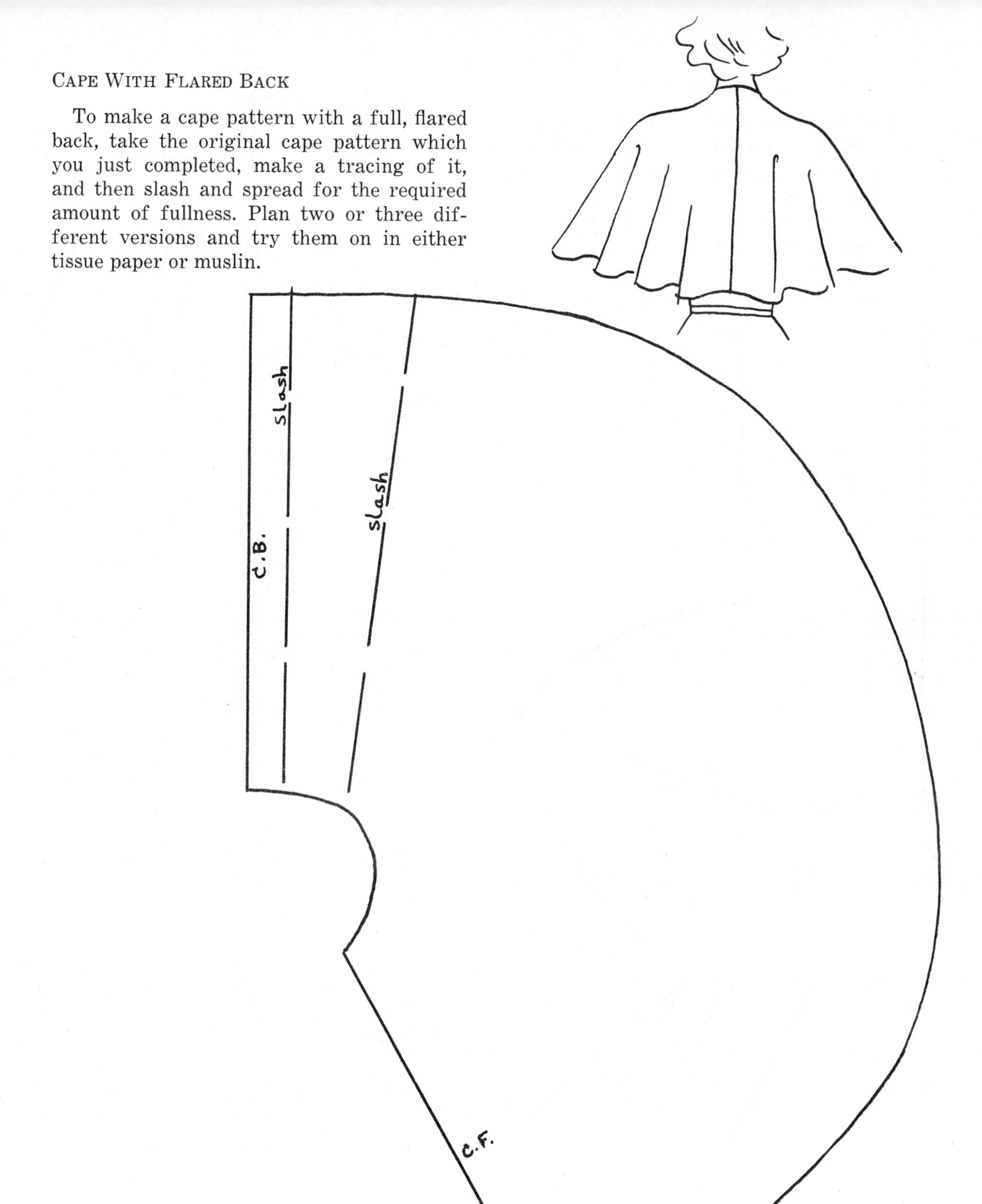

Cape With Drop Shoulder Detail

Again use your original cape pattern as a block. Make a tracing, and add style lines. Next, cut the cape apart on the style line and make a new tracing of each piece, this time adding as much flare as desired. Add seam allowance and facings.

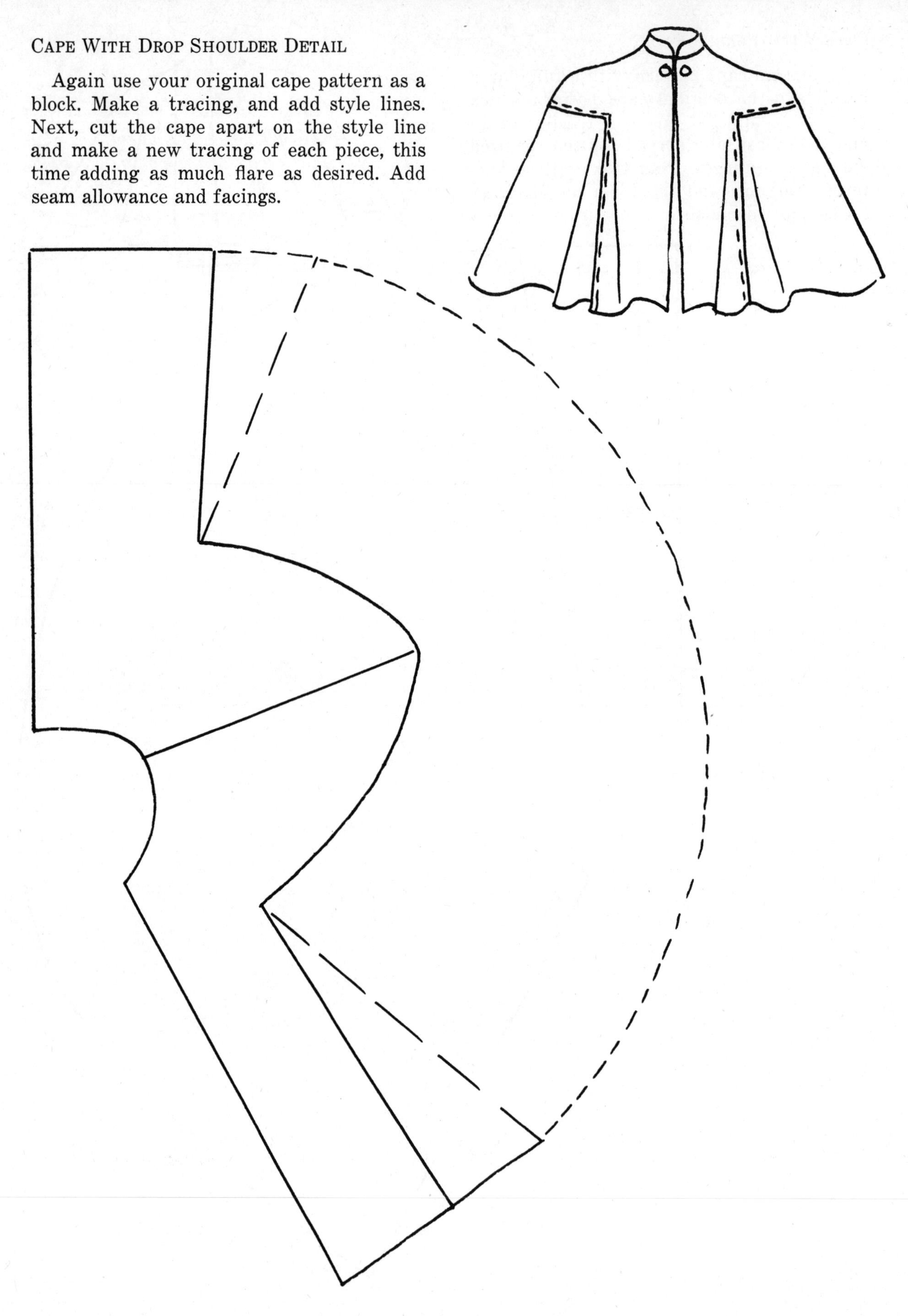

This diagram shows the lower pattern piece of the drop-shoulder cape. Seam allowance and flare have been added at the style line.

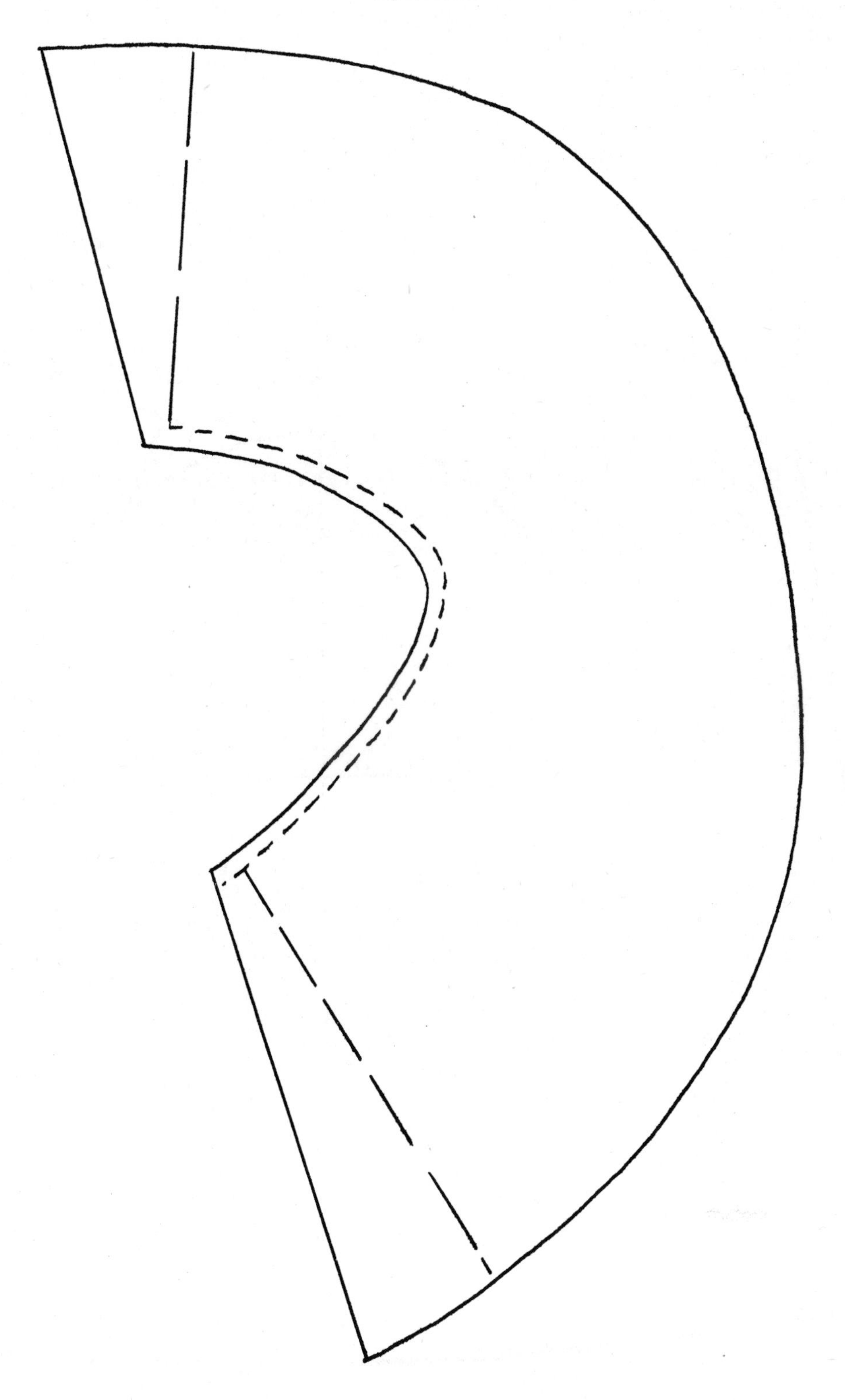

Box Cape

For a box cape, place the front and back blocks as shown.

The distance apart at the shoulder will be determined by the amount of fullness you wish to dart or gather.

The angle at which the blocks are placed will determine the fullness in the body of the cape.

The neck dart is optional.

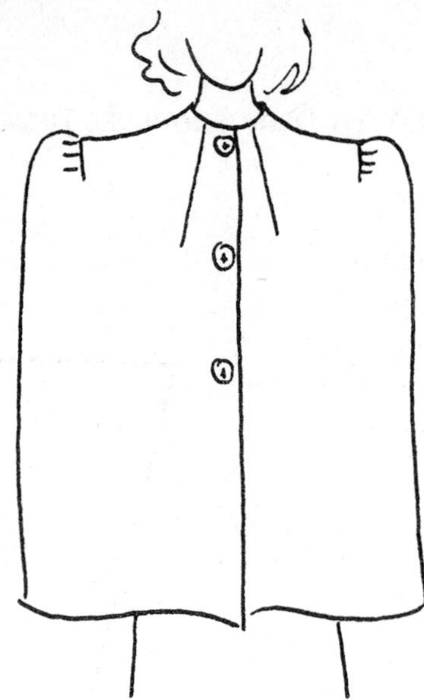

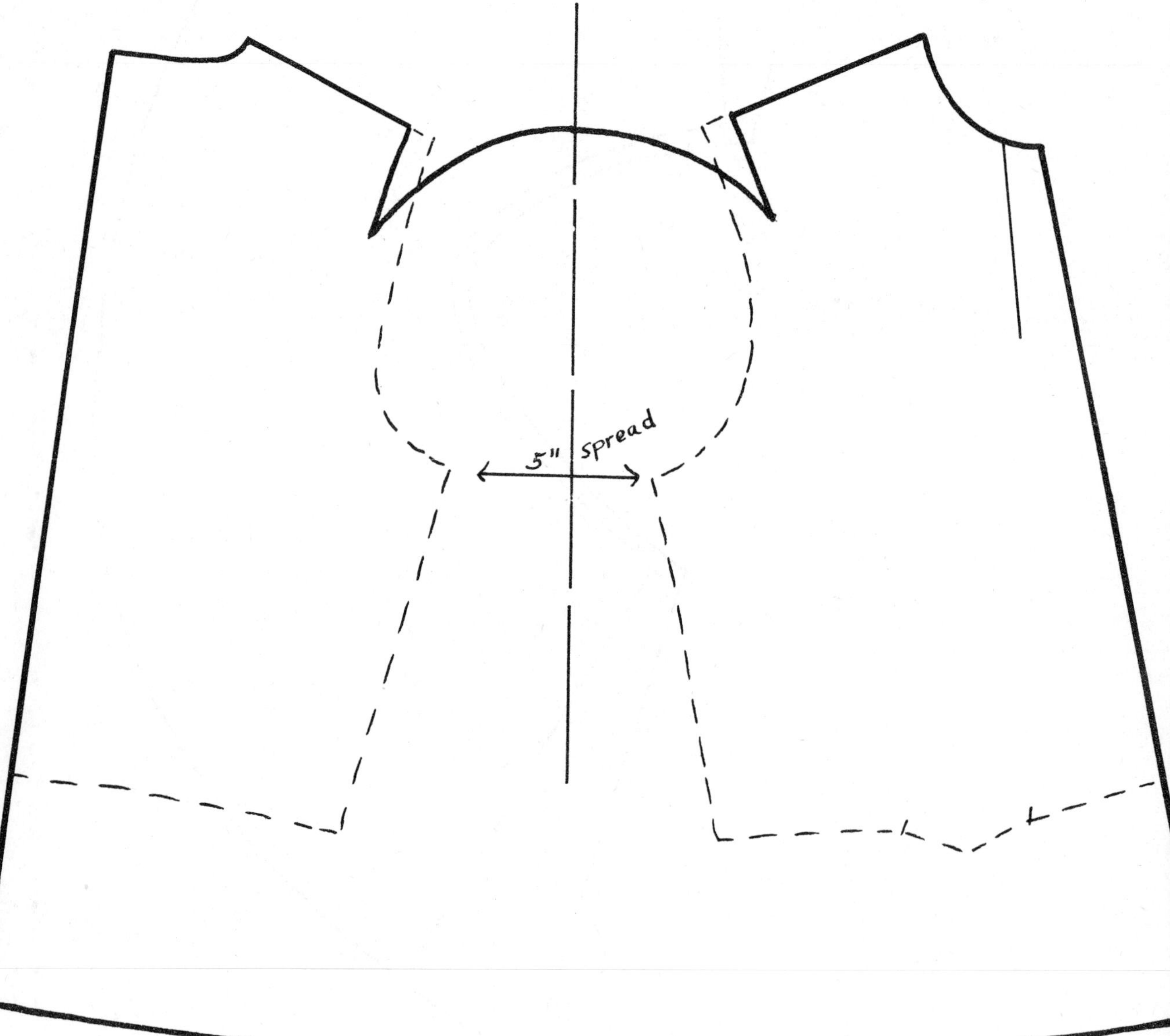

Drafted Hoods
#1

To draft hood #1, place your back and front bodice blocks together with shoulder seams overlapped, as shown in the diagram with dotted lines.

The solid line indicates the finished hood pattern.

The neckline of the hood must be the same as that of the garment to which the hood will be attached. The hood shown is larger than the bodice neckline because it is intended for a coat or suit and has a wide button lap.

Try out several hoods, pinning them together in muslin or tissue paper.

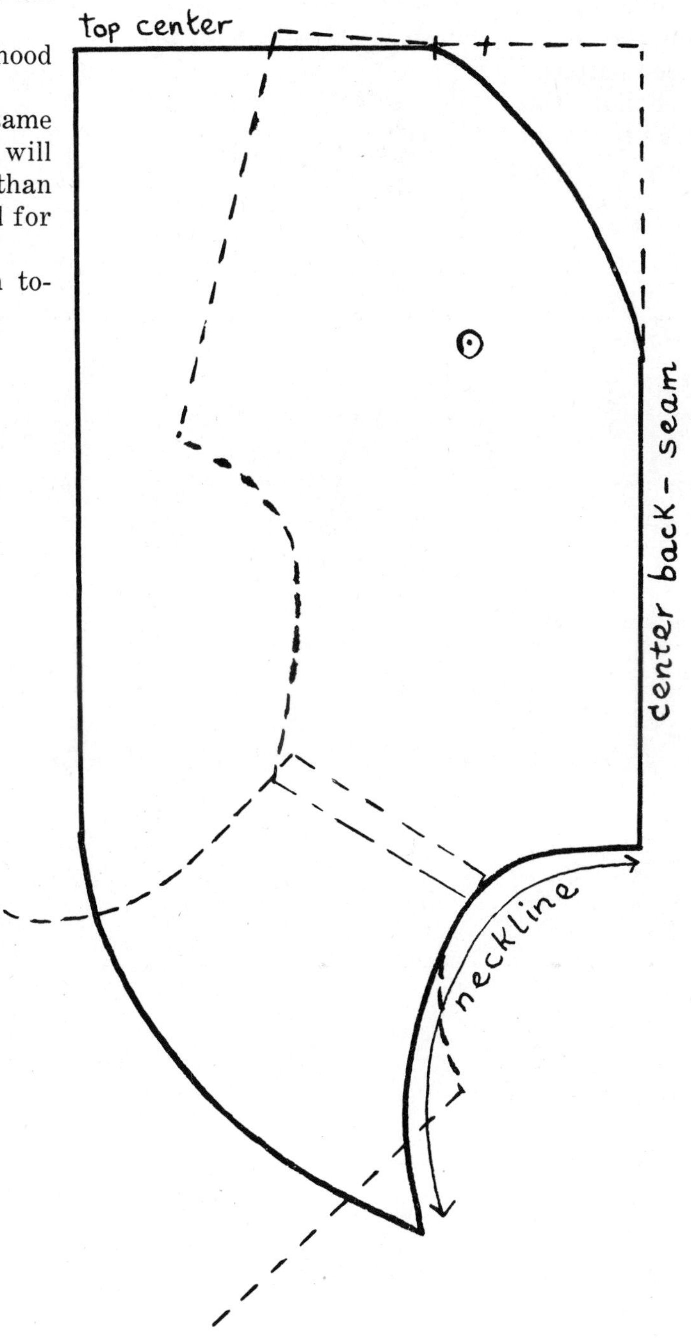

DRAFTED HOODS *(cont.)*
#2

Hood #2 is drafted almost entirely by measurement. The only part of the block which you need to trace is the neck. However, the neckline should be lowered ½ inch for the hood pattern.

Follow the measurements carefully. Be sure that your back-neck measurement is accurate *after* allowing for the darts.

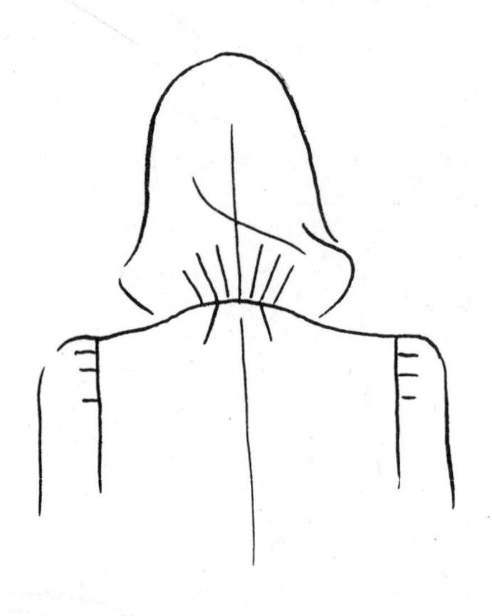

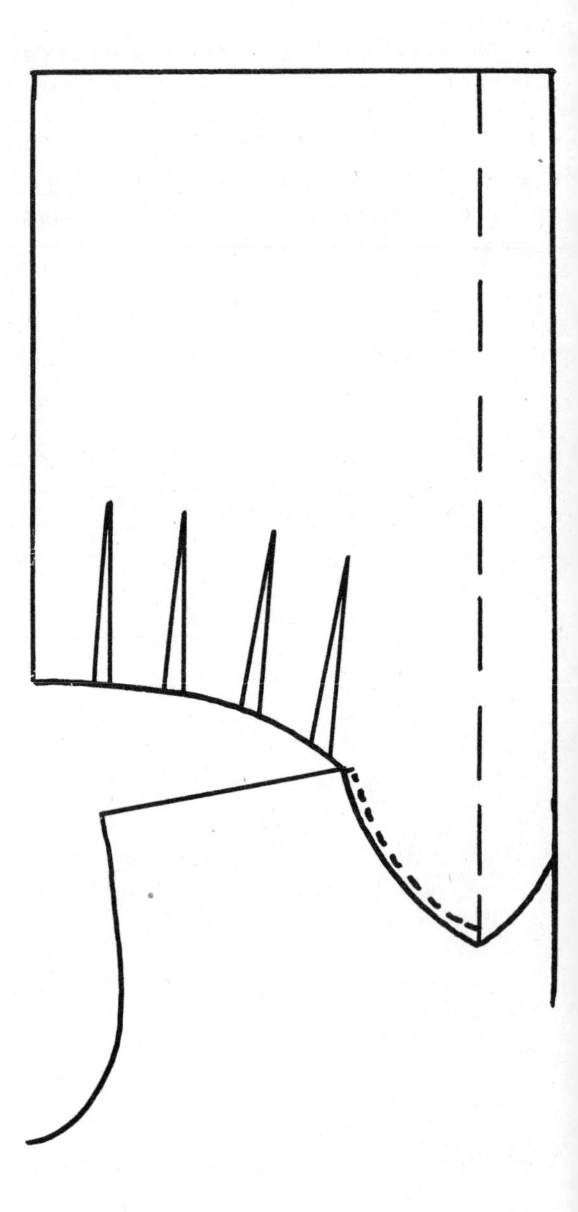

Single Button Suit Jacket With Tailored Notch Collar

1. Raise the neckline as indicated on Diagram B, step 1.

2. Continue the original neckline *out* 2¼ inches past the button lap.

3. Using a right angle, draw a line 1½ inches *up* from the neckline extension. This will establish the point of the lapel.

4. Draw in the lapel from the upper point to the waist.

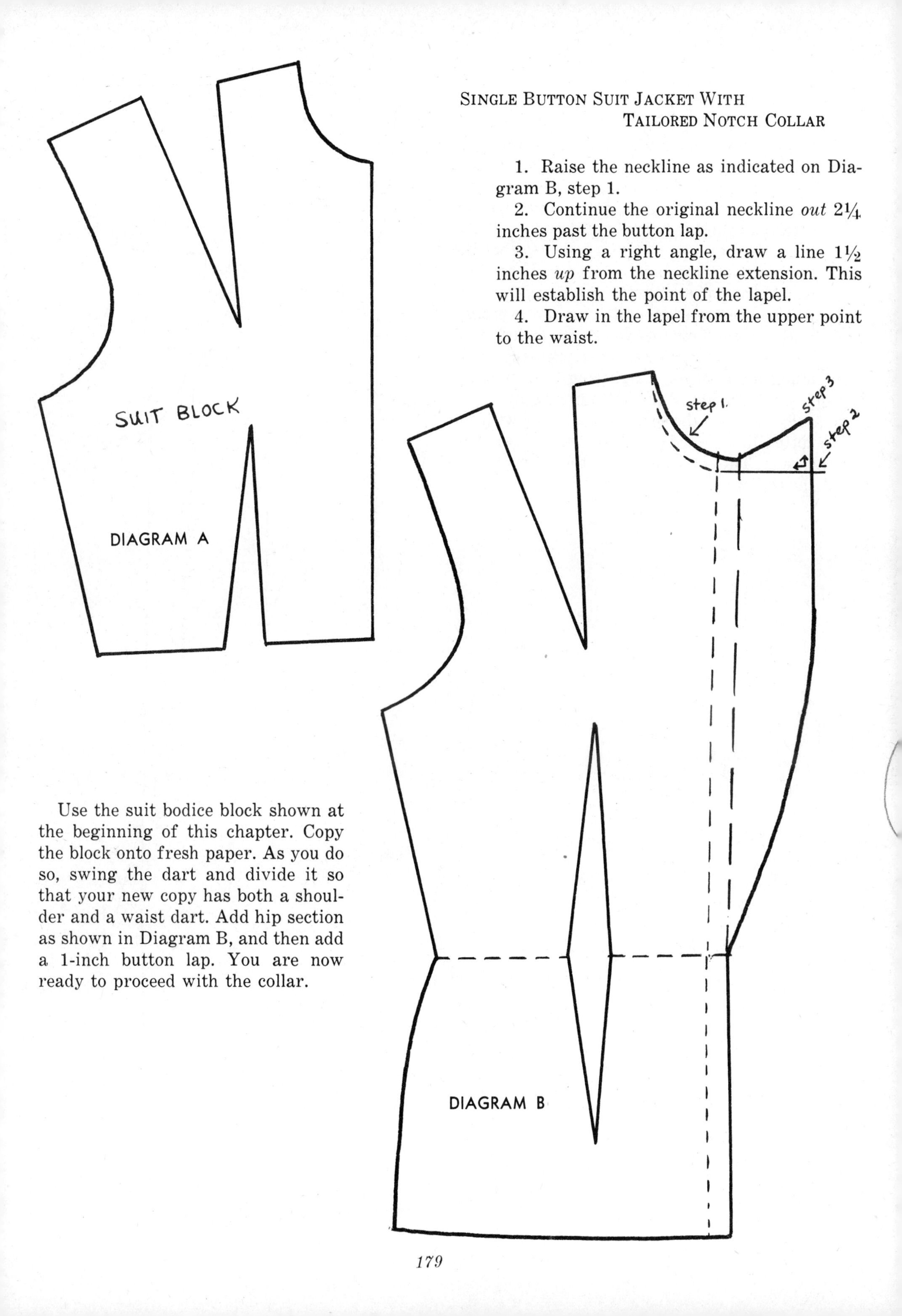

Use the suit bodice block shown at the beginning of this chapter. Copy the block onto fresh paper. As you do so, swing the dart and divide it so that your new copy has both a shoulder and a waist dart. Add hip section as shown in Diagram B, and then add a 1-inch button lap. You are now ready to proceed with the collar.

TAILORED NOTCH COLLAR *(cont.)*

5. Draw a straight line from the C.F. waist to a point on the shoulder 3/8 inch *in* from the neck. Extend this line past the shoulder several inches, as this line will locate your back neckline.

6. Now measure 1¼ inches *out* from the line you just drew, and from there to the C.F. waist draw another straight line; this line will be used to locate stitching and pressing.

7. On the first line you drew, measure off one half of the back-neck measurement. Make a mark, and, using a right angle, draw a line from that mark, 3 inches to the right.

8. Draw in the collar as indicated with the dotted line. Add ¼ inch to the C.B. neck as shown. This will allow for the turn over of the collar.

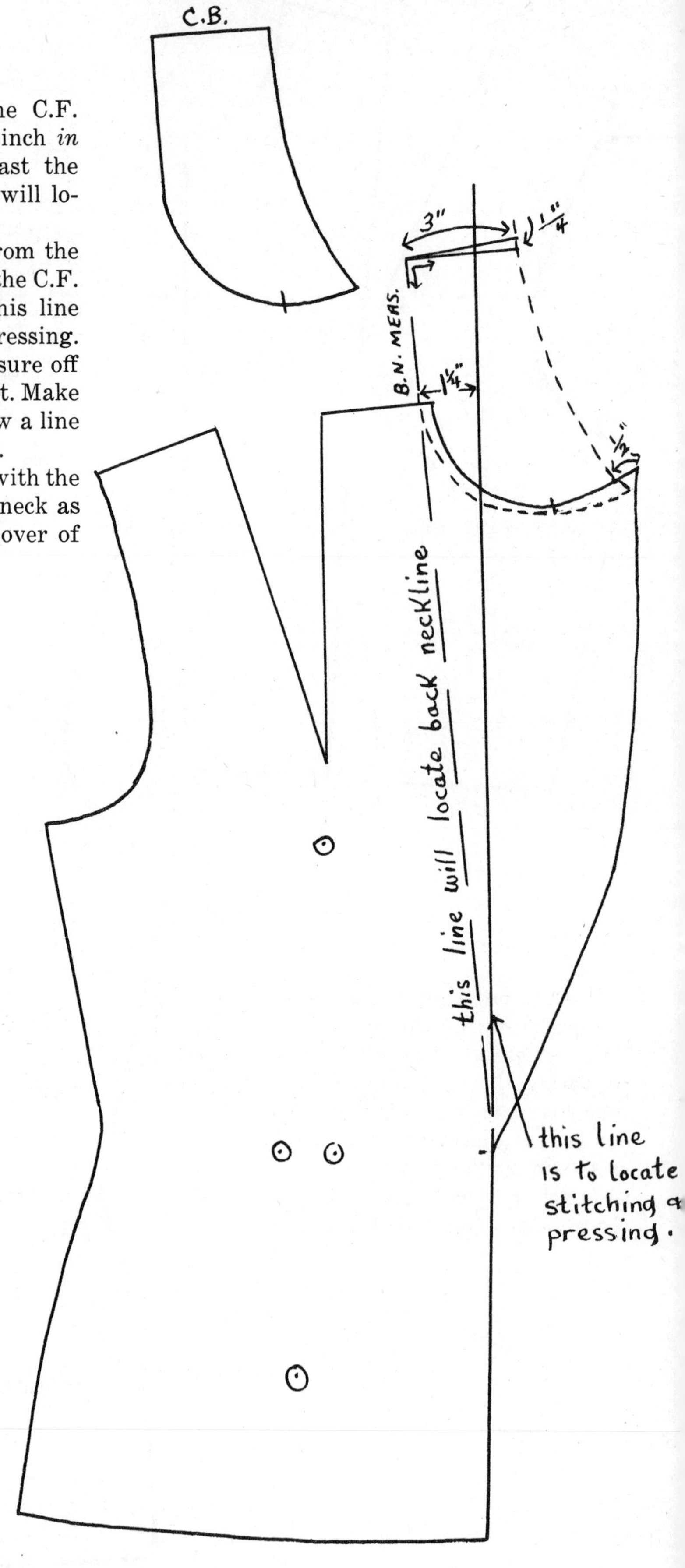

Tailored Notch Collar *(cont.)*

Details which you must learn to complete this pattern:

First, you need an inner lining for both the collar and the front facing. This lining is cut from tailor's canvas and the collar lining is stitched to the under collar to prevent the collar from wilting. The lining for the front facing is cut 1½ inches shorter than the front facing itself so that no needless bulk will be added to the hem of the garment. Both the collar lining and the facing lining are cut about ¼ inch smaller all around than the facing and collar; this is to prevent unnecessary bulk being added to the seams. The linings for the collar and the under collar are cut on the bias. The collar itself is cut on the straight of the goods, in one piece. The under collar and the canvas are usually cut with a seam down the C.B. to add body to the collar.

The collar and the front facing have to be slightly larger than the under collar and the body of the garment in order to allow for a nice roll.

If the garment has bound buttonholes, allow ⅛ inch more length to the front jacket for each buttonhole.

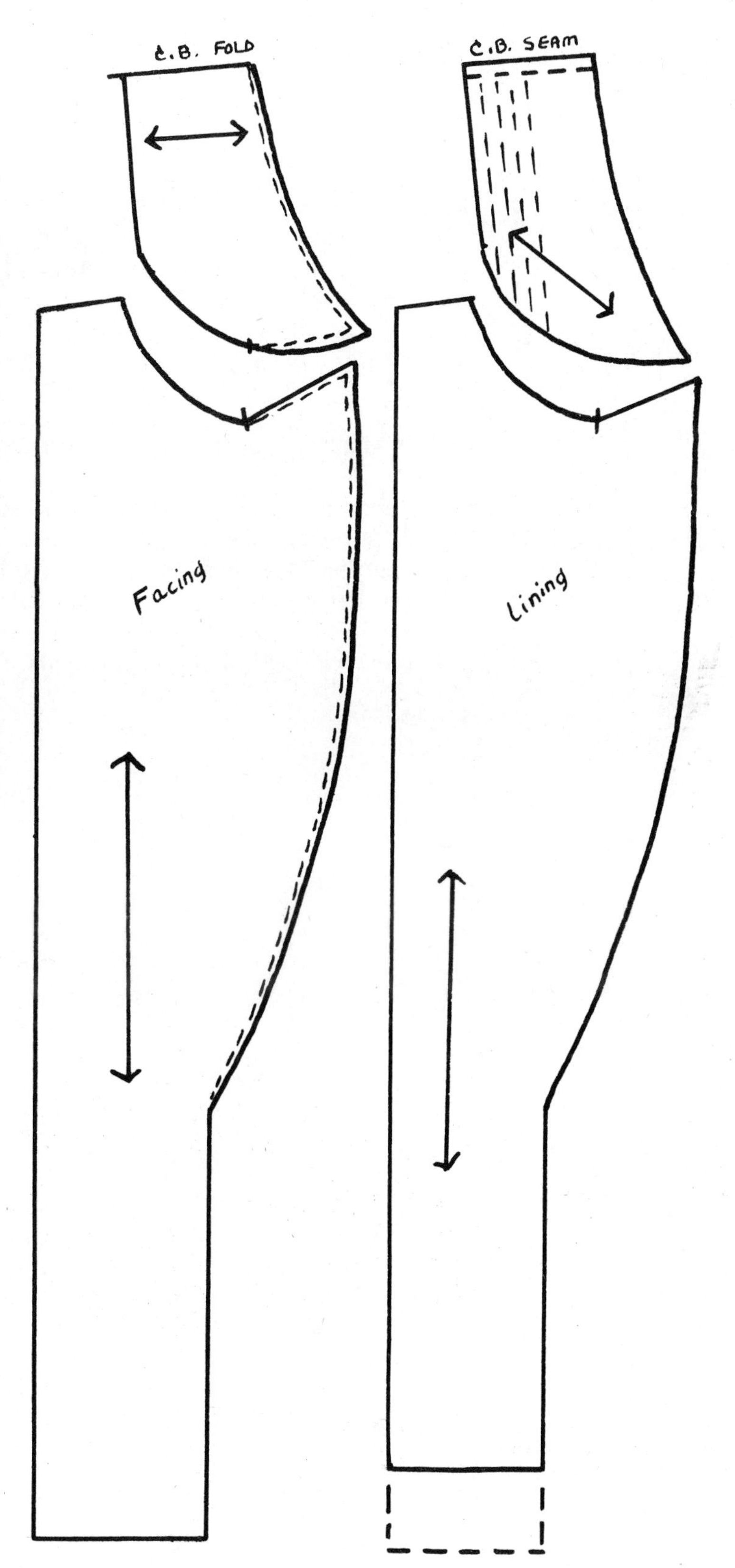

Chapter Twelve
Playclothes

In this chapter, panties, bras, slacks, shorts, and smocks will be discussed.

It is a good plan to develop your own blocks for these garments by continually altering and improving your pattern until you achieve as nearly perfect fit as possible. Rules will be given that will help you to make the basic patterns, which you can develop as you wish.

Unless you have a special form which is made for fitting slacks and other playclothes, fit these garments on yourself or on a friend.

Back Panty

To draft a panty pattern, begin with the skirt blocks and add a crotch to them.

Start with the back skirt block and proceed as follows:

1. Measure down the C.B. 14 inches. Use a right angle to draw a second line *out* 4 inches as shown on the diagram.
2. Again using the right angle draw a third line *down* 1½ inches.
3. Measure down the side seam 10 inches and make a mark — connect that mark to the 1½ inch line at the crotch. Make the line slope as shown in the diagram.

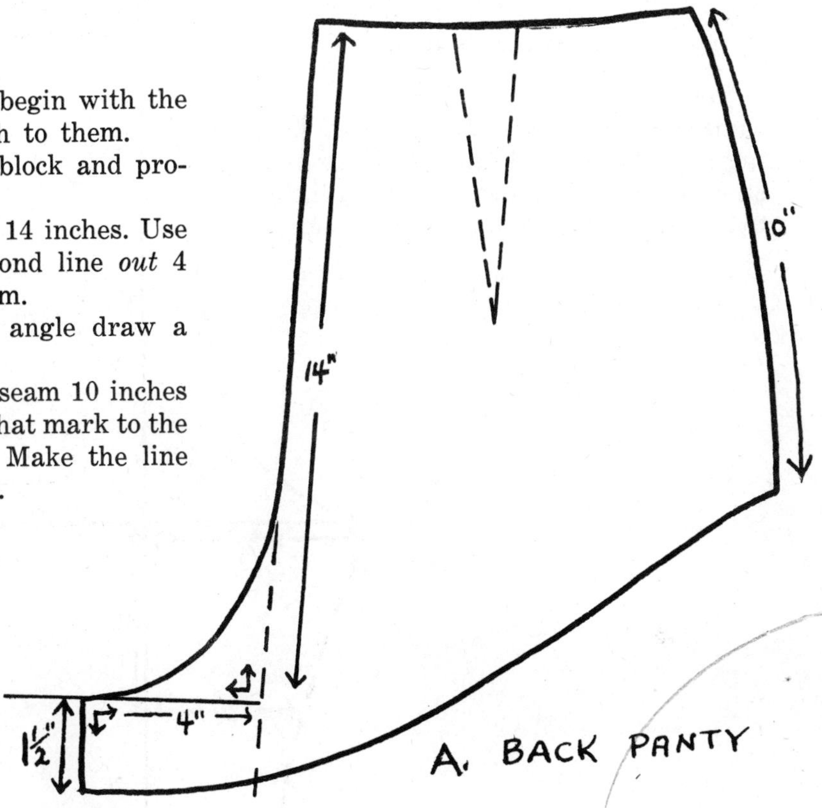

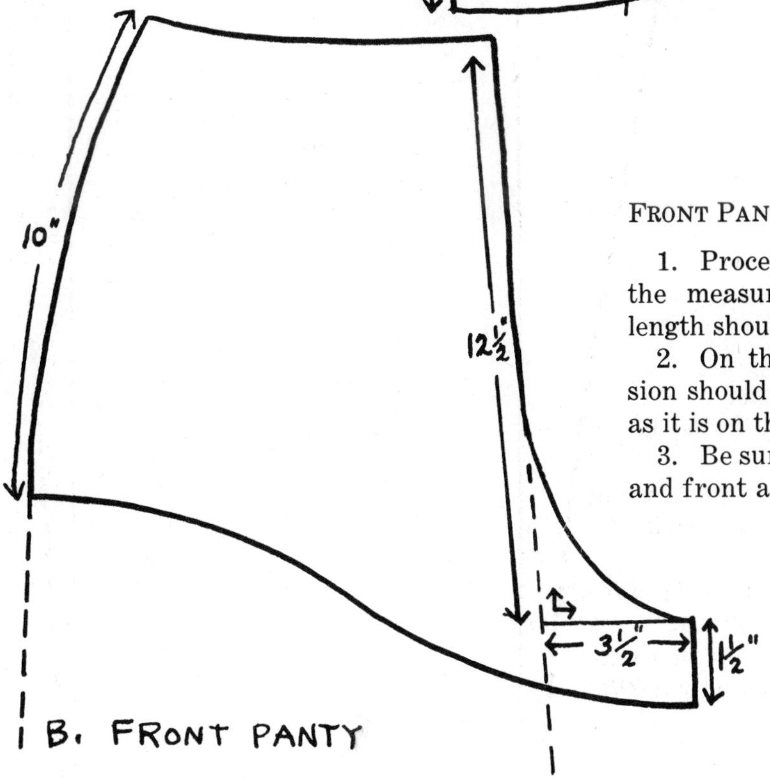

A. BACK PANTY

B. FRONT PANTY

Front Panty

1. Proceed as you did with the back; only the measurements will be different. C.F. length should be 12½ inches.
2. On the front panty, the crotch extension should be 3½ inches instead of 4 inches as it is on the back.
3. Be sure that the side seams in both back and front are the same.

Slacks — Drafting the Back

You can draft the slack pattern in the same way that you did the underpanty, allowing for a looser fit in the crotch. Or you can start by drawing a rectangle 40½ inches by 9½ inches as has been done in this diagram.

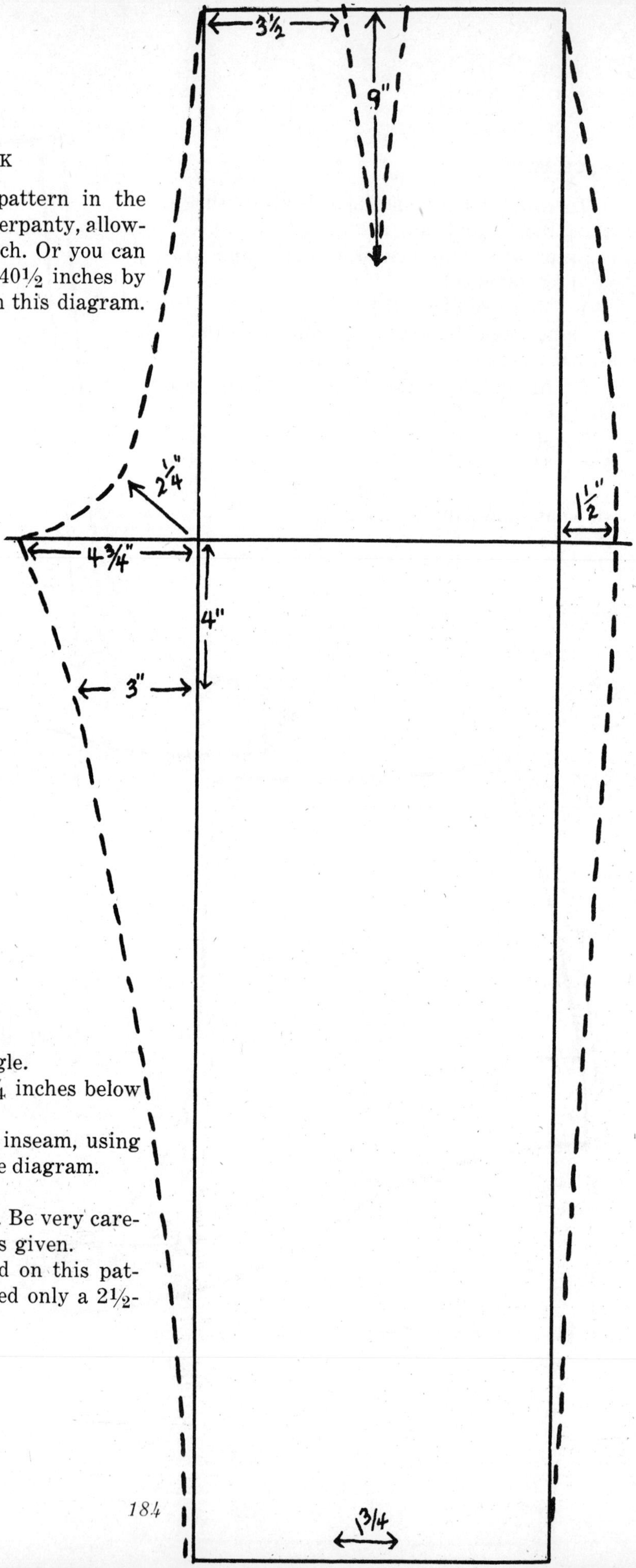

Directions

1. First draw in the rectangle.
2. Bisect the rectangle 13¾ inches below the top line.
3. Draw in the crotch and inseam, using the measurements shown on the diagram.
4. Draw in the side seam.
5. Place a dart at the waist. Be very careful to follow the measurements given.
6. Seams have been allowed on this pattern, so as a final step you need only a 2½-inch hem.

FRONT SLACK

To draft the front slack pattern, begin with a rectangle that measures 8 x 40 inches. Divide the rectangle at a point 12½ inches below the top line, and again 10 inches below the first division. Draw in the outline of the slack as shown in the diagram. Follow the measurements carefully.

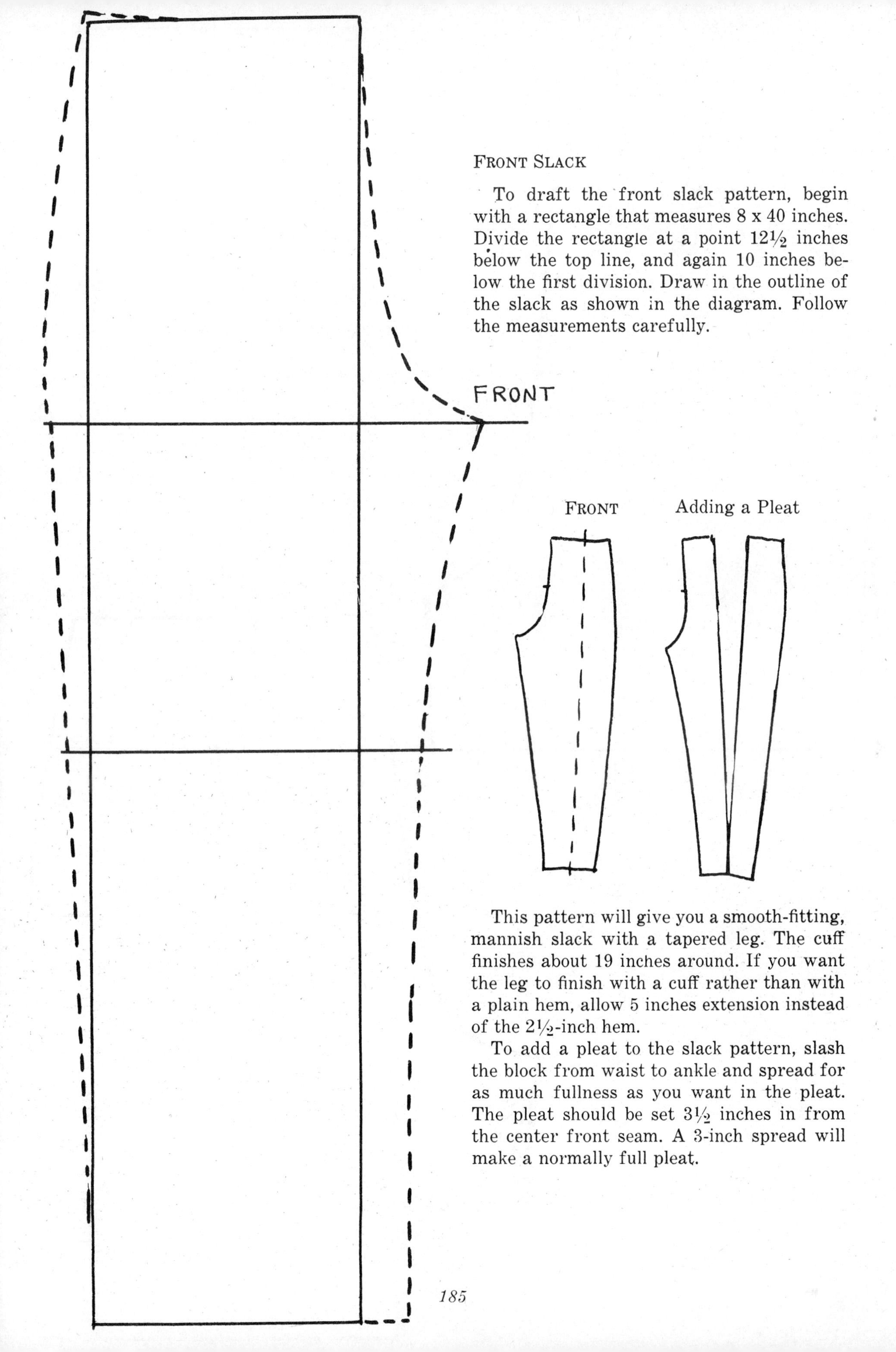

This pattern will give you a smooth-fitting, mannish slack with a tapered leg. The cuff finishes about 19 inches around. If you want the leg to finish with a cuff rather than with a plain hem, allow 5 inches extension instead of the 2½-inch hem.

To add a pleat to the slack pattern, slash the block from waist to ankle and spread for as much fullness as you want in the pleat. The pleat should be set 3½ inches in from the center front seam. A 3-inch spread will make a normally full pleat.

SHORTS

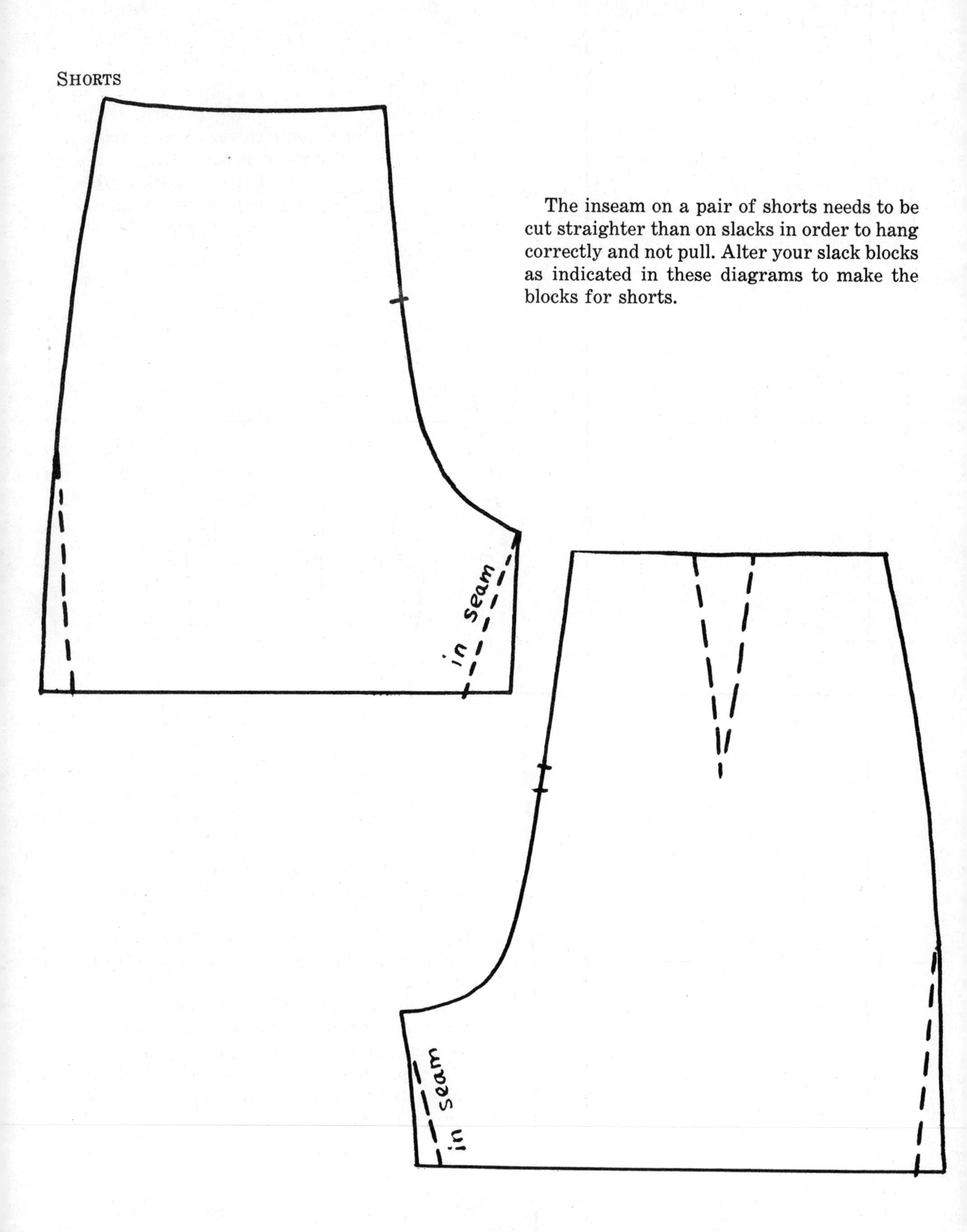

The inseam on a pair of shorts needs to be cut straighter than on slacks in order to hang correctly and not pull. Alter your slack blocks as indicated in these diagrams to make the blocks for shorts.

SMOCKS

Smocks must be cut rather loose. Use the dress blocks but deepen the armscye about ½ inch. The original outline of the dress blocks are shown with dotted lines.

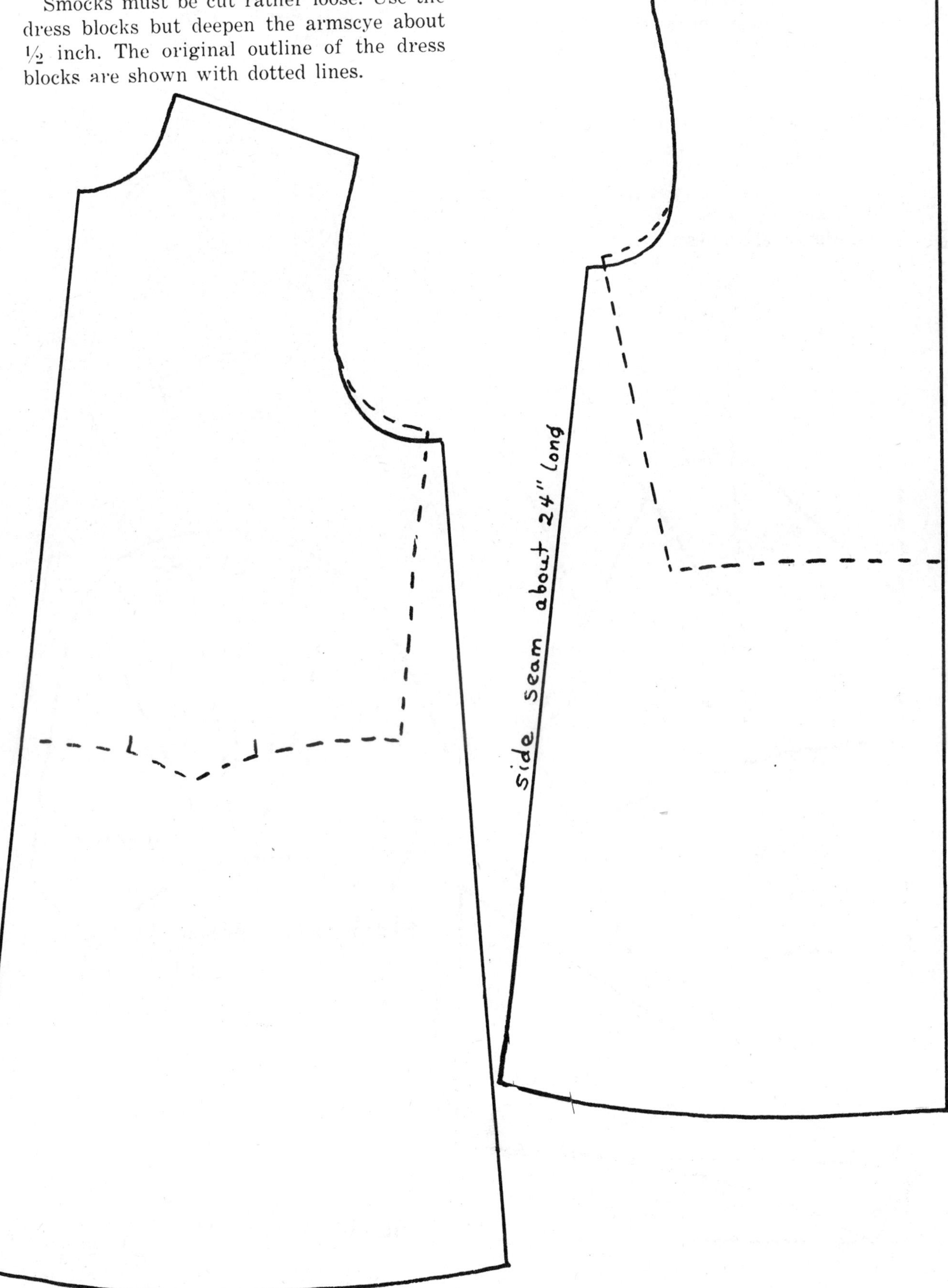

DRAFTED BACK BRA

The scale used here is ½ inch to the inch. Follow the diagram carefully, and finish by pinning both bra pieces together on the dress form or your own figure.

All fullness here is added at the top. Begin by drawing in the bra pattern on the shoulder block and then slash and spread the pattern for additional fullness.

DIAGRAM A

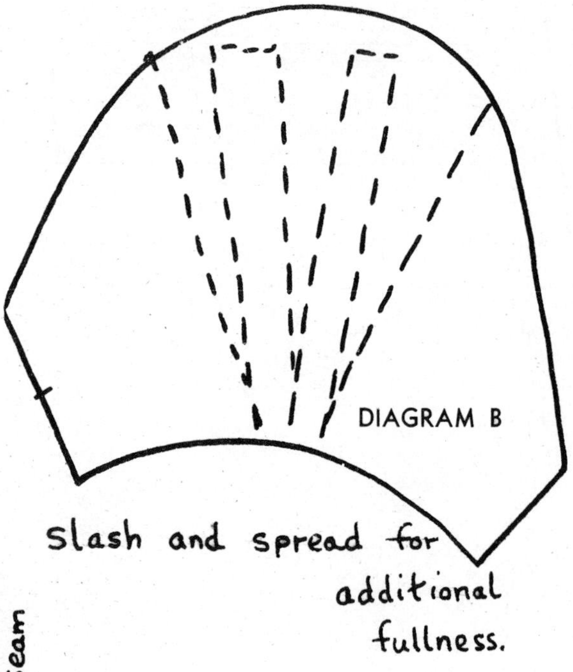

DIAGRAM B

Slash and spread for additional fullness.

DIAGRAM C

Side Seam

C.B.

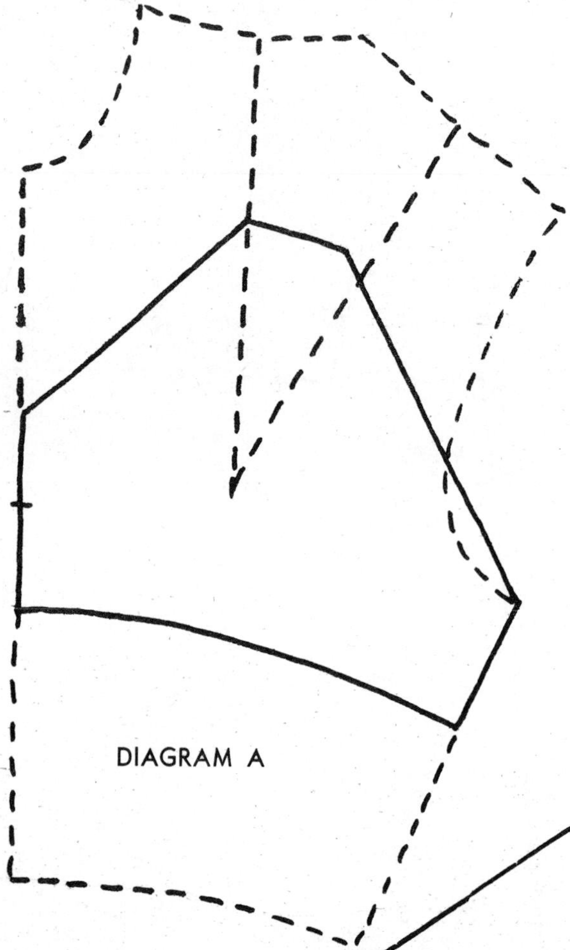

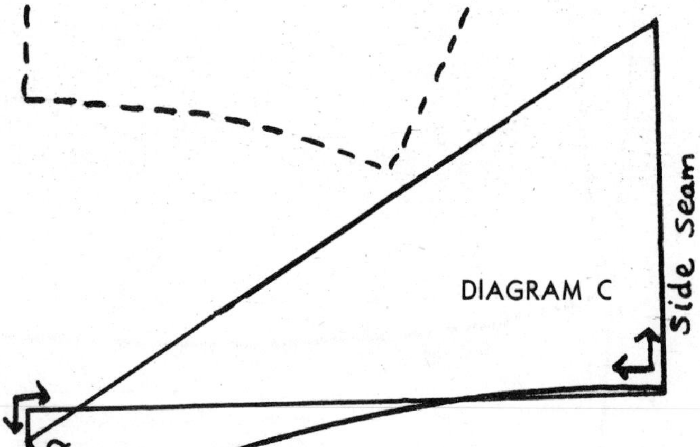

DIAG. C ← scale used for this piece ½" = 1"

BRASSIERES

A bra has to be fitted on a live model. You can do the preliminary work on a form, but for final fitting try it on a model.

Approximate your bra pattern by sketching it in on the dress blocks. Cut the pieces out in muslin or tissue paper and continue developing your pattern by working directly on the form.

The side seam on the back piece is 1¼ inches wider than the front. This is to allow for the finishing band that will be sewed onto the front. See sketch.

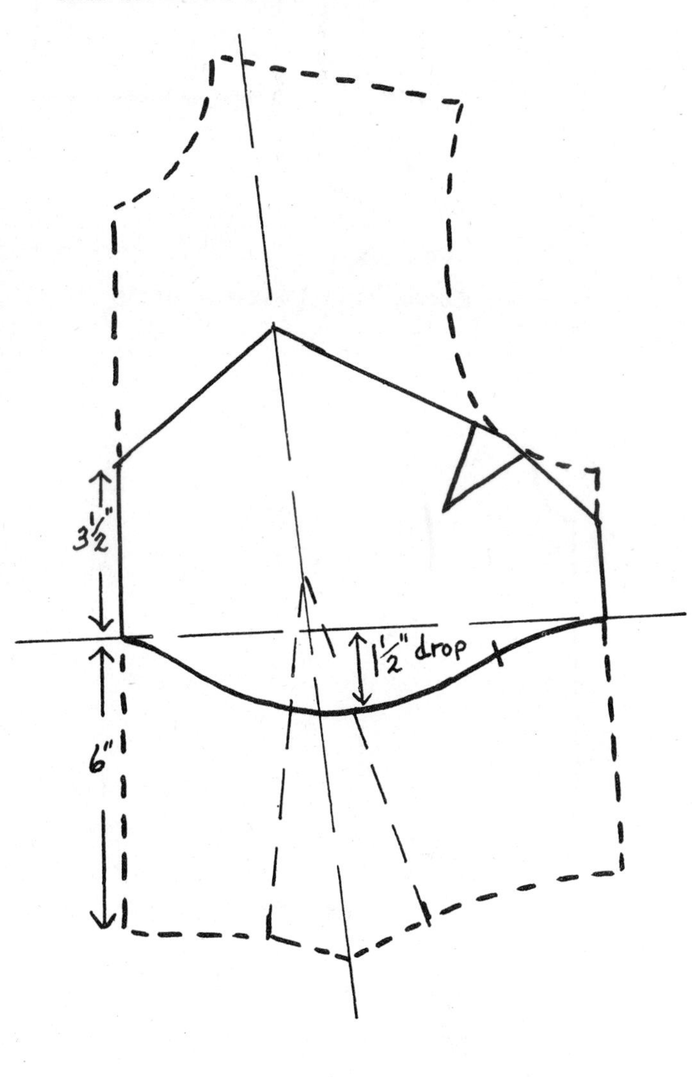

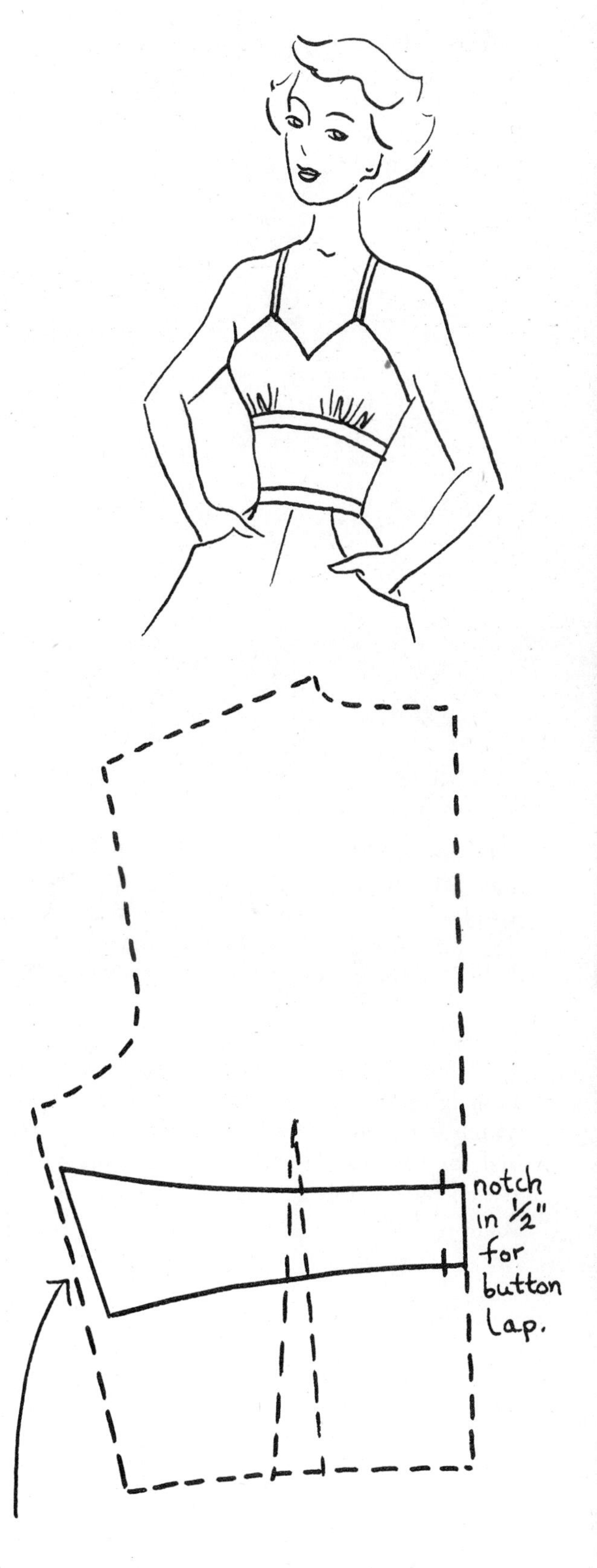

One-Piece Playsuit

A one-piece playsuit is apt to pull at the crotch when the wearer moves her arms. To avoid this, add about ⅝ inch of length to the side seams and taper it to nothing about half way to the center front.

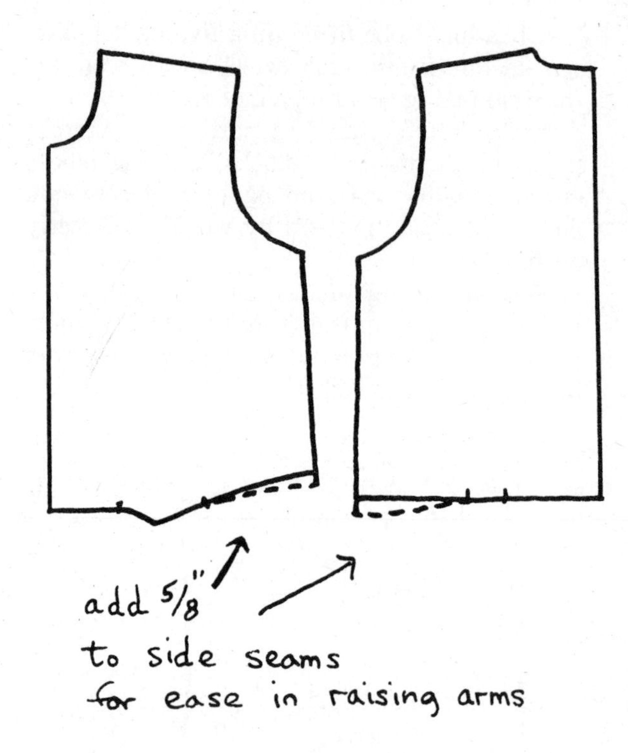

One-Piece Play Suit With Set-in Waistband

If the waistband is to finish 2 inches wide, make the pattern 3 inches wide in order to provide ½-inch seams on both sides. Also trim off 1 inch from both the shorts and the bodice or the garment will come out too long.

If the garment is to be buttoned up the front, add ½ inch to the center-front seam of the panty for a distance of about 8 inches. This is shown in the diagram. The ½ inch which you add to the front seam, plus the ½ inch of the seam itself, provides you with a 1-inch button lap.

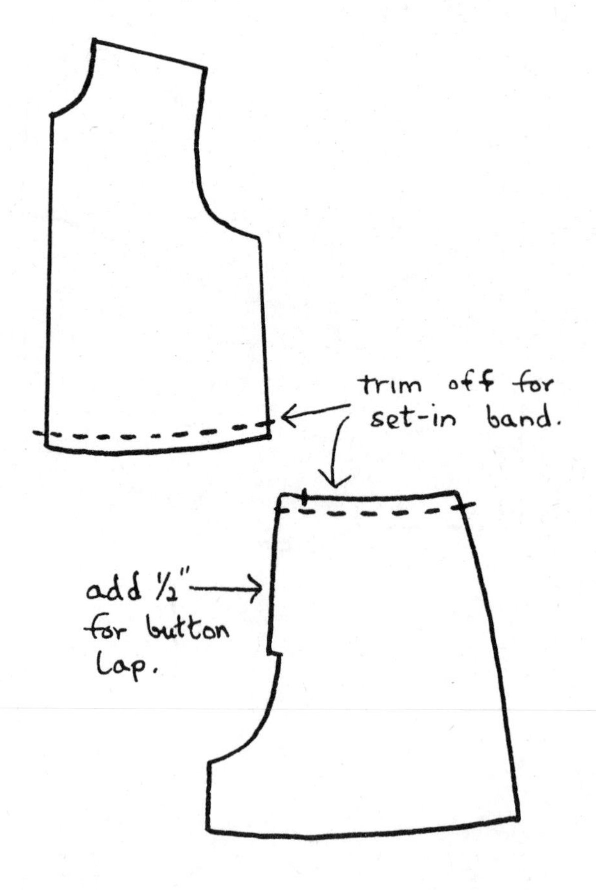

Cut the bodice as shown in the diagram. Fit it on the form for placement of the bustline dart. Be sure to add the little pointed extension at the center waistline. In making the panty and skirt patterns, take off the same amount at the center waist as you added to the bodice.

The three pieces are sewn together at the waistline. In setting in a zipper or a placket, use the two thicknesses of the panty and skirt just as you would if it were a single thickness.

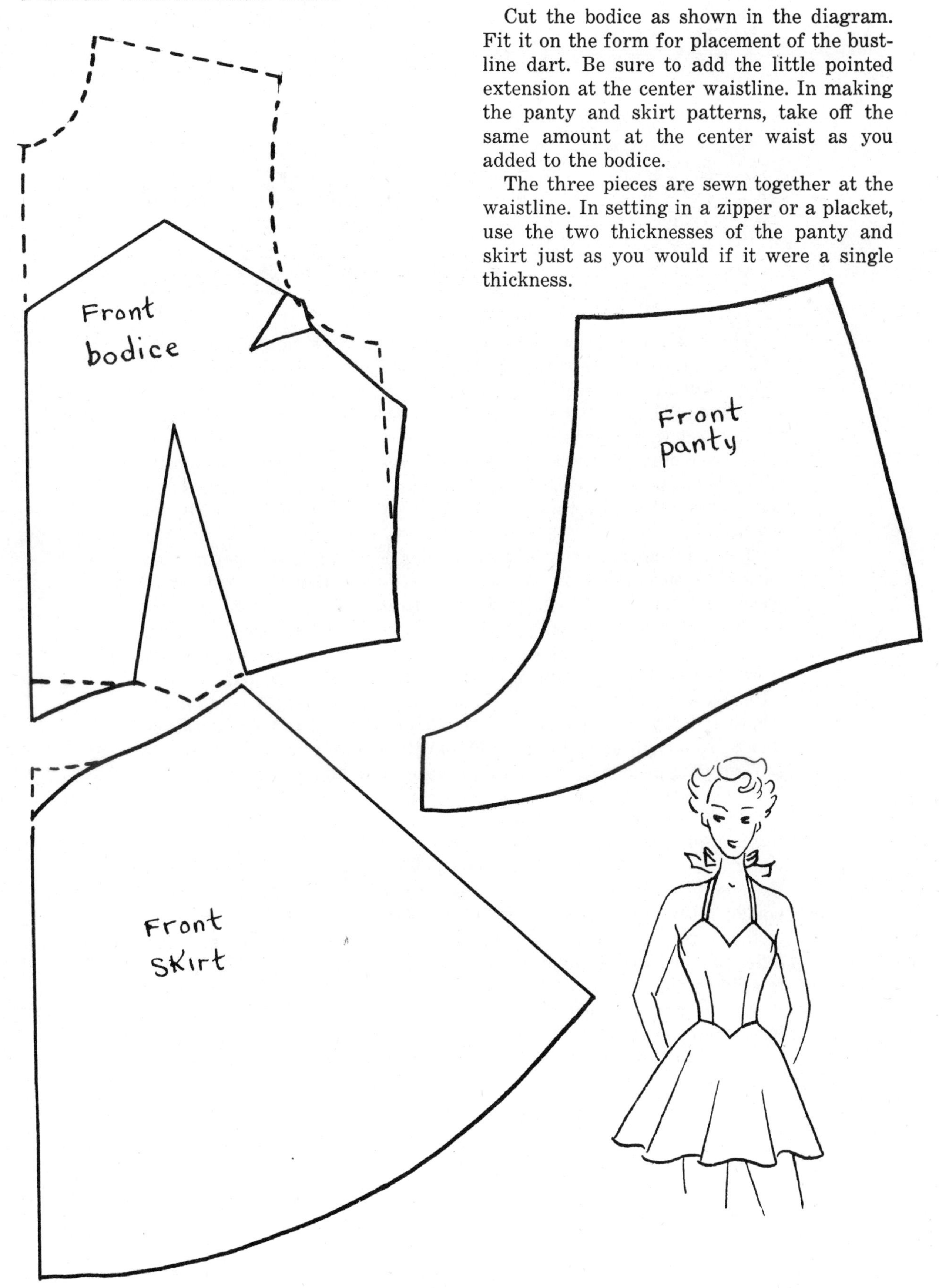

Chapter Thirteen
Children's clothes

There is no basic difference between children's clothes and those with which we have thus far been concerned. However, there are some fairly standard ideas of proportion which you should know, and of course you will have to have some basic blocks. The work on children's clothes here will be done in a size 4.

If you intend to work in the field of ready-to-wear as a designer, you will not be expected to provide blocks, but in almost all cases you will work with blocks that are standard with the firm for which you work.

For the homemaker who sews for her children, it will perhaps be easiest to purchase some commercial patterns in the size the child wears and make the blocks from the patterns. Be sure to select very simple patterns which will provide a darted back and front bodice, a plain skirt and plain sleeve, and panties or slacks. Alter the patterns to fit the child when making the basic blocks. Alter as little as possible. Waist measure, skirt or slack length, sleeve length, and bodice length are all you need to check. You will do well to take these measurements from clothes which fit the child rather than from the child himself, as it is practically impossible to get a small child to stand still long enough to take accurate measurements.

Pinafores, overalls, and box jackets are so uniform in proportion that complete patterns for all these garments are included. Naturally you are free to vary the proportions as you see fit, but it is important that you know what is standard, so that when you do change the proportions it will look deliberate. Nothing seems more "homemade," for instance, than a pinafore that is badly proportioned. There is a vast difference between a "homemade" look, and a "hand-sewn" look. Try to achieve the latter.

In order to demonstrate how simple it is to make children's patterns, four dress patterns will be shown. Only the fronts will be done here, as you can easily make the backs yourself if you wish to.

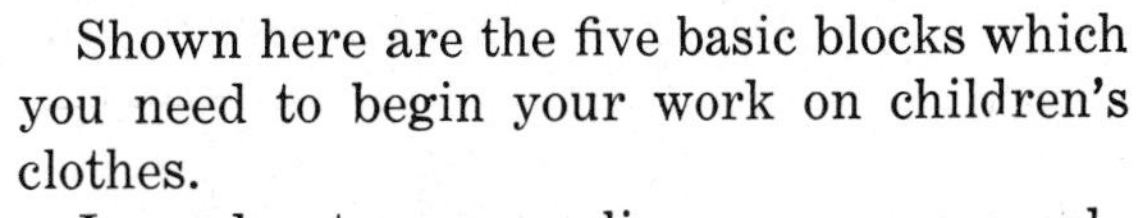

Shown here are the five basic blocks which you need to begin your work on children's clothes.

In order to personalize your own work, you will probably alter your blocks many times to suit your own ideas of fit or to keep up with changing style trends.

The slacks, overalls, and jacket pattern may be used for either boys or girls. A boy's shirt pattern can be made from the basic bodice blocks.

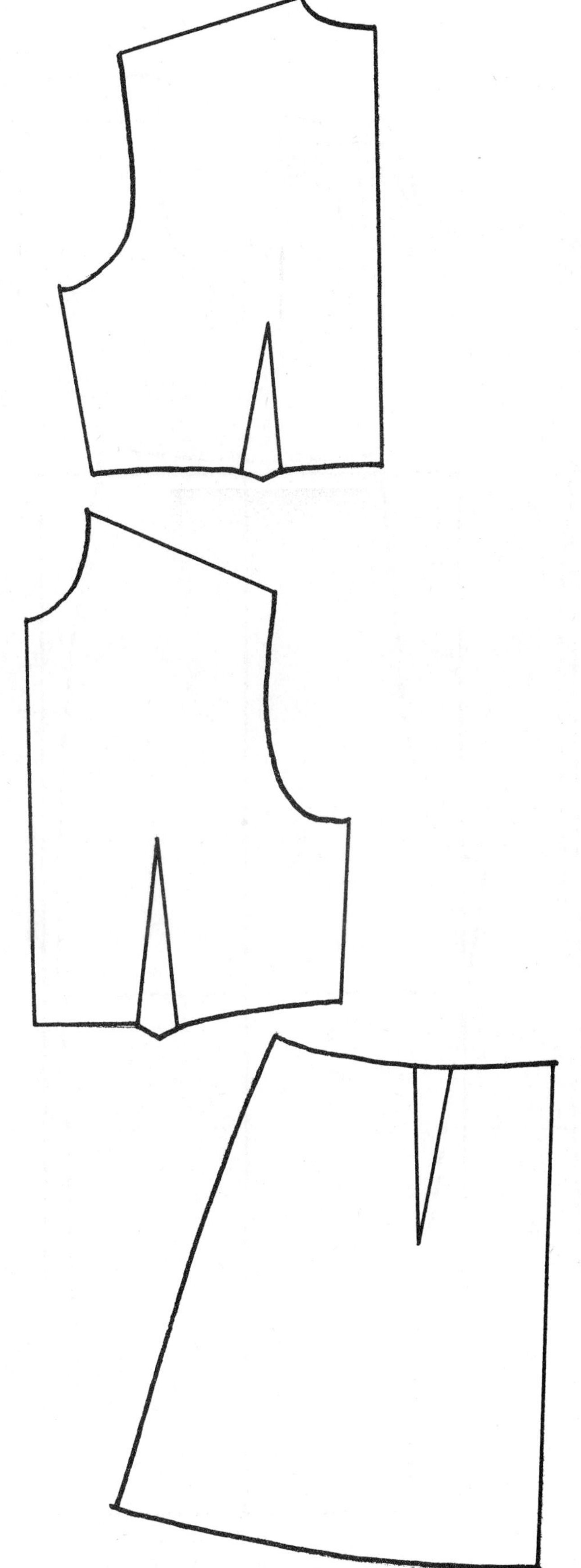

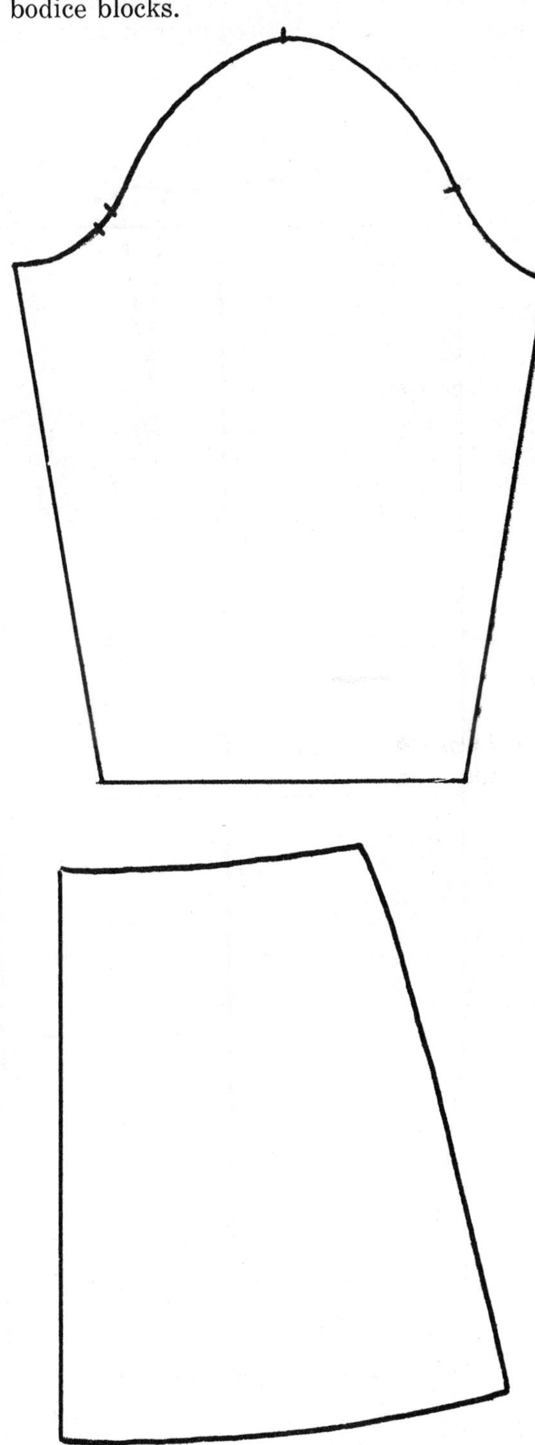

SLACK BLOCKS — SIZE 4

The scale here, as usual, is ¼ inch to the inch.

To make a pattern for boxer slacks, raise the waistline about 2 inches and add 2 inches of width to both front and back block. The raise at the waist is used to turn under for a casing for elastic.

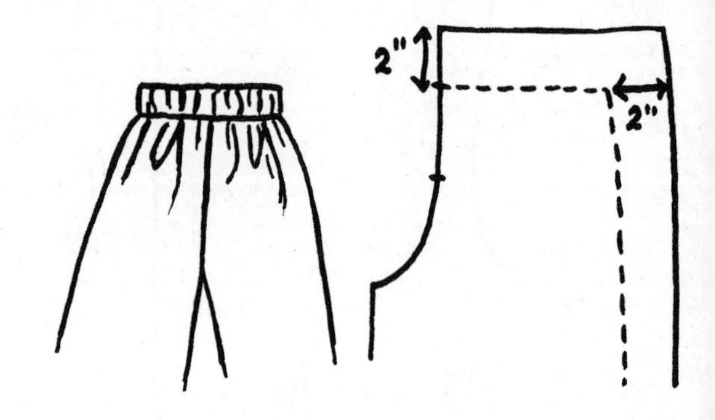

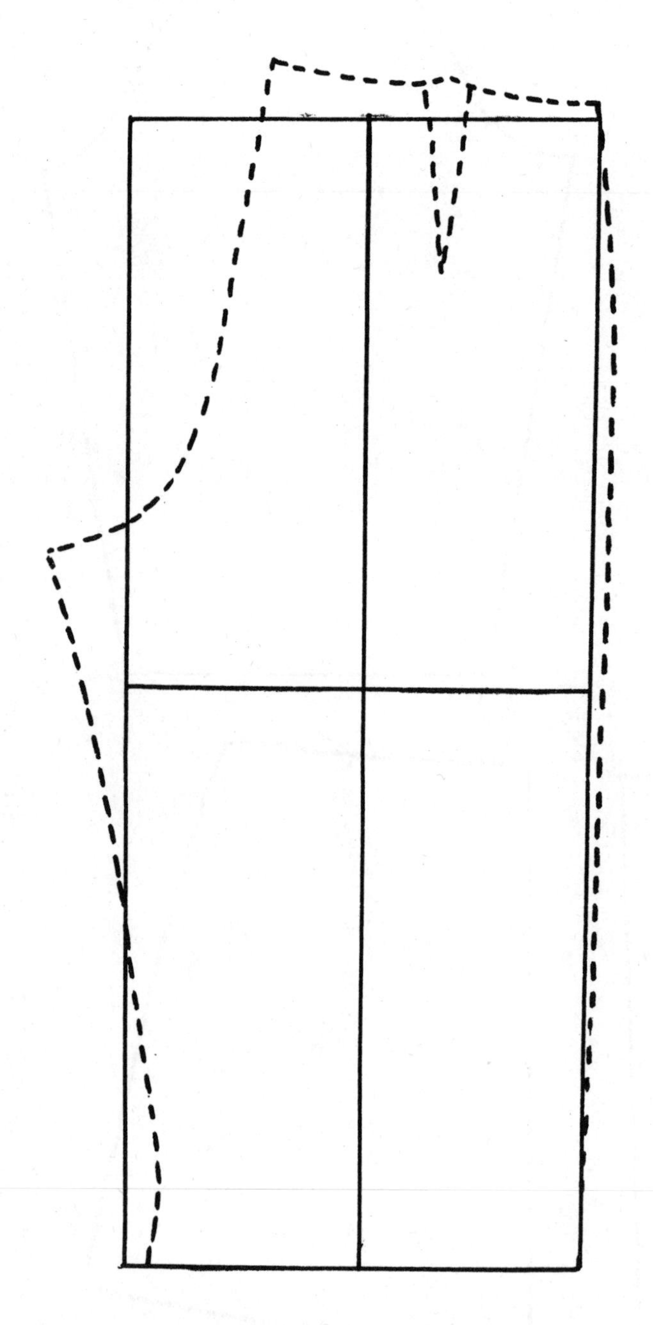

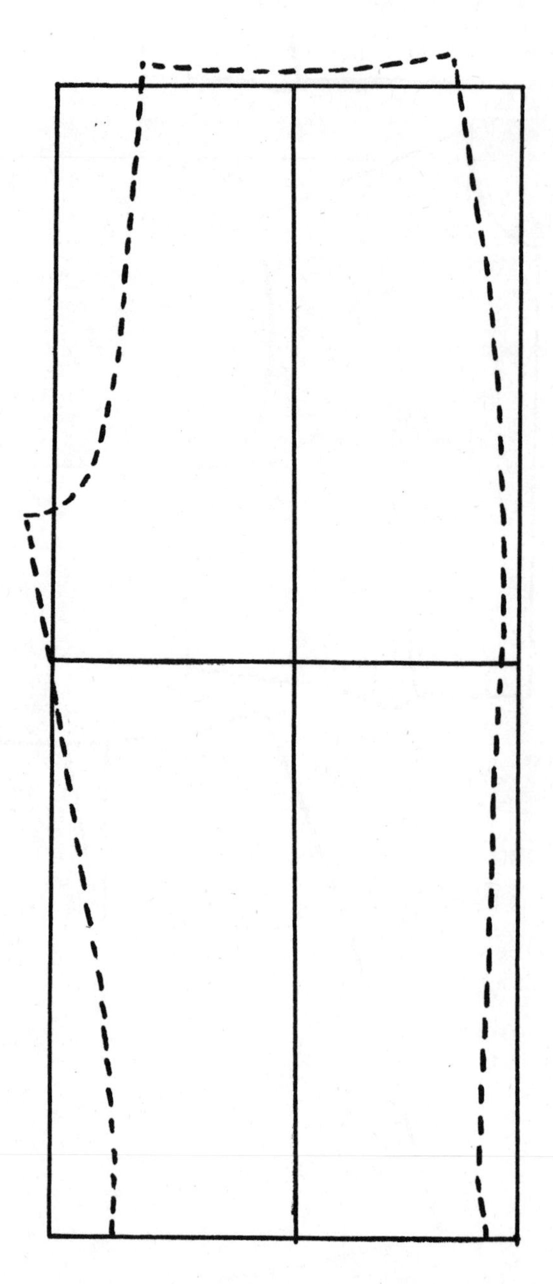

Under Panty and One-Piece Playsuit

This particular style of panty is the one that is generally used in little girl's clothes, since it is very simple to make. By experimenting, you may find that you can develop something better.

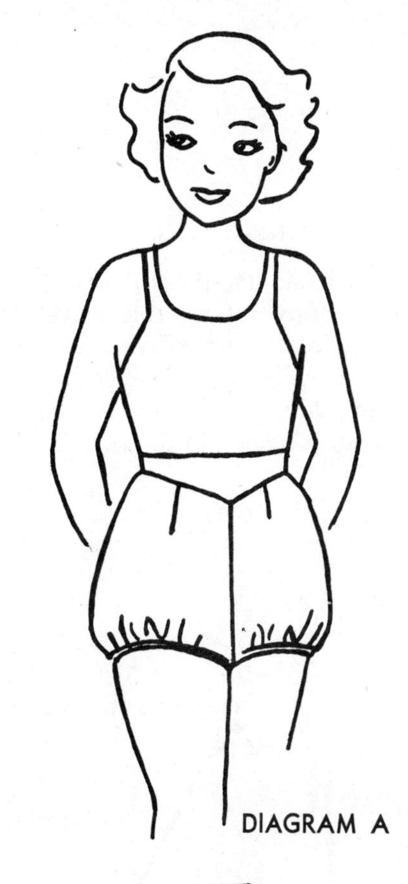

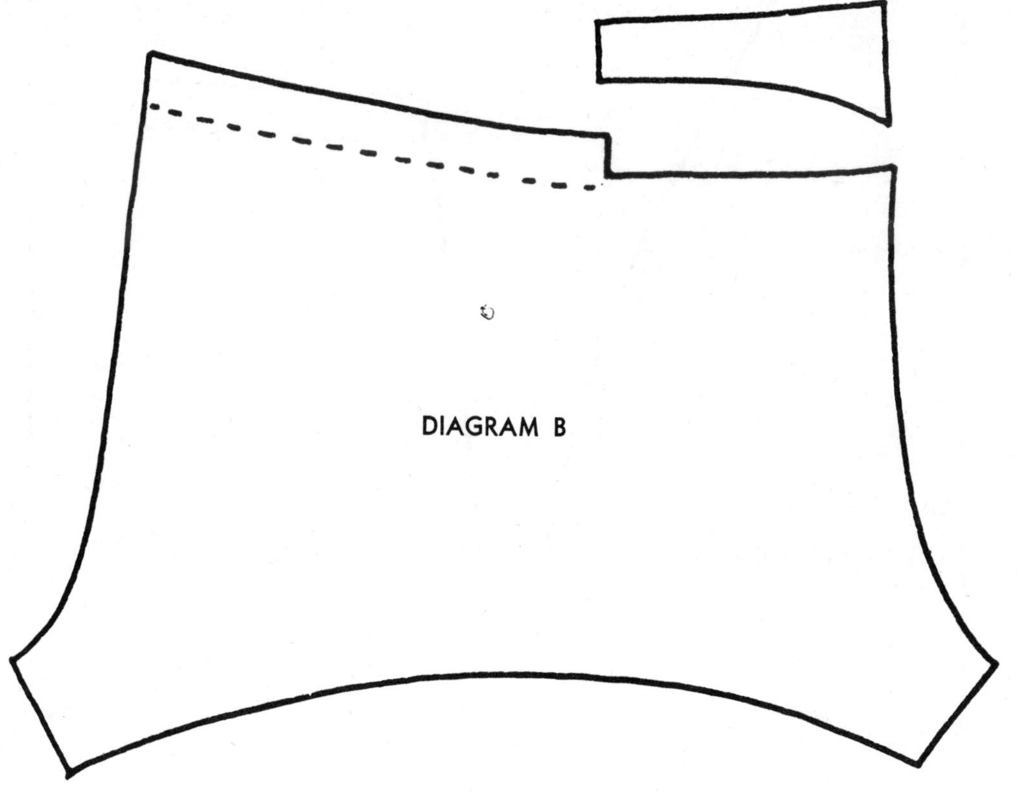

Play Clothing

This basic one-piece playsuit can be made up in many interesting ways. Having the front a stripe or print, and the back and straps a solid color is effective. An appliqué of the plain fabric may be used to add front interest as shown in the sketch.

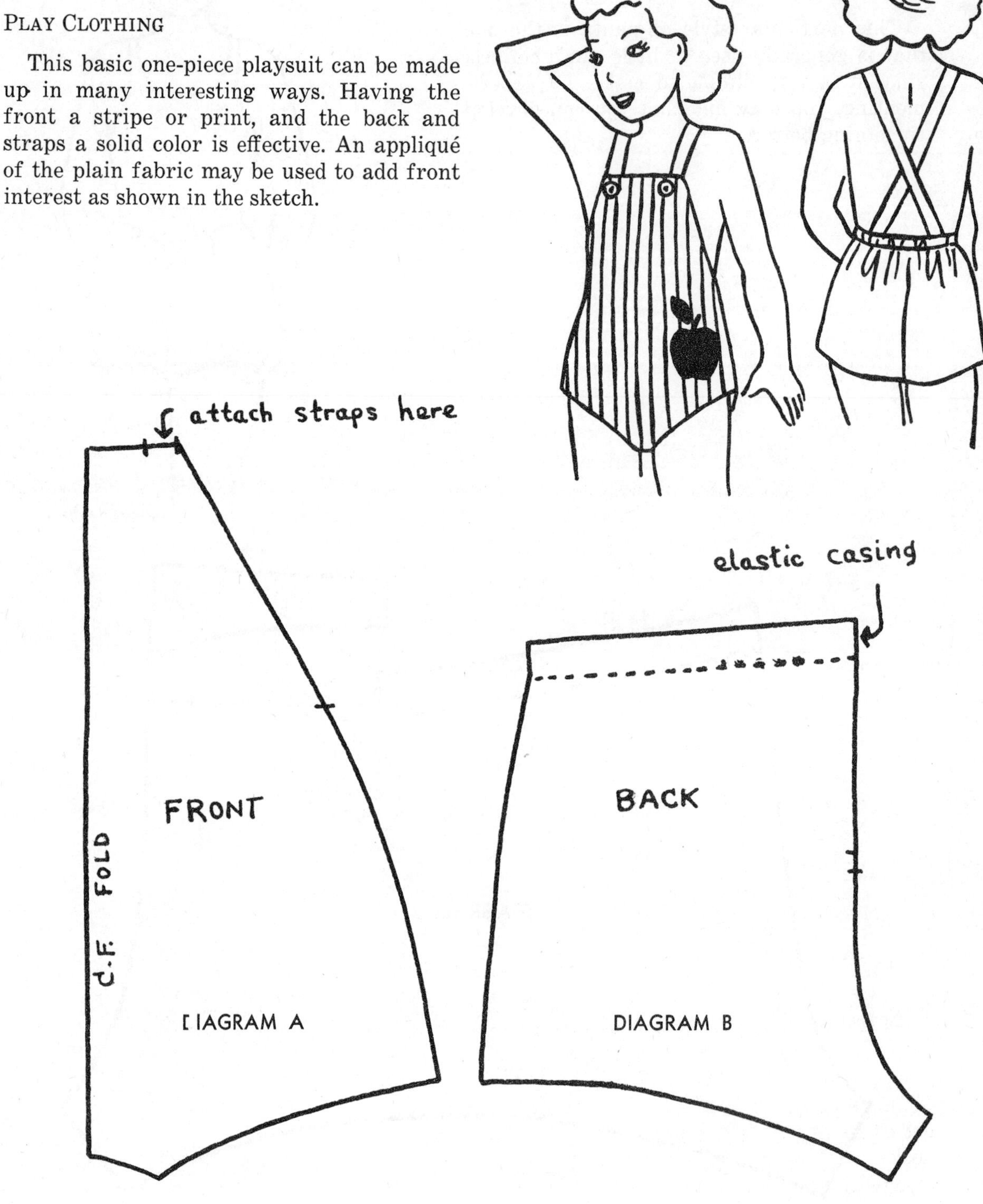

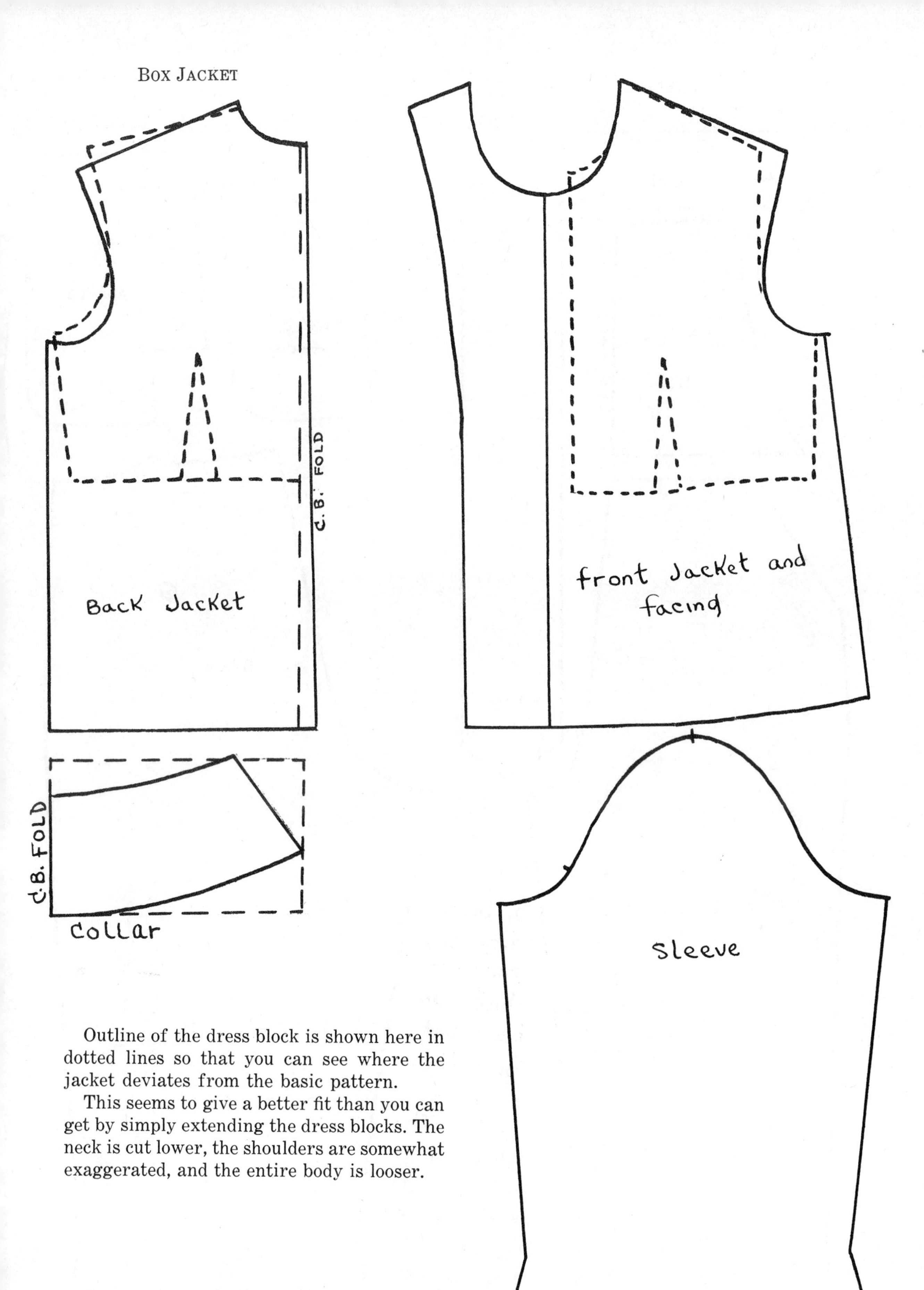

Outline of the dress block is shown here in dotted lines so that you can see where the jacket deviates from the basic pattern.

This seems to give a better fit than you can get by simply extending the dress blocks. The neck is cut lower, the shoulders are somewhat exaggerated, and the entire body is looser.

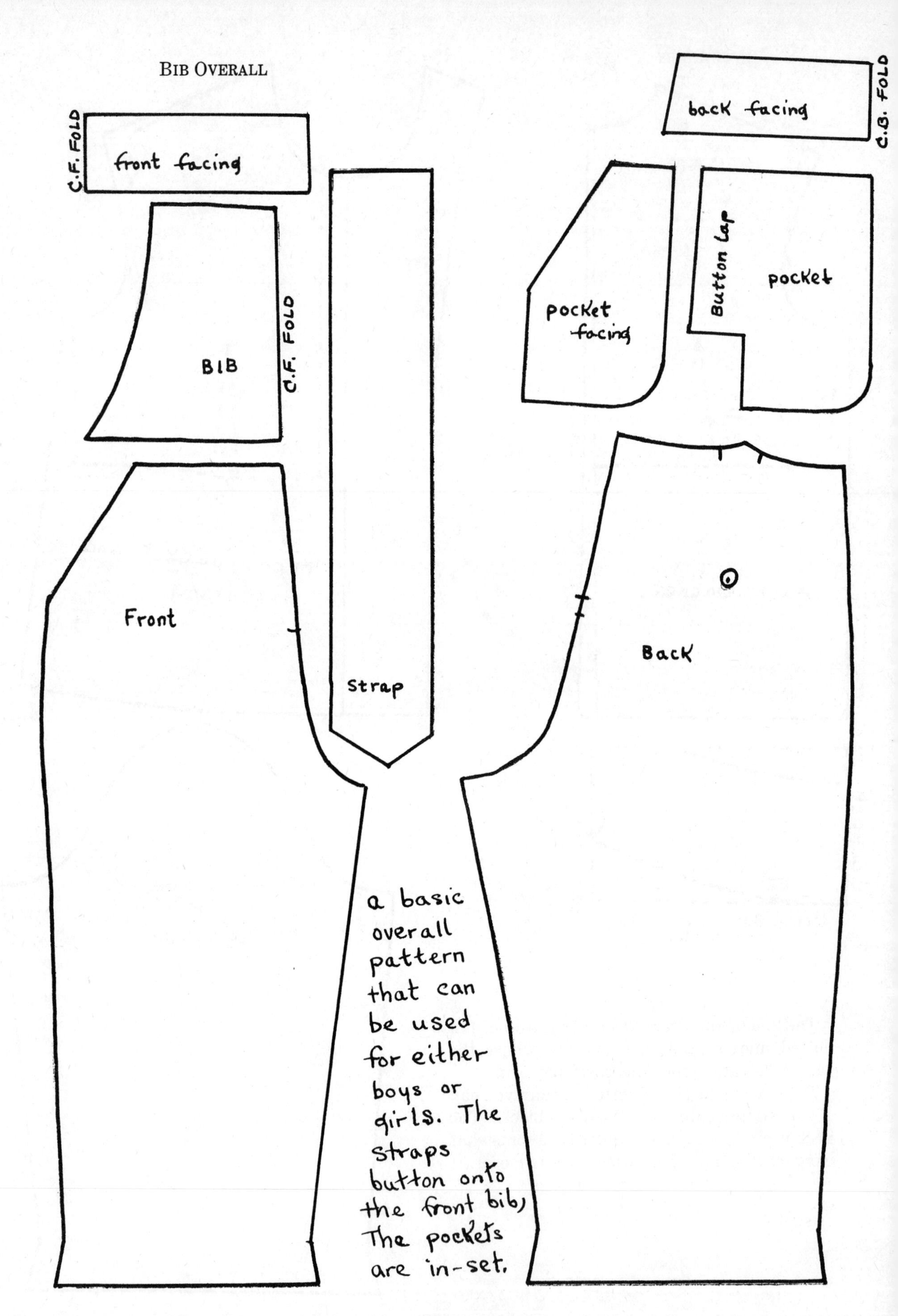
front facing
C.F. FOLD
BIB
C.F. FOLD
strap
back facing
C.B. FOLD
pocket facing
Button Lap
pocket
Front
Back
a basic overall pattern that can be used for either boys or girls. The straps button onto the front bib, The pockets are in-set.

Pinafore

A pinafore is such a basic garment in a little girl's wardrobe that it has assumed standardized proportions which should be kept in mind even though you are restyling the garment.

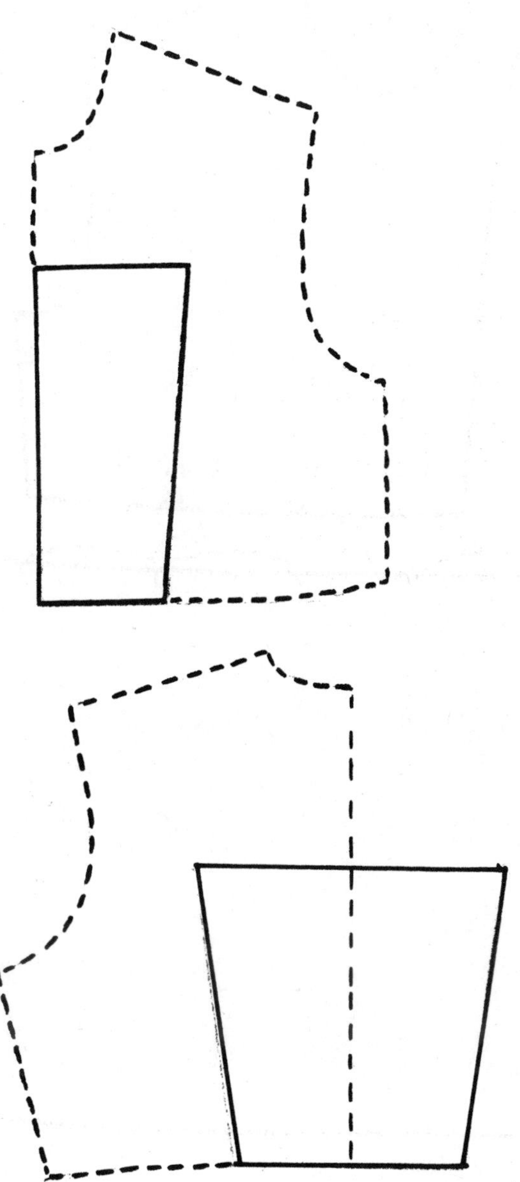

For a size #4 pinafore, the pattern pieces are usually proportioned as listed below.

front skirt	28 x 14	inches, 1 pc.
back skirt	18 x 14	inches, 2 pc.
sash	4 x 17	inches, 2 pc.
set-in belt	2 x 25½	inches, 2 pc.
strap	2 x 19	inches, 2 pc.
pocket	4 x 4½	inches, 4 pc.

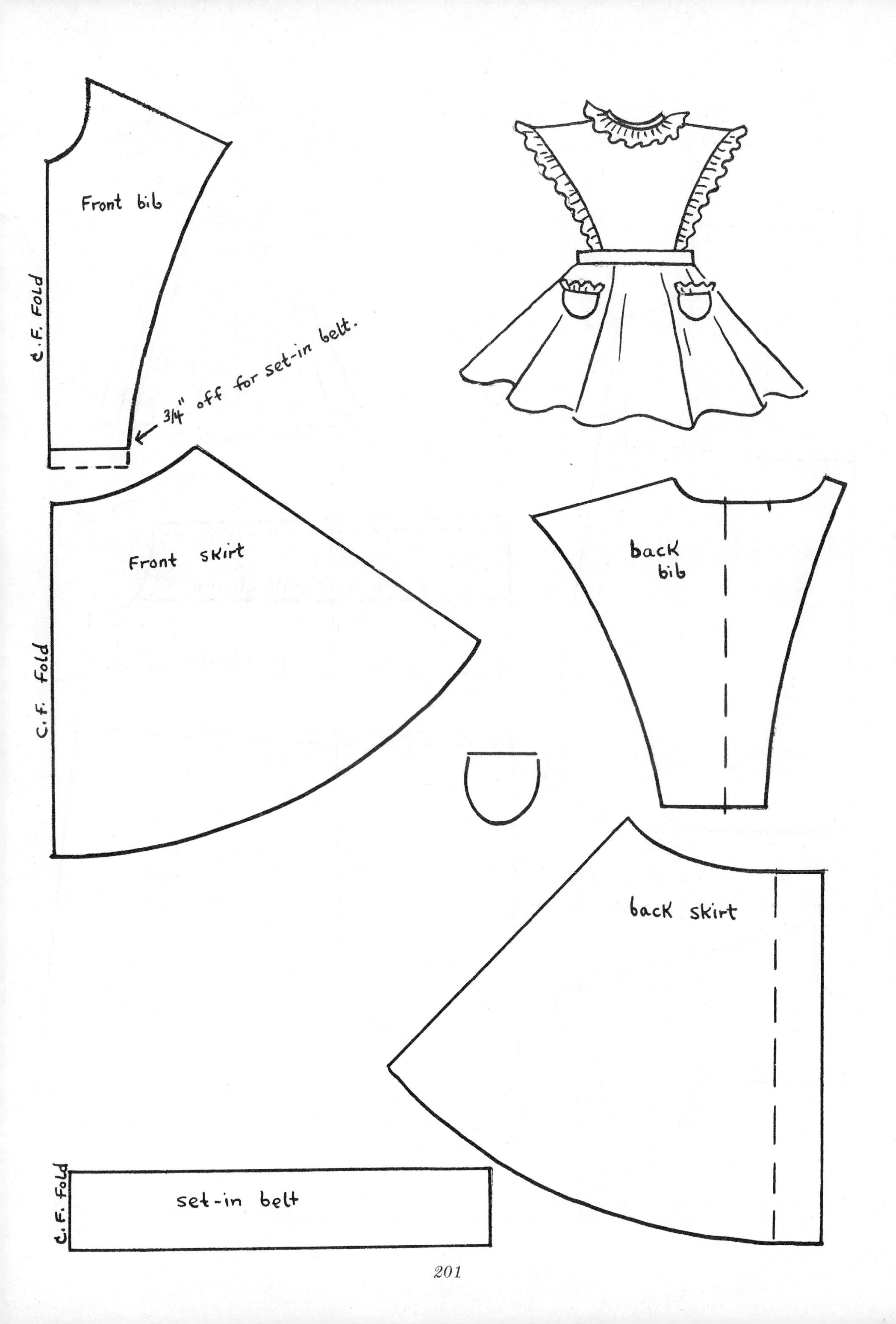
Front bib
C.F. Fold
3/4" off for set-in belt.
Front skirt
C.F. Fold
back
bib
back skirt
C.F. Fold
set-in belt

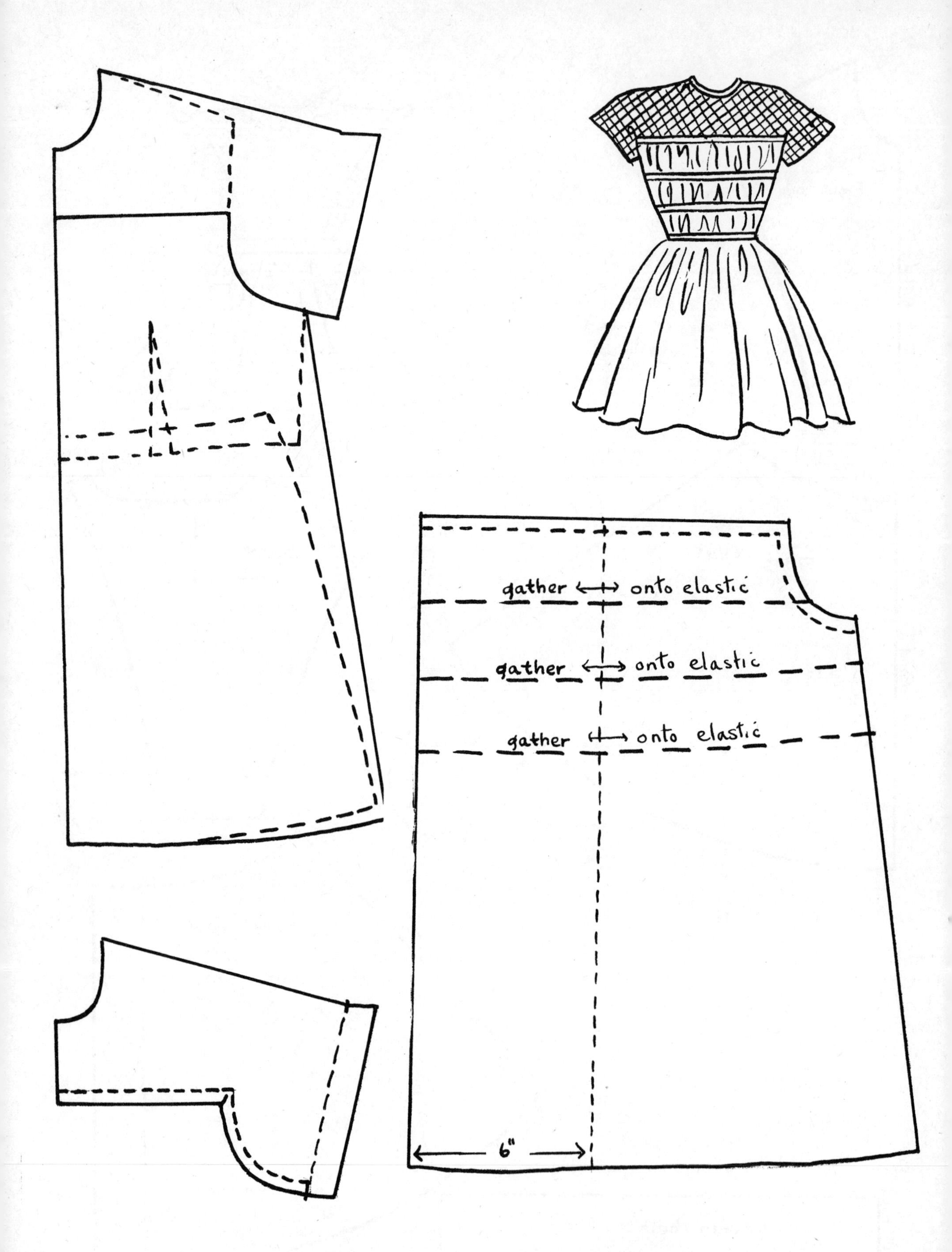
gather ↔ onto elastic
gather ↔ onto elastic
gather ↔ onto elastic
6"

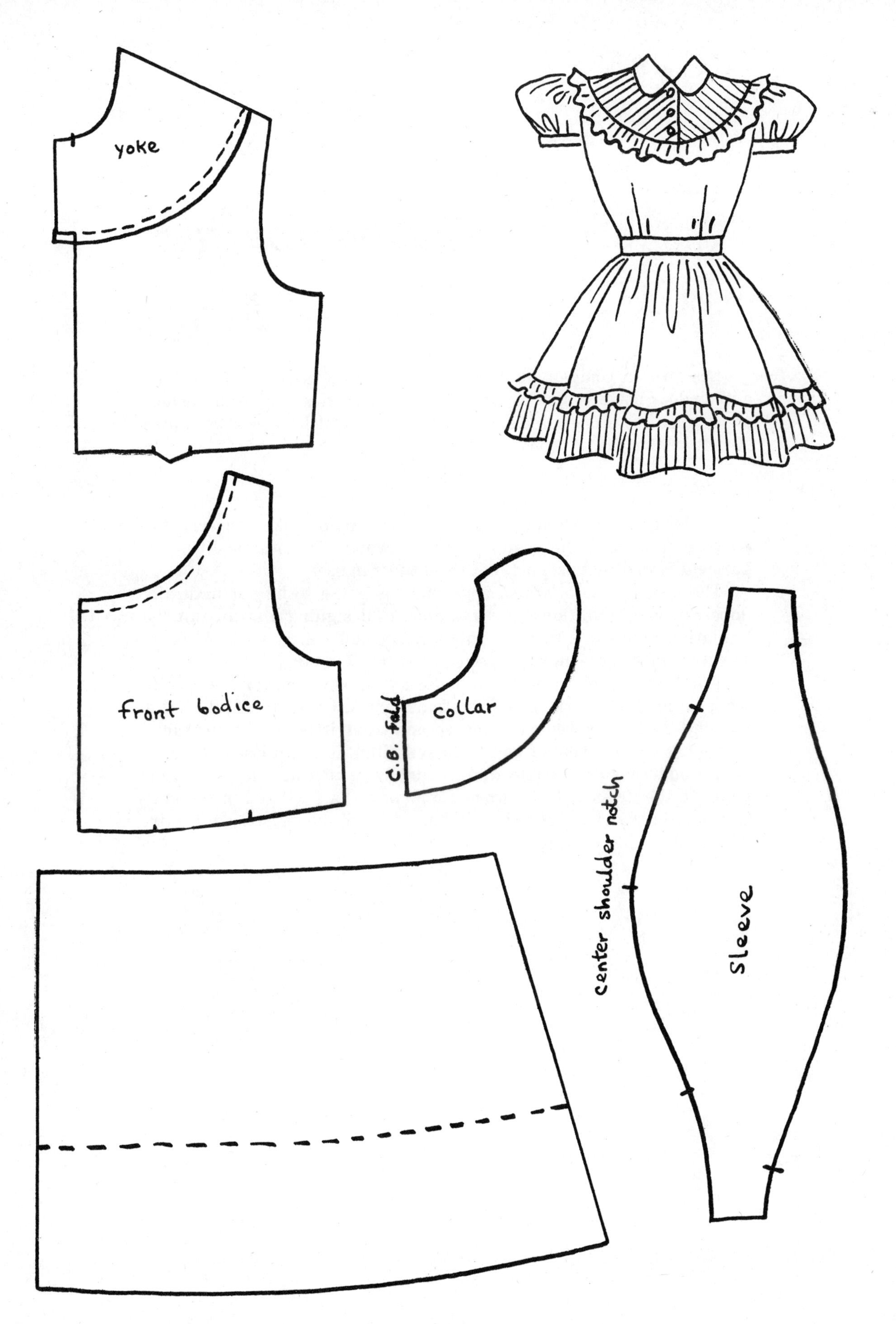
yoke
front bodice
C.B. fold
collar
center shoulder notch
Sleeve

Chapter Fourteen

Design

Design is a complex subject which takes years of study, and the author does not presume to cover the field but only to give the reader an outline. Use this outline as a foundation on which to build your own structure of ideas.

Function

In designing a costume, the first decision to make concerns the purpose for which the costume will be worn. The practicality of a garment is in direct proportion to its fitness in use.

The specific use to which a garment is going to be put naturally imposes some limitations. For example, in designing a swim suit the limitation imposed is that the suit must be sufficiently streamlined so as not to impede the movements required by swimming.

Another example is that of a house dress, which is worn primarily while doing housework. The limitations imposed here are, first, that it not impede free movement, and, second, that it be easily washable. In the case of an evening gown, the only limitation imposed is that it be as glamorous as possible, and, naturally, that it not offend current taste. If the dress is to be worn for dancing, a further limitation is imposed, in that it must not be hobble skirted, but must have a skirt which allows for wide, graceful movement.

Proportion

It may seem irrelevant to mention that clothing is made to cover human beings, but there have been periods when the human shape underneath the garment was completely ignored and the results were disastrous — at least in our eyes today.

The proportions of the human body seem to man to be the most beautiful there are; possibly because, being people, we consider our own kind spectacularly handsome. So, in considering the proportions of a garment, always guide yourself by the body which is being clothed. It is usually awkward looking to divide a garment anyplace except at the natural body divisions, such as the waist, bust, hips, etc. You will generally be safe in your proportions if you follow the body lines as they are indicated on a standard dress form. These lines have long been considered the most functional possible, and you will probably decide after much experimentation that the decision was just.

So plan your costume with great respect for the human proportions. Once a good basic shape has been planned, almost any fancy can be incorporated into a good design.

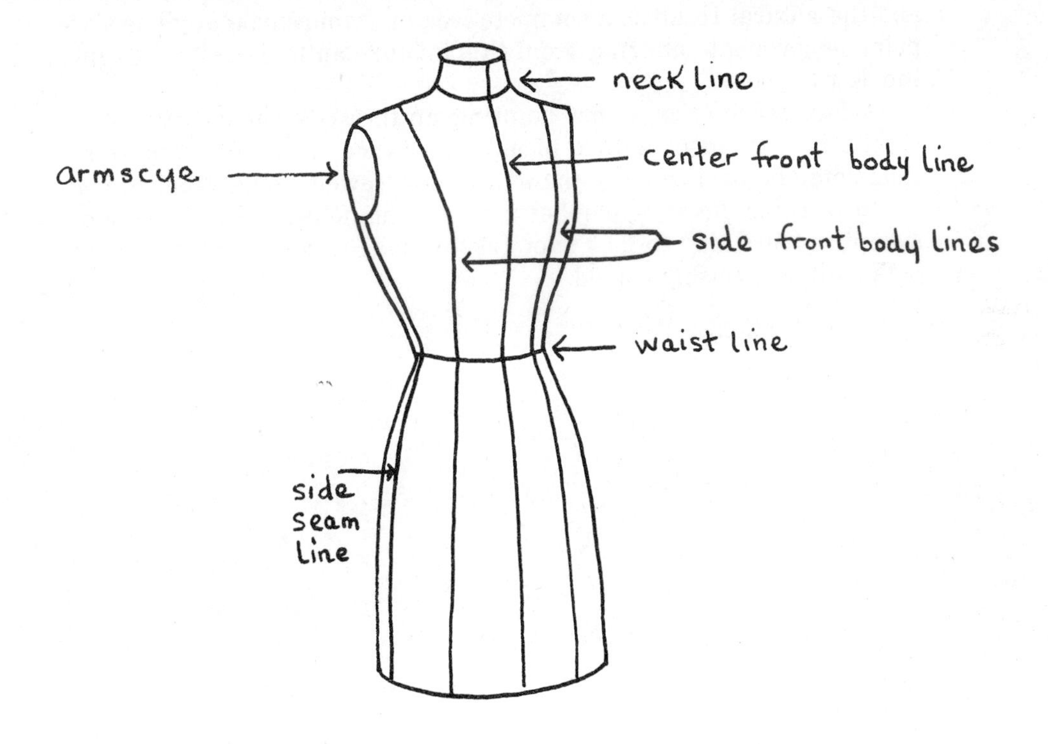

STYLE EMPHASIS

The best results come from a combination of paper planning and actual measuring and pinning on the dress form. Sketch your design roughly at first, considering only the basic shape and function of the costume. Then consider the treatment of your major style point, first deciding in what area the major style point is to be — whether it will be in the bodice, the skirt, or the sleeves.

Once the dominant style point is determined, it will govern whatever else you do to your costume. If you have chosen the sleeves for your major style point, you will necessarily have to subordinate the rest of the garment in order to emphasize the sleeves.

A common error is to overemphasize several parts of a garment, and the natural result is a complete lack of emphasis on any one style point. A garment suffering from this mistake automatically falls into the dowdy class.

A less grave error is not pointing up the style sufficiently, which results in a garment with a bleak appearance. This, however, sometimes may be overcome by the addition of jewelry or a fanciful belt.

In working out style emphasis, it is often helpful to go on window shopping tours, and to look over fashion magazines for ideas, not for details to be slavishly copied.

Texture

Texture is the quality of roughness or smoothness, coarseness or fineness, given to woven cloth by the manner in which it is woven, or by the material from which it is woven.

The concern of the apparel designer with texture is merely that of selection and combination, as the cloth has already been decided upon by a textile designer.

In making a selection, the primary function of the garment must be the first consideration. This may be expressed simply as "suitability to the occasion." For example, a rough tweed fabric would not be suitable for a summer evening gown, though a sheer cotton or silk would be eminently suitable. The tweed would be very much in place in a country suit or an all-purpose coat. So in selecting your fabric think, as always, of the function of the costume which you are planning.

In making interesting combinations of textures, you have to do more than select wisely for the garment's function. You either have to have some artistic perception or you will have to train yourself to appreciate textural values. We all know the beauty of a polished leather belt against a heavy tweed, or that of a silver pin on raw silk, but there are limitless possibilities in the way of textural combinations and it is the job of the designer to find them and to experiment with new and interesting combinations. Good taste must be your guide in this matter as in all others pertaining to design. In order to stimulate your awareness of the possibilities of textural combinations, spend some time seriously studying paintings, both of old masters and moderns.

You will probably find textures best illustrated by modern painting in objective and nonobjective abstracts. Since this is a visual experience, it cannot be expressed in words, so continue your study of design by acquainting yourself with modern paintings. Study them until you can experience a definite like or dislike for certain textural combinations. Then you will be able to trust your own taste.

Color

Color is another delicate subject, but if you have definite tastes and are without fear where color is concerned, you can depend entirely on intuition.

If you experience difficulty in making decisions where color is concerned, then it is essential that you learn the analogous and complementary color schemes, which mankind has been using since color was first introduced. Color cards demonstrating these color schemes can be found in any art or paint supply store.

Color and color combinations above and beyond those of the analogous and complementary color schemes are largely a matter of experience. Whenever you look at any color combination, decide instantly whether or not you like it and in a few months you will have developed some kind of color sense. In this way you will be training your perception of color, and it won't be long before you have a color sense on which you can depend.

There are a great many seemingly profound books written on color and its relation to emotions, and what this or that person should or should not wear. In my experience, color is something that should be chosen for its immediate appeal. If you cannot tell whether or not a color looks good on you or on a client, you are out of your element in designing and all the books on color in the world won't make it any easier for you to decide. But don't allow yourself to be unduly influenced by anyone who, for example, flatly states that a "brunette extrovert" should only wear navy blue or forest green! If the brunette extrovert looks dashing in coral or citron yellow, then by all means let her wear either or both.

If you like to show up boldly in a crowd, wear brilliant colors. But if you prefer to blend in with the scenery, choose your color accordingly. Don't follow the charts which recommend blue for blondes, green for red-heads, violet for over-fifties, etc., ad nauseum. If you are going to design clothes, the only chart to guide you is your own taste. Keep your eyes open to everything around you: nature, people, modern painting, textiles, politics, ceramics, everything with which you come in contact. You cannot help developing some sort of color sense. In any case, it will be your own — which is the important thing.